LEARNING RESOURCES CTR/NEW ENGLAND TECH.
GEN   GE197.S95 1997
Switzer, Jac   Green backlash :

3 0147 0002 3635 9

GE 197 .S95 199

W9-ACL-226

Switzer, Jacqueline Vaughn.

Green backlash

NEW ENGLAND INSTITUTE
OF TECHNOLOGY
LEARNING RESOURCES CENTER

GREEN BACKLASH

GREEN BACKLASH

The History and Politics of Environmental Opposition in the U.S.

Jacqueline Vaughn Switzer

NEW ENGLAND INSTITUTE
OF TECHNOLOGY
LEARNING RESOURCES CENTER

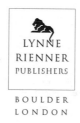

LYNNE
RIENNER
PUBLISHERS

BOULDER
LONDON

#35450525

Published in the United States of America in 1997 by
Lynne Rienner Publishers, Inc.
1800 30th Street, Boulder, Colorado 80301

and in the United Kingdom by
Lynne Rienner Publishers, Inc.
3 Henrietta Street, Covent Garden, London WC2E 8LU

© 1997 by Lynne Rienner Publishers, Inc. All rights reserved

Library of Congress Cataloging-in-Publication Data
Switzer, Jacqueline Vaughn.
  Green backlash : the history and politics of environmental
opposition in the U.S. / Jacqueline Vaughn Switzer.
    p.   cm.
  Includes bibliographical references and index.
  ISBN 1-55587-651-X (hc : alk. paper)
  ISBN 1-55587-635-8 (paperback : alk. paper)
  1. Anti-environmentalism—United States—History.
2. Anti-environmentalism—Political aspects—United States.   I. Title.
GE197.S95   1997
363.7'00973—dc20   96-43237
                                                                                  CIP

British Cataloguing in Publication Data
A Cataloguing in Publication record for this book
is available from the British Library.

Typeset by Letra Libre, 1705 14th Street, Suite 391, Boulder, Colorado 80302

Printed and bound in the United States of America

    The paper used in this publication meets the requirements
(∞) of the American National Standard for Permanence of
    Paper for Printed Library Materials Z39.48-1984.

    5   4   3   2   1

For those with
the courage of their convictions

Contents

Preface   xi

Introduction: The Roots of the Conflict   1
    The Evolution of Federal Policy, 2
    Preservation Versus Conservation, 4
    The Contemporary Environmental Movement, 7
    The Opening of the Policy Window, 10
    The Importance of Nomenclature, 12
    Notes, 15

PART I
CONFLICTS OVER LAND AND RESOURCES

1 The Early Land Use Battles   21
    The Creation of a National Public Domain, 22
    The Public Lands Question, 24
    The Evolution of an Organized Opposition, 26
    The Timber Opposition, 28
    The Utility Opposition, 31
    The Expansion of Opposition over Water Policy, 33
    Mining and Petroleum Industry Opposition, 36
    Enter the Preservationists, 38
    The Dispute over the Commons Continues, 39
    "Return the Public Lands to the West," 41
    Notes, 45

2 Ranchers, Predators, and Animal Lovers   49
    Livestock Grazing Law Disputes, 50
    Wildlife Management Issues, 59
    The Environmental Opposition and Animal Rights, 70
    Notes, 74

3 Farmers and Outdoor Recreationists   77
    The Agricultural Lobby, 79
    The Targets of the Opposition, 80

Agriculture's Impact on Environmental Policy, 86
The Outdoor Recreationists, 89
The Recreation and Off-Road Lobbies, 93
The "Real" Environmentalists? 96
Notes, 97

PART II
BUSINESS GETS ORGANIZED

4   How Industry Fights the Legislative Battle   103
An Overview of Industry Opposition, 106
The Extractive Resource Industries and
    Pollution Control, 107
The Nuclear Power Industry, 110
The Chemical Manufacturers, 111
The Automakers, 113
The Growth of Industry Alliances, 115
The Environmental Opposition's Legislative
    Allies and Enemies, 117
The Policy Legacy of the 104th Congress, 119
Business in the Legislative Arena, 124
Notes, 125

5   The PR Campaigns   129
Public Relations Campaigns, 130
The Initiative Campaigns, 133
Greenwashing, 135
Research Institutes and Think Tanks, 140
Imagemaking, 144
Effectiveness of PR Efforts, 146
Notes, 148

6   End Run: The Bureaucratic Arena   151
Avoiding the Public Limelight, 153
Taking Advantage of Vagueness, 154
Playing the "Advisory" Role, 156
Providing Orchestrated Commentary, 158
Bringing in the Experts, 159
Altering the Arena, 160
Delay and Sue, 163
Where Next? 165
Notes, 167

PART III
THE WAR AT THE GRASSROOTS

7 The Sagebrush Rebellion   171
   A Question of Federalism, *172*
   The Carter Connection, *174*
   Organizing a Rebellion, *176*
   The Rebels at the Statehouse, *178*
   The Sagebrush Rebellion Goes to Washington, *182*
   Out with a Whimper, *184*
   The Resurgence of Environmental Organizations, *186*
   The Aftermath of the Rebellion, *187*
   Notes, *189*

8 The Wise Use Movement   191
   Background and Development of the Movement, *194*
   The Umbrella Organizations, *200*
   The Grassroots Groups, *202*
   Movement Strategies, *205*
   The Environmental Movement's Response
      to Wise Use, *211*
   The Militancy/Wise Use Linkage, *212*
   Wise Use and Environmental Policymaking, *220*
   Notes, *223*

9 County Supremacy and the War on the West   227
   County Supremacy Groups and Leadership, *229*
   Battle Strategies and Issues, *231*
   Who's Winning the War? *239*
   Notes, *243*

10 The Property Rights Movement   247
    Perspectives on the Legal and Historical Issues, *249*
    The Property Rights Groups, *251*
    Regulatory Takings, *256*
    The Strategies, *264*
    Property Rights and the Environmental Opposition, *272*
    The Grassroots Movements in Perspective, *273*
    Notes, *276*

Conclusion: Environmentalism in the Balance   281
    The Policy Impact of the Environmental Opposition, *282*

Measuring Policy Success, *285*
The Continuing Salience of Environmentalism, *287*
Searching for Environmental Perspective, *290*
The Response by Environmental Groups, *292*
The Future, *294*
Notes, *297*

APPENDIXES

List of Acronyms   299

An Environmental History and Politics Time Line   301

Index   309

About the Book   323

Preface

On July 4, 1994—Independence Day—rancher Dick Carver started the motor of his 22-ton Caterpillar tractor in an act of civil disobedience against the United States Forest Service. In front of 200 supporters, he used the bulldozer to reopen a road into national forestlands without the government's permission. Carver, who is often pictured with a copy of the U.S. Constitution sticking out from his front shirt pocket, knew his action was illegal. As a commissioner in Nye County, Nevada, he was positioning himself to serve as one of the symbols of the environmental opposition in the United States.[1] Carver's act of civil disobedience exemplifies the green backlash—a growing resentment about the political and legal clout of the environmental movement and a distrust of the government's natural resource and environmental policies.

Many observers link the environmental opposition to antigovernment elements within both the conservative and libertarian movements. They question the opposition's claims about the size of its membership, as well as its effectiveness in shaping environmental policy. Yet Carver is one of many leaders in a large and diverse movement. *The Wise Use Address Book*, published in 1994, lists over a thousand names of "activists for property rights, jobs, communities, and access to federal lands."[2] They and their organizations represent individual property owners seeking to build vacation homes on land declared as protected habitat under the Endangered Species Act, off-road vehicle users seeking enhanced access to designated wilderness areas, state and local public officials attempting to gain control over public lands within their geographical jurisdiction, and workers in the extractive resource industries who believe that their jobs and way of life are being threatened by a distant Washington, D.C., bureaucracy controlled by idealists and radicals.

Traditionally, the individuals and groups represented by the grass-roots opposition have been concentrated in the rural West, although since the early 1990s the movement has spread nationwide, networked and organized by such umbrella groups as the Alliance for America, the Blue Ribbon Coalition, and the Center for the Defense of Free Enterprise. For the most part, these groups have tried to create the impression that there is a mass movement of disgruntled Americans dissatisfied with the direction in which policymakers are headed. They have tried to advance their policy goals by initiating new laws, by modifying existing environmental statutes and regulations, and by supporting lawsuits by private citizens who are trying to settle individual grievances against the government.[3]

In contrast to the recently conceived grassroots organizations (referred to by some observers as "astroturf" or phony grassroots groups because they are organizationally connected to or are funded by particular industries or businesses), the environmental opposition has a more enduring and traditional segment. This comprises business lobbies, individual corporations, and trade associations. However, rather than rely exclusively on conventional strategies, which involve lobbying within legislative venues,[4] these organized interests have increasingly tried to shape public opinion and exert influence in the bureaucratic arena, where they can affect the implementation and enforcement of laws and regulations.

While continuing to dispute the size and influence of its opposition, the mainstream environmental movement has begun to react with considerable alarm, especially since the 1994 elections changed the numerical majority and, to some extent, the ideological perspective of Congress regarding the role of the federal government and environmental stewardship. The real growth of the opposition groups, their early legislative victories, and the initially lethargic response by environmental organizations have made the contemporary green backlash a significant development for all who have concerns about the future direction of environmental policymaking.

OBJECTIVES

Much of the existing literature about the environmental opposition comes from journalists who have tracked contemporary organizations and industry lobbies on behalf of groups within the environmental movement, or from historians who have focused on early resistance to federal policy over natural resources. This book rests on the assumption that the seeds of discontent manifest in the current opposition to natural resource policy, along with a growing hostility toward environmental groups, were planted more than 200 years ago. They do not represent a novel threat to environmental protection. Rather, much of that discontent surfaced during the early years of western expansion and is seen in the colonial attitudes of eastern industrialists who exploited and overcapitalized the West. A primary objective of *Green Backlash* is to demonstrate that the more contemporary forms of opposition to the environmental movement and environmental protection generally, such as the wise use and property rights movements, have, at least in their rhetoric, a common, traceable ancestry. These historical roots began not as a resistance against what would later be called environmental ethics, but against federal resource policies that westerners felt were unfair and colonial in style.

Deriving from this, a second major objective of this book is to identify the changing role of the federal government in its natural resource policies. In the contemporary context, government is often seen as the steward of environmental resources. However, the contradictions in the role of the federal government as a promoter of settlement and industry and as a protector of natural resources are shown in its shifts in policy over time, over rivalries between different government agencies, and over debates between and within the major political parties. As former Colorado governor Richard Lamm writes,

> The federal attitude was that the West existed not as an entity in itself, but as a supplier for the needs of the nation in general. Believing this, it never wavered in its support of big business in the West, nor did it hesitate to exert its own power over the region. Its attitude, in turn, generated an antagonism in the West that grew and endures to this day.[5]

The attempts by early environmental activists, such as John Muir, to protect certain parcels of land from development and from anything more than minimal recreational use clashed directly with those of government officials, such as Gifford Pinchot, who favored an approach that allowed the multiple use of land and natural resources. This conflict set the stage for policy battles that remain unresolved. Whether deliberate or inadvertent, the alternating policy of encouraging and then discouraging the exploitation of resources has favored specific groups and industries over time, thus intensifying the fight of various lobbying groups for influence over government decisions.

A third objective of this book is to analyze the environmental opposition from a political perspective—to explain how the environmental opposition fits into the larger political process. It looks at how group opposition happens most often in reaction to policies proposed by other actors in the political system (usually members of environmental groups). It also examines the tactics used by business and grassroots groups in the environmental opposition, the venues they choose to press their demands upon the political process, and their linkages to other philosophical and ideological agendas, such as the modern conservative and libertarian movements.

My underlying thesis is that the groups commonly termed the "anti-enviros" are part of a complicated and complex movement that is more diverse than many observers have recognized. The chapters on the contemporary environmental opposition focus on how effectively these different groups have influenced environmental policy at each step of the policy process, from the setting and framing of the policy agenda through formulation, adoption, implementation, and evaluation.[6] The chapters suggest that their influence has varied in tandem with the ebb and flow of public opinion about the environment. This phenomenon, called the "issue-attention cycle,"[7] allows the opening of "policy windows," which permit an issue or a group (or a "policy entrepreneur") to bring a matter to the attention of policymakers.[8] The opening of the most recent policy window for the environmental opposition is evidence of a long but cyclical history of U.S. interest in the environment and the management of natural resources.

This book challenges many of the stereotypes and claims made by those who have characterized the business and grassroots segments of the environmental opposition as a monolithic entity that is funded almost totally by corporate fronts or is connected to an even larger conspiracy. It also seeks to explain why both the environmental opposition and the environmental movement have used negative characterizations of each other to promote their own goals and policy agendas. But it does not attempt to engage the reader in a debate over which advocacy group is more credible in its claims against the other. Rather, it is intended to be an objective analysis of the political forces shaping environmental policy in the 1990s. Ideally, the reader will make his or her own judgment about the validity of the arguments of the various groups and will gain a clearer picture of how green backlash developed historically and how it has impacted environmental policy in the United States.

PLAN OF THE BOOK

Green Backlash was written with a diverse audience in mind, from citizen activists along the continuum of the ideological spectrum to scholars seeking to place the environmental opposition in political, historical, or sociological perspective. Thus the Introduction is designed to provide the necessary background the reader might need to understand the nomenclature that identifies the diverse segments of the movement, their connections to one another, and the intricate relationship between the opposition and the environmental movement.

In keeping with the initial premise of the book—that the evolution of the environmental opposition can be traced to the period prior to the signing of the Constitution—Part I begins with a historical overview that introduces the first organized opposition to the government's environmental policies. These early land use battles set the stage for contemporary disputes over property rights, and many of the arguments used by those who opposed the federal government's control over the public domain are nearly identical to those being used today.

Part I concludes with a discussion of two distinct groups of land users: farmers and outdoor recreationists. Although both groups have important stakes in the decisions over land use, the targets and level of their opposition are quite different. Many agricultural organizations have vigorously sought and benefited from federal subsidies and have been less likely to oppose government regulation, with some members explicitly distancing themselves from leaders within the environmental opposition. Environmental organizations have vilified outdoor enthusiasts, from all-terrain vehicle owners to mountain bikers, while members of those groups call themselves "the real environmentalists" because they believe, as one of their leaders wrote, they represent "those of us who believe humans have a responsibility to use our natural resource[s] wisely."[9] Outdoor recreationists often work closely with other groups within the environmental opposition but have adopted and supported other natural resource issues as their own. Throughout Part I there is a discussion of the often changing role and policies of the federal government in resolving conflicts over land use, wildlife management, and the competing interests of agricultural and recreational users.

Part II shifts to a discussion of business and industry opposition to environmental policy, traditionally focused on the formulation, adoption, and implementation of policy. Using case studies, it reviews the traditional interest group strategies that have been used in the legislative arena to influence environmental statutes such as the Clean Air Act Amendments of 1990. It also looks at the way industry advocates have used the initiative process at the state level to advance their interests. The section then examines the public relations campaigns—called "greenwashing" by environmental groups—used by industry to soften the public's perception of its activities, including an analysis of the think tanks and legal foundations that provide much of the technical expertise and legal support for the environmental opposition. Chapter 6 identifies one of the most successful arenas wherein business has challenged environmental regulation: the bureaucracy. By choosing this forum, industry has managed to avoid the public spotlight and has used its technical expertise to influence policy implementation—a technique only now being matched by environmental organizations.

The next four chapters, in Part III, move to the contemporary wave of environmental opposition, beginning with the Sagebrush Rebellion of the late 1970s and early 1980s, which is discussed in detail in Chapter 7. Although there were earlier forms of opposition to the federal government's role in managing public lands, the Sagebrush Rebellion is the antecedent to today's more organized and geographically dis-

persed environmental opposition. The remaining three chapters out-
line the wise use movement, county supremacy advocates and the
"War on the West," and the property rights movement. Although some
observers have characterized the three as a single entity, they are separated here since many of the groups' adherents differ in their policy
goals, the forums in which they seek to advance their interests, and the
strategies they use. Part III concludes with a discussion about the alleged linkage between the grassroots organizations and industry, and
considers whether the green backlash is, as some observers argue,
closely connected to conservative and libertarian social movements or
to a broader antigovernment agenda.

The book's Conclusion ties together these disparate groups as it returns to the question about the impact the environmental opposition
has had on environmental policymaking. The chapter reviews the
salience of the environment as a political and social issue, the response
of the environmental movement to the opposition groups, and the
prospects for conflict and consensus in the future.

Coverage of the book's subject is historical within the separate sections on industry and the grassroots. For the reader's reference, a list of
acronyms is included in the Appendixes, as is a time line which sum-
marizes the overall development of environmental resource policy in
the United States.

ACKNOWLEDGMENTS

This book has been written with the belief that there is much more
agreement about environmental policy in this country than has been
suggested by government officials, the members of the environmental
movement, or their adversaries. I wish to thank all those who have
shared in my environmental education and have given me the opportunity to view their perspectives on the environmental policy debate,
especially those at the South Coast Air Quality Management District in
California and at Southern California Edison. I also have appreciated
the openness of those who responded to my requests for interviews,
completed surveys, wrote letters, and provided literature and other information as I attempted to gain a better understanding of their perspective and culture.

I gratefully acknowledge those who reviewed portions of the man-
uscript or provided guidance in its preparation: Leslie Alm, Ron
Arnold, Phil Brick, Todd Carney, Jon Lange, Carolyn Long, William
Lunch, David Meyer, Zachary Smith, Clyde Wilcox, and Stephanie
Witt, along with Aaron Hatch, who served as research assistant. The
staff at the Southern Oregon State College library helped me track

down obscure materials, and I wish to thank Anna Beauchamp, Deborah Hollens, and Anne Richards for their assistance. My special thanks go to editor-in-chief Don Reisman at Lynne Rienner Publishers, who generously shared his support and personal insight and believed in and guided this project from its inception.

NOTES

1. See Erik Larson, "Unrest in the West," *Time*, October 23, 1995, p. 52. Carver's story has been recounted in numerous other publications and has become one of the hallmark events in the burgeoning county supremacy movement discussed in Chapter 9 of this book.

2. *The Wise Use Address Book* (Bellevue, WA: Center for the Defense of Free Enterprise, 1994).

3. For a general discussion of the nature and tactics of these groups, see Phil Brick, "Determined Opposition: The Wise Use Movement Challenges Environmentalism," *Environment*, vol. 37, no. 8 (October 1995): 16–20, 36–42.

4. For an overview of interest group strategies, see the classic work of David Truman (*The Governmental Process* [New York: Knopf, 1951]) and of Earl Latham (*The Group Basis of Politics* [New York: Octagon Press, 1965]). See also Terry Moe, *The Organization of Interests* (Chicago: University of Chicago Press, 1980); Jeffrey Berry, *The Interest Group Society*, 2nd ed. (Glenview, IL: Scott, Foresman/Little, Brown, 1989); and Mark Petracca, ed. *The Politics of Interests: Interest Groups Transformed* (Boulder, CO: Westview, 1992). Case studies of how interest groups have attempted to influence environmental policy include Gary C. Bryner, *Blue Skies, Green Politics: The Clean Air Act of 1990*, 2nd ed. (Washington, DC: Congressional Quarterly Press, 1995); Richard E. Cohen, *Washington at Work: Back Rooms and Clean Air* (New York: Macmillan, 1992); and Charles E. Davis, *The Politics of Hazardous Waste* (Englewood Cliffs, NJ: Prentice Hall, 1993).

5. Richard D. Lamm and Michael McCarthy, *The Angry West: A Vulnerable Land and Its Future* (Boston: Houghton Mifflin, 1982), p. 11.

6. There are numerous versions of the policymaking model, including one developed by James E. Anderson, *Public Policymaking: An Introduction*, 2nd ed. (Boston: Houghton Mifflin, 1994), p. 37.

7. Political scientist Anthony Downs coined the phrase in his article "Up and Down with Ecology: The 'Issue-Attention Cycle,'" *Public Interest*, vol. 28 (1972): 38. Downs's five-stage systematic cycle begins with the preproblem stage in which the public's attention is not yet captured by an undesirable condition, but those affected by it gradually begin to become motivated to bring the problem to the attention of policymakers. In the second stage, a dramatic event or crisis leads to "alarmed discovery and euphoric enthusiasm" where the public believes that every problem can be solved; by the third stage, this is muted by the realization of the costs of solving the problem. Gradually, a fourth stage begins as interest declines, and the public becomes discouraged, threatened, or simply bored. This leads to a twilight fifth stage where the public's interest may sporadically be recaptured by crisis or additional intervening events, but where other issues crowd out the initial problem from the policy agenda.

8. For a discussion of the concepts of "policy windows" and "policy entrepreneurs," see John Kingdon, *Agendas, Alternatives, and Public Policies* (New York: HarperCollins, 1995). Kingdon theorizes that the policy process is a response to dynamics and actors within the political system. In his model, problems find their way to the political agenda—the problems to which government officials and others in the policy process pay serious attention—on the basis of two influences: the active participants in the policy process, such as institutional actors (the president, Congress, courts), and forces outside government, such as the media, interest groups, parties, and the general public. In addition, issues gain prominence due to a variety of factors such as crises, the gradual accumulation of knowledge about an issue, or political processes like a change in the control of Congress or the election of a new president. Problems, policies, and politics often come together at a critical juncture and result in the opening of a policy window, which allows an issue to gain consideration, often at the urging of policy entrepreneurs who take advantage of the opportunity and timing of internal and external forces and events.

9. Clark Collins, "Who Are the Real Environmentalists?" Blue Ribbon Coalition publication, n.d.

GREEN BACKLASH

Introduction:
The Roots of the Conflict

Concern about the environment has been called "one of the most profound and enduring social themes the world over in the last twenty-five years."[1] That observation no doubt stems from the realization that the environmental movement has not only shaped public opinion, but also has been responsible for sweeping legislative and regulatory initiatives.

Historian Roderick Nash has noted that opposing attitudes about the environment in the United States were first cast in the philosophical and social lives of the American colonists and the Native Americans who initially occupied the continent. Many of the early colonial ordinances reflected a protectionist ethic. Among these were William Penn's 1681 declaration that, for every 5 acres of land cleared, 1 must be left forested, and efforts by the Massachusetts Bay Colony to protect waterfowl from overhunting along its coastal regions in the early 1700s.[2] The indigenous population revered the environment and considered it a sacred responsibility to look after the land, with tribal beliefs encouraging the view that humans were part of the natural world, rather than its masters. Among the Iroquois, for example, other living creatures were viewed as possessing qualities of humanness and kinship, and there was an expectation that a hunter who killed more deer than needed would be punished.[3]

The early immigrants also brought with them a Judeo-Christian heritage in which God's bounty of natural resources was perceived as having been provided to satisfy humankind's material needs. That tradition can be seen in the aggressive and antagonistic Puritan attitude that insisted the wilderness be "tamed" and the land "improved," and in the utilitarian philosophy of European writers such as Jeremy Bentham and John Stuart Mill, who believed in the goal of maximizing the overall good for the greatest (human) number.[4] It is also found in the writings of John Locke, one of the philosophical forebears of the American Revolution, who saw wilderness as real estate to be owned and used.[5] Though, in 1626, the leaders of the Plymouth Colony began to regulate the cutting of timber to assure that sufficient quantities would be preserved, they and other early pioneers saw the subjugation of nature as integral to human progress—and they looked at their tech-

1

nology (the rifle, the axe, and barbed-wire fences) as agents in their mission.[6]

The raw, opportunistic attitude about land and resources was dominant well into the nineteenth century, as the nation was energetically expanding its boundaries. Even the intimidating Rocky Mountains presented only an inconvenience to the westward push of explorers and adventurers, including John Wesley Powell and the team of Meriwether Lewis and William Clark. Their discoveries and reports of the resource-rich West resulted in uncontrolled exploitation and the formation of political and economic coalitions that linked the extractive resource industries (especially timber groups), business (with chemical manufacturers at the forefront), ranchers, and agricultural water users. The early land use battles, which will be chronicled in Chapter 1, were due to conflicting purchase claims that arose during this period of rapid exploration.

The nineteenth century's model of exploitation of resources contrasts with an opposing concept of a land ethic, which began with the Ute Indians and was embraced by the early Mormon settlers, who developed the concept of stewardship over the land and its resources.[7] At the same time, there was a growing consciousness about preservation that is best illustrated by the romantic model, a philosophy that had its roots in the literary contributions of Jean-Jacques Rousseau, and continued in the nineteenth-century works of Americans such as George Perkins Marsh and the transcendentalists Henry David Thoreau and Ralph Waldo Emerson.[8] The romantic vision held the wilderness to be a symbol of innocence and purity, and saw virtue in the maintenance of land free from the corruptions of human development. It provided an alternate perspective on the place of humans in the environment, which led to the founding of the early nature organizations that focused on the protection of companion animals, wildlife, and game. These include the American Society for the Prevention of Cruelty to Animals (1866), the New York Audubon Society (1886), and the American Game Protective and Propagation Association (1911).

THE EVOLUTION OF FEDERAL POLICY: DISPOSING OF PUBLIC LANDS

The conflicting philosophical traditions about the place of humans in their environment are echoed in the history of the federal government's natural resource policies. As will be seen in later chapters, the federal government, from its elected leaders to its implementing agencies, has shifted its approach to environmental protection, largely dependent upon the winds of electoral change, public opinion, and technological advancement.

At least for the first seventy-five years of the nation's history, neither the concept of the land ethic nor the romantic vision had a strong influence on government policy. Although there were some elements of a preservationist mentality present in the early colonial resource policies, expansionist ideals rapidly overcame those sentiments. The rush for western lands was almost without check as explorers, speculators, and squatters rushed ahead of federal surveying teams, clearing the land and using the Preemption Act of 1841 to claim up to 160 acres at a cost of $1.25 per acre.

During this period, government policy was to sell its considerable landholdings as a means of generating revenue for its own operations. Land was sold directly to private individuals and, on occasion, as under the Land Ordinance of 1785 and the 1862 Morrill Act, was given to the states, which then sold the property to support education.[9] This applied to public lands the federal government had acquired either as spoils of war (through the cession of much of the Southwest after the Mexican War and the Treaty of Guadalupe-Hidalgo in 1848), negotiation (the Oregon Compromise of 1846), or through purchase (the Louisiana Purchase of 1803 and the 1853 Gadsden Purchase of Arizona).

As the government began to see greater revenue opportunities by maintaining a stake in the continual fees that could be generated from the development of natural resources, including minerals and timber, it started to change its policies. Prior to 1862, the federal government's policy had been to promote the rapid disposal of its land by sale to private individuals. After 1862, the policy's intent shifted to one that encouraged settlement and development. With this change was the general agreement that those lands not otherwise fit for systematic disposal and development would be permanently and efficiently managed by the federal government as part of what historian Samuel Hays calls the "gospel of efficiency."[10]

Passage of the Homestead Act in 1862 simply required potential claimants (a male or female citizen over age twenty-one or head of family) to pay a $10 filing fee and reside on the 160 acres of land for six months, making certain improvements to it, such as building a domicile.[11] (This created the myth that "free land" was available, as well as the belief among some historians that the opening up of the West served as a "safety valve" for the industrial laborers of the crowded cities in the East.[12] However, though the land was *disposed of* at low cost, its acquisition and maintenance was not necessarily inexpensive. In reality, the land was far from free: The cost of developing a homestead was more than the majority of urban dwellers and laborers could afford. Instead, most of the homesteaders were rural farm families and immigrants from northern and western Europe who came to the United States with capital in hand.)

The Homestead Act was followed by a string of land laws that became part of the federal policy of disposing of farmlands, including the
Timber Culture Act (1873), several Desert Land Acts (during the
1870s), the Timber and Stone Act (1878), and the Dawes Allotment Act
(1887). Eastern and western business interests saw these territories in
terms of untapped resources—minerals, timber, and land ripe for speculation. The widespread mismanagement and fraud in the land disposal process led to the formation of the first Public Lands Commission in 1879.

PRESERVATION VERSUS CONSERVATION

By the late nineteenth century, with open land becoming more scarce,
some of the private environmental organizations began having an impact on public policy. The federal government started to modify its earlier policies of selling the public lands at low cost and instead began establishing agencies and enacting legislation oriented more toward a
preservationist mission. That change is exemplified by several congressional actions, including legislation that authorized the president to reserve public lands as forest reserves under Section 24 of the 1891 General Revision Act (later referred to as the Creative Act); the creation of
national parks (Yellowstone in 1872 and Yosemite in 1891); and the
passage of the Rivers and Harbors Act of 1899, which banned pollution
of navigable waterways.

Regulatory involvement became even more prevalent after the
turn of the century, and, by the Progressive Era, a tug-of-war had already begun between the preservationists, led by naturalist and writer
John Muir, and by the federal government's leading conservationist,
Gifford Pinchot, appointed the first chief of the United States Forest
Service (USFS) in 1905. For the next fifty years, much of U.S. resource
policy was controlled by the USFS, the Bureau of Reclamation, and the
industry-related trade groups that lobbied the government to reject
the appeals of activists such as Muir, who sought to preserve the land
for aesthetic reasons, in favor of Pinchot's policies based on efficiency,
scientific management, centralized control, and organized economic
development.[13]

Despite their incorporation of some preservationist goals at the
turn of the century, federal policies have often been inconsistent and
contradictory to both the preservationist and the multiple-use, conservationist objectives. The Forest Service Organic Act of 1897, for example, established the government's intent to retain some forested
land under federal ownership to protect uncut forests from destructive
logging practices and fires. Under this policy, which was in effect for

several decades, timber harvesting from national forests was greatly limited. But after World War II, the demand for timber for housing construction led the USFS to revise its policy when the agency increased harvest levels and supported the practice of clear-cutting within national forests during the 1950s and 1960s. The USFS's subsidization of road building into logging areas made harvesting timber even easier.[14]

When the National Park Service (NPS) was originally created in 1916, Congress gave the agency two mandates that have produced considerable tension between environmental groups and members of the opposition. On the one hand, the NPS was given responsibility for conserving scenery, natural and historic objects, and wildlife, to "leave them unimpaired for the enjoyment of future generations." At the same time, the agency was asked to provide for the public's enjoyment of those features. As political scientist Zachary Smith notes,

> In an effort to provide more service for the public, the Park Service has been criticized by environmentalists for having a "Disneyland" mentality. For example, in the early 1970s, the Park Service and the Music Corporation of America (the concessionaire, at that time, in Yosemite National Park) together developed a master plan for Yosemite Valley that included, among other things, a significant expansion of visitor facilities, including the building of a convention center. MCA produced and distributed slick promotional brochures outlining the corporation's commitment to preserving park values. One read, "It's not just another American convention hotel. . . . All your worldly needs are provided for. . . . This isn't no man's land or primitive wilderness. This is civilization."[15]

In its efforts to satisfy the law's somewhat contradictory mandates, NPS policies have offended those seeking strict preservation as well as those groups supportive of enhanced public access and use.

Other controversies in resource policy have developed from the 1872 Mining Law, which is still in effect and is a major legislative target of the environmental movement. When this law was first enacted, the government encouraged new settlers to prospect for valuable minerals on public lands by offering them full title to surrounding lands for $5.00 per acre. However, there was never a requirement that the titleholder prove minerals were on the land within a specific time period following the staking of a claim. The policy has allowed thousands of acres of public lands to be tied up in nonproducing claims, with little revenue flowing back to the government and no attempts made to settle the lands as had been the law's original intent.

In other instances, although it might appear the government's policies were inconsistent, it is more likely that they reflected prevailing public attitudes that were out of sync with the ever-changing agenda of the environmental movement. After World War II, the federal government turned its attention from resource management to pollution-related issues in response to public concerns about widely publicized smog episodes in Donora, Pennsylvania, in 1948 and a similar incident in London in 1952. Although Congress made nominal legislative progress in dealing with pollution control issues with the passage of the Water Pollution Control Act in 1956 and the 1963 Clean Air Act, the major environmental organizations—the Sierra Club, the National Parks and Conservation Association (NPCA), and the Wilderness Society—remained focused on protectionism rather than pollution.

The efforts of these groups to expand wilderness designations and impede proposed hydroelectric projects, especially the Echo Park Dam within Dinosaur National Monument, became what Grant McConnell has termed "a turning point of historic significance."[16] A similar project, the proposed Glen Canyon Dam near the Arizona-Utah border, became the target of Sierra Club executive director David Brower, who transformed the environmental movement into a much more activist and, to some extent, militant political force.[17] Environmental activist and author Robert Gottlieb has described this period leading up to the 1960s as a time when

> the search for a common frame of reference, embedded in either management or protectionist language, had reached a certain impasse regarding the natural environment. With a complex relationship to the resource bureaucracies, an unresolved debate over technology and population, a growing expertise and lobbying focus, and an increasingly visible profile, conservationist and protectionist groups had managed to carve out for themselves a major role in the policy arena regarding resources and the natural environment. Yet these groups had failed to identify a common agenda even in the resources area, nor had they been able to respond to the urban and industrial realities that marked the Progressive Era and subsequently transformed the post–World War II order.[18]

As Gottlieb suggests, during this period environmental groups themselves became fragmented. The traditional groups continued to lobby for preservation, while new groups targeted the urban pollution caused by factory emissions, and still others focused on public health and sanitation issues or on consumer and workplace concerns. Some of these issues led to a divisiveness between labor and the environmental movement. "Bottle bill" legislation providing cash rebates for returnable containers, modifications to the Clean Air Act and the Endangered Species Act (ESA), and feared job losses due to new environmental regulations united labor and industry against projects proposed by environmentalists.[19] After World War II, new and distinctive groups began to emerge, made up of reformers, professionals, and radicals, transforming the movement from the late 1960s through the 1990s. The substantial growth in the number and membership of environmental groups in this period coincided with a responding period of environmental legislation and regulation that was virtually unchallenged until the Republican Party gained control of Congress after the 1994 congressional elections.

Within this thirty-year period, Congress reacted to not only the newly energized environmental movement, but also to a series of pivotal events: the publication of Rachel Carson's 1962 exposé of the pesticide industry, *Silent Spring;* a critical air pollution episode in New York City in 1966; author Paul Ehrlich's ominous predictions in his book *The Population Bomb* in 1968; and the highly publicized oil spill off the coast of Santa Barbara in 1969. By 1970, the United States was poised to enter a new environmental era, celebrated on January 1 with the signing of the National Environmental Policy Act (NEPA) (requiring environmental impact studies for proposed federal projects) and on April 22 with the observance of Earth Day.

THE CONTEMPORARY ENVIRONMENTAL MOVEMENT

Most observers credit Earth Day 1970 as the advent of modern environmentalism,[20] since it was accompanied throughout the new decade by the development of widespread public support and the creation of a new federal bureaucracy (the Environmental Protection Agency [EPA] in 1970, the revamped Nuclear Regulatory Commission in 1975, and the Department of Energy in 1977). Congressional initiatives during this decade included the Clean Air Act Amendments (1970), the Federal Water Pollution Control Act Amendments and the Federal Environmental Pesticide Control Act (1972), the Endangered Species Act (1973), the Safe Drinking Water Act (1974), the Toxic Substances Control Act and the Resource Conservation and Recovery Act (1976), the Federal Water Pollution Control Act Amendments and the Surface Mining Control and Reclamation Act (1977), and the National Energy Act (1978). An indication of the broad, public support for these bills was that many were passed during Republican presidential administrations.

At the same time, however, while environmental groups gained membership and political clout, and the federal government responded with new regulations and agencies to administer them, industry was gradually beginning to take notice. What had once been seen by industry as a nuisance movement was now recognized as something much more substantive. When environmental organizations secured places at the negotiating table that were previously reserved for business and trade groups, an industry-led countermovement, described in detail in Part II of this book, began to mobilize. Although earlier organizations such as the Conservation Foundation (1948) and Resources for the Future (RFF) (1952) had initially focused on efforts to better utilize natural resources, by the late 1970s, industry groups began to use their political expertise and financial resources in direct opposition to the mainstream environmental groups. From the Chemical Manufacturers Association to the Edison Electric Institute, business reentered a conservation debate in which it had been a noticeably passive participant.

In 1970, led by the utility industry, business mobilized against Earth Day with its own counterevents and public relations efforts, with some environmental groups responding with outright hostility. Activists presented Florida Power and Light with a dead octopus as a symbol of their allegations that the utility was responsible for the thermal pollution of Biscayne Bay, while a Commonwealth Edison speaker at the University of Illinois was disrupted by students throwing soot on one another and coughing vigorously. Government officials were not immune to the environmental groups' criticisms either. Antinuclear activists presented the Colorado Environmental Rapist of the Year Award to the Atomic Energy Commission, and Secretary of the Interior Walter Hickel, speaking at the University of Alaska, was booed off the stage when he spoke at an Earth Day rally to support the Alaska pipeline project.[21]

Though the 1980s began with a more conservative, Republican agenda,[22] there is disagreement among researchers about whether the environment became a less important issue to most Americans then. During the Reagan administrations from 1981 to 1988, the emphasis on deregulation and the accompanying cuts in the budget for the EPA devastated much of the legislative and attitudinal ground that had been covered in the previous decade.[23] Although public concern about the environment had been in a slow decline prior to 1980 as a result of a sluggish economy, high inflation, and international events such as the Iranian hostage crisis, reductions in staffing, research, and enforcement activities under the leadership of EPA administrator Anne Gorsuch and Interior Department secretary James Watt reignited the activists in the environmental movement. Sociologist Riley Dunlap's analysis of public opinion polls from this period shows a rejection of the Reagan administration's positions and an increasing commitment to protecting the environment—a comeback of sorts for a rejuvenated environmental concern.[24]

Environmentalists attempted to capitalize on this new momentum in 1990 by planning a twenty-year anniversary of Earth Day. This time, however, the mood and focus of the observance was quite different.

When Denis Hayes, the Stanford University student leader who had worked with Senator Gaylord Nelson to plan the 1970 event, took his proposal to major environmental groups in 1988, he argued that the event should be more global in scope. He said that Earth Day 1990 should be tailored to maximize media coverage and should focus on the theme of individual responsibility for environmental stewardship.

In retrospect, Earth Day 1990 was a public relations success for the environmental movement, with an estimated 200 million participants in 140 countries.[25] As Denis Hayes had wished, the media did publicize the event and used as their backdrop a scorecard on the still-unfinished environmental protection agenda.[26] However, Earth Day 1990 also underscored the widening gap between the more highly professionalized and sophisticated mainstream environmental groups (e.g., the National Resources Defense Council [NRDC] and the Environmental Defense Fund) and the grassroots organizations (e.g., the Gulf Coast Tenant Leadership Project and the Southwest Organizing Project), especially those developing in communities of color over the issues of environmental racism and toxic pollution.

A somewhat unexpected set of participants in the 1990 Earth Day observance were business and industry interests, who used the event as an opportunity to paint themselves with an environmental brush, part of an overall strategy called "greenwashing" that is explored further in Chapter 5. Earth Day became the mechanism by which companies touted their sense of corporate environmental responsibility and was a major step forward in their attempts to convince the public that industry had "turned green." Suddenly there was a rush to sign on to the "Valdez Principles"—ten corporate commitments to environmental protection drafted by the Coalition for Environmentally Responsible Economies (CERES)—created after the 1989 Alaskan oil spill caused by the tanker *Exxon Valdez*. Other companies attempted to gain consumers' support by seeking out "eco-approval" for products from two environmental certification companies, Green Seal and Green Cross.[27]

Despite the success of Earth Day 1990, public attention again seemed to have waned by the time the twenty-fifth anniversary of Earth Day was observed in April 1995. While the polls continued to indicate steady and broad support for environmental protection, many of the major organizations were struggling to meet payrolls. They were laying off workers, closing offices, and dealing with a declining membership base. They also faced a Congress and a president whose commitment and interest in the environment were overshadowed by other issues. Environmentalists who were comforted by President Bill Clinton's selection of Al Gore as vice president and Bruce Babbitt as secretary of the interior quickly became disenchanted with the president, who had not made environmental protection an issue during his 1992

campaign. Although Clinton was viewed as preferable to the only
other alternative—George Bush—candidate Clinton chose not to court
environmental groups' support and ignored their attempts to move the
environment nearer to the top of his policy agenda.[28]

Though Clinton, encouraged by Babbitt, did attempt several new
initiatives for environmental protection during his first term in office,
such as grazing reform and a new timber policy, he was successful in
convincing Congress to enact only a handful of important measures,
such as the 1996 Food Quality Protection Act and amendments to safe
drinking water laws. Analysts ascribe the failure to three factors: the
diffuse efforts to enact the bills, with too many interest groups pursuing
too many priorities; a determined bipartisan environmental opposition
that argued that enhanced protective efforts would harm property
owners, businesses, and local governments; and an increasing partisan-
ship in Congress, which favored a conservative agenda over a liberal
one.[29] After the 1994 congressional midterm elections, and the election
of a two-house Republican majority for the first time since 1946, the legislative arena returned as a key battleground for a growing grassroots
opposition dedicated to fighting the environmental movement.

As this brief overview indicates, the ebb and flow of public opinion on environmental issues has been coupled with federal policies
that, while gradually evolving in a preservationist direction, have reflected uncertainty and inconsistency by addressing the needs of different constituencies and balancing its roles as a promoter of industry
and protector of the environment. Those factors have further complicated the issues as the domestic policy process is increasingly influenced by global events such as U.S. involvement in the Persian Gulf,
famine in Africa, political instability in Mexico, and civil war in the
Balkan states, each of which affects the priority of the environment on
the policy agenda. The environment is an inevitable part of a cycle in
which other issues take over the public's attention and opportunities
develop for opposition movements and for individuals willing to capitalize on the lapse of public attention.

THE OPENING OF THE POLICY WINDOW

Political scientist John Kingdon describes the policy window as "an opportunity for advocates of proposals to push their pet solutions, or to
push attention to their special problems."[30] The window opens unpre-
dictably and infrequently, stays open for a short period of time, and
may close in response to a number of factors. Windows also are used by
policy entrepreneurs—individuals who invest their time, energy, reputations, and money—to promote an issue in expectation of a return or
future gain. Individual entrepreneurs are sometimes in the right place

at the right time, but they also take advantage of the way the policy-making process works and are able to make effective use of their resources, whether they involve a charismatic personality or a sophisticated understanding of the intricacies of the regulatory process.

Although I explain these factors in greater detail elsewhere in this book, an example here will illustrate how one contemporary policy entrepreneur has been able to use the opening of a policy window to his advantage. Charles Cushman, a former Los Angeles insurance executive, became involved in the environmental opposition in 1970 when he purchased a vacation cabin just inside the boundaries of Yosemite National Park. In 1978, as part of the Omnibus National Parks Act, the NPS adopted a policy to reduce private landholdings within the parks because they were incompatible with its intended purpose of preserving scenic wilderness areas. Funds were made available to purchase land held by inholders (people who own property surrounded by federal land), and, after several cabins were burned down, Cushman began organizing fellow property owners to oppose the NPS policy on inholdings, as well as later NPS plans to expand park boundaries and increase the number of parks under the agency's control. In 1978, he founded the National Parks Inholders Association and filed an unsuccessful suit against the NPS. But he was able to obtain the names of some 30,000 inholders nationwide and organized groups in fifty parks in the first year of the association's operation. The group's name was later changed to the National Inholders Association, expanding not only the organization's mission but its membership base as well by including those with permits to use federal land and those who own property outside the NPS system.[31]

The policy window opened for Cushman in the late 1970s for a number of reasons. His ability to organize inholders came at a time when the Sagebrush Rebellion (discussed further in Chapter 7) was beginning to unite landholders and extractive resource interests in the West. The election of Ronald Reagan in 1980 provided Cushman and other property rights advocates with a climate in which his group's issues received a highly receptive response from the president. As Kingdon observes, "the new Reagan administration provided a window for a host of players previously disadvantaged" who now realized they might get a sympathetic hearing with a new cast of characters.[32] Cushman was able to maintain the momentum throughout the 1980s until other environmental opposition groups also began to coalesce. With the redistribution of seats in Congress in 1994, the policy window remained open for Cushman and other entrepreneurs, even though President Bush lost his reelection bid in 1992 and a Democrat remained in the White House.

Cushman has been able to parlay his organization and rhetorical skills into leading one of the most powerful and militant segments within the environmental opposition: property rights activists. His success stems in part from efforts to magnify the apparent size and influence of his movement by the continuous creation of new groups with different names but purposes that are virtually identical. Although he works closely with wise use umbrella organizations such as the Center for the Defense of Free Enterprise (CFDFE), he has his own stable of organizations founded over the last few years, from the American Land Rights Association (ALRA) and the Multiple Use Land Alliance to the League of Private Property Voters, modeled after the environmental movement's League of Conservation Voters. He has also been successful at grassroots organizing, from orchestrating short-term campaigns against proposed marshlands protection to leading a boycott of companies that led them to drop their advertising during documentaries on grazing and ancient forests. He works the lecture circuit with other policy entrepreneurs, organizes letter-writing campaigns, provides training to local groups, and has been called "Rent-a-Riot" Cushman for his field organizing skills.[33]

The environmental opposition is noteworthy for a number of policy entrepreneurs like Cushman, many of them taking advantage of policy windows within their region or state. They have effectively used the same tactics as those pioneered by the mainstream environmental movement twenty years earlier, but they now have the added help of fax machines and the Internet, which enable instant and effective communication with members spread throughout the country. As Cushman himself has said, "We read their book on organizing," citing the ability of groups like the Wilderness Society and the Sierra Club to increase their membership and raise funds during the 1980s when Reagan appointee James Watt became the bane of environmentalists. Cushman has predicted that the Clinton administration "is going to scare a lot of people and we'll make lots of money"; and he told one reporter, "If your article is negative, I'll use it in my fundraisers."[34]

The policy window often closes when participants feel their issues have been sufficiently addressed, when they fail to get a return on their investment or resources, when a focusing event passes, when there is a recurrence of the same kind of personnel changes that opened the policy window initially, or when there is no readily available alternative to meet the needs of the policy entrepreneurs and their followers. The Conclusion of this book returns to these factors as a way of assessing the impact of the environmental opposition on public policy thus far and the implications of the movement for the future.

THE IMPORTANCE OF NOMENCLATURE

The terminology used in this book epitomizes the difficulty of trying to group the various participants of the environmental debate into a single entity. In 1994, journalist/private investigator David Helvarg's book *The War Against the Greens* profiled dozens of groups and individuals he termed "anti-enviros," who are part of a "counterrevolutionary movement that defines itself in response to the environmental movement of the past thirty years."[35] Within that movement, he includes a diverse list of interests, including extractive resource industries like timber and mining, property rights activists (developers and individual landowners), recreationists, western ranchers and corporate farmers, businesspeople, and militia members and conspiracy theorists. The movement, he says, has ties to the Reverend Sun Myung Moon and his business empire, conservative Washington, D.C., think tanks like the Heritage Foundation, and "the fringes of America's expanding underbelly of violence, where social causes become excuses for sociopaths motivated by fear, greed, and hatred, or private security agents working on behalf of outlaw industries."[36]

Helvarg is not alone in his assessment. Since 1990, most of the country's mainstream environmental groups and even organizations such as the New York Zoological Society have regularly published exposés on the groups Helvarg identifies in his book, with similarly ominous warnings about their power and influence. Scientists and writers Paul and Anne Ehrlich used the term "brownlash rhetoric" in their book *Betrayal of Science and Reason* to describe what they perceive to be a deliberate misstatement of scientific findings designed to support an anti-environmental world view and political agenda.[37] Liberal publications such as *The Progressive*, *The Amicus Journal* (published by the Natural Resources Defense Council), and *Mother Jones* have sounded comparable alarms about the threat posed by what they call the "anti-environmental movement."[38] The Center for Investigative Reporting and researchers at the Western States Center and Political Research Associates have lent their expertise and backed up the claims of the environmental groups. A few, notably the Audubon Society, have been more moderate in their rhetoric, viewing the creation of the wise use movement "as a wake-up call."[39] Phil Brick, one of the few political scientists to study the wise use movement, recognized the political and ideological coherence of the opposition and still speaks of "the rise of anti-environmentalism" as a form of resistance to the costs imposed by environmental regulations.[40]

The term "anti-environmental" is inaccurate, however, because it assumes those associated with the label are somehow philosophically "against" the environment, which is seldom the case. It is, in any event, unlikely that someone responding to a researcher's survey would stray from the socially acceptable response by willingly admitting that he or she is against the traditional goals of the environmental movement, such as clean drinking water or breathable air. In a less normative attempt at definition, journalist Gregg Easterbrook uses the term "unviros,"[41] but that, too, treats the players as if they were a single entity.

One of the goals of this book is to examine the legitimacy of commonly accepted stereotypes that portray those in the grassroots opposition as ill informed or easily misled about environmental issues. It is often assumed that these activists are politically unsophisticated westerners whose sole objective is to exploit the land for their own narrow use, with little concern for the future of the nation's natural resources. Many observers have also linked the environmental opposition to conservative, libertarian, or antigovernmental movements.

The interviews and surveys conducted during the writing of this book indicate that the environmental opposition is made up of a much broader constituency than has generally been identified. There is no singular occupational category to describe the opposition, nor is there a convenient political label. And while many of the organizations that are central to the grassroots activism of the movement are headquartered in the West, their membership base is slowly spreading to other regions of the United States and across demographic and socioeconomic lines. Property rights groups, such as the Pennsylvania Landowners' Association, have traditionally been stronger in the East than the wise use and county supremacy groups that tend to form in areas with access to larger tracts of public land. The terminology and descriptions used by individual members of the opposition provide some insight into their feelings about being called "anti-environmental." For example, one respondent admitted to being against "the radical preservationist movement," and another said she was engaged in "resource advocacy." One person noted that he did not oppose the environmental movement but supported multiple use in natural resource policy. A representative allied with the commercial fishing industry commented, "I do not have a problem with the environmental movement. I oppose the Crisis Industry." Others have equal amounts of contempt for environmentalists and for industry. As one woman wrote,

> First of all, I am not "anti-environmental." I care very much about the environment. I have spent a considerable amount of time in the woods, know quite a bit about the environment and raised orphaned and injured wildlife for several years. . . . I have no respect for big environmental groups and their $$$ leaders and I have no respect for big corporate owners or leaders who are ruthless and have no concern for people.[42]

For these reasons, the term "anti-enviros" is not used in this book. Instead, the more generic term "environmental opposition" is used, with some hesitation, to describe the focus of group strategy—environmental laws, regulations, policies, and the environmental movement—depending upon the individual or group involved. The next ten chapters will show how the environmental opposition developed, from the early land use battles to its contemporary counterpart, the property rights movement. The book returns in the Conclusion to reevaluate the nomenclature and the reasons why understanding the "environmental opposition" is less critical than understanding where it and the environmental movement fit in the larger political process.

NOTES

1. Timothy O'Riordan, "Frameworks for Choice: Core Beliefs and the Environment," *Environment*, vol. 37, no. 8 (October 1995): 4–9, 25–29. To assist the reader in gaining an overall sense of events, the time line in the Appendixes section provides some of the highlights in U.S. environmental history, including key legislative initiatives, group formation, and events that have contributed to public attitudes about the environment.

2. Roderick Frazier Nash, *American Environmentalism*, 3rd ed. (New York: McGraw-Hill, 1990), p. xi.

3. Gary Lee, "An Environmental History of America," *Washington Post National Weekly Edition*, December 12–18, 1994, p. 38. There are, however, conflicting views among researchers as to the impact of North American Indians on the environment, especially with regard to the hunting of game animals and the modification of forests and woodlands to create areas for grazing and agricultural use. Some have argued that our knowledge about the Native Americans' influence on the environment is more accurately a reflection of uncertainties about estimates of their population. See, for example, Karl Butzer, ed., "The Americas Before and After 1492," *Annals of the American Association of American Geographers* (September 1992); William Cronon, *Changes in the Land: Indians, Colonists, and the Ecology of New England* (New York: Hill and Wang, 1983); Michael Williams, *Americans and Their Forests* (Cambridge, England: Cambridge University Press, 1989); and Ronald Wright, *Stolen Continents: The Americas Through Indian Eyes Since 1492* (Boston: Houghton Mifflin, 1992).

4. See Jeremy Bentham, *Introduction to the Principles of Morals and Legislation* (Oxford, England: Clarendon Press, 1823); and John Stuart Mill, *Utilitarianism*, ed. with an introduction by George Sher (Indianapolis, IN: Hackett, 1979).

5. An expanded view of the early philosophical underpinnings of U.S. environmentalism can be found in Joseph R. Desjardins, *Environmental Ethics: An Introduction to Environmental Philosophy* (Belmont, CA: Wadsworth, 1993).

6. Nash, *American Environmentalism*, pp. 9–10.

7. Robert Gottlieb, *Forcing the Spring: The Transformation of the American Environmental Movement* (Washington, DC: Island Press, 1993), pp. 19–20.

8. See, for example, George Perkins Marsh, *Man and Nature; or, Physical Geography as Modified by Human Action* (New York: Charles Scribner, 1864); Henry David Thoreau, *Walden* (New York: Library of America, 1985), and *Maine Woods*, in *The Writings of Henry David Thoreau* (Boston: Houghton Mifflin, 1894); and Ralph Waldo Emerson, *Complete Essays and Other Writings* (New York: Modern Library, 1950).

9. See William L. Graf, *Wilderness Preservation and the Sagebrush Rebellions* (Savage, MD: Rowman and Littlefield, 1990).

10. See Samuel P. Hays, *Conservation and the Gospel of Efficiency* (Cambridge, MA: Harvard University Press, 1959). Hays has made an incredible

contribution to the historical understanding of U.S. environmental history, and his depth of detailed research on this period is without peer.

11. See Samuel T. Dana and Sally K. Fairfax, *Forest and Range Policy: Its Development in the United States* (New York: McGraw-Hill, 1980).

12. See Frederick Jackson Turner, *The Frontier in American History* (New York: Henry Holt, 1921). The safety valve theory is debunked by other historians, however, including Fred A. Shannon, "A Post-Mortem on the Labor-Safety-Valve-Theory," *Agricultural History*, vol. 19 (January 1945): 31–37.

13. Gottlieb, *Forcing the Spring*, pp. 23–24.

14. Frederick W. Cubbage, Jay O'Laughlin, and Charles S. Bullock III, *Forest Resource Policy* (New York: John Wiley and Sons, 1993), pp. 33–34.

15. Zachary A. Smith, *The Environmental Policy Paradox*, 2nd ed. (Englewood Cliffs, NJ: Prentice Hall, 1995), p. 61.

16. Grant McConnell, "The Environmental Movement: Ambiguities and Meanings," *Natural Resources Journal* (July 1971): 433.

17. See Conrad L. Wirth, *Parks, Politics, and the People* (Norman: University of Oklahoma Press, 1980).

18. Gottlieb, *Forcing the Spring*, p. 46.

19. Samuel P. Hays, *Beauty, Health, and Permanence: Environmental Politics in the United States, 1955–1985* (Cambridge, England: Cambridge University Press, 1987), pp. 298–300.

20. See, for example, Riley E. Dunlap and Angela G. Mertig, "The Evolution of the U.S. Environmental Movement from 1970 to 1990: An Overview," in Riley E. Dunlap and Angela G. Mertig, eds., *American Environmentalism: The U.S. Environmental Movement, 1970–1990* (Philadelphia: Taylor and Francis, 1992), pp. 1–10.

21. Gottlieb, *Forcing the Spring*, pp. 110–111.

22. See, for example, Laura M. Lake, "The Environmental Mandate: Activists and the Electorate," *Political Science Quarterly*, vol. 98 (1983): 16–20; and Robert Cameron Mitchell, "Public Opinion and Environmental Politics in the 1970s and 1980s," in Norman Vig and Michael Kraft, eds., *Environmental Policy in the 1980s: Reagan's New Agenda* (Washington, DC: Congressional Quarterly Press, 1984), pp. 51–74.

23. On the Reagan administration, see *Ronald Reagan and the Environment* (San Francisco: Friends of the Earth, 1982); and C. Brant Short, *Ronald Reagan and the Public Lands: America's Conservation Debate* (College Station: Texas A & M University Press, 1989). On the Bush administration, see Colin Campbell and Bert Rockman, eds., *The Bush Presidency: First Appraisals* (Chatham, NJ: Chatham House, 1991); Rae Tyson, "How Green Is Bush?" *USA Today*, September 18, 1991, p. 1; and Margaret E. Kriz, "The Selling of the 'Green President,'" *National Journal*, September 19, 1992, p. 2151.

24. See, for example, Riley Dunlap, "Polls, Pollution, and Politics Revisited: Public Opinion on the Environment in the Reagan Era," *Environment*, vol. 29, no. 6 (July–August 1987): 6–11, 32–37; Riley Dunlap and Rik Scarce, "The Polls—A Report: Environmental Problems and Protection," *Public Opinion Quarterly*, vol. 55 (1991); Louis Harris, "Public Worried About State of the Environment Today and in the Future," *Harris Poll*, no. 21 (1989): 1–4; and Robert Cameron Mitchell, "Public Opinion and the Green Lobby: Poised for the 1990s?" in Norman Vig and Michael Kraft, eds., *Environmental Policy in the 1990s: Toward a New Agenda* (Washington, DC: Congressional Quarterly Press, 1990), pp. 81–99.

25. See Robert D. McFadden, "Millions Join Battle for a Beloved Planet," *New York Times*, April 23, 1990, p. 1.

26. Gottlieb, *Forcing the Spring*, pp. 201–204. See also Gary Cohen, "It's Too Easy Being Green: The Gains and Losses of Earth Day," *New Solutions*, vol. 1, no. 2 (summer 1990): 9–12.

27. See, for example, Mark Potts, "The Greening of Big Oil," *Washington Post National Weekly Edition*, November 19–25, 1990, p. 22; "Seeing the Green Light," *The Economist*, vol. 317 (October 20, 1990): 88; and Eric Mann, "Environmentalism in the Corporate Climate," *Tikkun*, vol. 5 (March–April 1990): 61.

28. Notably, two early assessments of the Clinton administration make virtually no mention of his environmental record, either during or after his 1992 campaign. See Colin Campbell and Bert A. Rockman, eds., *The Clinton Presidency: First Appraisals* (Chatham, NJ: Chatham House, 1996); and David Stoesz, *Small Change: Domestic Policy Under the Clinton Presidency* (White Plains, NY: Longman, 1996). Other observers have been less than charitable, noting that Clinton's environmental policy appears based on years of costly research "devoted to the wrong problems." See Keith Schneider, "New View Calls Environmental Policy Misguided," *New York Times*, March 21, 1993, p. 1.

29. See John L. Cushman, "Few Environmental Laws Emerge from 103rd Congress," *New York Times*, October 3, 1994, p. B12; and Linda Kanamine, "Leaner Times Test Limits of Movement," *USA Today*, October 19, 1994, p. A1.

30. John Kingdon, *Agendas, Alternatives, and Public Policies*, 2nd ed. (New York: HarperCollins, 1995), p. 165.

31. This biographical sketch comes from a series of profiles of activists in William Perry Pendley's *It Takes a Hero* (Bellevue, WA: Free Enterprise Press, 1994), pp. 81–84. The publisher is part of the umbrella group Center for the Defense of Free Enterprise, coordinated by two other policy entrepreneurs within the environmental opposition, Allan Gottlieb and Ron Arnold.

32. Kingdon, *Agendas*, p. 168.

33. Cushman and his strategies have been widely profiled, especially by the environmental organizations he has targeted. See, for example, Margaret L. Knox, "The World According to Cushman," *Wilderness*, vol. 56, no. 200 (spring 1993): 28–31, 36; David Helvarg, "Grassroots for Sale," *Amicus Journal*, vol. 16, no. 3 (fall 1994): 24–29; Richard M. Stapleton, "On the Western Front," *National Parks*, vol. 67 (January–February 1993): 32–36; and Kate O'Callaghan, "Whose Agenda for America?" *Audubon* (September–October 1992): 80–89.

34. Knox, "The World According to Cushman," p. 36.

35. David Helvarg, *The War Against the Greens: The "Wise-Use" Movement, the New Right, and Anti-Environmental Violence* (San Francisco: Sierra Club Books, 1994), p. 9.

36. Ibid., p. 14.

37. See, for example, Nancy Simmons, "Eco-Investigation," *Wildlife Conservation*, vol. 95 (November–December 1992): 35; Richard M. Stapleton, "Green vs. Green," *National Parks* (November–December 1992): 32–37; Patricia Byrnes, "The Counterfeit Crusade," *Wilderness* (summer 1992): 29–31; and Paul R. Ehrlich and Anne H. Ehrlich, *Betrayal of Science and Reason: How Anti-Environmental Rhetoric Threatens Our Future* (Washington, DC: Island Press, 1996).

38. See, for example, Margaret Knox, "Meet the Anti-Greens," *The Progressive*, vol. 55, no. 10 (October 1991): 21–23; "Vote Vocally," *Amicus Journal* (fall 1994): 55; and Margaret Knox, "Wise Guys," *Mother Jones*, vol. 16, no. 1 (January–February 1991): 16.

39. O'Callaghan, "Whose Agenda for America?" p. 89.

40. Phil Brick, "Determined Opposition: The Wise Use Movement Challenges Environmentalism," *Environment*, vol. 37, no. 8 (October 1995): 19–20.

41. Gregg Easterbrook, *A Moment on the Earth: The Coming Age of Environmental Optimism* (New York: Viking, 1995).

42. The conclusion that the makeup of the opposition is more diverse than previously reported stems from interviews I conducted from 1991 to 1996, as well as a random survey and follow-up interviews conducted in 1995–1996 of activists in the wise use movement. Wherever possible, direct quotations from those interviewed or contacted for this book are attributed by source and date. However, some respondents asked that they not be specifically identified by name. See Jacqueline Vaughn Switzer, "Women and Wise Use: The Other Side of Environmental Activism," paper presented at the 1996 annual meeting of the Western Political Science Association, San Francisco, March 14–16, 1996, p. 6.

PART I

CONFLICTS OVER LAND AND RESOURCES

1

The Early Land Use Battles

SIGN OF THE TIMES: In 1910, in a speech delivered to the State Bankers Association of Washington, senatorial candidate Thomas Burke critiqued the federal government's land use policies and explained why many residents of the West were opposed to the eastern-based conservation movement:

> *The opinion seems to prevail in the East that the West is opposed to the conservation of natural resources. . . . [Conservation] is in more danger of shipwreck from its overzealous and intolerant advocates than from its avowed opponents. The people of the West believe in forest reservation based upon common sense and scientific principles. They believe in the necessity of protecting our forests against fire and preventable waste, in extending forest reservations over lands better adapted to forest growth than to farming, in preserving the forests on mountain sides and steep hillsides, and in the importance of reforesting deforested areas unsuited to agriculture. . . .*
>
> *But they do not believe in hoarding the wilderness. They do not believe in the sentimental fad that trees are entitled to more consideration than human beings. . . . The people of today have a right to share in the blessings of nature. There is no intention in the West to rob the future, but there is a determined purpose not to let a band of well-meaning sentimentalists rob the present on the plea that it is necessary to hoard Nature's riches for unborn generations.[1]*

Many of the contemporary battles in the United States over natural resources, land, and property rights that pit various interests against one another have their origin in disputes that date back to the early years of the nation's development. This chapter looks at some of the early skirmishes in the war over the public domain—defined as land owned by the federal government—from the late 1700s through the 1940s, and identifies the underlying disputes that are still unresolved. The majority of the early land use battles were focused on the West, where undeveloped land was abundantly available and federal control was less centralized and pervasive. Four periods of land use disputes can be identified during this time frame: The first was over the creation of a national public domain under the Articles of Confederation during the 1780s. The next set of controversies centered on the disposal of federal land, which began during the rapid western expansion of the early 1800s and continued for much of the century. The third stage began when various land users saw some common interests and formed a loosely organized but genuine environmental opposition to the government's imposition of fees and permits for use and access to the public land. Finally, beginning in the early 1940s, westerners organized in an attempt for an outright takeover of public lands from the federal government.

While many of the early disputes focused generally on the disposition of the public domain, there were additional policy issues involving the use of natural resources by various organized interests: the timber industry, utility companies, irrigation users and developers seeking expansion of navigable streams, and members of the mining and petroleum industry. The controversies that led to these disputes in the early history of the West grew into the contemporary Sagebrush Rebellion that is described in detail in Chapter 7. Although there was genuine agreement among policymakers and landholders that natural resources were important, valuable, and worth protecting, the argument was over how much of the land needed protection and for what purpose. The issues raised during the period from the 1780s to the 1940s have reappeared as a part of the evolution of environmental opposition that has dominated the land use debate during the 1990s.

THE CREATION OF A NATIONAL PUBLIC DOMAIN

The earliest disputes about what became the public domain began when the Articles of Confederation were being proposed in 1777 as a way of linking the states together in the interests of national unity after the American Revolution. One of the issues that formed the basis of land controversy was the relinquishing of state claims to territory immediately to the west of the original colonies. Virginia, for example, claimed much of what is now Kentucky; other claims were made by North Carolina over present-day Tennessee and by Georgia over land that extended all the way to the Mississippi River. The six states that claimed no western lands (Pennsylvania, New Hampshire, Rhode Island, Delaware, New Jersey, Maryland) were concerned about their relative lack of power, given the fact they were forced to levy high taxes on their citizens to help pay off the Revolutionary War debt. This was in sharp contrast to the other seven states that could potentially pay their portion of the war debts by selling their western landholdings, creating financial inequity during a fragile political period. The nonclaiming states refused to join the confederation without a cession of claims by the other states, which forced the Continental Congress to attempt to resolve the dispute.

Congressional leaders realized that the ratification of the confederation and national unification rested on a resolution of the lands dispute. In 1780, the Continental Congress pledged that if the claiming states ceded the lands west of the existing boundaries of the thirteen original states to the federal government, the land would be disposed of for the common benefit of the United States. The goal was to settle the ceded land and form states that would have the same rights, sovereignty, and independence as the original thirteen. The cessions began slowly and reluctantly, with New York becoming the first state to give up its claims in 1781 in hopes of keeping the confederation intact. The last cession did not take place until Georgia released its claims in 1802, doing so long after the Constitution was ratified and on the condition that the state receive $1.2 million in compensation for its land. The western lands ceded by the original colonies, as well as additional territory that the U.S. government conquered or purchased over the next century, became part of the national public domain. The cessions also represented conflicting policies. While the federal government agreed to manage the public domain for the benefit of all, it also sought to form new states but retained the title to the land and the authority to sell it to private parties.

In the public domain land, the federal government had a potential source of wealth. In 1782, the Continental Congress proposed the sale of the newly acquired public domain to discharge the national debt, a plan that surprised those who had expected the land to be given away to settlers.[2] Following that failure, in 1784, Thomas Jefferson proposed a public land ordinance that would divide the public domain into new states that would be admitted on an equal basis with the original thirteen, but the plan was never actually put into effect. A year later, the Land Ordinance of 1785 established the land survey system that is still used today, dividing the public domain into 36-square-mile townships, sections of 1 square mile (640 acres), and authorizing their sale at a minimum price of $1.00 per acre with a 640-acre minimum. The ordinance required the land to be surveyed in advance so the lands could be patented with clear title passing from the United States to the purchasers.

Another attempt to divide the public domain was made in 1787 with the Northwest Ordinance, an agreement that applied to the territory north of the Ohio River, which set forth specific requirements for the acquisition of territorial and statehood status as well as for internal governance. Under the ordinance, once a territory reached a population of 60,000, it would be admitted on an "equal footing" (with the same political and legal status) as the original thirteen, except that the new state did not have title to the land within its borders, which remained part of the public domain and could be sold. Initially, public domain land sales were financially disappointing, so Congress later revised both the price and the conditions of sale. Newly admitted states were also required to renounce their taxing power over public domain lands, and the majority of the southern states entered the Union only by agreeing to disclaim all rights to "waste or unappropriated lands" that remained in federal control.[3]

Those provisions were later recodified in Article 4, Section 3, of the Constitution of 1787, which gave Congress the power "to dispose of and make all needful Rules and Regulations respecting the Territory and other Property belonging to the United States." Historians and constitutional scholars argue that each state admitted to the Union after the original thirteen thus voluntarily gave up its claim to the land as a condition of admission. This enhanced the growing sectionalism that was beginning to develop as power was concentrated in the northern region of the nation and newly admitted states began to feel that they were on the periphery of decisionmaking.

THE PUBLIC LANDS QUESTION

From the very beginning, the federal government planned to divest itself of its massive landholdings, which by 1850 totaled more than 1.2 billion acres. It proceeded to do so through a variety of policies, culminating in the Homestead Act of 1862 by which homesteaders claimed 287 million acres, by granting another 328 million acres to the states as they were admitted to the Union, and by a series of legislative acts in the last quarter of the nineteenth century that were designed to encourage railroad development, tree planting, irrigation, and mineral production. Although the legislation intentionally reduced the federal domain to only 600 million acres by 1912, by transferring public lands into private hands, the policies also led to massive land fraud. Lands that were designed to be transferred to farmers ended up in the hands of land speculators, timber companies, and cattle companies that used a variety of schemes to acquire thousands of acres of cheap land. For example, the requirement that a homesteader bring water to a tract of land as a way of improving it was accomplished by throwing cupfuls on it, and aliases were often used to acquire land for the requisite six months before it was transferred to a landholding company. The expansion of the nation's economic base throughout this period allowed large corporations to dominate the political landscape all over the

country. Gradually, fears of economic monopoly began to lead to calls
for reform and, among conservationists, calls for the government to retain control of the remaining acreage within the public domain.[4]

In the last quarter of the nineteenth century, government scientists
who had previously focused on the individual issues of irrigation,
forestry, and grazing shifted to a more holistic view that became
known as "the public lands question." The management of natural resources, which previously had been segmented both scientifically as
well as administratively, was gradually integrated into a single problem with interdependent parts. That approach was first advocated by
George Perkins Marsh in his 1864 book *Man and Nature*[5] in which the
scholar and political leader argued that the fall of ancient empires
could be attributed to human abuse of the land, warning of a similar
fate for the United States.

Government scientists such as John Wesley Powell, Clarence King,
and members of the United States Geological Survey (USGS), along
with academic geographers and geologists such as Carl Ritter, Arnold
Guyot, and Joseph Henry, recognized that the West was scientifically
unique because of the variety of its altitude, latitude, topography, climate, and soil. They argued that proposed federal land use policies
should be dependent upon the availability of water and would, by necessity, have to be different from the more homogeneous regions of the
East and the Midwest.[6] Their studies began to influence policymakers
like Carl Schurz, who served as secretary of the interior from 1877 to
1881. Schurz was among those who urged a reversal of prior land use
policies that emphasized disposal of public lands. He favored a policy
through which the government managed and protected resources by
withdrawing some lands from the homestead laws. Such policymakers
were later joined by the man who would become the primary architect
of scientific management of resources within the federal government,
Gifford Pinchot.

Pinchot, a Yale-educated forester, became the central figure in the
development of federal land and timber policy following the turn of
the century. After studying silvaculture in Germany, where forestry
management was based on conservation, Pinchot worked as a private
consultant and managed the forests owned by the Vanderbilt family.
Compared with the romantic and preservationist views of Henry
David Thoreau or John Muir, Pinchot saw the public lands question
from an entirely different, utilitarian perspective. According to one observer, Pinchot and his group "made conservation a political movement between 1900 and 1910." Pinchot's essential achievement was "in
directing the energies and enthusiasm of the Progressive movement in
its early stages to conservation."[7] For Pinchot, the conservation movement was based on three principles:

The first principle of conservation is development, the use of the natural resources now existing on this continent for the benefit of the
people who live here now. . . . Conservation stands for the prevention
of waste. . . . The first duty of the human race is to control the earth it
lives upon. . . . The natural resources must be developed and preserved for the benefit of the many, and not merely the profit of the
few.[8]

Political scientist Christopher McGrory Klyza has characterized
the public lands question much more broadly, arguing that there were
three main conceptions of public interest that dominated this period:
economic liberalism, technocratic utilitarianism, and preservationism.[9]
Economic liberalism, which translated to minimal government intervention and opposition to government ownership of the public lands,
was the predominant attitude from the period following the Civil War
until the turn of the century. From the early 1900s, western governors
supported the idea that public lands ought to be transferred to the
states, which were perceived as being closer to the people. Meeting at
the Second National Conservation Congress in 1911, the officials asserted "the superior efficiency of state management"—a theme repeated at subsequent conferences of the Western States Governors.
Technocratic utilitarianism, most closely associated with the controversy over forestlands, became a more prevalent theme as Pinchot's influence grew and management, rather than preservation, was the underlying policy motif. Lastly, preservationism became the focus of how
best to protect the public lands, gaining momentum during the late
1920s and early 1930s. The effort was led by Robert Marshall, director
of the Division of Recreation and Lands in the USFS. Marshall criticized the agency's prodevelopment posture and the recreational emphasis of the NPS in his book *The People's Forests*.[10] He argued that the
more appropriate action for the public interest was to set aside land for
future generations to enjoy for aesthetic reasons. This ideal led to the
development of the Wilderness Society in 1935 and, later, the formation of interest groups that became the organizers of the mainstream environmental movement over the next four decades.

THE EVOLUTION OF AN ORGANIZED OPPOSITION

The tactics used in the early resistance to the government's land policies contrast markedly to those of the contemporary environmental opposition, which uses more sophisticated skills in building coalitions
and which fully exploits the most advanced of today's communications technologies. From the mid-nineteenth century until the period
after World War II, the opposition tried to influence policy through the

direct lobbying efforts of small groups of highly influential business and political leaders rather than by associations, trade groups, or political action committees.

This period is also marked by a shifting of allegiance by some groups, who initially supported government efforts to protect natural resources and then later developed an antagonistic relationship. During the Civil War, for example, mine owners in Nevada actively courted the federal government and sought statehood status for the territory with the expectation that their financial interests would enjoy the protection of the government. That presumption was underscored by President Abraham Lincoln, who signed Nevada's statehood bill on March 21, 1864, and a year later told newly elected senator "Big Bill" Stewart, "I am glad to see you here. We need as many loyal states as we can get, and in addition to that, the gold and silver in the region you represent has made it possible for the government to maintain sufficient credit to continue this terrible war."[11] Lincoln needed Nevada's mineral resources to support the war effort, and the mining industry's interests were secure until the war ended.

The attitudes of people like Stewart began to change after Reconstruction. He and other powerful western senators, including Henry Teller of Colorado, had become suspicious of "government experts" and their allegedly more scientific approach to managing public lands. Although they had intended to have the government's scientific teams survey the West for potentially irrigable lands, they belatedly realized that such studies could take years and would delay the development and settlement they supported. Along with other members of Congress who were supported by the cattle industry, railroad barons, and land promoters seeking to reduce the impact of federal land use restrictions, they fought eastern reformers bent on promoting the conservationist ethic.[12]

Just prior to the turn of the twentieth century, the cattle industry was dominated by eastern and European capitalists who used the open ranges of the West with little interference from the government. Land promoters fabricated stories of a West of flowing rivers and productive meadowlands, and there was little scientific evidence or first-hand knowledge of the region to contradict the pictures they painted for investors back East.[13] It is important to note that these interests, although not formally organized into groups in the sense political observers view them today, maintained a considerable amount of control over natural resource policy through their support of public officials and bureaucrats.

The opposition intensified after Congress passed additional legislation in 1888 to more scientifically and comprehensively survey the lands, followed by an orderly disposal process that would further encourage homesteading. Some large cattle companies proposed instead that the federal government release the territory to individuals, who would manage the lands and serve as stewards over it—a theme repeated in subsequent opposition to environmental policy discussed later in this book. The western senators sought to discredit the work of John Wesley Powell and other researchers who argued that the West was an arid land with minimal rainfall to support the grand development schemes of land promoters. Stewart and his allies persuaded Congress to push forward with development and expansion without further federal interference, while Powell argued for additional scientific study and orderly disposal of the land. In 1890, Stewart convinced his Senate colleagues to discontinue funding for Powell's irrigation survey, dismissing the scientists' contentions as unsubstantiated. In less than a quarter of a decade, western political leaders shifted from looking at the federal government as a defender of their mining, grazing, and development interests to seeing the government as intrusive and obstructive.

THE TIMBER OPPOSITION

While Stewart and his allies lobbied Washington, D.C., to free up the public lands for development and cattle grazing, a second front in the battle was brewing over the disposition of the nation's forest resources. The American Forestry Association, which first met in 1875, had as its objective "the fostering of all interests of forest planting and conservation on this continent."[14] The group was the primary lobbying and research organization for the scientific community and was successful in advocating the creation of a forestry division within the United States Department of Agriculture (USDA) and, in the 1880s, in securing congressional approval for studies of the condition of the country's forests.

In 1891, congressional amendments to legislation that later became known as the Creative Act gave the president the authority to create forest reserves from the public domain. President Benjamin Harrison designated fifteen reserves totaling more than thirteen million acres, with another fifteen reserves added by his successor, Grover Cleveland. To many westerners, the land that had been "theirs" now belonged to the federal government, locked up from their access by homesteaders looking for firewood as well as timber companies looking for profits. But at the same time, there were some timber company managers and municipal leaders who believed federal management was an essential element of a general forest policy that would limit competition and would help stabilize local economies dependent on forest products.

Despite claims that the land was already "locked up" by the turn of the century, Congress attempted to manage the West's natural resources while still making them accessible for private use. Part of the difficulty they faced, however, was in untangling the jurisdictional disputes over which agency ought to have authority over the land. In 1897, an amendment to the Sundry Civil Appropriations Act (now referred to as the Forest Service Organic Act), gave management powers to the Division of Forestry, a part of the Department of Agriculture. The forest reserves, however, were under the authority of the General Land Office in the Department of the Interior. Gifford Pinchot, named head of the Division of Forestry in 1898, lobbied President Theodore Roosevelt to transfer control of the forest reserves to his agency, renamed the Bureau of Forestry in 1901. Pinchot changed the direction of the agency, which had originally been established to assess, rather than manage, the nation's forests. He became active in promoting forestry research and sustained yield and fire suppression practices, but also argued that trees were to be used for human economic welfare. The bureau was besieged for information and advice, and Pinchot's businesslike approach and engaging personality brought the nation's largest forest owners and lumber companies into his circle of influence.[15]

The relationship, termed an "iron triangle," was comprised of the Bureau of Forestry, which provided expertise and an access point to government for lumber companies; the timber companies that assisted the bureau by providing private funds for forestry education and field training; and political support from timberworkers when the agency came under fire from Congress. The iron triangle was supported by the congressional norms of reciprocity and specialization, and strengthened by the close ties that had developed between corporate timber interests and the bureau. Pinchot, in turn, kept constituents at bay from members of Congress even when legislators failed to appropriate funds for his pet projects. The close relationship between what would eventually become the USFS in 1905 and the timber industry continued well after Pinchot left government service, and it later became one of the rallying points that fueled the environmental movement in the late 1960s.

Pinchot's work came to the attention of Theodore Roosevelt even before he became president upon the assassination of William McKinley in 1901. An avid lover of the outdoors, Roosevelt supported the efficiency concept enough to give Pinchot virtually free rein over the national forests and considerable unofficial influence over the nation's overall natural resource policies. Pinchot's influence was somewhat moderated, however, by interdepartmental rivalries: The USFS was a unit of the Department of Agriculture while the remainder of the public lands came under the auspices of the more highly politicized Department of the Interior, which was forced to answer to a broader range of constituencies, among them the Bureau of Fisheries, the Bureau of Indian Affairs, the Bureau of Mines, and the United States Fish and Wildlife Service (USFWS). Friction between the two agencies continues today.[16]

In 1903, Roosevelt appointed a Public Lands Commission, a body that gained tremendous support from the railroads and industrial leaders.[17] The commission supported public ownership of lands, but it also supported the continued disposal of small parcels of land suitable for farming to private owners under the homestead acts. Although this might initially sound like a conservationist's dream, to Pinchot and the dissenting members of the commission, only public ownership would guarantee maximum, rational (and therefore efficient) development.[18]

Pinchot was successful in building his power base as chief forester when Congress enacted the Transfer Act of 1905. The statute transferred all reserved lands from the Department of the Interior to the Department of Agriculture and provided that receipts from the sale of timber, water, and grazing rights would be placed in a fund for use in managing the preserves, which had come under Pinchot's control. In 1907, at Pinchot's urging, Roosevelt set aside an additional 16 million acres of valued timberland. What made the action especially aggravating to the timber industry was that the president's action came a few days before he signed the Agricultural Appropriations Act that prohibited the president from creating future reserves (renamed national forests under the bill) in the six northwestern states without the approval of Congress. There were two different perspectives about the president's action: To some, the action blurred the distinction between "stewardship" and "ownership" that westerners had taken for granted, creating a breach of faith. "To the angry West, the reserves were a calculated, radical, illegal departure from tradition, custom, and law, the stunning end of a century of progressive, civilization-building disposal and settlement, the beginning of federal landlordism."[19] But to others in the West, there was considerable support for the forest reserve policy. At the time, many opposed the unrestricted logging and grazing that took place on public lands, in large part because those activities affected water supplies.[20]

The forest controversy was further complicated by the presence of settlers who had left the South after the Civil War carrying with them a strong tradition of states' rights. Many of the residents of New Mexico, Arizona, and Nevada had little confidence in a distant federal bureaucracy that was telling them how to manage local resources, despite the fact that Pinchot had organized each national forest as a locally managed unit. Many Mormons in Utah opposed any federal intrusion into their lives, whether the battle be over polygamy or their use of the land.

An exception to this were Mormon residents of Salt Lake City, who were concerned about the water quality problems posed by unrestricted grazing and generally supported government measures.[21])

Some of the opposition appears to have had a decidedly sectional tone of East versus West, although that may be too simplistic an explanation of a dispute that involved many divergent interests. Led by well-financed lumber families from the upper Midwest, the tone of confrontation was set by such men as George Weyerhaeuser, Chauncey Griggs, and David Whitney. In 1907, these men were responsible for galvanizing the political support necessary to rescind the president's power to set aside additional forest reserves.[22]

Although the timber industry had gone on record as opposing federal regulation of forestry as early as 1883, it was not until after World War II that its interests became sufficiently organized to become an effective coalition. Two of the major industry groups, the National Lumber Manufacturers Association and the Forest Industries Council, began to once again press Congress for legislation to transfer existing forestlands to private ownership. By joining together the influential timber families who had dominated the industry for decades, the two groups paved the way for other natural resource groups to oppose government intervention.[23]

THE UTILITY OPPOSITION

One of the most powerful groups opposing the Roosevelt administration's land policies was the utility industry, which cultivated congressional converts representing a variety of regional interests. Southern representatives envisioned and supported the growth of great cities as a result of an expanded energy grid, and they resented conservationists as meddlesome busybodies. They also joined the utilities because they saw the government's land policies as an intrusion on their sovereignty at a time when states' rights was still a compelling issue. Western members of Congress felt that by placing large portions of their states in reserve, the federal government had denied them the opportunity to develop their resources, shortchanging the potential for growth. Midwestern and eastern members of Congress supported the utilities as part of an overall prodevelopment ethic.[24]

There are several reasons why the utility industry was more active in its attempt to influence the policy process than were other organized interests. From its earliest beginnings, the hydroelectric industry had been characterized by centralized control. Power development involved financial risks, was highly technical, and required firms to interlock numerous units to provide continuous service at maximum efficiency. In 1909, thirteen companies controlled one-third of the commercial waterpower in the United States; three years later, ten groups controlled three-fifths of the generated power output, forming the basis of what would later be called the "water monopoly."[25]

Under Interior Department regulations, power companies were required to obtain right-of-way agreements for irrigation ditches, reservoirs, and access across federal lands to construct hydroelectric plants. In California, the Edison Electric Company received permission to set up a power plant in the forest reserves under a special act of Congress in 1906. To bring uniformity to the law, Pinchot and the USFS drew up a standard permit agreement that included specific terms of the access easement and an allowance for fees to be charged the utilities.

In an argument that would later become the basis for contemporary property rights debates, the power companies argued that the government could not control running water on public lands because water rights stemmed from state, rather than federal, law. In 1908, a U.S. Circuit Court judge disagreed with the power companies' argument, upholding the USFS fees and permit system.

Seeking another arena for their case to be heard, the utilities turned to Congress, seeking limits on the fees the USFS could charge, but still demanding perpetual leases for access. The hydroelectric lobby argued that it was unfair to expect their companies to make a substantial investment in a project knowing that the lease could be revoked at any time. The legislation failed to pass after it was sharply criticized by President Roosevelt, so the companies sought a private meeting with federal officials to work out a compromise agreement. That, too, proved unsuccessful.

Undaunted, the power companies devised a way around Pinchot's permit system. Instead of attempting to get access to federal lands under the forest provisions of the 1897 Forest Service Organic Act, they did so under a loophole in the law that permitted them to enter the national forests under the guise of gaining access to mining property.

The government countered by withdrawing mineral permits for the lands and arguing that the lands were needed by the USFS for administrative purposes or as potential sites for ranger stations. On those sites where the power companies had already constructed plants, the attorney general's office sought to evict them, and on sites where no construction had occurred, the permits were revoked on the grounds that the land had been held strictly for speculation. This left the utilities little choice but to accept the USFS permit system in order to expand their hydroelectric programs, which made up 42 percent of the developed power in the western states by 1916.[26]

Though they accepted the permit system and the lease restrictions, utilities balked at any attempt by the federal government to levy fees for access to public lands. Meeting in Portland in 1915, the members of the Western States Water Power Conference protested the fee systems devised by the Departments of Agriculture and the Interior, relying upon the argument of military preparedness. Under the guise of patriotism, they pointed out the need for the immediate development of waterpower to manufacture nitrates used in ammunition. As allies, they brought in the Aluminum Company of America and the American Newspaper Publishers Association, both of whom depended upon waterpower to operate their facilities for the production of aluminum and newsprint.[27] Although power companies had cultivated considerable support in the Senate and were able to stall legislation for several congressional sessions, they did not have enough clout to prevent passage of the Federal Water Power Act of 1920. The bill set the stage for public regulation of hydroelectric power and securely established the federal government's control over waterpower on public lands. In part, that power came about as a result of the realization that major energy projects were beyond the resources of private capital, as well as demands by some westerners that the federal government should be responsible for paying for development in the region.

THE EXPANSION OF OPPOSITION OVER WATER POLICY

In 1878, Powell published his study of western land in a controversial report to Congress that made recommendations for sweeping changes in the use of water on public and private lands. Much to the dismay of members of Congress supported by land speculators, Powell concluded that finite water supplies would limit the amount of land available for settlement unless the federal government became involved in major irrigation projects.[28]

Water returned as a major resource issue in 1888 when Congress authorized the USGS to measure and study groundwater and irrigation, a follow-up to earlier studies by the Army Corps of Engineers of navigable streams, drainage, and floods. The studies resulted in the formation of two groups in opposition to federal water policy: farmers and water users in the West dependent upon the federal government for irrigation funding, and commercial interests seeking greater usage of the nation's inland waterways.

The federal government's involvement in these issues expanded in 1894 with passage of the Carey Act, which provided funding for western irrigation projects. Led by George H. Maxwell, Nevada congressmember Francis Newlands, and the Homecroft Society, a coalition of water users sought support from eastern business interests by convincing them that irrigation would increase homesteading in the West and, eventually, would open up new markets for their goods. Maxwell quickly won the support of groups like the National Board of Trade, the National Business Men's League, and the National Association of Manufacturers, and in 1900, he convinced both political parties to adopt platform planks that called for federal construction of irrigation projects.[29]

In 1901, Newlands attempted to convince his congressional colleagues to support a plan to finance western irrigation projects by creating a reclamation fund composed of proceeds from the sale of western lands, arguing that this would allow the West to pay for its own development. Although the plan was initially opposed by eastern interests who felt the proposal would give an unfair advantage to western farmers, the Reclamation Act (also known as the Newlands Act) had Pinchot's and Roosevelt's support, and it passed in 1902. The statute led to the development of an extensive system of western dam projects and the establishment of the Reclamation Service under the USGS. In 1907, the Reclamation Service was separated from the USGS, and in 1923, it was renamed the Bureau of Reclamation.[30]

The Reclamation Service promptly ran into a host of problems as it became apparent that demands for water greatly exceeded supply. Water rights claimed and granted by the state courts were often conflicting, and there was little scientific information on how much water was actually available. Speculators continued to buy up large tracts of land, making coordination of development projects haphazard.

In several states, support and opposition to the government's irrigation policies were split by internal disputes among farmers, cattle ranchers, and sheep graziers, which reduced their impact as a united front. Small landowners supported the federal government's water policy and sought protection in the Newlands Act requirement that water could be delivered to units no larger than 160 acres. Large agricultural interests opposed the Bureau of Reclamation's policies because they limited their ability to gain access to publicly developed water. Wyoming cattle owners believed settlers and the growing number of forest reserves were reducing the amount of land with adequate water supplies for their use. Sheepherders in Arizona and New Mexico protested the forest reserves established to protect water supplies for the Phoenix area because the government's actions encroached on what was already a limited supply of grazable forage. For the most part, these groups were successful in stopping the expansion of the government's reserve program.

While attempting to spread the conservation ethic to the West, the Roosevelt administration simultaneously turned its attention to the East. At the same time the irrigation battles were brewing, water users also had an impact on policies related to the nation's inland waterways.

Navigable streams were perceived to be the savior of smaller communities that could depend upon them for cheap transportation, and new interests were formed to promote inland navigation to compete against rising railroad transportation costs. Massive canal and dredging projects were proposed, but they were intensely opposed by the Army Corps of Engineers, which doubted their economic feasibility.

To encourage the government to move forward with the projects, waterways enthusiasts formed the National Rivers and Harbors Congress to lobby legislators to increase funding for river development. The group's president went so far as to propose that the Army Corps of Engineers be eliminated and replaced by a civilian department of public works. A Chicago-based group, the Lakes-to-the-Gulf Association, and the St. Louis Business Men's League spearheaded a proposal to build a 14-foot channel from Chicago to New Orleans to increase the region's economic growth. They were later joined by the Latin-American Club of St. Louis, composed of business leaders seeking to open up markets not only in South America, but also with Asia as the Panama Canal neared completion.[31] The proposals were considered unfeasible and were blocked by both the Corps and by eastern Republicans in Congress, turning the dispute into a sharply partisan one.

The debate shifted to what came to be known as the "multiple-purpose approach" in which the problem was approached in totally different terms. Whereas previous policies had treated rivers simply as navigable waterways, new proposals took into account the management of the rivers as a source of drinking water, the development of power, flood control, and irrigation. President Roosevelt codified the policy with creation of the Inland Waterways Commission in 1907.

As part of the multiple-purpose waterways policy, the federal government embarked upon a plan that required hydroelectric companies to pay a portion of the cost when a waterway was improved, such as the creation of a dam. Opposition by the power companies led to a congressional stalemate that halted all waterpower development on the navigable streams at a time when it proceeded rapidly on the public lands.[32]

Another source of opposition to water policy emerged in the South, where developers sought support for a federally financed drainage program. Business interests attempted to convince Congress of the advantages of reclaiming swamplands along the Mississippi River and formed short-lived organizations like the National Drainage Congress and the National Drainage Association. Other interests attempted to gain congressional support for a federally funded flood control program—an issue that gained credibility following disastrous flooding throughout the Mississippi valley in 1912 and 1913. The flooding led to creation of a nationwide organization, the National

Reclamation Association, which sought funding for numerous water-shed and reservoir programs.

But neither the drainage proponents nor flood control advocates were able to mount sufficient opposition against the Army Corps of Engineers and the debate over the technical merits of various proposals. Western senators entered the fray by arguing that the southern Democrats were ignoring their irrigation project needs. The resulting compromise, the Federal Water Power Act, marked a defeat for the concept of multiple-purpose usage and deflated the opposition to the government's water usage policies.

MINING AND PETROLEUM INDUSTRY OPPOSITION

After the discovery of gold in California in 1848, the mining rush suddenly took off, with the federal government encouraging settlement and development throughout the West despite the fact the United States had declared war against Mexico in 1846. At the time, much of the region was under the control of the U.S. Army because Mexico had not yet fully ceded its claims to the territory that later became Arizona, California, Nevada, New Mexico, Texas, and Utah. When California became a state in 1850, the U.S. government still had no laws in place to govern mineral claims, especially on public lands. Miners resisted attempts by Congress to develop leasing, fees, or permit systems, eventually convincing President Millard Fillmore to support a laissez-faire policy, and it was not until 1866 that the first mining legislation was enacted. The mining policies reinforced homestead laws that gave settlers title to both the land and any resources below it, opening up huge parcels in the West to speculators who obtained the land cheaply and fraudulently, with claim inspections made only infrequently.

The 1872 Mining Law, which codified provisions in two previous acts, gave the western states virtually unlimited power over hard-rock mining policies. The federal government did not have the administrative ability or mechanism to implement a more encompassing law (the USGS was not established until 1879 and the Bureau of Mines did not exist until 1910) to regulate mining on public lands and relied instead on the military to maintain order. In essence, these early policies were extralegal, developed by the mining industry through informal codes and the establishment of mining districts that later became a privatized policy regime.[33]

In 1906, the Roosevelt administration addressed concerns about mining and land fraud by placing 50 million acres of land in reserve from further sales and ordered the USGS to review the amount of coal on public lands in order to set prices at fair market value. The reserve policy led Wyoming representative Frank Mondell to remark, "The West is facing probably a serious coal famine next winter because it is impossible to acquire government land for new mines."[34] After review, some land that had been set aside as reserves was determined to be non–coal bearing; other parcels were proposed for lease, with the government retaining royalty rights. Opposition by other western members of Congress foiled the president's leasing proposal, so Roosevelt turned to an administrative remedy. He ordered the USGS to revalue the coal-bearing lands at higher prices to reduce speculation and reopened their sale.

A similar reserve plan was implemented for phosphate and oil, with the federal government withdrawing land from sale, the USGS reviewing the holdings and classifying them after determining their value, and the lands placed back on the market for sale. The oil industry sought further protection, however, and asked the secretary of the interior to close oil land to further entry by agricultural or mineral interests and to develop a leasing plan as the government had done for the utility industry. The National Conservation Association, which had been organized by Pinchot in 1909, opposed the leasing concepts proposed in Congress, although the industry worked successfully toward a compromise that allowed the federal government to retain ownership while leasing mineral rights to private companies.

The mining lobby was almost totally controlled by investors who counted on the support of three senators, George Hearst of South Dakota, Simon Guggenheim of Colorado, and William Clark of Montana. Hearst made a fortune in gold, Guggenheim in silver and in ore processing, and Clark in copper; each was backed by the eastern establishment, although the financiers lost some of their clout with a downturn in economic conditions, especially the silver crisis of 1893–1896.

By the turn of the century, the power of the mining industry was weakened by a growing antimonopoly, anticorporate mood that would usher in the Progressive Era and set the stage for a new preservationist ethic. The change in public opinion was coupled with several legislative actions after World War I that reopened the public mineral lands to leasing. In addition to opening up millions of acres of oil, coal, potassium, and helium lands, Congress gave each state treasury a sizable royalty on minerals accruing within its borders—compromises that blunted the mineral lobby's opposition to the leasing policies developed decades earlier.

The oil and mineral lobby's influence was also reduced by political events. The lobby was at first encouraged by the shift from a Democratic to a Republican White House in 1920 with the election of Warren Harding. They were further heartened by the presence in the administration of Herbert Hoover, who had a background as a mining consultant and served as secretary of commerce to Harding and Calvin Coolidge before becoming president in 1928. However, Harding made several controversial cabinet appointments, which led to a series of scandals that reduced the industry's credibility and, eventually, its influence on policy. Harding's secretary of the interior, Albert B. Fall, and two oil company officials, Harry Sinclair and Edward Doheny, were involved in the Teapot Dome scandal of 1924 in which Fall was accused of receiving almost $400,000 in bribes for approving fraudulent lease permits on naval oil reserves in California and Wyoming. The scandal led to a full review of federal petroleum leasing policies as well as the Federal Corrupt Practices Act of 1925, which required the reporting of campaign contributions and expenditures. In 1931, Fall was sentenced to a year in prison; Doheny and Sinclair were acquitted of the bribery charges.[35]

ENTER THE PRESERVATIONISTS

The initial shift in public opinion about environmental protection in the late 1800s and early twentieth century came about as a result of the philosophical debate between conservation and preservation. The term "conservation" was originally derived from the idea of storing floodwaters in reservoirs for future use, gradually evolving to encompass a much broader spectrum of issues. In its early years, conservation enjoyed the support of scientists and engineers who agreed with the concept of efficient planning, as well as support from companies seeking managed use of natural resources.

A sharply opposing view grew out of the desire of eastern game organizations and groups like the Boone and Crockett Club to transfer forest reserves into parks and game preserves—hence the name "preservationists." When their efforts were opposed by western cattle associations who feared the loss of grazing areas, the preservationists turned to Pinchot—whom they perceived to be their ally. However, Pinchot believed wholeheartedly that forest reserves should be developed for commercial use rather than preserved from it,[36] thus he became the de facto leader of the conservationists and set up the philosophical debate over land use that continues today.

Preservationists, who became the vanguard of the contemporary environmental movement, looked at the same legislation as the conservationists but saw an entirely different picture. For example, they viewed the Forest Service Organic Act of 1897 as an opportunity for protecting forest reserves from commercial exploitation, while conservationists saw it as a way of efficiently managing timber sales.

The conflict was not limited to western lands: A controversy in New York's Adirondack State Park epitomized the contrasting perspectives. The preservationists, led by the New York Board of Trade and Transportation (which sought to protect the water supply for the

Erie Canal) and the Association for the Protection of the Adirondacks (consisting of owners of estates within the park boundaries), had successfully fought for inclusion of a provision in the state constitution that prohibited all timber cutting in the park. Although the provision was initially planned as a temporary measure to prevent wanton cutting, the preservationists later sought to keep the land "forever wild." Pinchot disagreed with the plans. With about 60 percent of the land within the park under private ownership, he tried unsuccessfully to have the acreage condemned and the state's holdings consolidated. His hope was that the state's management of the lands would allow the timber cutting that was denied to private landholders.[37]

A similar controversy was being waged in California, and from it, John Muir emerged as the leader of the growing preservationist movement.[38] The newly formed Sierra Club had successfully persuaded Congress to incorporate the Hetch Hetchy valley into Yosemite National Park, but the organization faced a challenge from the city of San Francisco, which sought to use a reservoir site in the valley for its water supply.[39]

Muir, the Sierra Club, and American Civic Association president J. Horace McFarland argued to President Roosevelt that the area had been set aside for recreation and as natural wilderness; Pinchot and his National Conservation Association believed that the water supply constituted a more important use in the public's interest. After a decade of controversial dispute, the conservationists won in 1913 when a measure approving the Hetch Hetchy Reservoir was passed in Congress.

The Hetch Hetchy debate was the first of many similar disputes between the two sides over the use of public lands. Related controversies arose over the commercial use of land within Glacier National Park and a proposal to set aside the Calaveras Big Trees as a national park. Pinchot worked to have areas with potentially valuable timber included as national forests, rather than national parks, so that he could maintain greater control over the use of the land.

The preservationists picked up new allies as they sought to have Congress create a bureau devoted to protection of the national parks, a move vehemently opposed by Pinchot and the conservationists. Buoyed by a growing number of tourists, new groups (travel agencies, railroad interests, and highway associations) joined with recreationists, women's organizations, and nature clubs to lobby Congress to establish the NPS as a part of the Department of the Interior in 1916.

THE DISPUTE OVER THE COMMONS CONTINUES

These early struggles over the public domain have often been characterized as a dispute over the use of the commons (meaning resources held in common in the public trust).[40] Initially the federal government had conflicting policies of managing and protecting the commons while at the same time arranging for the disposal and exploitation of the public domain. Gradually, the government adopted a more conservationist, and later, preservationist role. By the early twentieth century, led by representatives of the extractive resource industries, a segment of opposition began to form that sought to change the rules governing the commons to convert public lands to private property.

In 1907, the Denver Public Lands Conference marked the first organized western opposition to the federal government's land and timber policies, with the majority of the representatives from Wyoming and Colorado. The initial purpose of the meeting, chaired by Montana senator Tom Clark, was to force the federal government to turn the public lands over to state control. But although the convention delegates were in agreement over their opposition to being charged fees, they were themselves split on whether to actively confront the president. Many perceived Roosevelt and Pinchot as friendly toward their interests, and thus the convention produced relatively minor resolutions dealing with USFS administrative practices.

Representatives of the two states then formed the National Public Domain League in 1909, attacking Pinchot, and Roosevelt and Taft and their administrations' policies through press releases and conventions in order to broaden their base of support. Their goal was to convince the public that the public lands be ceded to the states—a proposal that received little congressional backing and even less support from the Taft administration and his new interior secretary, Richard Ballinger. Although the league tried to pass itself off as a grassroots effort to counter Pinchot's conservationist policies, in fact it was a publicity office staffed by only a few individuals. More "grassroots" organizations followed, such as the Western Conservation League, a publicity mill founded by L. K. Armstrong, the editor of the *Northwest Mining News*.[41]

These opposition groups were short-lived, failing to attract a broad base of support and lacking an essential element required for policy success: strong, popular leadership. Still, these early-twentieth-century land use conflicts provided a starting point for the contemporary Sagebrush Rebellion, the county supremacy and wise use movements, and property rights groups, which will be discussed later in this book.

Eventually, the battle became more politicized and partisan, with western Democratic officials critical of land policies produced by a Republican administration. Conservation became a potent campaign issue, with the recurring theme that the states were in a better position to administer natural resources than was the federal government. Sectionalism was fostered by western newspapers like the *San Francisco Chronicle,* which criticized government proposals to purchase land in the East that had been denuded by timber companies, arguing that western tax dollars were being used for the benefit of the East.[42] At the 1912 Democratic National Convention, western leaders introduced a plank into the presidential platform calling for the transfer of all public lands to the states, but they received little support for their efforts. A resolution that called for an investigation of corruption and fraud within the USFS also failed.

With the election of the Democrat Woodrow Wilson in 1912, western interests thought they had once again found a political ally; just prior to his inauguration, Wilson noted that "a policy of reservation is not a policy of conservation." When a delegation of Colorado Democrats met with Wilson in May 1913 and asked him to cede the national forests to the states, he refused and continued his predecessors' policies of federal control.

For the next fifty years, the issues of protecting natural resources and managing the public lands would continue to simmer on the policy agenda, stirred periodically by the winds of electoral change from Democratic to Republican administrations. President Herbert Hoover, for example, declared in 1929 that the federal government should end its role as landlord in order "to place our communities in control of their own destinies. . . . Western states have long since passed from their swaddling clothes and are today more competent to manage much of their affairs than is the federal government." When the Democrats took control of the House of Representatives in 1931, the Hoover proposal was shelved, and the remaining 173 million acres of land in the public domain remained firmly under federal control.[43]

It is important to note, however, that the foundations of the antifederal ethic were well formed before the advent of World War I; and although the targets of the opposition changed periodically, the antiregulatory philosophy established during these early land battles would be seen again during the third period of this evolution of opposition.

"RETURN THE PUBLIC LANDS TO THE WEST"

The fourth period in the evolution of opposition to federal policies began in the mid-1940s when representatives of the western livestock industry began once again to organize a takeover of federal lands. This new opposition was initiated by a group of 150 cattle and sheep ranchers who met in Salt Lake City in August 1946 to tackle their common enemy: the federal bureaucracy.

What made this attempt to privatize the public lands somewhat different from previous efforts was the presence of a powerful member

of Congress, Nevada senator Pat McCarran, who orchestrated many of
the meetings that followed. McCarran was the leader of the Cow Bloc,
a group of senior members of Congress who had made their way
through the rigid seniority system to gain control of both the Senate
and House public lands committees. A militant antifederalist, McCarran exercised considerable influence in Congress as chair of the Judiciary Committee and the Appropriations Subcommittee.[44]

McCarran's allies were Senator Edward Robertson of Wyoming (a
sheep rancher who was the former vice president of the Wyoming
Stock Growers Association) and his House counterpart, Frank Barrett
of Wyoming, who as chairs of their respective lands committees relied
upon the support of the American National Livestock Association and
the National Wool Growers Association. The two factions pooled their
resources as the Joint National Livestock Committee and met again in
Denver in early 1947 to develop a plan to buy 145 million acres of federal land at prices from $0.09 to $2.80 per acre, with 10 percent down
and thirty years to pay.[45]

The Cow Bloc and its constituent supporters in the livestock industry relied upon a number of tactics to gain support for their proposals. Using the slogan "Return the Public Lands to the West," they
convinced several members of Congress to introduce bills that would
sell federal land to private owners by promising that the revenues
would be used for public education, as had been the policy during the
nineteenth century. In 1946, for example, New Mexico senator Carl
Hatch sponsored legislation to sell two-thirds of his state's lands; Representative Barrett made a similar attempt but skipped the provision
about education. Robertson proposed a bill that called for the establishment of state commissions to evaluate all public lands, including
national parks and monuments, to see if they could best be used in
some other way.[46] During the 79th Congress, a total of fifty-eight similar bills were introduced, any one of which, if enacted, would have
opened up the western landgrab.

Another tactic of the livestock industry was to appeal to the public's growing fears about communism. J. Elmer Brock, vice president of
the American National Livestock Association, criticized the conservationist policies of the government by saying, "We are tired of being
bossed around by a bunch of Communist-minded bureaucrats. We
don't want to be like a slice of Russia."[47] In an article in the *Denver Post*,
Brock referred to his opponents as bungling officials and pool-hall conservationists, "all predacious and most of them tinged with pink or
even deeper hue."[48] In a somewhat ironic alliance, western critics of
the government bureaucracy joined with eastern members of Congress
who criticized the Grazing Service for subsidizing the livestock industry. The subsidization level was significant: In 1941, Congress appro-

priated $5.2 million to operate the agency but collected less than $1 million in fees from ranchers because the grazing fees were so low.

In addition to taking on the grazing agency, Representative Barrett scheduled hearings on the USFS's policies in seven western states in 1947, placing notices in various stock publications urging those with complaints against the service to come to testify. In Wyoming, the audience was composed almost entirely of stockmen, who "yelled, stamped [and] applauded every time someone leveled a charge at the Forest Service. Stockmen with gripes were permitted to ramble on, while those seeking to preserve resources and Forest Service employees were cut short after a few minutes."[49]

The hearings became so one-sided that they lost credibility; one scheduled in Arizona was canceled because preservation interests were organized to counter Barrett's rhetoric. The committee members faced similar hostility when they appeared in California, Utah, and Nevada, with the press referring to the proceedings as "The Wild West Show." The final hearing report was ignored and denounced by the secretary of agriculture.

The rebellion of the 1940s was not stopped by legislation, but by the forces of public opinion, led by crusading journalists who helped shape the public's attitudes toward the environment. In 1947, Bernard De Voto, one of the most prominent literary figures and writers of the day, wrote the first of a series of columns in *Harper's* magazine in which he criticized the powerful cattle and sheep associations for overgrazing western lands and then attempting to purchase them at below-market prices. De Voto was a respected historian who was able to reach a broad audience and struck a responsive chord among the public.

In his column, "The Easy Chair," De Voto explained to the general public the substance of the Robertson bill, and argued that the lands never belonged to the states or to individuals in the first place.[50] De Voto believed that the lands could not be "returned" because they had been publicly owned ever since their acquisition from France, Spain, Mexico, and Great Britain. Using carefully crafted language, and with science on his side, De Voto exhorted his readers:

> If the West cannot control the exceedingly small number of people whose program would destroy it, the rest of the country will have to control them for the West's sake and its own. Up to twenty Western votes in Congress might be swung to support that program, and such a bloc might be enough to hold the balance of power. But your Representative has a vote that counts as much as any other. Better make sure that he does not cast it on this issue in ignorance of what is at stake.[51]

De Voto was joined in his crusade by Lester Velie, who wrote for the popular magazine *Collier's*. Velie used dramatic USFS photographs of rangeland that had been overgrazed in contrast to lush, managed acreage along with statements from government officials to warn the public about what was happening to the public lands. Quoting the secretary of agriculture, Velie wrote:

> Already, more than half our range and farm land has been seriously injured . . . and 280,000,000 acres of crop and grazing lands have been either ruined or destroyed. One hundred million acres of former cropland are no longer suitable for cultivation. Another 100,000,000 acres are in serious condition. And finally, still another 150,000,000 acres are subject to erosion in some degree. America's topsoil, when John Smith and Miles Standish came to these shores, averaged about nine inches in depth. Today, topsoil averages about six inches for the nation as a whole, the result of land abuse.[52]

De Voto's and Velie's columns began to attract the attention of western governors like Colorado's Lee Knous, who warned the livestock leaders that there was no public support for their plan. Diverse groups led by Kenneth Reid of the Izaak Walton League, the National Farmers Union, and game protection associations began to support the USFS as did several of the region's newspapers. A USFS landscape architect, Arthur Carhart, lent his preservationist and wilderness expertise to the effort to gut the landgrab as well. The preservationists and journalists joined together as the Natural Resources Council of America and acted as a united front against the Cow Bloc. Before long, McCarran and his Senate allies began to retreat, recognizing that their legislation had insufficient backing within Congress.

Although the cattle and sheep interests were unsuccessful in getting congressional support for an outright sale of the public lands, they did manage to sabotage much of the bureaucracy that administered them. The Cow Bloc successfully slashed appropriations for the grazing field service budget from $1,070,360 to $373,000, which meant that there could only be one office in each state to regulate 145 million acres of rangeland used by more than 20,000 ranchers. They then set their sights on funding for the 80 million acres of grazing lands administered by the USFS.[53]

For the time being, this end run through the appropriations process effectively ceased any federal regulation of grazing practices and became a model that would be used in later years by other organized interests frustrated by their inability to progress through the legislative arena. It also placed the agencies that administer the federal lands in a precarious position between a public that was rediscovering Muir's preservationist ethic and powerful industry constituencies that controlled members of Congress who would ultimately oversee their budgets and future. While the preservation lobby effectively blocked the legislative transfer of public lands, it was also made aware of the fact that the organized interests that opposed it had many other tools with which they could fight. By using such tactics as taking advantage of loopholes in the law, lobbying legislators directly, or appealing to public opinion, the environmental opposition learned during the period from the 1780s to the 1940s that there were numerous strategies and venues that could be used to shape public policy.

NOTES

1. Quoted in Roy M. Robbins, *Our Landed Heritage: The Public Domain, 1776–1936* (Lincoln: University of Nebraska Press, 1962), p. 373.

2. See V. Webster Johnson and Raleigh Barlowe, *Land Problems and Policies* (New York: Arno Press, 1954).

3. This interpretation is at the heart of the contemporary property rights movement's perspective on public ownership of land. See Wayne Hage, *Storm over Rangelands: Private Rights in Federal Lands*, 3rd ed. (Bellevue, WA: Free Enterprise Press, 1994), pp. 35–38.

4. For more on the land fraud that occurred during this period, see Stephen A. Douglas Puter, *Looters of the Public Domain* (New York: Da Capo Press, 1908).

5. George Perkins Marsh, *Man and Nature; or, Physical Geography as Modified by Human Action* (New York: Charles Scribner, 1864).

6. See Wallace Stegner, *Beyond the Hundredth Meridian: John Wesley Powell and the Second Coming of the West* (Boston: Houghton Mifflin, 1954). See also Charles F. Wilkinson, *Crossing the Next Meridian: Land, Water, and the Future of the West* (Washington, DC: Island Press, 1992), pp. 236–237.

7. Grant McConnell, "The Conservation Movement—Past and Present," *Western Political Quarterly*, vol. 7 (1954): 464–466.

8. Gifford Pinchot, *The Fight for Conservation* (New York: Doubleday, 1910), p. 46.

9. Christopher McGrory Klyza, *Who Controls Public Lands? Mining, Forestry, and Grazing Policies, 1870–1990* (Chapel Hill: University of North Carolina Press, 1996), pp. 11–26.

10. Robert Marshall, *The People's Forests* (New York: Smith and Haas, 1933). For more on Marshall's philosophy and life, see James M. Glover, *A Wilderness Original: The Life of Bob Marshall* (Seattle, WA: Mountaineers, 1986).

11. Ted Morgan, *A Shovel of Stars: The Making of the American West, 1800 to the Present* (New York: Simon and Schuster, 1995), p. 232.

12. See, for example, Richard O'Connor, *Iron Wheels and Broken Men: The Railroad Barons and the Plunder of the West* (New York: Putnam, 1973); and Dana Lee Thomas, *Lords of the Land: The Triumphs and Scandals of America's Real Estate Barons from Early Times to the Present* (New York: Putnam, 1977).

13. See William L. Graf, *Wilderness Preservation and the Sagebrush Rebellions* (Savage, MD: Rowman and Littlefield, 1990), pp. 19–34.

14. Henry Clepper, *Professional Forestry in the United States* (Baltimore, MD: Johns Hopkins University Press, 1971), p. 20.

15. For additional information on Pinchot, see Martin L. Fausold, *Gifford Pinchot: Bull Moose Progressive* (Syracuse, NY: Syracuse University Press, 1961);

Alpheus T. Mason, *Bureaucracy Convicts Itself: The Ballinger-Pinchot Controversy* (New York: Viking, 1942); M. Nelson McGeary, *Gifford Pinchot, Forester-Politician* (Princeton, NJ: Princeton University Press, 1960); James Penick Jr., *Progressive Politics and Conservation: The Ballinger-Pinchot Affair* (Chicago: University of Chicago Press, 1968); and Harold T. Pinkett, *Gifford Pinchot, Private and Public Forester* (Urbana: University of Illinois Press, 1970).

16. For more on the division of responsibility among federal agencies charged with forest management, see Frederick W. Cubbage, Jay O'Laughlin, and Charles S. Bullock III, *Forest Resource Policy* (New York: John Wiley and Sons, 1993), pp. 283–319.

17. The first Public Lands Commission was appointed in 1879.

18. Samuel P. Hays, *Conservation and the Gospel of Efficiency* (Cambridge, MA: Harvard University Press, 1959), p. 69.

19. Richard D. Lamm and Michael McCarthy, *The Angry West: A Vulnerable Land and Its Future* (Boston: Houghton Mifflin, 1982), p. 216.

20. See, for example, Harold K. Steen, *The U.S. Forest Service: A History* (Seattle: University of Washington Press, 1976); David A. Clary, *Timber and the Forest Service* (Lawrence: University Press of Kansas, 1986); and Robert A. Ficken, "Gifford Pinchot Men: Pacific Northwest Lumbermen and the Conservation Movement, 1902–1910," *Western Historical Quarterly*, vol. 13 (1982): 165–178.

21. Graf, *Wilderness Preservation*, p. 64.

22. Robbins, *Our Landed Heritage*, pp. 348–349.

23. For a more detailed explanation of the role of the industry, see Samuel T. Dana, *Forest and Range Policy* (New York: McGraw-Hill, 1956).

24. See Jerome G. Kerwin, *Federal Water-Power Legislation* (New York: Columbia University Press, 1926), p. 154.

25. Ibid., p. 45.

26. Hays, *Conservation and the Gospel of Efficiency*, pp. 74–80.

27. Kerwin, *Federal Water-Power*, pp. 210–211.

28. See John Wesley Powell, *Report on the Lands of the Arid Region of the United States, with a More Detailed Account of the Lands of Utah* (Washington, DC: U.S. Geographical and Geological Survey of the Rocky Mountain Region, 1878).

29. Hays, *Conservation and the Gospel of Efficiency*, pp. 6–11.

30. For a more detailed accounting of the activities leading up to the passage of the legislation, see Wilkinson, *Crossing the Next Meridian*, pp. 231–247.

31. Hays, *Conservation and the Gospel of Efficiency*, pp. 91–95.

32. Ibid., p. 121.

33. See Klyza, *Who Controls Public Lands?* pp. 27–36.

34. Robbins, *Our Landed Heritage*, p. 353.

35. See M. R. Werner and John Starr, *Teapot Dome* (New York: Viking, 1959); James Leonard Bates, *The Origins of the Teapot Dome* (Urbana: University of Illinois Press, 1963); and M. E. Ravage, *The Story of Teapot Dome* (New York: Republic, 1924).

36. Hays, *Conservation and the Gospel of Efficiency*, p. 41.

37. Ibid., pp. 190–192.

38. See Michael P. Cohen, *The Pathless Way: John Muir and the American Wilderness* (Madison: University of Wisconsin Press, 1984); Stephen Fox, *John Muir and His Legacy* (Boston: Little, Brown, 1981); Frederick Turner, *Rediscovering America: John Muir in His Time and Ours* (New York: Viking, 1985); and Linnie M. Wolfe, *Son of the Wilderness: The Life of John Muir* (New York: Knopf, 1945).

39. For a history of the Sierra Club and the Hetch Hetchy controversy, see Michael Cohen, *The History of the Sierra Club, 1892–1970* (San Francisco: Sierra Club Books, 1988).

40. For more on the concept of the commons, see Garrett Hardin, "The Tragedy of the Commons," *Science,* vol. 162 (1968): 1243–1248.

41. Graf, *Wilderness Preservation,* pp. 129–130.

42. Robbins, *Our Landed Heritage,* p. 374.

43. Ibid., pp. 413–418.

44. See Jerome Edwards, *Pat McCarran: Political Boss of Nevada* (Reno: University of Nevada Press, 1982); and Fred E. Whited, *The Rhetoric of Senator Patrick A. McCarran,* unpublished Ph.D. thesis, University of Oregon, 1973.

45. Lester Velie, "They Kicked Us Off Our Land," *Collier's,* July 26, 1947, p. 21.

46. Dyan Zaslowsky, "Does the West Have a Death Wish?" *American Heritage,* vol. 33, no. 4 (1982): 34.

47. Lester Velie, "They Kicked Us Off Our Land II," *Collier's,* August 9, 1947, p. 80.

48. Graf, *Wilderness Preservation,* p. 168.

49. Zaslowsky, "Does the West Have a Death Wish?" p. 35.

50. The definitive biography of De Voto is by Wallace E. Stegner, *The Uneasy Chair* (Garden City, NY: Doubleday, 1974).

51. Bernard De Voto, "The Easy Chair," *Harper's,* vol. 197 (July 1948): 110, 112.

52. Velie, "They Kicked Us Off Our Land II," pp. 72–73.

53. Velie, "They Kicked Us Off Our Land," p. 40.

2

Ranchers, Predators,
and Animal Lovers

SIGN OF THE TIMES: The fairy shrimp, a twenty-two-legged crustacean that measures less than an inch long, lives in freshwater vernal pools. The shrimp, which were offered protection under the Endangered Species Act in 1994, have a life span of one to three months, laying their eggs in the pools and then dying when the pools dry up. Dormant eggs hatch with the next winter's rain. The shrimp have delayed the redevelopment of an air force base, the expansion of an airport, and the building of major housing developments in three California counties. California governor Pete Wilson is not a shrimp supporter. "You can find the damned thing in every puddle and drainage ditch in twenty-seven counties. I don't know how endangered it can be. But it's endangering economic development."[1]

Governor Wilson's sentiments are consistent with the views of many of those within the environmental opposition. His comments about the protection of endangered species stem from very different perspectives on the relationship between humans and animals, and the laws that regulate that relationship. Ranchers and hunters, for example, have historically viewed animals as food, as predators, or as the source of their livelihood. Early nature lovers observed nongame animals in what later came to be known as the "appreciative use" of wildlife,[2] or expressed their concern for animal welfare and rights. Later activism would focus on the importance of preserving animal habitats and, subsequently, on a concern for the entire ecosystem. This evolution of attitudes about animals and their habitats has been punctuated by specific controversies that continue as key elements of the contemporary environmental opposition.

At the heart of these conflicts are those who believe that no animal should be killed or exploited for any purpose or through any by-product of human activity; those who support protection only when a species becomes endangered; those who support protection only for species that are endangered and are clearly proven to be of importance

49

to humans and/or the ecosystem; and those who subscribe to the view that animals are simply a resource for human use, that extinction is a natural process, and oppose all attempts at management.

When the issue has been the use of animals in medical experimentation or hunting, the wearing of fur, or the methods by which animals are bred for food, there is another influential segment of the environmental opposition that has piggybacked on to the traditional issues of grazing rights and species protection: groups organized against animal rights activists within the environmental movement. The environmental opposition, although fragmented by sometimes differing perspectives, has brought together divergent interests into a powerful political movement by capitalizing on various groups' common interests.

The issues have become more complex because many of the conflicts are regional (centered in the West) or limited to a specific segment of ideological adherents, such as those who oppose the utilization of animals in circuses and rodeos. There has also been an increasing proliferation of state and federal agencies with authority to regulate and protect the land, the animals upon it, and the way they are managed or, as some observers see it, exploited. This chapter examines the growth of the environmental opposition that has developed in the twentieth century over three interrelated issues—livestock grazing, wildlife management, and animal rights—as a way of illustrating how different interests have attempted to influence environmental policies using a variety of political strategies and resources.

LIVESTOCK GRAZING LAW DISPUTES

It is doubtful whether most American consumers understand the complex system by which meat finds its way from the range to their dining room tables. That lack of understanding helps to explain one of the most vitriolic aspects of opposition to the U.S. environmental movement and regulation: the debate over grazing rights. Ranchers view livestock as a business and seek to maximize their profits using whatever methods work efficiently and economically, which often involves obtaining leases to graze their animals on public lands. Members of environmental groups see grazing as despoliation and as one of the factors that have led to the destruction of valuable wildlife habitat and wilderness areas.

Range livestock ranches (the source of most of the nation's meat supply) rely upon the dry, unirrigated rangelands as pasture, deriving their income from the sale of the animals or their wool. Ranchers use the rangeland grasses as a seasonal source of feed for their cattle and sheep; when drought or other factors reduce the amount of available rangeland, the animals' weight drops, there is a higher incidence of disease and death, and a resulting reduction in profits. There are only two other food sources to use in place of rangeland: feed produced on the irrigated land belonging to the rancher or purchased feed, both of which increase the total cost of production. Having an accessible, inexpensive, and productive source of rangeland for livestock becomes a critical element of a successful ranching operation, a key factor in the ability of the rancher to provide meat to the market at a price that is attractive to both the producer and the consumer.[3]

Using the cheapest food source—open rangeland—also means finding adequate sources of water for livestock to drink. Cattle, for example, tend to stay near water sources and will seldom travel more than 4 miles from water in search of forage. When water sources are widely scattered, cattle graze unevenly, leaving forage far from the water sources relatively untouched and grazing heavily nearest the water. Toward the end of the ranch cycle, the cattle are shipped to farmers who "finish" them on grain or concentrated feeds for delivery to slaughterhouses.

Sheep ranchers, in contrast, rely more extensively on range forage to meet a much larger proportion of their total annual feed requirements than do cattle ranchers. Unlike cattle, which are allowed to roam and forage freely, sheep must be herded from one grazing area to another, adding additional labor costs to the production formula but allowing better rangeland utilization. Sheep also do not need an available water supply and can rely upon morning dew for as long as a month or more. As a result, sheep can graze areas of the West that are unsuitable for cattle.[4] However, for both sheep and cattle ranchers, finding adequate affordable rangeland is complicated by the fact that the majority of western land is owned by the federal government or by individual states, both of which require ranchers to obtain permits for their use. Owners of private rangeland charge as much as five times the rate charged by the government, further reducing the ranchers' potential profits.

The development of an organized opposition to the government's grazing policies began in the West in the mid-nineteenth century when chaos and anarchy predominated on the open range. Livestock owners grabbed the choice grazing areas (including those in the public domain), fencing their cattle in against armed raids by competitors. As more and more cattle and sheep were fed on increasingly less acreage, forage became depleted and many ranch owners went bankrupt in the late 1880s. The struggle for western land intensified as farmers and homesteaders transformed grazing land into cropland, and livestock owners began pressuring the U.S. government to lease the lands within the public domain to them for grazing. In some states, cattle associations joined together to pool their herds and define their property rights by group enforcement of claims. As they worked out agreements on grazing, breeding, branding, and disease containment, the livestock associations became formidable political powers.[5]

Local community boosters hoping to attract eastern settlers who would homestead in the rural West faced off against the livestock industry, which responded by attempting to gain control of state politics and lobbied against homestead legislation. The grazing dispute was fostered by intense feelings of sectionalism—especially among eastern "cattle capitalists" and railroad magnates who dominated the industry during Reconstruction. They had no desire to share the West's resources—whether rangeland, timber, or minerals—with settlers and tourists.[6]

The federal government has had a pivotal role in this issue by regulating grazing on its lands. The Department of the Interior attempted to exclude cattle and sheep from forest reserves in the 1890s, but relented in 1898 and issued cattle and sheep grazing permits for most areas in its jurisdiction. Regulations issued at the time warned that the stock owners used the forest only as a privilege and not as a right, and that the secretary of the interior could exclude them entirely at his discretion.[7] That fact has been in dispute in the debate over grazing rights on public lands ever since and has been responsible for maintaining the influence of a powerful coalition of livestock groups.

At the turn of the century, groups like the American Cattle Growers Association appealed to Congress to open up the public domain rangeland in addition to the forest preserves, setting off an all-out war with farmers, with the first skirmishes in the state legislatures. With the creation of the Public Lands Commission in 1903 came proposals to open up the range with grazing leases—a step viewed by western newspapers as monopolistic and a threat to further homesteading.[8]

Beginning in the mid-1920s, stock associations were divided on how best to resolve the conflict between their desire for autonomy and the recognized need for some orderly and stable system for managing grazing. Some livestock groups supported a transfer of lands to the states or to private owners, while others believed a federally administered leasing system was a more cost-effective solution. Unlike other environmental policies such as timber management, there was little scientific expertise to rely upon (the Society of Range Management did not form until after World War II), and the preservationist movement was more concerned at the time with scenic areas than with the open range.[9]

The issue moved slowly through the political system, not only because of the differences among the livestock groups, but also because of turf disputes between the Department of Agriculture and the Department of the Interior as to which agency should manage a proposed leasing program. From 1929 to 1932, President Herbert Hoover complicated resolution further by introducing several unsuccessful proposals to transfer federal lands to the states. The president's recommendations were opposed by groups like the Arizona Cattle Growers Association, the California Cattlemen's Association, and the Wyoming Stock Growers Association, who still wanted the land ceded to private ranchers, and by homesteading interests.[10]

In 1934, a compromise bill, introduced by Colorado representative Edward Taylor, was supported by the Roosevelt administration and livestock producers who realized the need for some type of stable grazing program. Under the Taylor Grazing Act, each agency allocates a portion of the lands it administers as forage for game animals, with the remainder made available to livestock ranchers who pay grazing permit fees based on a complex formula called an animal unit month (AUM). Enforcement of the Taylor Act and the issue of the appropriate grazing fee level have been highly politicized since the legislation was enacted. Ranchers sought major concessions from the Department of the Interior, including low-cost grazing fees and a somewhat casual approach to grazing claims founded on custom rather than law, while Interior Department officials wanted scientific management of the land use. The grazing issue was further complicated by the fact that most lands were under the jurisdiction of the Department of Agriculture rather than the Interior Department, giving the latter agency little authority to negotiate. Both agencies were protective of their bureaucratic turf and often extended their interdepartmental rivalry by courting the ranchers and livestock associations in an attempt to expand their jurisdictions.

Initially, 14,653 grazing licenses were issued in thirty grazing districts, covering 1.5 million cattle and over 6 million sheep. The permits limited the number of animals that could be grazed on each allotment, although the actual numbers were based on historic grazing patterns rather than on any scientific basis. The initial permits were issued annually, even though the act authorized ten-year licenses. But the ten-year license required the ranchers to calculate carrying conditions; and since annual licenses did not do so and were routinely renewed, there was little push for the longer-term licenses.

From 1935 to 1959, grazing permits were administered by several agencies, including the Division of Grazing, which was later renamed the Grazing Service. In 1946, as part of a presidential reorganization plan, the Grazing Service and the General Land Office merged to form the Bureau of Land Management (BLM), where grazing came under the jurisdiction of the Division of Range Management. The BLM served in a largely custodial capacity, with the permittees and local advisory boards holding most of the decisionmaking power over implementation of the grazing law. Their work was supervised by the National Advisory Board Council (NABC), which worked closely with the National Wool Growers Association and the American National Livestock Association. The NABC also contributed money toward the salaries of those who were employed to administer the lands, allowing the regulators to be supervised by those who were regulated.[11]

Many observers believe the livestock industry has "captured" the agencies that regulate it, a term used to describe the ways organized interests' influence becomes so pervasive that an agency loses its autonomy and neutrality in making policy.[12] The industry's domination of the political process is virtually unprecedented. In the late 1940s, for example, livestock interests successfully convinced several western members of Congress to sponsor legislation that drastically cut appropriations for the Department of the Interior's administration of the grazing districts. As a result, some local Grazing Service offices were closed, and the industry decided to capitalize on its success by campaigning for legislation to sell western public lands on a preferential basis to the ranchers who were using them at the time of sale. The ranchers' primary argument was that they were historically accustomed to using the land and that it was grossly unfair, illegal, unconstitutional, immoral, and communistic for the federal government to continue holding on to it.[13]

In 1959, the BLM published the first of several reports that indicated the lands were being severely overgrazed, a charge repeated in subsequent reports by the General Accounting Office. The reports reinforced the image that ranchers were selfishly using the range in disregard for the public interest and doing so at the public's expense through the low level of fees charged in comparison to those paid for grazing on private rangeland.[14] Congress responded with passage of a series of laws that signaled a dramatic change in policy. The 1960 Multiple Use and Sustained Yield Act granted the USFS additional authority over grazing within the national forests. Environmental organizations, which were beginning to turn their attention to the grazing issue, hoped to earn the support of Presidents John F. Kennedy and Lyndon B. Johnson, both of whom appeared to have an interest in natural resource issues. In 1964, the establishment of the Public Land Law Review Commission, whose mission was to make recommendations on public land management, reinforced the government's intention to continue its ownership of the remaining federal lands.

Attempts by the federal government to remedy a problem that had been building for decades brought out the livestock industry's big guns in opposition to these measures, as well as to other attempts to reduce the amount of land available for grazing. In 1961, the federal government proposed converting one-third of a million acres of Utah grazing lands into Canyonlands National Park, a move the state's governor, George Dewey Clyde, said he would oppose "to the last ditch."[15] Ranchers were accustomed to controlling what they perceived as "their" land, especially land with usable natural forage that they felt would otherwise be wasted.

The tenor of the debate intensified with passage of the Classification and Multiple Use Act of 1964, which called for federal lands to be made available for purposes other than grazing, and the Federal Land Policy and Management Act (FLPMA) of 1976, which enhanced the powers of the BLM and restored its authority to regulate grazing rules. Although both laws enjoyed the support of a broad range of environmental organizations, some groups, such as Friends of the Earth and the Wilderness Society, considered the BLM incapable of implementing the law.

The Contemporary Grazing Debate

"No Moo by '92" . . . "Cattle Free by '93" . . . "Cattle Galore by '94" . . . "Cattle Alive by '95": These bumper-sticker sentiments from environmental groups and livestock owners typify the rhetoric that characterizes differing positions on the grazing issue. The environmental movement's criticisms of the livestock industry became more strident in the 1980s and 1990s, led largely by the Sierra Club, the Wilderness Society, and the coalition group Rest the West, formed in 1990 specifically to work for livestock-free wilderness on federal land. Environmental group pressure was coupled with a demographic change that weakened western control over key congressional committees that had historically protected ranchers from federal intervention. As the urban population increased and their constituencies looked to the land for recreational purposes, Congress felt less inclined to bend to the ranching lobby as it had in previous years. New voices from the environmental community became a countervailing force that shifted the balance of power in some communities in the West, especially in California. That state's mammoth delegation, although it seldom unites on any single issue, has often been able to block proposals aimed at obstructing or impeding the implementation and enforcement of environmental laws and regulations.

Despite the onslaught and accompanying negative publicity, the livestock associations have remained united in their lobbying efforts, backed up by vocal constituencies that can be counted on to show up at public hearings and rallies. More recently, the grazing lobby has added to its list of supporters representatives of other extractive resource industries and environmental opposition groups like the Oregon Lands Coalition, all of whom are fighting federal intrusion over the use of public lands.

Although the FLPMA underscored once again the government's desire to retain ownership of the public domain, environmental groups have charged that current grazing laws and practices are severely flawed. The organizations charge that the policies have resulted in the subsidization of the livestock industry by taxpayers and allow the continuation of ecological damage caused by mismanagement and misuse of federal lands. The first charge is based on the imbalance of fees issues as well as the fact that taxpayers pick up the cost of improvements to rangelands, such as cattle guards, stock ponds, and signage.

But they are even more adamant about the damage caused by livestock, especially to scarce riparian areas alongside streams and springs. Livestock require tremendous amounts of water and, in foraging, destroy food stock for native species. When they congregate into small areas, their hooves trample the ground cover, leading to soil erosion and stream sedimentation.[16]

For those reasons, grazing issues are not likely to disappear from the environmental movement's agenda. While some attempts at compromise have been suggested, such as a Sierra Club proposal to allow grazing on those portions of the public lands where ranchers agree to abide by strict range management regulation while banning it on areas already damaged, other groups feel any compromise is actually capitulation to the enemy.

Although the shift in demographics and public opinion has had some impact, the forces of electoral change are even more powerful because the members of the 104th Congress managed to stall an issue that had been one of President Clinton's major environmental promises. When former Arizona governor Bruce Babbitt was appointed secretary of the interior by President Clinton in 1993, the initial plan was to raise the $1.86 per AUM grazing fee on public lands to nearly $5.00 to make the fees closer to the cost of grazing on private lands, estimated at about $8–$10 per AUM. Over the next several months, the administration's proposal repeatedly came under attack by western senators, who vowed to retaliate by lobbying against other policies Clinton supported. Several senators introduced their own grazing fee package, which would have raised fees a modest 25 percent, and Babbitt countered with an announcement that he would administratively raise fees to $4.28 per AUM and place restrictions on pesticides, water availability, the length of the grazing season, and leasing conditions.[17]

Western senators, in a classic example of how the system of checks and balances works in Washington, D.C., responded by attacking the Interior Department's budget, which had not yet received full congressional approval. A House/Senate conference committee worked out a compromise that would have raised fees to $3.45 by 1997, which prompted western senators to filibuster the appropriations bill for the agency. By late 1993, Nevada senator Henry Reid and the supporters of reform withdrew the grazing compromise from consideration, allegedly in exchange for votes the president needed for approval of the North American Free Trade Agreement (NAFTA).[18]

In 1994, Babbitt continued his attempts to move grazing reform through Congress, but in a move that angered environmental organizations, he forced controversial BLM director Jim Baca to resign his position. When the Republicans took control of Congress after the 1994 elections, the grazing fee issue reappeared in an altogether different partisan form, although Babbitt continued to press for new range rules that encouraged conservation but did not require congressional approval. Environmental organizations including the NRDC argued that Babbitt's regulations did not go far enough and would continue to encourage overgrazing. Babbitt appeared to concede defeat to the livestock industry in December 1994 when he announced he was deferring a decision on the fee structure to the new Congress and postponed implementation of the new grazing regulations.

Livestock associations like the National Cattlemen's Beef Association complained that the regulations would be a death knell to the industry. "Under the guise of constraining a few bad actors out there, they [take] a sledgehammer on the entire industry, while not doing anything to take the bad actors off the land. It's not a carpet bombing of the industry. It's more like death by strangulation," one association official said.[19] The livestock lobby then turned to the new Congress to reinforce its opposition to any fee increases or attempts to further regulate grazing, drawing a rebuttal from activists ranging from antitax advocates who see the federal grazing program as a multi-million-dollar giveaway to environmentalists and hunters to mainstream environmental groups.[20]

As a result of Babbitt's deferment on grazing policy, grazing fees not only did not go up as the Clinton administration and environmental groups had planned, but they actually went down 19 percent. The annual fee reverted to a formula established by the Public Rangelands Improvement Act of 1978, which takes into account factors such as production costs and wholesale meat prices, which brought the fee down from $1.98 per AUM in 1994 to $1.61 in 1995—the lowest price since 1988.

Whereas livestock associations have been at the heart of this segment of the environmental opposition, the less visible side of the grazing lobby comprises the major corporate interests who hold the bulk of the nation's 28,000 grazing permit holders. While the cattle

and sheep groups have attempted to portray themselves as representatives of small farms and ranchers, the profile of ranching in the
United States has changed. Today, the top 10 percent of the permit
holders control about half of the nation's public grazing land. Only
12 percent of the permit holders are listed by the federal government
as small operators. One California rancher controls permits for
nearly 5 million acres of public land in Nevada and California—an
area as big as the state of Massachusetts. Other major permit holders
include the J. R. Simplot Company of Idaho, which owns food-pro-
cessing and chemical companies as well as several high-tech firms,
the Mormon Church, and the Japanese conglomerate Zenchiku Corporation. Even the habitat protection group the Nature Conservancy
holds permits for 250,000 acres in California, using cows to trim unwanted plants in the spring in hopes of restoring native perennial
flowers. Unlike the majority of the livestock grazing permit holders,
however, the Nature Conservancy has said it does not oppose a
grazing fee increase.[21]

The issue of grazing rights has also become inextricably linked
with the property rights movement discussed in Chapter 10. Among
the organizations advocating that linkage is the Nevada Agricultural
Foundation, which helped fund a study of western grazing rights by
Frank Falen and Karen Budd-Falen, two Wyoming attorneys who have
frequently served as legal counsel for the environmental opposition.
The Falens note that BLM regulations recognize a "grazing preference"
or permit to graze on federal lands, which they argue is a type of property or property right protected by the Constitution, rather than a privilege revocable at will by the government. The permits have a monetary value (since they can be purchased and taxed), and, therefore,
federal agencies should be required to pay compensation to the permit
holders if the right to graze is taken away.[22]

By tying the fee issue up in Congress, and by expanding the
grazing issue into the legal morass of regulatory takings, the grazing
lobby has managed to maintain the status quo despite a substantial ex-
penditure of energy by environmental organizations. Although the fate
of grazing fees is tied in part to the winds of electoral change, livestock
advocates are also moving their battle into the judicial arena in hopes
that a more conservative, Republican-appointed judiciary will support
their cause. But environmental groups, accustomed and effective at
using litigation as a political strategy, have used other statutes besides
grazing laws to try to force the federal government to limit grazing. In
a 1996 suit brought by the Oregon Natural Desert Association, the Oregon Natural Resources Council, the Pacific Rivers Council, the Portland Audubon Society, and Trout Unlimited, a U.S. District Court
judge agreed that livestock producers must comply with state stan-

dards under the Clean Water Act. The judge ruled that the USFS must obtain the state's assurance that grazing operations on federal lands will not pollute streams and rivers before granting new grazing permits. The environmental groups had submitted photographs to the court that showed that cattle had trampled the stream banks and dropped manure in the stream, violating clean water laws. The case indicates the tenacity of environmental organizations in their attempts to further reduce, if not altogether ban, grazing in riparian areas.

WILDLIFE MANAGEMENT ISSUES

Wildlife management issues have often been the source of conflict in the United States, whether the issue is protection of a single species like the marbled murrelet under the ESA or the restriction of cougar hunting in Oregon. There are several factors that make these issues somewhat different from other policies that have led to an organized environmental opposition. Often the opposition to wildlife management policies has been localized rather than nationwide. A single rancher's battle against a local USFWS official has been the norm, and attempts to reform the ESA had been the result of regional skirmishes with federal agencies up until the 1994 elections when the Republicans gained control of Congress. When USFWS goals have conflicted with those of agencies with powerful constituencies (like the BLM), the political fragility of the ESA became apparent. Even some legislators who originally supported the ESA in concept now believe it has become a tool of environmental groups seeking to shut down the nation's extractive resource industries.

The government has made some effort to ameliorate the growing opposition to its wildlife policies through cooperative programs and incentives, rather than clashing with groups head on. For example, Interior Secretary Bruce Babbitt implemented the "Safe Harbors" program in 1995 to encourage private landowners to create habitats for endangered species without facing land use restrictions if they decide later to develop the land. The program provides incentives to developers who create or improve habitats that could then attract endangered species. One beneficiary of the incentive program was the Pinehurst Resort and Country Club in south-central North Carolina, which agreed to improve habitats for the red-cockaded woodpecker on the resort's land. The object of such provisions is to assure landowners that the ESA is not as inflexible as its critics believe, although only a handful of habitat conservation plans have been approved thus far. While the Clinton administration prided itself on its lack of a confrontational style in dealing with the environmental opposition, many compromise proposals satisfied neither environmentalists nor those who opposed legislation like the ESA.

Two closely related wildlife management issues have thus become central to the environmental opposition: predator control and endangered species protection. These policies have become two of the most potent rallying points for hundreds of diverse groups and have created the perception that the environmental opposition represents a massive outpouring of public sentiment for political change.

Predator Control

American wildlife law has traditionally focused on animals considered dangerous to people or livestock, such as wolves, bears, mountain lions, alligators, eagles, coyotes, foxes, snakes, and bobcats. Other animals that have occasionally been regulated include those that compete with human society for scarce resources, like harbor seals that eat salmon or sea otters that eat abalone, and pest animals like crows, rats, skunks, and starlings.[23]

U.S. policies and attitudes toward predators have followed a clearly discernible but inconsistent historical path. As early as 1630, the Massachusetts Bay Company paid trappers a one-cent bounty for killing wolves, a practice that continued with western expansion. Along with bounties, the government became more proactive in 1705 when the Pennsylvania Colony hired the first government predator control agent to kill wolves using public funds. As the human population expanded in the 1800s, cheap strychnine poisoning became the easiest way to kill unwanted species, replaced eventually by steel-jawed traps and rifles. The public's attitude toward the killing of predatory or unwanted animals was uniform approval of the practice, since at the time, most people accepted the concept of human supremacy over the land.[24]

By the late nineteenth century, the USDA's Office of Economic Ornithology and Mammalogy (later named the Division of Biological Survey [DBS], and then the USFWS) began studying more efficient ways to poison rodents, pest birds, and predators, largely at the behest of cattle and sheep owners who estimated they were losing millions of dollars in livestock annually. By 1905, the policy changed from theory to practice when the USFS began paying trappers to kill wolves on national forest grazing lands, and by 1915, a full-fledged federal predator eradication effort was under way.

In 1924, western zoologists began to question the government's "vermin" control program because nontarget animals were being rapidly eliminated and some were believed to have already become extinct. Economic interests were at stake, they noted, because predatory animals also controlled the rodent population that competed with livestock for grass. Government biologists scoffed at their concerns, arguing that even if large predators were eliminated from the United States, they still survived in Canada and Mexico. One DBS biologist, E. A. Goldman, told the American Society of Mammalogists Conference in 1924, "Large predatory mammals, destructive to livestock and game, no longer have a place in our advancing civilization."[25]

A financial relationship existed at the time that would further frame the policy debate. In 1918, the DBS began working with local governments, livestock associations, and sheep and cattle ranchers paying a tax on livestock to fund trapping operations. The concerns of scientists (including a 1930 petition signed by 148 researchers criticizing the predator control program) and the newly emerging concepts of balance of nature and ecology were overcome by the financial support generated by the ranchers. Pressure by the National Wool Growers Association to give the secretary of agriculture authority to pursue predators and other pest animals on public and private lands resulted in the passage of the Animal Damage Control Act (ADCA) in 1931. The legislation funded a plan for predator and rodent control that allowed the agency virtually unlimited power in eradicating any animals ranchers and farmers wanted eliminated. The act allows for all "injurious" species to be destroyed, although Congress repealed the authorization for killing bald eagles in 1940 because they are part of America's political symbolism.

The government's policies on wildlife management have not been limited to carnivores and have been sometimes inconsistent. In the late nineteenth century, for example, human egg gatherers and plume hunters nearly wiped out the gull population along the New England coast, prompting local Audubon societies to hire wardens to protect the remaining nests. After the turn of the century, public sentiment changed, wildlife refuges were established, and the growth of landfills (which became immediate attractants for gulls foraging on garbage) expanded not only the gulls' numbers but also their range. The success of the refuge program had an unintended consequence: The gulls became a nuisance species—posing dangers to aircraft, contaminating water supplies, and driving out other native birds.

After the Great Depression, the government abruptly changed its wildlife policy and undertook efforts to kill gulls, destroy their nests, and poison their eggs. In most cases, the efforts failed and only encouraged the gull population to move southward. Today, a poison originally used to kill starlings is used on specific gull colonies to allow rare seabirds to flourish in what one Audubon Society official referred to as "weeding a garden."[26]

Opponents of the government's predator eradication programs first turned their attention to saving wildlife in the nation's national parks. When the NPS was created in 1916, it exterminated wolves and mountain lions in parks such as Yellowstone. It opposed trapping and poisoning in the mid-1920s, and eventually adopted a policy of wildlife protection and study within the parks. An unwritten rule remained, however, that what lived outside park boundaries was fair game. Within the parks, this created, in essence, "outdoor zoos" or islands of natural conditions in which remnants of native fauna were preserved for scientific, educational, and aesthetic interest.[27]

The federal government engaged in decades of virtually unlimited eradication through programs like the ADC and the USFWS program PARC (Predatory Animal and Rodent Control), which in 1963 laid 39,910 traps, spread 151,942 pounds of poison grain, prepared 708,130 poisonous baits, and set 64,921 "coyote-getters" (a type of spring gun loaded with poison). As the nation's major environmental organizations became more active in the 1960s and 1970s, they relied upon science to bolster their efforts to protect wildlife. In order to convince Congress and the president that eradication programs were not effective, they relied upon three federal studies: the 1964 Leopold Report, the 1971 Cain Report, and the 1980 Andrus Report. The studies—audits produced by biologists rather than trappers—dealt specifically with public concerns over predator poisons' contamination of the food chain, inhumane methods used to trap animals, and the accidental trapping of nontargeted endangered species. All three reports expressed doubt about the need for predator control and were highly critical of the methods being used by PARC. In addition, the audits were highly critical of PARC as "a semi-autonomous bureaucracy whose function in many localities bears scant relationship to real need and less still to scientific management."[28]

Since then, an ongoing battle has raged between environmental groups that accuse the government of mismanagement and western ranchers, who have successfully lobbied to keep the ADC program alive and well funded for decades.[29] As the livestock industry regrouped and became more organized in its lobbying efforts in the 1970s and 1980s, President Ford relaxed the ban, and President Reagan removed most limitations on renewed use of poisons in 1982.[30]

The issue of predator control has become entwined with the issue of endangered species protection as members of the environmental opposition, environmental groups, and public officials have attempted to reconcile the conflicting goals of protecting some animals at the expense of others.

Protecting Endangered Species

If any one animal epitomizes the conflict of perspectives on the relationship of humans to animals between the environmental movement and the environmental opposition, it is the wolf. By the 1880s, the government's policies had essentially eradicated the wolf in the eastern United States, and by 1914, most had been killed in the western plains states, with a only a few pockets persisting in the Southwest in the early 1920s. For all practical purposes, by World War II the wolf no longer posed an economic threat to livestock or game.[31]

At the same time the livestock industry was engaged in policy warfare over predator control, another battle line was being drawn by environmental organizations seeking to expand wildlife protection policy. In 1966, Congress enacted the Endangered Species Preservation Act (ESPA), the vague provisions of which indicated the government's intentions to protect, conserve, and restore species threatened with extinction. Although the ESPA was never successfully implemented, a politically savvy Congress responded to the intense lobbying of the growing environmental movement with the enactment of additional wildlife protection statutes such as the Wild, Free-Roaming Horses and Burros Act (1971), the Marine Mammal Protection Act (1972), and the Bald Eagle Protection Act (1972).

The apex of wildlife management legislation was the 1973 passage of the Endangered Species Act, setting clear guidelines to prevent the destruction of animal and plant diversity. The legislation was designed to conserve threatened species through the development of a listing program and a protection component, with the USFWS and the National Marine Fisheries Service given responsibility for administering the law. The measure focused on the preservation of the critical habitat upon which a species depends—a policy that is central to the opposition to the law both in principle and in practice.

Although the ESA provided complete legal protection for the wolf, the law was not fully implemented. In Minnesota, for instance, the Department of Natural Resources rejected the notion that the wolf had ever been a threatened species in that state.[32] At the urging of farmers, the USFWS had enacted rules permitting the killing of wolves that could be identified as predators—a policy challenged by environmental groups in 1978. In *Fund for Animals v. Andrus*, a U.S. Federal District Court judge ruled that the USFWS could trap wolves only after a significant predation had occurred and that efforts must be directed at capturing rather than killing.[33]

Subsequently, state agency discretion and varying legal interpretations of the ESA's mandate "to conserve" species has significantly affected the implementation of the law and has led to renewed battles between ranchers and environmental groups. The issue came to a head in 1995 when the USFWS reintroduced twenty-nine wolves from Canada into Yellowstone National Park in Wyoming and parts of central Idaho in an effort to build up the region's population to 200 animals. The government implemented the multi-million-dollar program to restore the area's natural balance and to reduce the region's burgeoning elk and deer populations, despite intense resistance.

Opposition to the reintroduction program came from a variety of organizations and individuals. Groups such as the Montana Stock-growers Association opposed the program because they feared the wolves would leave the park's boundaries to attack their livestock, even though provisions allow ranchers to kill wolves under certain conditions. In October 1995, a Billings, Montana, rancher was found guilty of shooting to death one of the Yellowstone male wolves despite his claim that he thought it was a wild dog. He had killed the endangered animal outside the park's boundaries, but the wolf was still protected under federal law. In February 1996, the rancher was sentenced to six months in prison and fined $10,000—a penalty one observer argued was merely the federal government's way of "flexing its muscles, bullying everyone to make sure its program succeeds."[34] The case further galvanized those who believed the government's reintroduction program was ill conceived, reinforcing the belief that both the federal government and the environmental movement were appropriate targets for the environmental opposition's activists.

The debate has pitted various wildlife and livestock organizations against one another, with little evidence that the reintroduction debate will be settled in Yellowstone or any other region. One organization, Defenders of Wildlife, set up a $100,000 fund to pay ranchers fair market value for any livestock kills attributable to the wolves. An environmental opposition group, the Wyoming-based Abundant Wildlife Society of North America, has used dramatic photos of animals killed or mauled by wolves as evidence that the government's reintroduction program is misguided.

State government officials added their voices in opposition as well. In January 1995, the Montana legislature joined the debate by passing the following resolution:

> Whereas the United States Congress has sanctioned the reintroduction of wolves into the Yellowstone Park ecosystem by federal agencies; and
> Whereas most areas of the United States do not presently have populations of wolves;
> Now, therefore, be it resolved that if the United States government is successful in its efforts to reintroduce wolves into the Yellowstone Park ecosystem, the U.S. Congress be urged to take the steps necessary to ensure that wolves are also reintroduced into every other ecosystem and region in the United States, including Central Park in New York City, the Presidio in San Francisco, and Washington, D.C.[35]

A Montana state representative who supported the resolution, and who is also a cattle rancher, said the reintroduction program would force him "to stand by while our business is torn apart, piece by piece. What other businessperson would stand by and watch that sort of thing?"[36]

Congressional opposition to the wolf reintroduction plan was based on a variety of arguments. Alaska representative Don Young, chair of the House Resources Committee, questioned the program's cost, estimated to total $6.7 million through the year 2002. Idaho representative Helen Chenoweth proposed opening up the park's herds to hunters instead as a way of culling the elk and deer. None of the proposals went very far.

The arguments on both sides of the reintroduction issue consist of equal parts of passion and politics. Environmental groups have argued that wolves are intelligent and docile animals that represent harmony with nature; ranchers who have less enthusiasm for the symbolic issues portray them as killing machines.[37] One observer has characterized the wolf reintroduction program as the "line in the sand that divides the old West from the new. Both sides want us to see this as a distillation of all endangered species conflicts, as a simple question of either/or."[38]

USFWS and NPS officials consider the program an unqualified success. They note that the wolves have begun to breed, are restoring the predator/prey balance without killing livestock, and are good for tourism, replacing grizzly bears as the number one animal attraction in Yellowstone National Park. But western members of Congress have responded to an unconvinced constituency and have successfully cut the program's budget and reduced staff. Environmental organizations have solicited private donations to try to bridge the gap and keep the program going, with more wolves slated to be reintroduced in the late 1990s.

The environmental opposition has been especially adept at bringing diverse interests together to fight the ESA, using the umbrella organization Grassroots ESA Coalition (GESAC) as its focal point. It requires no membership fee and is made up of an estimated 350 other organizations with 4 million members who have "joined" by making a donation or allowing their name to be used as a participating group. Formed in 1994 and managed by wise use policy entrepreneur Chuck Cushman out of his Battle Ground, Washington, headquarters (home to several other environmental opposition organizations he coordinates), GESAC's mission is to reform the ESA. The group argues that the ESA has failed to conserve endangered and threatened animals and plants and has wasted scarce conservation resources by "engendering a regulatory regime that has violated the rights of individuals ... destroyed jobs, devalued property, and depressed human enterprise on private and public lands, hidden the full cost of conserving endangered species by foisting those costs on private individuals, and imposed significant burdens on state, county, and local governments."[39]

Clearly GESAC's grievances closely parallel those of the property rights movement with which it is aligned, although its list of participating groups includes a wide range of other opposition organizations, from California Women in Timber to the U.S. Taxpayers Association and the Family Water Alliance. At the heart of GESAC's proposed reforms are issues focused on the rights of states to control their own lands and resources, reducing costs of conservation, and "voluntary, incentive-based programs to enlist the cooperation of America's landowners and invigorate their conservation ethic."[40]

A second source of opposition to species protection has come from developers and private landowners, many of whom have joined forces to fight implementation of the ESA. They are especially opposed to the process that allows individuals as well as organizations to petition the government to declare a species as threatened or endangered. Petitions can be used to hold up projects already under development while the USFWS completes habitat and population studies.

Along the southern California coast, some of the state's most valuable real estate is also the home of the California gnatcatcher, a small bird listed as a threatened species, as well as home to about fifty other species in danger of becoming threatened. The NRDC petitioned for the bird to be listed as threatened to preserve more than 200,000 acres of prime coastal habitat. In 1992, the Southern California Building Industry Association and regional transportation agencies filed suit, arguing that the scientific study on which the listing was based was significantly flawed. In 1994, a federal district court agreed, vacating the listing in a decision environmental groups termed "a significant setback."

Those opposed to the ESA point to a list of similar species that have at least initially thwarted developers' plans, including the golden-cheeked warbler of Texas, the red squirrel of Arizona, and the Colorado squawfish. In Texas, for example, the warbler's listing set off a series of unintended consequences that drew diverse segments of the community together in opposition and led to the formation of the Hill Country Landowners Coalition. The coalition's members, composed primarily of property owners in the two counties affected by the listing of the warbler, another bird, and several species of small cave insects, mobilized to fight two local bond issues that would have purchased nearly 30,000 acres of land for the birds' habitat. The coalition argued that if the federal government wanted the habitat so badly, they ought to pay for it, rather than expecting local citizens to ante up additional tax dollars to pay for the land.

The Hill Country Landowners Coalition used a traditional interest group strategy to achieve at least a partial victory against the federal government: They broadened their potential membership base by joining with others who also felt threatened. The 3M Company initially announced it was delaying a multi-million-dollar expansion of its research and development center, and another developer stopped work on a major shopping center, all because of questions over the warbler's habitat. In the Texas hill country, the fate of a small songbird or a minuscule insect paled in comparison to families looking for economic security who felt potential jobs might be lost, providing a common rallying point around which the opposition could coalesce. They were joined by taxpayers' groups and those who simply believed the government had no business telling them what to do and, even more, expecting them to pay for the intrusion into their lives. Another citizens' group complained when a winding road on which numerous accidents had occurred could not be straightened because the work might interfere with the bird's habitat.

One of the two bond measures passed, the other failed, and the project was scaled back. The private companies later paid millions of dollars in permits in order to continue with their projects, and citizens balked as their taxes went up. But the coalition was able to stall the habitat protection program and an estimated $150–$300 million bond issue because it effectively mobilized interests other than its own.

In Clark County, Nevada, the emergency listing of the desert tortoise as an endangered species in 1989 brought construction to a standstill. The USFWS tried a novel approach in the ongoing development-vs.-species battle. The agency agreed to allow development to continue on about 22,000 acres of tortoise habitat near Las Vegas in exchange for an agreement that required strict conservation measures to be taken on 400,000 acres of BLM land. In this way, the agency authorized the "incidental" loss of protected species as long as a comprehensive conservation plan was in place. Under the arrangement, livestock grazing in the preserved area was eliminated entirely and off-road vehicle use was strictly limited. The habitat conservation plan was funded by $10 million in developer fees, ranging from $250 to $550 an acre—a proposal that raised the ire of local ranchers who felt they had lost out to the monied development lobby.[41]

The ESA has been the focus of several property rights organizations that will be discussed in Chapter 10, but one bears mention here. The Coalition of Arizona/New Mexico Counties for Stable Economic Growth, or simply the Coalition of Counties, was initially formed in 1989 in Catron County, New Mexico, to address public land grazing issues. Since its inception, it has broadened its mission and has targeted the USFWS and the USFS, filing several intents of notice to sue the agencies over ESA recovery plans for the spikedance minnow, loach minnow, and the Mexican spotted owl. Unlike several other anti-

ESA groups, the Coalition of Counties includes among its members the elected representatives of more than a dozen counties in two states.[42] Like many of the ESA opposition organizations, the Coalition of Counties is focused on regional issues (in this case, the listing, critical habitat designation, and recovery plans for local species) rather than on generalized disagreement over the law.

Opposition flared when implementation of the ESA threatened large federal projects, including the infamous case of a tiny fish, the snail darter, and the Tennessee Valley Authority's Tellico Dam.[43] In 1989, a Salt Lake City biochemist, Peter Honigh, asked that the spotted frog, found in clusters from Alaska to Utah, be listed as an endangered species. Utah's senator, Jake Garn (who once argued that the ESA was intended to cover grizzly bears and bald eagles rather than "minor species"), led the political opposition. Garn sought to stop the frog from being listed because he feared it would stop progress on the Central Utah Project, a massive series of reservoirs and aqueducts, and the Jordanelle Dam near Heber City, Utah. Garn sought $1 billion in federal funding for the project, which allowed Utah to tap into the Colorado River system.

The ESA has also come under attack from members of the public who do not coalesce into organized interests but who express varying levels of opposition to its implementation. Despite generalized support for the concept of species protection, there is evidence that most Americans have little understanding of the relationship between human activities and habitat destruction, and a limited familiarity with endangered species as a whole. One USFWS-sponsored study, for example, found that only one-fourth of the respondents knew that endangered manatees are not insects.[44]

Not surprisingly, the study found that support for the ESA varies in relation to the amount of behavior change involved. Most of the respondents indicated that they favored the development of different water uses over the protection of a species. When asked if they would be willing to absorb higher energy costs to protect an endangered species, the respondents' answers were dependent upon the nature of the species involved. As species become less "likable," public support for their protection dropped sharply. While 92 percent favored the protection of bald eagles, and 74 percent favored protection of crocodiles, the figures dropped to 47 percent for the Eastern indigo snake, 42 percent for the Furbish lousewort, and 38 percent for the Kauai wolf spider.[45]

Aside from a lack of support for spending public funds on species deemed less deserving of protection, a general dissatisfaction with the ESA's recovery programs has been fueled by press accounts of extraordinary efforts by the USFWS to protect those species. The Houston toad, one of the most endangered amphibians in the United States, was listed by the USFWS in 1970, and seven years later, a critical habitat was designated. That habitat included three counties in southeast Texas, including seven sites in Harris County, which includes metropolitan Houston. The USFWS was ridiculed in the press when it was pointed out that one of the sites included a shopping center, an industrial park, and several large apartment complexes. No toads had been sighted there, and the development had made much of the site unsuitable for the toads. Still attempting to follow what was obviously a flawed policy, the USFWS then ordered its regional office to acquire Ellington Air Force Base, one of the other Harris County critical habitat sites. The regional office responded, "We are unsure as to how to go about acquiring Ellington Air Force Base, but will maintain contacts with people in Houston. If and when the AFB comes up as surplus property we will attempt to acquire it." Public outcry led the USFWS to drop the urban designations altogether.[46]

Publicity over the USFS efforts to protect the habitat of the Kirtland's warbler was the source of ridicule for that agency as well. The bird winters in the Bahamas and then migrates to the jack pine forests of northern Michigan to nest. The habitat was originally created as a result of wildfires that cleared the older growth and ensured the species' existence. The USFS once started a 200-acre prescribed burn to create additional habitat, but the fire raged out of control, burning 25,000 acres, destroying or damaging forty-one homes, and killing one firefighter.[47]

The federal government's difficulty in implementing its own wildlife management programs is illustrated by an issue that has polarized groups in the Pacific Northwest. In 1995, a federal advisory panel recommended that the National Marine Fisheries Service capture and kill sea lions that congregated at fish ladders near Everett, Washington. The sea lions are a protected species under the federal Marine Mammal Protection Act, but they have taken up residence at the Ballard Locks and have almost decimated migrating runs of steelhead trout, another endangered species. In the mid-1980s, an average of 1,600 steelhead swam through the locks and into the Lake Washington watershed to spawn, but by 1994, that number had dwindled to 70. Animal rights activists, including the Humane Society of the United States, immediately threatened to sue.

Similar stories, repeated by radio talk show hosts and chronicled in the conservative press, have led to much of the public's disillusionment and hostility over the ESA and the government's ability to implement it successfully. Regardless of the scientific arguments for protecting indicator species, or environmental groups' concerns about protecting critical habitats, incidents like these provide cannon fodder for those who perceive the government as mismanaging its resources at the expense of jobs and economic development.[48]

THE ENVIRONMENTAL OPPOSITION
AND ANIMAL RIGHTS

The highly volatile issue of animal rights and welfare is one in which the government is caught in a no-win situation in its attempt to formulate environmental policy. No matter what decisions are made, a well-organized and quickly mobilized vocal coalition of activists is prepared to put pressure on policymakers. Some of these interests have become part of the environmental opposition and have added their political clout and membership base to the wise use and property rights movements by taking up as their own issues that are totally unrelated to animals. The front page of one group's newsletter, for instance, included an article on how environmental groups had blamed the wise use movement for the 1995 bombing of the federal building in Oklahoma City and a second story on how the president of the California Forestry Association had been assassinated by a "radical environmentalist" whose purpose was "to intimidate property rights and Wise Use activists."[49] Wise use groups, in turn, have welcomed these activists under their umbrella as a way of demonstrating the diversity of their membership.

On the one side of the animal rights debate are groups opposed to the killing or exploitation of animals regardless of purpose. The political and philosophical mission of the groups involved has been compared to a crusade, and increasingly, several of the organizations have adopted strategies as radical as any other organized interest in this country. The animal rights groups are diverse in their interests, as well as in their resources: Some focus on antivivisection, some on the eating of meat, while others protest the wearing of furs. Another segment of the movement is opposed to circuses and zoos, believing them cruel and inhumane.

Although a few of the animal rights groups are part of a worldwide movement, others are local organizations dedicated to the humane treatment of animals in pet shops and animal shelters, and are usually referred to as "animal welfare organizations." Both segments are of relatively recent origin, with the exception of the American Society for the Prevention of Cruelty to Animals, which was formed just after the Civil War. It was followed by a wide range of groups like the Anti–Steel Trap League and, in the late twentieth century, more militant groups like People for the Ethical Treatment of Animals (PETA), the Animal Liberation Front, and such individual species protection groups as Help Our Wolves Howl and the Crustacean Liberation Front, which protests the harvesting of lobsters.

Although animal rights activists have a wide agenda of concerns, some of them have become a vocal and powerful source of opposition to environmental policies, using litigation and protest activities as their primary strategies. Members of environmental groups usually want to preserve an entire native ecosystem and protect or restore its original species. In some cases, they support the eradication of foreign species or species whose population has been distorted by earlier human intervention. Many animal rights activists do not discriminate between the worth of native and foreign, or introduced, species. They oppose all efforts to support one kind of animal by killing another. The Humane Society of the United States, for instance, filed a court action to obtain a temporary halt to a BLM policy (which had the support of the Audubon Society and the Defenders of Wildlife) of shooting and poisoning ravens to protect the declining population of California desert tortoises. The Humane Society also led the legal efforts against plans by biologists at the San Francisco Bay National Wildlife Refuge to trap and kill foxes that feed on the endangered California clapper rail, despite support for the program by members of the local Sierra Club.[50] Similar suits have been filed to protect wolves (Fund for Animals) and bobcats (Defenders of Wildlife) from eradication under the ADCA. The more radical groups have protested the government's policies over the use of animals for medical research, restaurants that serve meat, furriers, and wild animal dealers. A spokesperson for Last Chance for Animals calls medical researchers "the scum of the earth. They're no better than what the Nazis or slave traders did."[51] Otherwise innocuous companies like Taco Bell, Burger King, Kentucky Fried Chicken, leather furniture stores, and the makers of Hormel chili have repeatedly had their property defaced or vandalized because their products use meat or animal hides.[52]

What makes the animal rights groups such an interesting element of the environmental opposition is that many initially sprang from the early nature appreciation groups that later evolved into the environmental movement. The groups had similar ideological and philosophical roots, but their interests began to diverge over some government policies to restore critical habitats of one species at the expense of another. As a result, they have become hostile to some organizations within the environmental movement when they believe these groups do not adequately protect the rights of every animal, regardless of circumstance. PETA, for example, has urged its members to call the toll-free telephone numbers of groups like the National Wildlife Federation (NWF) to tie up the lines with abusive calls, thus costing the environmental groups money and wasting their staffs' time. PETA has criticized the NWF for being supportive of hunting and not proactive on the implementation of animal rights legislation.[53]

On the other side of the issue are the organizations that make a distinction between animal rights and animal welfare, arguing that extremist groups would "put millions of Americans out of work by closing every business, industry, and recreation that uses animals." Groups like Putting People First, formed in 1990 by Kathleen Marquardt, "represent the average American who drinks milk and eats meat, benefits from medical research, wears leather, wool, and fur, hunts and fishes, owns a pet, and goes to zoos."[54] Marquardt calls the animal rights activists "zealots" and says Putting People First has been responsible for helping defeat two incumbent members of Congress who they argued were apologists for the animal rights line, as well as filing formal complaints with the Internal Revenue Service and other government agencies about the groups. PETA leaders, in turn, call Putting People First "an abusers-rights movement. They do not want people to make humane choices. It's Neanderthal and it's degrading."[55]

To enhance the membership base of Putting People First, estimated at about one-tenth that of PETA, Marquardt has enlisted the aid of still another group that has frequently organized in opposition to the environmental movement and to the government's policies: hunters. The group has founded a program called Hunters for the Hungry, which provides venison for needy families as a way of countering the animal rights groups' claims that Marquardt's organization is indifferent to life.

What sets groups like Putting People First apart from those like PETA is a completely different perspective on the role of humans and animals. PETA national director Ingrid Newkirk has been quoted as saying, "Six million people died in concentration camps, but 6 billion broiler chickens will die this year in slaughterhouses." The group's chair told the *New York Times,* "We feel that animals have the same rights as a retarded human child." Marquardt dismisses such emotionalism as nonsense: "They insist every form of life is equal: humans and dogs and slugs and cockroaches."[56]

It is unlikely that groups with such differing perspectives are ever going to sit down together—one of the factors that has pushed the evolution of the environmental opposition to one of its most radical phases. When groups like these perceive that there is little common ground between them, policy stalemate results and the potential for frustration and violence becomes almost inevitable.

Sport Hunting

Sport hunters have at various times been on both sides of the issue of environmental protection and are thus a somewhat difficult interest to analyze. Some hunting groups compare their goals to those of environmental organizations and see themselves as true conservationists. Many hunters argue that they are dedicated to culling, rather than killing, animals and that they are in this sense protecting the public interest by maintaining a healthy balance of wildlife and resources. The basis of that belief stems from a long history that began in England and made its way with the first colonists to arrive on American shores.[57]

When the first settlers arrived, they brought with them a sense of stewardship that held the rights of wildlife in the public trust. Colonial laws set limits on the length of the hunting season, bag limits, and the use of hunting techniques like netting and poisoning to maintain a sustained yield. State game agencies were later created to enforce hunting laws, followed by statutes permitting the sale of hunting licenses to limit the number of hunters and to provide a stable source of game agency income. The state agencies' dependence upon license sales has made them understandably sensitive to pressures from the hunting lobby, which has grown in membership and political clout.[58]

Although more recent in terms of political history, opposition to hunting has been vocal and intense. Defenders of wildlife turned to issues of class during the mid-to-late nineteenth century. Those who hunted for food were considered ill bred in comparison to the elite, upper-class hunters who pursued game for pleasure. New terms like "pot hunting" and "pot shot" were used derogatorily to refer to poorly skilled, lower-class individuals hunting to put food in their pots and on their tables.[59]

There has been a strong historical linkage among hunters, recreational fishers, and environmental groups, who have not always been at the opposite ends of the political spectrum. President Theodore Roosevelt's views on animals and their habitats came about in large part due to his experiences as a hunter and as a member (along with Gifford Pinchot) of the elite Boone and Crockett Club. At the turn of the century, groups like the Sierra Club joined Roosevelt in a broad consensus that argued for the "right use" of resources and wilderness, claiming that the application of scientific technique would reduce spoilage of wilderness areas.[60]

That same linkage holds true today. The supporters of recreational fishing have asked the National Marine Fisheries Service to protect dwindling stocks of fish from the excesses of the commercial fishing industry. The issue has become particularly important in Florida, Texas, and California, where fishing enthusiasts have joined environmental groups seeking a ban on gill and entanglement nets. In 1992, the publisher of *Florida Sportsman* led a campaign called "Save Our Sealife" and enlisted the support of the Florida Conservation Association, the Florida Wildlife Federation, and a half dozen other environmental groups to obtain signatures for a state constitutional amendment to end netting in Florida waters. The American Sportsfishing Association and fishing equipment manufacturers contributed funding to the $1.3 million campaign, but most of the contributions came from rank-and-file anglers. This time, the opposition to the environmental movement came from the commercial fishing industry, which lost out when nearly 72 percent of Florida's voters approved the ban in 1994.[61]

There is still an element of the environmental movement, composed of groups such as the Fund for Animals, the Committee to Abolish Sport Hunting, and other animal rights activists, that has developed a politically sophisticated and well-funded public appeal to limit hunting within the National Wildlife Refuge System, sabotage hunting events, and flout hunter harassment laws. But the hunting and fishing organizations are more likely to be on the side of the environmental movement than to oppose it. Although there are still some hard-core environmental groups that perceive sport hunters and anglers as the enemy, they no doubt have more in common than either side realizes.

NOTES

1. "A Not-So-Simple Tradeoff: Regulations vs. Jobs," *Congressional Quarterly Weekly Report,* June 17, 1995, pp. 1702–1703.

2. Samuel P. Hays, "From Conservation to Environment: Environmental Politics in the United States Since World War II," *Environmental Review* (fall 1982): 19.

3. See Wesley Calef, *Private Grazing and Public Lands: Studies of the Local Management of the Taylor Grazing Act* (Chicago: University of Chicago Press, 1960), pp. 3–24.

4. Ibid., pp. 33–34.

5. See Gary D. Libecap, *Locking Up the Range* (Cambridge, MA: Ballinger, 1981), pp. 18–19.

6. See Wayne Hage, *Storm over Rangelands* (Bellevue, WA: Merril Press, 1994). Hage's perspective is built on his experience in the livestock industry, as well as on his service as an outspoken member of the wise use movement and a party in a series of property rights disputes.

7. Samuel P. Hays, *Conservation and the Gospel of Efficiency* (Cambridge, MA: Harvard University Press, 1959), p. 57.

8. Ibid., pp. 61–62.

9. Christopher McGrory Klyza, *Who Controls Public Lands? Mining, Forestry, and Grazing Policies, 1870–1990* (Chapel Hill: University of North Carolina Press, 1996), p. 111.

10. Ibid., pp. 111–112.

11. Phillip O. Foss, *Politics and Grass* (Seattle: University of Washington Press, 1960), pp. 135–136.

12. See James Q. Wilson, *The Politics of Regulation* (New York: Harper and Row, 1980).

13. Calef, *Private Grazing,* pp. vii–viii.

14. Libecap, *Locking Up the Range,* pp. 65–74.

15. Edward Higbee, *Farms and Farmers in an Urban Age* (New York: Twentieth Century Fund, 1963), p. 109.

16. See Rose Strickland, "Taking the Bull by the Horns," *Sierra*, vol. 75 (September–October 1990): 46–48; George Wuerthner, "How the West Was Eaten," *Wilderness*, vol. 54 (spring 1991): 28–37; and George Wuerthner, "The Price Is Wrong," *Sierra*, vol. 75 (September–October 1990): 38–43.

17. Klyza, *Who Controls Public Lands?* pp. 2–4.

18. Rose Ellen O'Connor, "Senate Braces for Showdown on Grazing Reform This Week," *The Oregonian*, March 17, 1996, pp. D1, D7.

19. Allan Freedman, "Clash of Interests and Ideology Threatens Grazing Overhaul," *Congressional Quarterly Weekly Report*, March 9, 1996, pp. 609–612.

20. O'Connor, "Senate Braces for Showdown," p. D1.

21. Timothy Egan, "Wingtip 'Cowboys' in Last Stand to Hold On to Low Grazing Fees," *New York Times*, October 29, 1993, p. A1.

22. See Frank J. Falen and Karen Budd-Falen, "The Right to Graze Livestock on the Federal Lands: The Historical Development of Western Grazing Rights, " *Idaho Law Review*, vol. 30 (1993–1994): 505–524.

23. George Cameron Coggins and Parthenia Blessing Evans, "Predators' Rights and American Wildlife Law," *Arizona Law Review*, vol. 24, no. 4 (fall 1982): 822–823.

24. Thomas R. Dunlap, "Values for Varmints: Predator Control and Environmental Ideas, 1920–1939," *Pacific Historical Review*, vol. 53, no. 2 (1984): 143–146.

25. Ibid., pp. 147–148.

26. Andrew Neal Cohen, "Weeding the Garden," *Atlantic Monthly*, vol. 270, no. 5 (November 1992): 78.

27. Dunlap, "Values for Varmints," pp. 158–159.

28. David Todd, "Wolves—Predator Control and Endangered Species Protection: Thoughts on Politics and Law," *South Texas Law Review*, vol. 33, no. 3 (July 1992): 461, 489

29. For the Sierra Club's perspective on the ADCA, see Donald G. Schueler, *Incident at Eagle Ranch* (San Francisco: Sierra Club Books, 1980).

30. Coggins and Evans, "Predators' Rights," pp. 848–856.

31. Todd, "Wolves," p. 461.

32. See Janice Goldman-Carter, "Federal Conservation of Threatened Species: By Administrative Discretion or by Legislative Standard?" *Boston College Environmental Affairs Law Review*, vol. 11 (1983): 63–104.

33. 11 ERC 2189 (D Minn 1978).

34. Gwen Florio, "Montana Ranchers Blame Wolf Issue on Washington," *The Oregonian*, March 17, 1996, p. A15.

35. Cited in Renee Askins, "Releasing Wolves from Symbolism," *Harper's*, vol. 290 (April 1995): 16.

36. Florio, "Montana Ranchers," p. A15.

37. See, for example, Rick McIntyre, *A Society of Wolves* (Stillwater, MN: Voyageur Press, 1993); and Rocky Barker, *Saving All the Parts: Reconciling Economics and the Endangered Species Act* (Washington, DC: Island Press, 1993), pp. 175–198.

38. Askins, "Releasing Wolves," pp. 15–17.

39. "Statement of Principles for Reform of the Endangered Species Act," Grassroots ESA Coalition, Battle Ground, Washington, July 10, 1995.

40. Ibid.

41. Tom Kenworthy, "Desert Tortoise Shows Difficulty of Saving Threatened Species," *The Oregonian*, March 28, 1993, p. A24.

42. Kevin Bixby, *A Report on the County Movement* (Las Cruces, NM: Southwest Environmental Center, 1992), pp. 8–10.

43. There is a considerable literature on the Tennessee Valley Authority controversy. See, for example, William B. Wheeler, *TVA and the Tellico Dam* (Knoxville: University of Tennessee Press, 1986); and William Chandler, *Myth of the Tennessee Valley Authority* (Cambridge, MA: Ballinger, 1984).

44. Richard J. Tobin, *The Expendable Future: U.S. Politics and the Protection of Biological Diversity* (Durham, NC: Duke University Press, 1990), p. 49.

45. Ibid., p. 274.

46. Ibid., pp. 160–163.

47. Ibid., pp. 8–9.

48. For an overview of the ESA's implementation, see Tim W. Clark, Richard A. Reading, and Alice L. Clarke, eds., *Endangered Species Recovery: Finding the Lessons, Improving the Process* (Washington, DC: Island Press, 1994).

49. The articles are found in the spring 1995 issue of the *People's Agenda*, published by Putting People First, an environmental opposition group.

50. Cohen, "Weeding the Garden," p. 82.

51. William G. Tapply, "Who Speaks for People?" *Field and Stream* (June 1991): 49.

52. A listing of animal rights groups' attacks in the United States, Canada, and Great Britain can be found in *The People's Agenda* (April 1995): 2–11.

53. Tapply, "Who Speaks for People?" p. 49.

54. Phil McCombs, "Attack of the Omnivore," *Washington Post*, March 27, 1992, p. B1.

55. William Plummer and Margie Sellinger, "A Fur-Shure Warrior's PETA Peeve," *People,* October 19, 1992.

56. McCombs, "Attack of the Omnivore," p. B4.

57. For an overview of the British version of U.S. hunting issues, see Richard H. Thomas, *The Politics of Hunting* (Aldershot, England: Gower, 1983).

58. See Todd, "Wolves," pp. 469–470.

59. Robert Gottlieb, *Forcing the Spring: The Transformation of the American Environmental Movement* (Washington, DC: Island Press, 1993), p. 30.

60. Ibid., p. 23.

61. George Reiger, "Good Vibes," *Field and Stream* (April 1995): 16–17, 22.

3

Farmers and Outdoor Recreationists

SIGN OF THE TIMES: In November 1962, a seven-year-old California boy, Scott Turner, went to look for lizards in a canyon near his home and found the previously open land was now restricted to organized play. Homes were being constructed in a nearby canyon, further limiting the open space nearby. He wrote the following letter to President John F. Kennedy:

> Dear Mr. President: We have no place to go when we want to go out in the canyon because there ar [sic] going to build houses. So could you set aside some land where we could play? Thank you four [sic] listening. Love, Scott

A Department of the Interior official responded,

> Dear Scott: . . . We are trying as hard as we can, President Kennedy and I, to do just what you asked—"to set aside some land" where you can play—not in groups with supervision, but just roaming around by yourself and finding out how you relate to the earth and the sky.[1]

The desire to "relate to the earth and the sky" is deeply interconnected with decisions about how land is used, and it is one of the key motivations that has led to differences in perspectives over environmental resources. As western expansion opened the lands for settlement, farming expanded from homesteaders whose plots fed their families into agribusiness—farm operations owned by multinational corporations or large family-run farms. Issues related to land use and natural resources were of critical concern to farmers, who, like other interests that were attempting to shape the nation's resource management policies, gradually formed coalitions and began to engage in political activism. Farmers, like ranchers who approach the land as a resource and potential source of profit, have often clashed with environmental groups who want the land to remain undisturbed or, at the very least, more extensively regulated and managed by the government.

The farm segment of the environmental opposition was later joined by another group with a stake in how the land ought to be managed. After World War II, the economy accelerated, and along with it came a population boom coupled with increasing commercial and residential development. More families meant more demands for housing, which further encroached upon "open" land. At the same time, increased leisure time for recreation, the increased availability of automobiles, and the expansion of the nation's surface transportation system became a part of American culture.

This combination of factors put new pressures on the land and its resources. It was almost inevitable that clashes would begin to take place: farmers competing with developers over zoning as housing spread from the urban core into the country, the agriculture industry reacting to new government regulations as environmental groups sought more controls on air quality and biocide use—a term now used to describe the application of both herbicides and pesticides. Other disputes arose as families sought greater access into wilderness areas to explore their natural surroundings and discovered some areas had been designated for limited public access to preserve their pristine state or wildlife.

In each of these instances, there was a gradual development of opposition to what was perceived as government intrusion engineered and controlled by powerful environmental groups. The agriculture industry believed that most members of environmental groups were unfamiliar with farm operations and therefore unsuited to direct policy; outdoor recreationists opposed both the government and environmental organizations seeking limitations on their ability to use "public" lands and to restrict their ability to enjoy the outdoors.

Many environmental historians have focused on the role of farmers as one of the major groups initially opposed to the environmental movement and the government regulations it spawned. But like many of the organized interests and individuals opposed to environmental regulation, the terms "farmers" and "agricultural opposition" are somewhat misleading. There is no single, monolithic entity that represents agricultural interests; the industry is widely fragmented. Although farmers have joined agricultural groups to pursue their individual interests, they have been less likely to become activist members of lobbying organizations to secure collective benefits. There is also a separate segment of agriculture that represents the interests of farmworkers, the majority of whom are highly supportive of government regulation over issues such as biocide exposure and worker safety. What is somewhat ironic about the agricultural lobby is its dependence upon the federal government for subsidies and other forms of assistance and its simultaneous resistance to what is perceived as regulatory intrusion into farm culture and operation.

Sugar growers, for example, were very supportive of the price support provisions of the 1981 Agriculture and Food Act. The statute established a USDA program to guarantee sugar growers about $0.18 a pound for raw cane sugar, a program that a 1993 GAO report said costs American consumers $1.4 billion a year in higher prices because the world free-market price is only $0.15 a pound. But at the same time the Florida Sugar Cane League and the American Sugarbeet Growers Association have lobbied for continued support of federal subsidies for their products, they have been accused by environmental groups of resisting federal attempts to reduce the use of phosphate fertilizers that are seeping into the waters of the sensitive Florida Everglades ecosystem. As one Florida sugar cane grower sees it, "I've put up with all these environmental laws, paid all these taxes. Why can't the government do something for us?"[2]

This chapter begins with a brief overview of the development of organized agricultural interests, followed by a description of their occasional forays in the political arena over environmental issues. It then proceeds to an explanation of the role of farm organizations and agricultural interests within the environmental opposition.

The second half of the chapter focuses on the role of outdoor recreationists—a segment of the environmental opposition comprising a variety of groups seeking greater access to public land for their use and enjoyment. The majority represent off-highway vehicle (OHV) groups and equestrian associations joined together in such national umbrella organizations as the Blue Ribbon Coalition (BRC).

While recreational use of public land is not a new issue, it has become a more salient one in recent years, targeted by the environmental movement as one of the reasons why additional federal regulations are imperative. Environmental groups have sought to have the wilderness preserved for solitude, contemplation, and the appreciation of nature; they perceive devices along the lines of snowmobiles and jet skis as ruining their outdoor experience. That has touched a nerve among outdoor recreationists, who also consider themselves nature lovers and "true environmentalists," caring just as much about the outdoors and its resources as those in the mainstream groups.

THE AGRICULTURAL LOBBY

It was not until after the Civil War that farmers began to organize their interests, beginning with the National Grange of the Patrons of Husbandry in 1867. The first Grange was established in Washington, D.C., and modeled after the Masonic order. Its purpose was to protect farmers against corporate monopolies and to provide opportunities for cooperative buying and selling. Particular animosity was leveled at the railroad barons, who were given millions of acres of land by the government. By 1874, more than 20,000 Grange organizations had been established throughout the United States, with more than three-quarters of a million members.[3]

Early farm organizations were closely linked to nonagriculture issues that affected farmers' ability to make a profit, such as currency inflation, civil service reform, and tariffs. Interest in purely political issues began to wane around 1880, and the groups shifted their strategy to opening "Grange stores," which grouped orders for farm machinery and supplies, providing material benefits for their members. By the 1920s, an estimated 8,600 farm groups had emerged, from the Farmers Alliance to the National Agricultural Wheel, but their emphasis shifted to the problems of rural isolation and specific commodities. Gradually, as federal farm policy moved from a regulatory focus to one of direct support for producers, the grassroots agrarian protest movement became a more traditional, albeit small, Washington, D.C., lobby.[4]

After World War II, many small farms consolidated, and organizations shifted their focus to commodity-specific problems, although many of the groups did not develop a Washington presence until the 1980s. Later, they were joined by public interest groups and mergers of trade associations. Today, the farm lobby represents a variety of interests and organizations. One researcher divides the organizations into six groups, further subdivided as "primary" or "supportive" on the basis of whether they represent distinct policy positions or whether they have positions that are expressed through coalition-based lobbying. The six groups are producer organizations, producer/agribusiness organizations, agribusiness middlemen organizations, supplier facilitator organizations, public interest groups, and agribusiness and food firms.[5]

One of the most venerable and powerful of the agricultural groups is the American Farm Bureau Federation (AFBF), formed in 1919. From the very beginning, an internal philosophical debate raged between those who felt the group should focus on education and those who wanted the group to be more politicized to lobby for improved economic conditions. The AFBF has its own lobbyists and additional advocates in nearly every state capital. The group's experiences are parallel to the debate that has become the focus of most of the agricultural lobby even today: work for direct member benefits like subsidies (many of which are short term and subject to electoral shifts) or for long-term policy change to affect issues related to agriculture.

THE TARGETS OF THE OPPOSITION

For generations, farm practices had been based primarily on custom and intuition rather than science. Some of this changed in 1862 with passage of the Morrill Act, which granted each state 30,000 acres of public land that it could sell. The sale of the land was designated to create a fund to establish colleges of agriculture and the mechanical arts, later termed "land grant colleges," giving the teaching of these disciplines federal support for the first time. As agricultural science became more specialized and standardized in these institutions, farmers reluctantly began to change their operations. The targets of their opposition to preservation and environmental policies have been diverse and, until recently, somewhat narrow.

After World War I, economic issues and drought hit farmers head-on, with thousands of acres of productive land destroyed or ravaged by prior inappropriate farm practices. Political mobilization became a necessity for farmers who needed the financial assistance of the federal government to repair the entire agricultural sector of the economy. In 1933, members of the AFBF and other farm groups convinced Congress and President Franklin D. Roosevelt of the gravity of the situation and successfully lobbied for passage of the Agricultural Adjustment Act (AAA) of 1933. The legislation gave the secretary of the Department of Agriculture the authority to pay farmers to reduce the amount of acreage in production in surplus crops in order to restore farm purchasing power.

The idea behind the law was to reduce the amount of crops and livestock produced, thus driving up prices that would then stabilize farm income. In theory, the concept of supply and demand was sound, but in practice, there was urban outrage at the thought of paying people not to do something. Public opinion against the AAA steamrolled with press disclosure of an emergency hog-reduction program in which 500 million pounds of pork were to be removed from the U.S. market, along with a 2-billion-pound reduction in production of pork products. Editorial writers jumped on the bandwagon as they described how "6 million little pigs were plowed under."[6] In 1936, the U.S. Supreme Court declared the AAA unconstitutional, leaving control of agricultural production to the states under Article 10 of the Constitution.

To replace the AAA, the AFBF and other groups then embarked on a new strategy, lobbying for passage of the Soil Conservation and Domestic Allotment Act of 1936 that paid farmers to restore and maintain soil fertility by growing soil-building crops that would be plowed under rather than harvested. Although the measure received the support of most farm organizations, a ripple of opposition was beginning to form from some commodity groups—notably the dairy industry—that criticized the government's "regimentation" of farmers.[7] In one sense, federal intervention in the form of the soil conservation program was welcomed as a way of restoring a valuable commodity. But federal assistance also meant federal intrusion in the eyes of many farmers.

Subsidy policies have a number of unintended consequences that have been targeted by environmental groups as a waste of limited resources. The USDA's disaster aid program, for example, provides farmers with millions of dollars worth of free crop insurance each year, encouraging riskier planting decisions, less care in crop management, and, in some cases, exploitation of land that is marginally productive. In that sense, disaster aid works as an anticonservation policy.[8] Farm subsidy programs were reevaluated in 1996 as part of the Clinton administration's efforts to balance the budget and, in part, to demands by competing interests seeking funding for their own programs.

Many environmental policies have united farmers against the EPA and other federal agencies or policies, such as wetlands designations that are perceived to be haphazard and to dictate land use, or ESA regulations that tie up thousands of acres of valuable farmland. The agricultural lobby has also rallied against laws regulating air quality, non–point source water pollution, and biocides.

Farmers have opposed two provisions involving state and federal air quality regulations: dust control and open-field burning. In almost every case, however, they have lost out to state air quality agencies mandated to reduce emissions from activities like burning fields or cropland after harvest and controlling naturally occurring "fugitive" dust. With the passage of the 1990 Clean Air Act Amendments, the agricultural lobby was eclipsed in its efforts to protect its interests by the more powerful utility industry and chemical manufacturers that faced a more significant threat from proposed legislative revisions. As a result, the farm lobby's efforts have largely been limited to input on regional and state implementation plans to comply with federal pollution control requirements.

Although water availability has always been a source of concern for agricultural users, in recent years the debate has shifted to non–point source pollution. Nonpoint sources include runoff from fields or feedlots for livestock that contaminate water supplies. The EPA has identified agriculture as the leading source of water pollution in the United States, causing river impairment, species endangerment, and fish kills. The issue was specifically addressed in the 1972 Clean Water Act and in the subsequent State Nonpoint Source Management Program. But unlike air quality regulations, water pollution laws have been a less salient political issue and less stringently enforced or interpreted for a number of reasons totally unrelated to any political action on the part of the agriculture lobby. One study of the effectiveness of the nation's attempts to clean up its water noted that the 1972 Clean Water Act was initially vetoed by President Nixon, who recognized the seriousness of the water quality problem but made an economic trade-off between supporting funding for water pollution controls and the cost of fighting the war in Southeast Asia. The president's veto was overridden by Congress, but the legislation resulted in weak and incomplete standards for identifying water quality problems. In that sense, farmers have benefited from the federal government's attention to more identifiable sources of water contamination, differences in the way each state reports its watershed health that lead to inadequate water quality data, discontinuity and lack of federal funding, and institutional conflicts.[9]

The protection of food supplies from infestations by insects, pollution, weeds, and disease is an enduring agricultural problem, and science has become a partner in finding new and more powerful biocides to combat them. Although farmers welcomed the majority of the provisions of the 1947 Federal Insecticide, Fungicide, and Rodenticide Act (FIFRA) because it required that chemicals work as the manufacturers claim they will, they have chafed at the law's implementation by the USDA. The law requires that all pesticides be registered for specific uses under the standard that the substance will not cause any "unreasonable risk to humans or the environment, taking into account the economic, social, and environmental costs and benefits of the use of [the] pesticide."[10]

The indiscriminate and widespread use of pesticides gained public attention in 1962 with the publication of Rachel Carson's *Silent Spring*, which condemned the chemical industry and farmers who used their products. Subsequently, in the 1970s, the federal government banned several of the most widely used pesticides including dichlorodiphenyltrichloroethane (DDT), the focus of Carson's widely read book. However, new pesticides have replaced DDT and other banned applications, with many farmers continually using substances that environmental groups like the National Toxics Campaign believe are injurious to human health.

One controversy over pesticide use involves the nation's wildlife refuges. In 1908, President Roosevelt established the country's first refuge dedicated to waterfowl, the Lower Klamath Refuge along the border between California and Oregon, with the adjacent Tule Lake Refuge added in 1928. Farmers opposed establishment of the refuges from the very beginning, arguing that it was wasteful not to use the valuable acreage for agriculture. In 1964, Congress agreed, leasing 22,000 acres within the two refuges for production of potatoes, onions, and sugar beets. Thirty years later, one environmental organization, the Oregon Natural Resources Council, sued for enforcement of federal law that says no pesticides can be used on refuges unless a scientific review panel agrees there is no threat to wildlife and waterfowl. When the USFWS was forced to implement its own regulations banning the use of pesticides on the leased land, angry farmers in the Klamath Basin accused the government of "regulatory overkill" that would cause them economic hardship.[11]

The agricultural lobby's arguments have centered on one major economic reality: Without some use of biocides, crop yields will decline and consumer prices will go up. The farm lobby's position has been that environmental groups have exaggerated the threat posed by pesticides. In one highly publicized incident during California's spraying against Mediterranean fruit flies in the early 1980s, an aide to Governor Jerry Brown (who was actually seen as a supporter of the environmental movement) drank a bottle of the pesticide Malathion to demonstrate it was not harmful to humans. Unconvinced, environmental groups continue to press Congress to restrict biocide applications even more.

Another target of the agricultural lobby has been the Food, Drug, and Cosmetic Act's Delaney clause, which was enacted in 1958 to govern safety in food additives and other products. Safety is measured in terms of its risk to laboratory animals, an evolving area of scientific dispute that seeks to determine the probability of an event or exposure and the subsequent health and environmental effects. Risks are difficult to assess, and it is even more difficult to quantify the level of harm to humans or animals, since levels are expressed in mathematical terms with a high degree of uncertainty.[12]

In a rare show of unanimity, environmental groups, pesticide manufacturers, and farmers worked together on a revision of the Delaney clause, which President Clinton signed in 1996 as the Food Quality Protection Act. The groups agreed the law was outdated, since it banned even minuscule amounts of pesticides on processed food. The new legislation formalized a safety standard that requires "a reasonable certainty of no harm" for all foods treated with pesticides, defined as no more than a one in a million chance of getting cancer from a lifetime of exposure. The EPA is required to test about 9,000 agricultural chemicals, with an emphasis on their safety for children, who are the most susceptible to chemical toxins.[13] The consensus among the stakeholders on this issue signaled a more conciliatory attitude toward safety and risk than has generally been exhibited in other pesticide controversies involving farmers and environmental organizations.

Incidents of pesticide poisoning among farmworkers have become a rallying point for many environmental and labor organizations that charge employers with sacrificing worker safety in the pursuit of profit. Public and media concern over the problem has been erratic, highlighted by occasional coverage like the 1960 television documentary *Harvest of Shame* or the fines levied on seven physicians in 1980 by California's Occupational Safety and Health Administration for failure to report that they had treated fifty-four farmworkers for apparent pesticide poisoning.

One of the most highly publicized clashes between environmental groups and agriculture occurred in 1988–1989 when the NRDC hired Fenton Communications, a public relations firm, to increase public awareness about toxic pesticides. The EPA had announced plans to remove the chemical diaminozide, known as Alar, from the market as part of its ongoing decertification and phaseout of chemicals with low but unacceptable levels of toxicity. Fenton Communications focused on an NRDC report, *Intolerable Risk: Pesticides in Our Children's Food*, and claimed that the chemical, used on about 5 percent of the U.S. apple crop primarily to improve appearance, was potentially dangerous to children, although the EPA said the study was flawed. Worried consumers reacted by calling their children's schools and demanding that all apple products be taken off the menu. Grocery stores pulled products off shelves, and legislators called for a total ban on Alar and fruit sprayed with the chemical. As a result of the controversy, the apple industry estimated its growers lost billions of dollars in revenues, and the apple market was devastated for years afterward.

The incident provoked bitter hostility against the NRDC and the environmental movement by many in the agriculture industry, who felt the entire issue had been orchestrated as a publicity stunt to raise funds for the organization. Critics alleged that Fenton Communications, which gave CBS News's program *60 Minutes* exclusive rights to the story, used research performed by scientists on the payroll of the NRDC. They also charged the firm with setting up a front group, Mothers and Others for Pesticide Limits, with actress Meryl Streep as its spokesperson. Streep subsequently appeared before a Senate committee and appeared in a series of television commercials in which she washed broccoli in laundry detergent. Apple growers attempted to fight back by hiring their own public relations firm, Hill and Knowlton, and spent $2 million in advertising that alleged the media had exaggerated the story. Eleven apple growers later filed suit against the NRDC, CBS, and Fenton Communications, but they were unsuccessful in their litigation. The Alar controversy, many later agreed, was a masterful strategy by the NRDC, although it raised questions about the group's credibility as well as how the media handled the issue. Some observers believed the press had been duped by the environmental group through manipulation of the release of the story at news conferences and in interviews with celebrities. Others argued that the publicity brought the issue to the attention of both the public and policymakers, with the means justifying the end result. Years later, industry groups continued to defend the use of Alar, and the question of what constitutes an acceptable risk of pesticide use on food remained unanswered.[14]

Farmers have also ridiculed claims by environmental organizations like Friends of the Earth and the National Toxics Campaign against biotechnology applications, food irradiation, and the use of bovine somatotropin, a naturally occurring growth hormone used to boost milk production.[15] Farmers argue that these scientific advances make foods safer for consumers and make agriculture more productive. But their lobbies in Washington, D.C., have been ineffective against the environmental and natural foods movements, which have questioned the reliability of many of the studies because they were funded by industry or have shown concern that more long-term research is needed.

In contrast to these lobbying efforts on specific issues, a number of observers have argued that there has been a major shift of opinion about the environment by farmers in the last two decades. A study of one of the most popular agricultural magazines, *Farm Journal*, showed that in the early 1970s, columnists deplored the banning of pesticides and ridiculed the environmental movement with articles on "natural food cults" and one titled "Will You Go to Jail over Erosion?" But less than twenty years later, the editors of the magazine introduced a monthly section called "Environment Today," started a "Stewardship Campaign," and published articles urging compliance with environmental regulations. One researcher believes such editorial changes represent a profound transformation and a sea change in public opinion, despite continuing partisan differences.[16]

AGRICULTURE'S IMPACT ON ENVIRONMENTAL POLICY

Some observers believe farmers and the agricultural lobby have not played an especially prominent role in opposing the environmental movement until recently and question their overall political clout on environmental issues. Even agribusiness interests are often perceived as being less hostile and contentious than are their support industries or corporate interests in general, perhaps because they have been less visible in their opposition. Others feel that Congress is still easily influenced by the farm lobby, especially in specific states where it is the legislator's primary constituency.[17]

One difficulty in assessing the role of farmers in the environmental opposition is that there is no bloc that can be identified by either the public or by policymakers as "the agricultural lobby." Its interests are diverse, fragmented, and, more recently, often represent different points on the ideological spectrum. This diversity makes it difficult for decisionmakers to address issues to a singular entity or for interests to speak with a unified voice. Many of the groups representing agricultural interests have actually been very supportive of the environmental movement in recent years, especially those representing grassroots interests. The American Agriculture Movement (AAM), for example, formed in 1977, produced a cadre of grassroots leaders who later went on to organize agricultural workers to protest biocide policies and working conditions. Agricultural interests have also formed multi-interest coalitions rather than attempting to single-handedly tackle the policy process. Coalition building has proved to be a successful mechanism for achieving policy goals, especially when those goals are narrowly defined. For smaller farm groups, coalition building may be the only practical political strategy available.

Another problem that makes it hard to measure the clout of agricultural interests and farmers in general is the lack of precise information on their levels of political activism. Only a quarter of the AFBF's 4 million members, for example, are farmers. The rest are individuals who purchase inexpensive AFBF insurance and get automatic membership. This would seem to undermine the contention that all AFBF members share an anti-environmental agenda, or that there are millions who are politically active in farm groups. Farmers often work side by side with environmental groups rather than always opposing them. In Texas, for example, cotton farmers have joined with environmental organizations seeking to end an aerial Malathion spraying program that was initially designed to eradicate boll weevils, small insects that are the scourge of the industry. But the spraying had a number of unintended consequences, including reduced crop yields, because it allowed other insect pests like the army worm to raid the fields. Environmental groups protesting the spraying were joined by farmers who grow organic crops or use nonchemical methods of weevil control and who were forced to join the mandatory program.[18] There is also some evidence that agriculture group membership nationwide is on the decline. The General Social Survey conducted by the National Opinion Research Center found that the percentage of individuals reporting they belonged to a farm group dropped from 4.3 percent in 1974 to 3.7 percent in 1994.[19]

Like other interests, agricultural groups face an ever-expanding list of policy areas to scrutinize and must decide how involved they wish to become on behalf of their members. Few groups have the capability of tracking the legislative and regulatory process both in Washington, D.C., and in the states when their political agenda becomes more and more extensive. The AFBF, for instance, like many other conservative groups, lists among its policy targets the Voting Rights Act of 1965, the World Court, the Equal Rights Amendment, statehood for the District of Columbia, gay rights, the National Biological Survey, and one-world government. Because of its broad agenda, this has led one observer to characterize the AFBF as "the nation's largest anti-environmental organization,"[20] a generalization that seems fallacious given the group's membership size and diversity of policy targets. The breadth of its legislative agenda may actually weaken its ability to have an impact in any one area. But despite its membership size and political longevity, the AFBF does not represent the views of all farmers nor all segments of the agriculture industry. As cited in the boll weevil and Delaney clause examples, there has been a gradual move toward less contentious relationships with environmental groups and, in some cases, cooperative agreements that are exemplary of a slight shift away from a politically conservative agenda.

Today, most agricultural organizations have focused on internal nonpolicy activities and the provision of member service benefits, such as inexpensive insurance policies, rather than attempts to directly influence public policy through traditional lobbying in Washington, D.C. Their participation in the policy process has been selective, and in some ways, even reluctant, in comparison to other organized interests. State legislators and members of Congress are no longer as responsive to the rural vote as they were in the nineteenth and early twentieth centuries because the political demographics of the country have changed. Declines in the number of farms and farmers have given urban interests a strong edge in policymaking. In the first half of this century, the rural vote was courted and disproportionate to the representation afforded those who lived in cities. In 1962, for instance, Burlington, Vermont, with a population of 33,000, had one state senator to match the one senator representing the town of Victory, with a population of only 48, in effect giving the rural residents of Victory more clout than their neighbors in urban Burlington. Former Georgia governor Eugene Talmadge once told supporters he did not bother to campaign in counties where streetcars ran. The growth of urban areas and the accompanying political power they have amassed have, as historian Edward Higbee noted, brought the country to a point where "the era of strong rural interest at the political pork barrel is near its end."[21]

The statistics on the number of farms and amount of land in farm acreage explain why the interests of rural voters no longer play such a critical role in environmental decisionmaking. In 1974, the U.S. Bureau of the Census estimated that there were 2.31 million farms in the United States; twenty years later, that number had dropped to 2.04 million, a 1 percent drop from the previous year's total and following a historical pattern of decline. In 1978, 1.01 billion acres of land were being farmed; in 1994, the figure was down to 975 million acres. While the South continued in 1994 as the region with the largest number of farms, led by Texas, decreasing numbers of farm acreage occurred in states that were experiencing the greatest increase in urbanization, such as California and Washington.[22] The loss of each farm equals a loss of an agricultural constituent who is often replaced by an urban one.

Lastly, the agricultural lobby has not been as successful as other groups in engaging in protest—one of the most visible strategies of organized interests. The 1978–1979 AAM invasion on Washington, D.C., and the "tractorcade" around the Capitol were not focused on environmental regulation but, rather, on price supports and other economic issues.[23] As one woman from Pennsylvania put it, "We farmers are not the kind of folks who march around with picket signs. We've got too much work to do back on the farm."

THE OUTDOOR RECREATIONISTS

The Puritan settlers who came to North America in the seventeenth century brought with them a Protestant work ethic that considered idleness sinful—a societal value that persisted until the transformation of American society in the nineteenth and twentieth centuries.[24] The average work week was 69.8 hours in 1850; then it gradually began to decline, dropping to 60.2 hours in 1900 as a result of Progressive Era reforms, but still leaving little time for the pursuit of any recreation other than socializing or spectator-oriented activities. Until the 1930s, organized labor pushed for a 30-hour workweek despite massive business resistance. To industry, leisure time was equated with "crime, vice, the waste of man's natural capacity, corruption, radicalism, debt, decay, degeneration, and decline." Daily work hours rose again in response to World War II, especially in manufacturing, escalating more than seven hours between 1940 and 1944. After the war, many women sought a shorter workweek, but their demand was outweighed by an emerging climate of consumerism and a desire to have more purchasing power.[25]

The federal government was only marginally interested in preserving its land for nonproductive recreational use throughout most of the late nineteenth century, although by 1900, that policy began to change. In 1890, there were only three sites set aside as national parks; by 1900, the figure had risen to twelve with the inclusion of national historical and military areas. And by 1910, forty-four sites had been designated, the majority of which were national monuments rather than wilderness areas. However, the number of individuals who had the time to see these sites remained relatively low by today's standards: Less than 200,000 people made park or monument visits in 1910.[26]

Wilderness Preservation

One of the noncommercial land use issues that developed after the Progressive Era and during the early development of the preservationist ethic described in Chapter 1 was whether the lands in the public domain should be set aside or open to very limited recreational use, or opened to additional public access. The issue began to focus on the federal government's definition of what portion of the public domain lands should be designated as wilderness and therefore set aside. In 1921, the forest supervisor of the Gila National Forest in New Mexico, preservationist supporter Aldo Leopold, defined wilderness as a roadless, continuous stretch of country devoid of trails, cottages, or other human artifacts—a definition that guided federal policy for the next seventy-five years.[27]

The government's effort to set aside wilderness areas is reflected in the fact that between 1930 and 1945, the areas administered by the NPS grew from 55 to 180, in area from 10 million acres to 24 million acres, and in visitors from 3 million to 30 million.[28] Leopold's goal of preservation conflicted with a new generation of Americans just discovering a new passion: the outdoors. Outdoor recreation finally became recognized as a primary policy goal rather than as an incidental or accidental result of other federal objectives.[29] The keyword that exemplified this shift in policy direction was "multiple use," which meant that public land use included recreation as well as extraction of resources.

After World War II, the entire concept of recreation changed, in large part because the automobile greatly enhanced Americans' ability to see the great outdoors. In 1940, for example, annual passenger car vehicle miles of travel (VMT) was about 250 billion; by 1950, the figure had risen to 364 billion, by 1960, to 588 billion, and by 1970, to 917 billion. Growth slowed during the 1970s with the Arab oil embargo and increases in fuel prices, but still climbed to 1.1 trillion VMT in 1980 and 1.5 trillion in 1990.[30] As the number of cars increased, there was a dramatic expansion of the nation's surface transportation system, making remote wilderness areas suddenly accessible to millions of Americans. In 1904, the nation had 204,000 miles of surfaced roads; twenty years later, that figure had jumped to 567,000, and by 1934, the total miles of surfaced roads climbed to 1,164,000. After World War II, road building resumed in earnest, with 1.9 million miles of road surface in 1950, 2.6 million in 1960, 2.9 million in 1970, and 3.9 million in 1980.[31] Much of the increase was due to the creation of the federal interstate highway system, which made travel not only easier but faster. Families found they could get to recreation areas more quickly, giving them more time to spend outdoors.

There were two important results of this societal change. The first impact was the development of a direct conflict with landowners who suddenly found urban dwellers camping out on their doorsteps. City residents thought nothing of spreading a picnic blanket on a picturesque hillside while ignoring the fact that the land might belong to a private property owner. This led to frequent skirmishes between property owners who unsuccessfully posted No Trespassing signs on their land and city folks who assumed that undeveloped land was theirs for the trampling. Noisy automobiles scared livestock and killed wildlife, destroying the pastoral farm lifestyle.[32] Hunters particularly raised the ire of the farmers. As one Iowa man complained in a letter to the editor of the *Des Moines Sunday Register,* "I don't know about the other farmers, but I for one will do anything to discourage these weekend killers from coming to my farm."[33]

The second impact was that initially both outdoor recreationists and environmental organizations pressured Congress to establish and set aside scenic areas. In many regions of the United States, this meant the reassignment of land from old uses to new ones that fit the needs of the growing urban population at the expense of rural dwellers. The nation became deeply divided on the wilderness-vs.-recreation issue in the late 1950s and early 1960s. On the one hand, Congress supported the public's desire for enhanced recreational opportunities when it created the Outdoor Recreation Resources Review Commission in 1958 to study public recreation needs and resources. Upon the commission's recommendation, the federal Bureau of Outdoor Recreation was established in 1962. Three years later, passage of the Land and Water Conservation Fund Act set up the process by which user-generated fees would enable the federal government to fund land acquisition and development of recreational areas.

But the groups had contradictory reasons for seeking congressional protection for the wilderness. Environmental groups like the Sierra Club and the Wilderness Society sought to have the areas set aside, preserved and protected from human intrusion, while recreationists wanted them to be made even more accessible to the public. The congressional response was to add more sites to both the wilderness and the recreational system. There were 168 sites (national parks, monuments, historical and military areas, and parkways) designated in 1945, 182 in 1955, and 214 in 1965.[34]

While the public cheered congressional efforts to open up more public lands for recreation, other environmental organizations like the Izaak Walton League and the NPCA sought to have more lands set aside, drafting the first of six attempts to enact a wilderness preservation bill in 1956. These long-established organizations were the vanguard of the fledgling environmental movement that would grow rapidly in size and influence over the next twenty years.

The initial opposition to the wilderness preservation legislation came from western governors and members of Congress who feared that the designations would prevent the development of massive projects needed to bring water to rapidly expanding cities in California and Colorado. Additional opposition was raised by representatives of the timber, livestock, and mining industries. Despite the extractive industries' efforts, Congress forged on with several measures that reflected the conflict between the conservationist and the preservationist ethic. President Lyndon Johnson signed two critical pieces of legislation in 1964: the Wilderness Act and the Classification and Multiple Use Act. The idea of convincing Congress to set aside wilderness lands had been promoted in the late 1940s by Howard Zahniser, director of the Wilderness Society, but environmental groups' efforts were stymied for nearly twenty years as other issues like the proposed Echo Park Dam took precedence. After several legislative attempts at passage in intervening years, the 1964 Wilderness Act was a compromise between preservationists, who managed to achieve a statutorily designated wilderness system, and opponents among the environmental opposition, who gained concessions over mining access, grazing, and recreational use.[35]

The Classification and Multiple Use Act made explicit the goals of preserving, balancing, and accommodating all potential uses of the public lands. It also gave the BLM authorization to inventory and classify the lands it managed, a process some observers believe suggested that some of the lands would continue to be owned by the federal government.[36]

The government's intention to preserve more wilderness lands was reflected in the 1976 FLPMA and the Roadless Area Review and Evaluation (RARE) required under the Wilderness Act. FLPMA reiterated the concept that federal lands would remain in public ownership and gave the BLM authority to develop a long-range plan for the lands it administered, similar to the jurisdictional powers of the USFS. RARE included an inventory of USFS lands that could potentially be added to the National Wilderness Preservation System. It was accompanied by a similar BLM survey of the unreserved public domain lands scattered throughout the West.

One controversy that surfaced almost immediately involved the NPS, which felt this series of wilderness preservation laws, administered by other agencies, might limit visitors (and thus the NPS budget). Over the years, the NPS had seen its jurisdiction broadened to cover an increasing number of facilities, from national cemeteries and military parks to national seashores. When the NPS was created in 1916, there were 54 sites covering 6 million acres and 358,000 visitors; when the Wilderness Act was signed in 1964, there were 203 sites over 26 million acres drawing 111 million visitors.[37] The NPS was slow in implementing both the spirit and the letter of the law, creating its own exemption zones where the act did not apply and proposing an extensive road network for the Great Smoky Mountains National Park. Similar conflicts developed between the USFS and groups like the Sierra Club, which eventually brought suit to force compliance with the law. Additional conflicts surfaced in 1968 with the passage of the Wild and Scenic Rivers Act.

Much of the outdoor recreationists' political efforts have been led by owners of motorized recreational equipment, who have attempted to secure funding and enhanced accessibility to roads and trails. Many of the areas they sought to use had been set aside in the wilderness legislation of the 1960s and 1970s, and there had been little success in changing the federal government's direction. In 1991, they seized legislative success with the Symms National Recreational Trails Act, which had been attached as a rider to a federal highway bill. The legislation established a $30 million per year appropriation for backcountry trail construction. Since that time, their legislative and policy interests have broadened considerably, as the following profile of the off-road lobby shows.

THE RECREATION AND OFF-ROAD LOBBIES

The structure and strategies of the recreation and off-road lobbies are remarkably similar to those of most organized interests, with a strong national umbrella organization, a nationwide representation of state groups, and their local affiliates. The national organizations serve as the primary locus for lobbying, media contact, and as an information source for the state and local groups. The national organizations also provide expertise the smaller groups lack, as well as serving as a central clearinghouse so the lobby speaks as a unified voice on issues of importance to its members. What has made the OHV lobby somewhat more impressive than that of other groups is that it brings together such a broad band of recreational users, from motorcycle enthusiasts and four-wheel drive clubs to mountain bikers and snowmobilers. These recreationists have united with a common purpose even though they maintain their individual user-group identity.

The largest of the national umbrella groups is the Blue Ribbon Coalition (BRC), founded in 1987 with the motto "Preserving Our Natural Resources for the Public Instead of from the Public." Its monthly national magazine notes the group is "dedicated to the preservation of all forms of Off-Road Recreation in an environmentally responsible manner." Like all of the groups profiled in this book, however, the BRC has its own definition of what constitutes environmental responsibility.

The organization's power stems from its executive director, Clark Collins, and the nineteen members of its board of directors, which almost exclusively represents western states. This is not to imply that the issue of expanding access to wilderness areas for motorized recreational use is a purely regional one. For although BRC serves as the umbrella group for hundreds of state OHV organizations in the West, such as the Utah Trail Machine Association, the Colorado Off Highway Vehicle Coalition, and the Arizona State Association of 4 Wheel Drive Clubs, it also works with nonwestern groups such as the New England 4-Wheelers, the Association of Wisconsin Snowmobile Clubs, and the Pennsylvania Trail Riders Association. Similar organizations exist on the local level in almost every state, including the Tucson Rough Riders (a four-wheel drive club), the Lakeville [Minnesota] Sno-Trackers, and the Mt. Scott [Oregon] Motorcycle Club.

In recent years, the BRC has lobbied for less protective revisions in the ESA and has become more allied with the wise use movement discussed in Chapter 10. While the initial thrust of the organization may have been oriented toward member services and communication among its myriad individual groups, the organization has become more politicized in the last few years. Collins has commented that

> Democrats and Republicans alike should support reasonable access to our national resources for recreation and our natural resource industries. . . . It has always troubled me [that] so many of the folks we have trouble with say they are for the working people while they support environmentally extreme legislation that drives industry right out of the country.[38]

Other organizations that are typically more service oriented to their members have also begun to take a more proactive interest in the environmental debate, expanding their concerns to legislation related to the designation of wilderness areas, the creation of forest reserves, and the ESA, which has the potential of limiting public passage to previously accessible areas. Groups like the American Motorcyclist Association, the United 4 x 4 Association, the Wildlife Legislative Fund (a hunter's group), and the American Horse Council have also begun to take a more active interest in the environmental debate. By expanding their agenda to include issues that go beyond the recreational use of wilderness areas, they expand their membership base but at the same time run the potential danger of diluting their influence on topics of special interest to their members. By becoming an integral part of the wise use movement, they enjoy the benefits as well as the costs of that affiliation.

The off-road users' groups are strongly allied with the companies that manufacture and sell off-highway vehicles and products, many of whom advertise in the BRC magazine—large manufacturers like Yamaha, American Honda, Polaris, Suzuki, and Kawasaki are joined by parts dealers (e.g., Mikuni Racing Carburetors), individual vehicle dealerships (e.g., Rocky Mountain ATV), and recreational clothing outlets (e.g., Thor Racing Apparel). They are also represented in Washington, D.C., by the International Snowmobile Industry Association, the Motorcycle Industry Council, the American Recreation Coalition, and the Specialty Vehicle Institute of America. This accumulation of allies has made the BRC among the most well-connected lobbies in Washington.

Financial and political support for the BRC comes from other sectors as well. Corporate contributors represent a wide range of firms, from Idaho's multi-interest J. R. Simplot Company (cattle, high-tech and food processing) to the Grand Targhee Resort in Wyoming. Extractive resource interests have joined the BRC as corporate sponsors, such as timber/paper giant Boise Cascade, the Western States Petroleum Association, and the Rocky Mountain Oil and Gas Association. Support for OHV legislation has also come from extractive industry groups like the Oregon Lands Coalition. While individual members and the smaller local and state organizations provide financial support through their membership contributions, the industry and corporate interests provide advertising revenues to the BRC.

What makes this threatening to environmental organizations is the belief that outdoor recreation groups are subsidized and controlled by industry and corporations with a stake in selling their products or further extraction of natural resources. One study commissioned by the Wilderness Society and written by the consulting firm MacWilliams Cosgrove Snyder suggested that environmental organizations expose the connection between Japanese commercial interests and groups like the Blue Ribbon Coalition because they have provided "substantial support" to the BRC.[39] In response, one BRC official says that these companies are simply members who support the organization's goals and that environmental organizations have overstated the importance of corporate dollars in their overall financial profile. The fact that companies like Kawasaki advertise in the BRC's newsletter is no more an indication that the company controls the group's political agenda, the official said, than similar advertising revenues received by the more sophisticated publications of environmental organizations.[40] A typical issue of the Sierra Club's magazine featured advertisements for Pentax cameras, General Motors, and North Face outerwear, while *E: The Environmental Magazine* included ads for a washing machine sold by White Westinghouse, Troy-Bilt Manufacturing's chipper-vac, and Nashbar bike apparel. Clearly, businesses support, through advertising or direct contributions, both environmental groups and those considered part of the environmental opposition. That support, however, does not in and of itself back claims that the organizations are fronts for or financed by large corporate interests.

Although there are hundreds of other recreational users, they are not nearly as politically active as those allied with the BRC. For instance, numerous recreational vehicle groups like the National RV Owners Club, Loners on Wheels, and Escapees, Inc., were established during the 1970s and 1980s, primarily as member-service organizations. One of the largest, the Good Sam Recreational Vehicle Club, has over 660,000 members who attend the group's annual "Samboree" and network with other clubs for rallies, tours, and safety clinics. Since many of these groups use well-established campgrounds (both commercial and publicly owned), they are less motivated to join in the effort to open up the more pristine wilderness areas.

THE "REAL" ENVIRONMENTALISTS?

To many of the mainstream environmental organizations, the imagery of the motorized recreationist is that of a rogue motorcycle rider running roughshod over virgin forest carpets or pristine desert sand, scattering endangered species and plants in his or her wake. The ruts left in the landscape frequently bear out that imagery, although many recreation groups also are working to restore trails. Groups like the National Parks and Conservation Association have rallied against the use of snowmobiles because of the noise they cause, "replacing the solitude and quiet that once defined the winter landscape."[41]

Over the last five years, motorized recreation interests have been especially critical of environmental organizations because they believe that they represent a lock-up-the-land mentality that would limit wilderness use only to an elite few.

As the BRC's Clark Collins writes:

> So who are the real environmentalists? Are they the green advocacy groups who crank out millions of "hate mail" letters, opposing everyone's activities but their own? Or are they those of us who believe humans have a responsibility to use our natural resources wisely? . . . Are the real environmentalists the timber workers and ATV riders who take a week-end to build a bridge for handicapped access to a nature trail? Are the real environmentalists the 4 wheel drive club members who volunteer to clear a river of abandoned cars and other debris? Are the real environmentalists the snowmobile club who helps with their wildlife agency's winter feeding program? Are the real environmentalists the motorcycle riders who help the forest service replant a burn area?[42]

Neither side is "right" or "wrong" in its arguments—the groups simply do not share the same perceptions about what wilderness policy should be and how the land ought to be used. To one group, preservation is the only way to maintain the wilderness; to the other, the "public" in public lands means that there ought to be more, not less, wilderness opened to their use. That dichotomy, and the resulting demonization of recreational users by the environmental movement, has made wilderness preservation one of the more volatile issues within the land use debate.

NOTES

1. The story of Scott Turner is found in the introduction of a special report published by the U.S. Department of the Interior, *The Race for Inner Space* (Washington, DC: Government Printing Office, 1964).

2. David Hosansky, "Florida Sugar Growers Edgy as Farm Bill Debate Nears," *Congressional Quarterly Weekly Report*, May 13, 1995, pp. 1311–1315.

3. Orville Merton Kile, *The Farm Bureau Through Three Decades* (Baltimore, MD: Waverly Press, 1948), pp. 4–6.

4. William P. Browne, *Private Interests, Public Policy, and American Agriculture* (Lawrence: University Press of Kansas, 1988), pp. 14–15, 18.

5. Ibid., pp. 30–38.

6. Kile, *The Farm Bureau*, pp. 207–208.

7. Ibid., p. 241.

8. Karl Zinsmeister, "The Environmentalist Assault on Agriculture," *Public Interest*, no. 112 (summer 1993): 92.

9. See Robert W. Adler, Jessica C. Landman, and Diane M. Cameron, *The Clean Water Act Twenty Years Later* (Washington, DC: Island Press, 1993).

10. Federal Insecticide, Fungicide, and Rodenticide Act, 7 U.S.C. 136 (section 3[c][5] and section 2[bb]).

11. Brent Walth, "Pesticides Might Return to Klamath Refuges," *The Oregonian*, September 3, 1995, pp. A1, A15.

12. There are a variety of opinions on what constitutes an acceptable risk and how policymakers ought to respond. For contrasting views, see, for example, Richard B. Belzer, "The Peril and Promise of Risk Assessment," *Regulation*, vol. 14 (fall 1991): 40–49; Susan G. Hadden, *A Citizen's Right to Know: Risk Communication and Public Policy* (Boulder, CO: Westview, 1989); and Paul Slovik, "Perceived Risk, Trust, and Democracy," *Risk Analysis*, vol. 13 (1993): 675–682.

13. Rick Weiss, "Clinton Signs Pesticide, Gambling Legislation," *The Oregonian*, August 4, 1996.

14. The accounts on the extent of the Alar incident vary considerably. See, for example, Timothy Egan, "Apple Growers Bruised and Bitter After Alar Scare," *New York Times*, July 8, 1991, p. A1; Elizabeth Whelan, "Apples Revisited," *Wall Street Journal*, March 16, 1992, p. A14; Ron Arnold and Alan Gottlieb, *Trashing the Economy: How Runaway Environmentalism Is Wrecking America* (Bellevue, WA: Free Enterprise Press, 1994), pp. 330–340; "The EPA Is Looking for a Few Bad Apples," *Newsweek*, February 13, 1989, p. 65; and "How a PR Firm Executed the Alar Scare," *Wall Street Journal*, October 3, 1989, p. A22.

15. See Christopher L. Culp, "Sacred Cows: The Bovine Somatotropin Controversy," in Michael S. Greve and Fred L. Smith Jr., eds., *Environmental Politics: Public Costs, Private Rewards* (New York: Praeger, 1992), pp. 47–65.

16. Mark Sagoff, "The Great Environmental Awakening," *American Prospect* (spring 1992): 39–47.

17. See John Mark Hansen, *Gaining Access: Congress and the Farm Lobby* (Chicago: University of Chicago Press, 1991).

18. Sam Howe Verhovek, "In Texas, an Attempt to Swat an Old Pest Stirs a Revolt," *New York Times,* January 24, 1996, p. A7.

19. Robert J. Samuelson, "Join the Club," *Washington Post National Weekly Edition,* April 15–21, 1996, p. 5.

20. See Paul Rauber, "Down on the Farm Bureau," *Sierra,* vol. 79 (November–December 1994): 32.

21. Edward Higbee, *Farms and Farmers in an Urban Age* (New York: Twentieth Century Fund, 1963), pp. 118–119.

22. National Agricultural Statistics Service, U.S. Department of Agriculture, *Farm Numbers and Land in Farms* (Washington, DC: Government Printing Office, July 28, 1994); and Bureau of the Census, U.S. Department of Commerce, *Statistical Abstract of the United States, 1994* (Washington, DC: Government Printing Office, September 1994), p. 665.

23. See *Farm Policy: The Politics of Soil, Surpluses, and Subsidies* (Washington, DC: Congressional Quarterly Press, 1984), pp. 77–87.

24. For a discussion of the transformation of the work ethic, see Neala Schleuning, *Idle Hands and Empty Hearts: Work and Freedom in the United States* (New York: Bergin and Garvey, 1990).

25. Juliet B. Schor, *The Overworked American: The Unexpected Decline of Leisure* (New York: Basic Books, 1991), pp. 74, 77–78. Schor argues that the consumer boom was driven by employers' ability to get long hours from employees, locking the nation into a pattern of work and spend that eliminated leisure time. For a contrasting view, see Phillip O. Foss, *Conservation in the United States: A Documentary History, Recreation* (New York: Chelsea House Publishers, 1971), pp. 3–9.

26. Bureau of the Census, U.S. Department of Commerce, *Historical Statistics of the United States: Colonial Times to 1970* (Washington, DC: Government Printing Office, 1975), p. 396.

27. Aldo Leopold, "The Wilderness and Its Place in Forest Recreational Policy," *Journal of Forestry,* vol. 29 (1921): 718–721.

28. William L. Graf, *Wilderness Preservation and the Sagebrush Rebellions* (Savage, MD: Rowman and Littlefield, 1990), p. 198.

29. Foss, *Conservation in the United States,* p. 12.

30. "Annual Motor Vehicle Miles of Travel and Fuel Consumption," *American Automobile Manufacturers Association Facts and Figures, 1994* (Washington, DC: American Automobile Manufacturers Association, 1994), p. 65.

31. Federal Highway Administration, U.S. Department of Transportation, *Highway Statistics: Summary to 1985* (Washington, DC: Government Printing Office, 1986), pp. 187–188.

32. See Samuel P. Hays, *Beauty, Health, and Permanence: Environmental Politics in the U.S., 1955–1985* (Cambridge, England: Cambridge University Press, 1987), p. 288.

33. In Higbee, *Farms and Farmers,* p. 96.

34. Bureau of the Census, *Historical Statistics,* p. 396.

35. See Christopher McGrory Klyza, *Who Controls Public Lands? Mining, Forestry, and Grazing Policies, 1870–1990* (Chapel Hill: University of North Carolina Press, 1996), pp. 76–91.

36. Ibid., p. 116.

37. Bureau of the Census, *Historical Statistics*, p. 396.

38. Clark L. Collins, "Bipartisan Politics," *Blue Ribbon Magazine* (March 1995): 3.

39. MacWilliams Cosgrove Snyder, *The Wise Use Movement: Strategic Analysis and Fifty State Review* (Washington, DC: Environmental Working Group, March 1993), p. 49. See also John D. Echeverria and Raymond Booth Eby, eds., *Let the People Judge: Wise Use and the Private Property Rights Movement* (Washington, DC: Island Press, 1995), p. 29.

40. Author interview with Adena Cook, public lands director, Blue Ribbon Coalition.

41. See Todd Wilkinson, "Snowed Under," *National Parks*, vol. 69, nos. 1–2 (January–February 1995): 32.

42. Clark Collins, "Who Are the Real Environmentalists?" undated column.

PART II

BUSINESS GETS ORGANIZED

4

How Industry Fights
the Legislative Battle

SIGN OF THE TIMES: Contrasting views on the 104th Congress and environmental policy:

> *Quite simply, we are engaged in total war over the future of the environment.*
>
> —Carl Pope, Sierra Club executive director

> *If we don't close down the Environmental Protection Agency, we at least put a snaffle bit on them and ride the pony down. They're out of control.*
>
> —House Majority Leader Dick Armey (R-Texas)[1]

> *This legislation is not reform. It is a full frontal assault on protecting public health and the environment.*
>
> —Carol Browner, Environmental Protection
> Agency administrator[2]

There are two primary differences among the various segments of the environmental opposition outlined in this book: the nature of the groups' grievance and the venue and political strategies they choose to seek redress. The majority of the grassroots organizations, for instance, evolve from an individual's personal grievance (such as a rancher being told his permit to graze on public lands is being withdrawn). The rancher may join fellow livestock owners with similar interests, and they may have enough momentum to work collectively as a small, short-lived group. Grassroots organizations tend to rely upon strategies like letter-writing campaigns and demonstrations as a way of attracting the attention of the public and, eventually, of elected officials who make environmental policy. Their approach has been direct but tends to be unsophisticated and limited by a lack of resources with which to press forward their agenda.

In contrast, business interests are more likely to be experienced in dealing with environmental legislation and regulation at both the federal and state levels, and they may have shared grievances that allow them to form coalitions, giving them additional political clout. Industry groups have more at stake in the environmental debate because they are usually the parties responsible for picking up the cost of compliance with most statutes and rules. One EPA study of past and predicted costs of providing a clean environment jumps from $26 billion in 1972 to $160 billion in 2000 (expressed in 1986 U.S. dollars). As a percentage of the gross domestic product (GDP), those numbers would more than triple, from .09 percent of GDP in 1972 to 2.8 percent in 2000. More important, government agencies would pick up about 40 percent of the direct costs of public and private pollution control activities in the United States; the remaining 60 percent is the responsibility of business.[3] As more information about longer-term pollution problems becomes available, such as the addition of new toxic waste sites to the Superfund National Priorities List, those figures are expected to jump dramatically.

Since the stakes are so high, business has a greater incentive to use its considerable financial resources and to focus on the legislative arena wherein it can attempt to influence policy by making campaign contributions. Although individual corporations are prohibited by federal election law from making campaign contributions to members of Congress, they may contribute as part of a political action committee (PAC). In the 1993–1994 election cycle, for example, PACs contributed nearly $190 million to congressional candidates, with business-related PACs accounting for half of the top twenty contributors to federal candidates.[4] Neither grassroots organizations nor individuals can even begin to compete with industry on that level, which helps explain why the legislative arena has long been a favorite target of business interests.

Any analysis that attempts to profile the way business interests have dealt with environmental policy in the legislative arena almost requires a "before" and an "after" review. The "before" period is comprised primarily of the landmark legislation that was initially enacted in the 1960s and 1970s, such as the Clean Air Act (1963), the Water Quality Act (1965), the Wild and Scenic Rivers Act (1968), the Federal Water Pollution Control Act Amendments (1972), the Endangered Species Act (1973), the Safe Drinking Water Act (1974), and the Toxic Substances Control Act (1976).

Although there has often been a perception that industry has always been the environmental movement's greatest adversary, in actuality business was somewhat slow to respond to these early legislative initiatives proposed by the environmental movement. Historian Samuel Hays has observed that, initially, the environmental movement "was looked on with fascination, but as its influence increased in the late 1960s and early 1970s, this perception turned to incredulity and fright."[5]

During the 1980s and the first half of the 1990s, many of those landmark pieces of legislation were fine-tuned with incremental changes and amendments, with only a handful of major bills enacted that broke new ground, such as the Comprehensive Environmental Response, Compensation, and Liability Act (1980), better known as Superfund. Many industry trade associations did not become fully engaged in actively fighting environmental legislation until this period, relying upon the industry-sympathetic Reagan and Bush administrations to keep the environmental movement and regulatory agencies in check from 1981 until 1993.

A 1993 survey conducted by the *National Law Journal* and Arthur Anderson Environmental Services found that the nation's top corporate legal officials felt the businesses they represent were caught "in an environmental vise—squeezed by ever-closer scrutiny and harsher penalties, while the complexity and breadth of green laws and regulations make full compliance impossible."[6]

But all that changed in 1994—the "after" phase—when Republicans took control of both the House and the Senate. Even though environmental policy was not one of the initial targets of the new Republican majority, it was included under the umbrella concept of "regulatory reform." It began to emerge in a variety of policy initiatives, from attempts to eliminate the Department of Energy and reduce the budget of the EPA to reopening the debates over risk assessment, drilling for oil in the Arctic National Wildlife Refuge (ANWR), and financial compensation to landowners affected by environmental statutes.

This chapter looks at industry opposition to environmental regulation within the legislative arena and business response from the early 1960s through the 104th Congress. Since it is impossible to chronicle the response of organized business interests to every piece of environmental legislation during that period, several case studies are used to illustrate the strategies and tactics used by various groups toward a number of legislative initiatives.

There are several important assumptions that have been made about industry that have colored this typical analysis. Contrary to what has been the usual assessment, business, like other segments of the environmental opposition, is not monolithic. From a historical standpoint, its resistance to environmental regulation developed slowly, incrementally, and somewhat haphazardly as each affected industry group felt the impact of the legislative and regulatory process at different points in time. From a political standpoint, business opposition has rarely been united because it mirrors the variations in re-sources among the various organized interests themselves. The lack of cohesiveness reflects the fact that environmental legislation has often pitted one industry against another, sometimes making coalition and alliance formation difficult at best.

AN OVERVIEW OF INDUSTRY OPPOSITION

One of the ways business interests have organized themselves has been through the creation of various trade associations—a widely accepted industry strategy that is akin to the coalition building of various groups within the environmental movement. Trade associations perform valuable services for their members, whether in lobbying Congress or in shaping the forces of public opinion, as will be discussed further in Chapter 5. For those reasons, this chapter looks at business opposition on an industry-by-industry basis as a way of examining the differences among the organized interests. There are three common themes to industry opposition in general, although certainly there are exceptions and companies that do not fit the model presented here.

First, business has attempted to minimalize compliance wherever possible as a way of reducing implementation costs, most of which result from the installation of new pollution control technology or the threat of paying civil sanctions. For some firms, opposition to government intrusion has been imperative for one simple reason: The cost of environmental regulations threatens a company's ability to make money and there is little incentive for voluntary compliance. For others, there is real disagreement over some of the goals of environmental protection, although not in the broad sense. It is unlikely that a chief executive officer (CEO) would take a public stand against clean air, but there might be a potential for objection if the goal were a less tangible resource, like preserving the scenic quality of the views from the rim of the Grand Canyon.

Second, industry interests have used their resources at several access points within the legislative process. Whereas traditional forms of interest group strategy such as lobbying have focused on the drafting of legislation and testifying at public hearings, attention is increasingly being paid to the markup sessions of congressional committees, in which the actual legislative language of a bill is developed and informally amended. These sessions are less visible to the public and generally underreported by the media. Members of Congress have the ability to press their constituents' interests in these sessions and to propose amendments that totally alter the sponsor's original legislative intent.

In a Senate Agriculture Committee hearing on the FIFRA Amendments in 1988, for example, Minnesota Republican senator Rudy Boschwitz pushed forward an innocuous-sounding amendment that required that "whenever tests . . . are required by more than one state or federal agency, such tests . . . shall be coordinated and synchronized among the agencies so as to avoid unnecessary repetition and redundancy." The amendment had been widely referred to as the Chemical Specialties Manufacturers Association (CSMA) Amendment, no doubt because CSMA's political action committees had given Boschwitz at least $30,000 when he ran for reelection in 1984. The amendment would have greatly complicated or delayed the efforts of states to write stiffer pesticide regulations. However, in this case, though industry succeeded in getting a legislator to advance their cause, they were not successful with the remainder of the committee. The measure failed on a 14:4 vote.[7]

Lastly, business opposition to environmental regulations usually waxes and wanes in response to the forces of public opinion, as the last section of this chapter indicates. When conservative public attitudes are reflected in massive electoral change, as they were in the 1994 electoral cycle, there is a gradual (and in some rare instances, sweeping) change in environmental policy. Business uses electoral change as a policy window, becoming more activist and taking advantage of the opportunity to push forward legislative proposals more likely to gain support within a partisan, conservative Congress. The sustainability of the conservative momentum and its accompanying tide of deregulation will determine how proactive organized business interests will be during the remainder of the 1990s.

THE EXTRACTIVE RESOURCE INDUSTRIES
AND POLLUTION CONTROL

Air and water pollution occupied most of the congressional environmental agenda for twenty years between the mid-1950s and the mid-1970s and thus became the focus of opposition by the extractive resource industries. Beginning with the Eisenhower administration's Water Pollution Control Act of 1956, the next two decades saw a steady flow of water quality legislation: the 1965 Water Quality Act, the 1970 Water Quality Improvement Act, the Federal Water Pollution Control Act Amendments of 1972, the 1974 Safe Drinking Water Act, and the 1977 Clean Water Act. Similar legislation focused on the very visible problem of air pollution: the 1963 Clean Air Act, the 1967 Air Quality Act, and Clean Air Act Amendments in 1970 and 1977.

Passage of these bills provided Congress with an image of "doing something" about pollution while at the same time providing environmental organizations with a very visible enemy in the form of smokestack polluters and wastewater dischargers. The extractive resource industries conveniently and accurately fit the role of villains, since many had operated without significant federal regulation for decades.

Business began its assault on pollution legislation by arguing that the regulations the bills created would destroy America's industrial edge over its competitors. Those arguments gained considerable credence during the economic hard times of the late 1970s, when double-digit inflation and rising unemployment rates became more important in public opinion polls than clean air and water.

The timber, pulp, and paper industries were among the first to recognize the potential impact of environmental regulation, in part because they were being hit hard not only by the new pollution laws, but also by initiatives to increase the amount of federal land designated as wilderness or allocated to national parks, as seen in Chapter 1. Groups like the National Lumber Manufacturers Association joined individual timber companies in attempting to block several of the land use bills, although they were unable to defeat the Land and Water Conservation Fund Act in 1965, which set up funding mechanisms for wilderness acquisition.

The timber lobby was even less successful in fighting the air and water pollution laws since many companies had already established decades-long reputations as bad neighbors in communities where mills produced acrid odors or fouled local streams. They became easy targets for environmental groups that pointed to smokestacks as evidence of the industry's indifference to pollution control.

Environmental organizations also targeted energy producers, especially the coal and petroleum industries that epitomized the smokestack imagery of pollution. Weak attempts to counter the plethora of air quality bills were made by the petroleum industry's Committee for Air and Water Conservation (1966) and by subsequent groups like the American Petroleum Association and the American Petroleum Institute.

The coal coalition, as it came to be known, represented a pooling of interests by the nation's major producers. In 1959, the idea of a permanent industry trade association took the form of the National Coal Policy Conference (NCPC), representing the coal producers, mining equipment firms, electric utilities, and coal transporters like railroads and barge lines. By 1970, the coalition consisted of a four-tier political machine made up of state and regional trade groups at the grassroots level, national trade associations like the National Coal Association, interindustry associations like the American Mining Congress (AMC), and industry advisory councils. The four tiers presented a consistent and unified front on two major issues: air pollution controls and strip mining.[8]

Initially, the NCPC focused on its members' self-interests—promoting the use of coal over other fuels. But with the growth of the environmental movement during the 1960s, the group turned its efforts to dampening the impact of air pollution controls by opposing federal regulation and enforcement, coordinating its efforts with the United Mine Workers.

Like many of the extractive resource groups, the NCPC provided its members with advice on the technicalities of the new environmental legislation, producing *A Guide to the 1967 Air Quality Act* and a political action handbook for its members. In that sense, the NCPC did not overtly lobby Congress as much as it did provide advice and direction for its members. The group dissolved in 1971, in part due to tensions with the union as well as a reduction in competition among coal, gas, petroleum, and other fuel producers.[9]

Its replacement was the previously lethargic National Coal Association, which became more politically active when it established a full-time lobbying staff in 1972, using as its spokesperson former congressmember Carter Manasco. The use of former members as lobbyists became a strategy adopted by many of the extractive resource industries and trade associations. Manasco's presence also helped the industry to lure current members of Congress to its receptions and social gatherings.[10]

Somewhat ironically, eastern utilities joined environmental groups in the battle over the 1977 Clean Air Act Amendments. Under previous versions of the law, utilities were permitted to use the most cost-effective means possible to meet the law's emissions standards, which generally meant power plants would rely upon low sulfur coal from western states. By lobbying Congress together, the two sides gained support for language mandating utilities to attain percentage reductions of sulfur dioxide emissions instead of the sulfur content of the coal itself, thus protecting the eastern segment of the industry that mined coal with a higher sulfur content.[11]

Petroleum firms have been engaged in a dual effort that requires them to be active not only in lobbying in the legislative arena, but also in attempting to clean up their image, as will be outlined further in the next chapter. One of their legislative aims was to lessen the impact of the Pollution Prevention Act of 1990, which, among other provisions, enhanced the pollution reporting requirements of the Toxics Release Inventory originally required by the 1986 Emergency Planning and Community Right-to-Know Act. This legislation did not force the petroleum industry to conduct its operations any differently, but, by making the data public, it provided environmental groups with fuel for their own anti-industry assault.

The interests of the mining community have historically been represented by the American Mining Congress, whose members consist primarily of westerners engaged in the extraction of uranium, silver, copper, and iron. The AMC's members have become considerably more active since the 1970s, individually contacting members of Congress and expanding their political influence to lobby interindustry-oriented issues ranging from air pollution to grazing fees.

Perhaps the industry's biggest success story has been its ability to stall repeated calls for change in the 1872 Mining Law. By consolidating its varied interests and joining forces with grassroots groups, the mining industry has mystified environmental leaders who still contend that the country's policies on the use of public lands represent a giveaway of its natural resources. The industry convinced Republican leaders to include what Interior Secretary Bruce Babbitt called "a cosmetic, industry-written 'reform' bill . . . in the fine print of the [1995] budget reconciliation bill, where it will escape public attention."[12]

Unlike some of the other extractive industries, however, much of the mining industry's political efforts have been centered on state-level associations. Although mining is conducted almost everywhere, it is most concentrated in states wherein concerns are not easily translated into national-level political activism. The Nevada Mining Commission, for example, has focused its efforts on lobbying its own state's governor and senators, who then carry their concerns back to Washington, rather than relying exclusively on the AMC.

As this overview indicates, the extractive resource industries have relied upon traditional strategies of organized interests, like the direct lobbying of members of Congress, with mixed results. What is especially important to note is that most of their efforts have been in response to the initiatives of environmental organizations, rather than proactive in support of their own agendas.

THE NUCLEAR POWER INDUSTRY

In comparison to the extractive resource industry's lobby, the highly proactive nuclear power lobby has been matched against an equally well organized antinuclear element within the environmental movement. Fears of radiation and contamination and public awareness campaigns by groups like Greenpeace have been countered by a series of industry-sponsored organizations and lobbies. In the early 1960s, for example, the Atomic Industrial Forum worked against attempts to change the jurisdiction of the Atomic Energy Commission, which later became the Nuclear Regulatory Commission, fearing the agency might be given even more regulatory power over the industry.

The United States Council for Energy Awareness (USCEA) does not attempt to hide its utility affiliation in its publications or organizational literature. USCEA was founded in 1980 as a private, nonprofit organization comprised of nearly 400 groups around the world "that have an interest in energy and electricity" and as a response to the 1977 incident at the Three Mile Island nuclear power facility. Accused by environmental groups as being a front group for the nuclear power industry, the organization admits in its brochures that it promotes an increased reliance upon nuclear energy as a way of meeting the nation's energy needs. The group points out the ten-year-long process of building a new power plant as the rationale for educating the public now about issues such as radiation and nuclear waste.

In 1994, the industry regrouped as the Nuclear Energy Institute, incorporating four Washington, D.C.–based nuclear energy organizations: the American Nuclear Energy Council (ANEC), the Nuclear Management and Resources Council, USCEA, and the nuclear activities of the Edison Electric Institute. Each of the four arms of the organization is responsible for dealing with a separate function; USCEA, for example, retained its role of developing a national communications program, while ANEC is responsible for the group's government affairs activities. Its bylaws, like the group's public brochures and literature, clearly promote "the safe utilization and development of nuclear energy" and "a unified nuclear energy industry approach to address and resolve nuclear regulatory issues and related technical matters."[13]

For environmental critics to designate industry trade associations and their nonprofit educational awareness organizations as "front groups" may be misleading and unjustified. Does ANEC constitute a front group as environmental groups have claimed? If the term implies that industry is hiding its intentions behind a facade, then the group's agenda is hardly hidden. The organization's literature is explicit about its goals and activities, although some observers seem more concerned about the organization's innocuous-sounding name. That does not imply duplicity, however, any more than does the similarly innocently named Environmental Working Group, a Washington, D.C.–based watchdog organization that others might consider a "front" for the environmental movement.

THE CHEMICAL MANUFACTURERS

In 1872, seventeen sulfuric acid manufacturers joined together to deal with the common problems they faced of safety, labeling, and tariffs, becoming the oldest chemical trade association in the Western Hemisphere, followed four years later by the American Chemical Society.

Historian Samuel Hays credits chemical manufacturers with the most extensive business environmental opposition, citing the early 1950s efforts of the industry's main trade group, the Manufacturing Chemists Association (MCA).[14] While the chemical manufacturers worked extensively to thwart efforts by environmental groups to control the use of agricultural pesticides, they mounted a coinciding public relations campaign to reassure a worried public that chemical additives in food were perfectly safe. The chemical industry was also the first to establish a publication exclusively devoted to environmental issues, *Chemecology*.[15] But MCA was rarely engaged in litigation and, according to one industry observer, "was more concerned with avoiding possible antitrust problems that could come from concerted industry action."[16]

By the late 1970s, environmental organizations and public opinion had shifted congressional interest from pollution control (primarily, the more visible problems of air and water quality) to emerging concerns over the health effects of toxic and hazardous substances. In 1977, the industry, led by Dow Chemical Company, established the American Industrial Health Council as an alliance against an Occupational Safety and Health Administration cancer policy. In 1979, the MCA changed its name to the Chemical Manufacturers Association (CMA), and the organization stepped up its lobbying efforts under the direction of a powerful new president, Robert A. Roland, who had previously served as president of the National Paint and Coatings Association.

This represented more than just a cosmetic name change, however. As one chemical maker noted, "There was an awful lot of hoping that if we didn't do anything [about government intervention] it would go away. . . . The industry got precisely what it wanted [from the trade group]—which was not much." Roland immediately moved the organization into a position of advocacy. "We're going to be more visible. We've changed our name so that there is going to be no mystery about what we are. We represent chemical manufacturers and we're damn proud of it."[17] Still, CMA's efforts to take a more proactive stance came almost a decade after the first Earth Day and at a point when the environment had already become an element of U.S. political culture.

In recent years, chemical manufacturers have joined the agricultural lobby over the issue of food additives, only this time the battle has been over acceptable levels of risk. Industry faces new attacks on potentially carcinogenic substances because new technology has given the EPA new tools with which to determine the highest level of exposure to a pesticide or other chemical at which there are no observed adverse effects in laboratory animals, considered the "acceptable daily intake." Tolerance levels, and therefore the degree of threat to human health, can now be measured in parts per trillion, which is the equivalent of one second's exposure in 32,000 years.[18]

The chemical industry has also fought efforts by environmental groups like Greenpeace to ban the use of chlorine, which has been suggested as a possible cause of as many as 12,000 bladder and rectal cancers annually when consumed in chlorinated tap water. Stratospheric chlorine, a constituent element of chlorofluorocarbons (CFCs), has also been implicated as being responsible for damage done to the earth's ozone layer and potentially related increases in skin cancer.[19] An estimated 85 percent of all pharmaceuticals, 96 percent of all pesticides, 98 percent of all municipal water treatment, and much of the paper, plastics, and baking industries depend upon chlorine as a component or disinfectant. Consumers would face an estimated $90 billion in additional costs to find a replacement, according to a Boston consulting firm hired by the industry.[20]

Paralleling the concerns of other industries, chemical companies have chafed at the implementation of requirements that they disclose the quantities and locations of releases of toxic chemicals. Individual companies have lobbied members of Congress with chemical plants in their district, hoping to avoid the expansion of pollution reporting requirements, even though the pollution prevention programs are largely voluntary.[21]

CMA has a permanent staff in Washington, D.C., but depends primarily on its member companies, with more than 200 task forces monitoring issues facing the industry, from the adequacy of energy supplies to international health and safety concerns. CMA is also a part of the Council of Chemical Associations, an informal consortium of more than fifty other associations in the chemical industry.[22]

But much of the chemical manufacturers' efforts have been low profile and undertaken at the bureaucratic level, rather than in the glare of the legislative arena, as will be discussed in greater detail in Chapter 6. High-profile incidents like the explosion that sent a cloud of dioxin over Seveso, Italy, in 1976, or the Bhopal chemical spill in India have made many of the nation's larger firms hesitant to lobby publicly for major changes in existing environmental laws for fear of being perceived as insensitive to health risks.

THE AUTOMAKERS

One industry group that appears to have been successful in limiting the impact of environmental regulation through the implementation of traditional lobbying efforts has been the automotive industry. Hit hard by a series of clean air act regulations, the industry has built an effective coalition and maintained a legislative presence in Washington that has only rarely been beaten by the environmental lobby.

The automakers first began to tackle environmental groups in the battle over the 1970 Clean Air Act Amendments when their lobbyists convinced the House of Representatives to scuttle more stringent auto emissions standards, claiming that the cost of such controls was prohibitive. In the Senate, however, the industry faced a tough battle against Maine's Edmund Muskie, a potential Democratic presidential candidate who hoped to deny President Richard Nixon the support of environmentalists. Muskie had targeted automobiles because such mobile sources as cars, trucks, and buses are the biggest sources of ambient, or outdoor, air pollution. He managed to convince his colleagues to enact legislation requiring a 90 percent reduction in tailpipe emissions by January 1, 1975, with an escape clause permitting the EPA to grant the automakers a one-year extension if necessary. In conference, the House agreed to the timetable with little industry resistance.

The passivity of the automakers to such a sweeping and costly change has been explained by one observer as a result of the industry's strong financial position at the time, since there was little competition from imports. The industry was also not well known for its lobbying expertise on Capitol Hill; General Motors did not establish a Washington lobbying office until 1969, and the industry's narrow base of support was confined to Midwest legislators.[23]

But in an illustration of their emerging influence, the automakers successfully pressed Congress to allow them the one-year extension called for in the law, claiming that the proposed emissions standards were technologically unfeasible. EPA administrator William Ruckelshaus initially refused to grant the extension, so the industry sued and Ruckelshaus capitulated.

In the negotiations over what would eventually become the 1990 Clean Air Act Amendments, the automakers relied heavily on their chief legislative ally, Michigan representative John Dingell, whose position as chair of the House Energy and Commerce Committee placed him in a position to control the debate over tailpipe emissions. Dingell, who had both political and financial support from the automotive industry, packed the Subcommittee on Health and the Environment with members who supported a watered-down bill, attempting to reduce the potential for further reductions in tailpipe emissions. The subcommittee chair, California's Henry Waxman, was unable to satisfy the concerns of the environmental groups that he represented, although there was eventually a compromise agreement reached between the two powerful congressional leaders.[24]

Unlike the battle over the 1970 amendments, the automotive industry worked to adopt a unified approach and often collaborated with the United Auto Workers and the oil companies on various issues. As one environmental group lobbyist commented, "They did their work and we often saw them on the Hill when no one else was there. They came out smelling like a rose."[25] When the Clean Air Act Amendments were finally signed into law by President George Bush on November 15, 1990, the resulting legislation allowed Congress, rather than the EPA, to determine tailpipe emission standards new vehicles must meet. The measure also included a clean fuels program that had been strongly opposed by the oil companies. But the automotive industry could have been in far worse shape had it not been for Dingell's lobbying position on its behalf and the president's willingness to compromise on other aspects of the bill to satisfy automakers' demands.

THE GROWTH OF INDUSTRY ALLIANCES

Although the narrowness of some environmental legislation affects only a single segment of industry, there have been some instances where business leaders have joined together to strategize against a much broader environmental agenda, as was the case in the late 1970s with the formation of the Western Regional Council (WRC). The WRC included top executives from several of the intermountain West's largest banks, utilities, and energy corporations who saw a common enemy in the EPA's clean air regulations. This private-sector group, which included several high-level public officials such as former Utah governor Calvin Rampston, was formed in part to counter the efforts of the Western Governors Policy Office, which represented officials from ten Rocky Mountain and Southwest states. Bruce Rockwell, chairman of Colorado National Bank, called WRC "a no-nonsense group" with none of "the Chamber of Commerce–type crap."[26] WRC was patterned after several earlier state-level groups like the California Business Roundtable, as well as its national counterpart, the National Business Roundtable.

One of the strengths of the WRC was that it used the highest-level officials in each company as its representatives, relying upon CEOs who made a powerful impression when lobbying public officials and agency staffers. The logistics for the group were handled by a private consulting firm, Bonneville Associates, that set up the meetings with top White House aides and did the research and monitoring of legislation for the WRC's members, freeing them of that responsibility. Member companies paid $5,000 each to participate, with ad hoc committees formed to handle issues like leasing regulations for publicly owned coal, the implementation of President Jimmy Carter's energy policies, and a bill that would have barred the eight largest oil companies from obtaining mineral leases on federal land.[27]

There are occasions when an omnibus bill forces business into coalition building. Perhaps the most notable case involving this strategy was the debate over the 1990 Clean Air Act Amendments. Since so many types of companies were affected by the proposal, it was inevitable that alliances would be formed. Representatives of the steel industry found themselves opposing proposed emission controls on coke ovens, just as dry cleaners and gas station owners joined together to blunt proposals on toxic pollutants emitted by their businesses. A second reason for the reliance upon coalitions was the tremendous cost associated with compliance. President Bush had threatened early on to veto any clean air act legislation that exceeded the projected costs of his own proposal by more than 10 percent. Congressmember John Dingell alerted his industry constituents to the struggle that lay ahead of them given the more organized and vocal environmental lobby; the result was the formation of the Clean Air Working Group (CAWG) in 1988. Comprised primarily of Washington, D.C., representatives of industry trade groups, its membership numbered nearly 2,000 at the height of the air pollution negotiations. Divided into ten separate teams headed by a lobbyist whose industry was directly affected by the issue, CAWG actively fought each amendment to the legislation and proposals submitted by its environmental group counterpart, the National Clean Air Coalition. It was also effective in discouraging individual companies from cutting their own deals with environmentalists or members of Congress in an attempt to maintain industry cohesiveness.[28]

An example of one of the ongoing alliances that is likely to remain active well into the twenty-first century is the Alliance for Responsible Atmospheric Policy, known formerly as the Alliance for Responsible CFC Policy. Characterized by Greenpeace as an anti-environmental group because "the Alliance's real goal is to slow down the timetable for phasing out CFCs,"[29] the organization's tactics are similar to those of the hundreds of other trade associations that monitor legislation and advocate industry positions. Its representatives testify before congressional committees and lobby committee staffers much like any other organized interest would do for its members.

Established in 1980, the alliance coordinates its 250 industry members' efforts to influence global and domestic policies on ozone protection and global warming. In its literature, the group notes that it seeks "a reasonable transition period" between the phaseout of CFCs and the implementation of new ozone protection technologies, as well as to limit the adoption of state and local ozone protection policies it considers "unnecessary and inconsistent with the Clean Air Act and the Montreal Protocol."[30]

It is here where the perspectives of industry and environmental groups collide. As Kevin Fay, counsel to the alliance, noted in his testimony before the House Subcommittee on Energy and Environment,

"Depending upon the 'politically correct' vantage point, the ozone depletion story is either about industry and technology bringing about global destruction in pursuit of financial gain; or in the alternative, environmentalism and social engineering out of control."[31]

Industry response to the concept of coalition building to affect environmental policy has been varied. More than 1,000 businesses worldwide have supported the International Chamber of Commerce's Business Charter for Sustainable Development, and others have adopted policies in compliance with the Global Environmental Management Initiative, which states that businesses can, and must, make environmental management an integral part of their strategy for success.[32]

Other companies attempted to outrun or preempt the environmental movement on their own by moving forward with research or new internal policies before the legislative wheels caught up with them. AT&T, for example, was at the vanguard within the industry to research substitutes for CFCs and formed the Industry Cooperative for Ozone Layer Protection as an alliance among CFC users. The cooperative includes corporate rivals like Northern Telecom, Boeing, British Aerospace, Ford, General Electric, Motorola, Texas Instruments, and dozens of others who have become allies.

With partisan support on their side, business alliances in the 104th Congress were relatively secure. The National Association of Manufacturers' 13,500 members, for example, presented a united front in support of the "Contract with America" and its regulatory flexibility for businesses faced with environmental compliance problems. Similar statements have come from groups representing smaller companies, like the National Federation of Independent Businesses, which is part of the Project Relief coalition lobbying for passage of the contract's provisions. "Big businesses have the resources, the experience, and the batteries of lawyers to handle this. Small businesses just can't keep up. The Contract is the first time small businesses have seen anything positive coming from legislative leadership," says a group spokesperson.[33]

THE ENVIRONMENTAL OPPOSITION'S
LEGISLATIVE ALLIES AND ENEMIES

While the environmental movement has relied upon current and former members of Congress like Edmund Muskie, Morris Udall, George Miller, and Henry Waxman to shepherd their policy agenda through the legislative maze, a somewhat unique set of factors, including a large number of retirements and open seats, set the stage for a revision of major environmental policies in 1994. In the Senate, the retirement of such key environmental advocates as Tim Wirth opened the door for conservative Republicans and put such continuing Democratic members as Max Baucus in the rare position of being in the political minority.

The environmental opposition expected its legislative momentum to escalate as a result of the 1994 midterm elections. Democrats had held the majority in the House of Representatives since 1949, the longest period of single-party control in the nation's history. But when the Republicans picked up an unexpectedly large gain of fifty-two seats in the House, giving them an initial 230:204 majority over the Democrats, it appeared a conservative, partisan window was about to open. Environmental groups felt their agenda was threatened by a loosely knit coalition of conservatives dominated by westerners among the seventy-three Republican newcomers, thirty-five of whom beat House Democratic incumbents.

Republicans who had previously been ineffective in pushing legislation sought by industry interests now found themselves in the majority. In the Senate, Republican John Chafee of Rhode Island, who was also a key player in the crafting of the 1990 Clean Air Act Amendments, became chair of the Environment and Public Works Committee, lending an aura of experience to one of that body's most important legislative committees. In the House, Republican representative Don Young of Alaska positioned himself in the enviable position as chair of the Public Lands and Resources Committee, which oversees his state's major industry, petroleum. Considered the most powerful (and perhaps the most colorful) of the environmental opposition's allies, Young once angrily flourished an oosik—the penis bone of a walrus—at his policy nemesis, the director of the USFWS, Mollie Beattie. Young also once referred to what he called "elitist environmentalists" as a "waffle-stomping, Harvard-graduating, intellectual bunch of idiots."[34]

Alaska's Frank Murkowski was Young's Republican counterpart in the Senate, and Alaska's other Republican senator, Ted Stevens, chaired the Governmental Affairs Committee, which has some jurisdiction over the USFS, giving the state unparalleled clout over natural resource policy. Stevens's power was magnified by his position as the second highest ranking Republican on the Appropriations Committee. The three Alaskans targeted policies that previously had gotten nowhere in the Democratic-controlled Congress: logging restrictions in the Tongass National Forest, revisions of the Alaska National Interest Lands Conservation Act, and opening up the ANWR to oil exploration.[35]

Among the most vocal members of the western House coalition in the 104th Congress was Representative Helen Chenoweth of Idaho, who defeated two-term Democratic incumbent Larry LaRocco with 55 percent of the vote as part of the Republican sweep in 1994. Her victory was also tied to LaRocco's support for the Clinton administration's land use proposals as the lone Democrat in the state's four-member congressional delegation. The Idaho representative insisted upon being referred to as "Congressman Chenoweth" and endeared herself to members of the militia movement and anti-abortion groups with legislative proposals, comments, and appearances on their behalf. Her environmental targets included the ESA (her fund-raising events have included the endangered sockeye salmon on the menu) and mining legislation. During the campaign, she called for metal mining in a state recreation area.[36]

Not all of the opposition has come from westerners, however. David McIntosh came to the House from Indiana as a thirty-six-year-old freshman in 1994 after serving as a special assistant to the White House at age twenty-nine during the Reagan administration. Under President Bush, McIntosh was executive director of Vice President Dan Quayle's Council on Competitiveness. The council was credited with gutting key provisions of environmental legislation that had come out of prior sessions of Congress. Speaker Newt Gingrich named McIntosh as chair of a new, specially created Subcommittee on Growth, Natural Resources, and Regulatory Affairs as a way of continuing the pro-industry work he had done during his tenure on Quayle's staff.

THE POLICY LEGACY OF THE 104TH CONGRESS

Both environmental groups and their opponents initially expected that the partisan personnel changes would be paralleled by policy changes. Environmental organizations warned their members that the new Congress would dismantle long-standing regulations; opposition groups geared up to do just that. Some Democrats did defect from their party, joining Republicans in what was called an "indirect approach" to environmental regulatory reform.[37]

In addition to expecting that its influence would be expanded through the sheer number of Republican members, the environmental opposition realized that policy change would also require structural change within Congress itself. The Republican leadership responded by restructuring various committees and subcommittees, and by slashing committee staff positions to dilute the power of longtime Democratic staffers.

One of the eliminated committees was the House Merchant Marine and Fisheries Committee, which had been in existence for 107 years prior to the Republican takeover. Initially, staffers had no idea what would happen to their archival records or the jurisdiction of the committee, which in the past had been responsible for oceanic issues from the Long-Range Plan for the Panama Canal to the International Maritime Conference.[38]

To reflect changes in environmental priorities, a number of committees were renamed. The Energy and Commerce Committee had the word "energy" dropped from its name and its jurisdiction narrowed, losing control over the TransAlaska Pipeline; the Committee on Natural Resources became the Committee on Public Lands and Resources; the Public Works Committee became the Transportation and Infrastructure Committee; and the Committee on Science, Space, and Technology was renamed the Committee on Technology and Competitiveness with an expansion of its jurisdiction.

In addition to changes in its own organization, the 104th Congress took aim at several federal agencies that implement environmental policy. The Department of the Interior was one of nine cabinet agencies targeted by the Republican majority, which managed to close down the Bureau of Mines under a compromise plan that eliminated the bureau but stalled efforts to end mine worker health and safety programs. Congress also defunded the Office of Technology Assessment, a legislative branch agency created in 1972 to provide independent analysis on the consequences of new technologies.[39]

Congress was also reflecting voter antipathy toward the policies of the Clinton administration and the party in power. Conservative efforts to overhaul environmental policies began innocuously with the unveiling of the Republicans' "Contract with America" in September 1994. Drafted by then-Congressmember Newt Gingrich of Georgia, House Republicans and congressional candidates pledged the reforms they would bring to a vote during the first 100 days of the 104th Congress if they took control of the House. The contract itself did not appear to be an attack on the environment, and in fact, the word "environment" did not even appear in the 400-page document. Although environmental groups were already alarmed by the magnitude of the Republican victory, it was somewhat belatedly that environmental organizations began to realize that interwoven in the contract's ten major proposals were a series of reforms and recommendations that could potentially undermine much of the environmental protection legislation that had been created and fine-tuned over the past three decades. If nothing else, the "Contract with America" promised to complete the Reagan administration's environmental agenda with new faces in support of its provisions. While some environmental activists initially sounded the alarm about the potential damage that the contract might cause, even the most astute political pundits had no idea there would be so many Republicans elected to Congress who would attempt to implement the proposed reforms.

Initially at least, many of the proposals seemed focused on regulatory reform that on the surface amounted to little more than cutting red tape and streamlining various administrative procedures. But a more thorough reading of the document, and the legislation that rapidly sprang from it, indicates that the Republicans were out to radically change American environmental policy. Many of the conservatives' proposals were attached to spending bills that were less visible but that Interior Secretary Bruce Babbitt called "a sneak attack."

The new Republican majority perceived, at least initially, that there were subtle changes in the way Americans looked at environmental protection. The lack of a clear consensus on environmental goals and lukewarm executive branch support had limited the 103rd Congress's efforts to implement an ambitious agenda during President Clinton's first two years in office. Congress managed to enact only one new piece of environmental legislation, the California Desert Protection Act, despite attempts by the Democratic-controlled body to revamp several key statutes that were up for reauthorization.

Their efforts were stymied by Republicans who managed to tack on provisions that called for cost-benefit analyses of all environmental laws, and the perception that voters wanted less government regulation in their lives. Although Americans have consistently viewed themselves as environmentalists or sympathetic if not active on environmental issues, a September 1994 Cambridge Reports survey showed that 31 percent of those questioned thought there was too much government involvement in environmental protection, up from 9 percent in a 1989 survey. But those attitudes appear to be in a state of flux as voters demonstrate their uncertainty over how to approach environmental protection. In the midst of the 1994 election, a similar survey showed that 53 percent of the respondents said they would sacrifice economic growth for the environment.[40]

Nonetheless, candidates seized upon the antiregulatory momentum and promised constituents that the new Congress would look after local residents' jobs, cut red tape, and keep environmental protection goals in balance with economic development. The message worked, not only in Congress, but at the state level as well. After the 1994 elections, Republicans controlled the governorship of thirty states, including eight of the nine most populous states in the nation, and made substantial gains in state legislatures.

There are a number of environmental issues that conservatives within the 104th Congress prioritized, several of which grew out of the "Contract with America." The first three proposals were labeled "the unholy trinity" by some environmental leaders: risk assessment, the revision of the Endangered Species Act, and revisions in surface and drinking water laws. Despite intensive lobbying efforts by conservative groups, the majority of the legislative proposals stalled completely due to continuing public support for environmental protection that was reflected in lawmakers' unwillingness to support such drastic changes in policy.

In the case of risk assessment, for example, the environmental opposition was led by a coalition of industries that argued that billions of dollars are being spent by industry on problems that pose virtually no threat to human health or that result in a minimal improvement in environmental quality. Standards have been set so high, it is claimed, that they threaten not only a company's viability but result in virtually no environmental benefit at enormous costs in jobs and economic savings. By assigning a benefit figure to reducing the risk, and a cost figure for compliance, the industries believe the nation could better prioritize its limited resources.[41] Several bills were introduced that would have forced federal agencies to justify any new regulations regarding risk, part of the Republicans' overall assault on government rulemaking. Cost-benefit analysis would also be required of any federal project costing $1 million or more.[42]

Extractive resource industry representatives were partially behind efforts to reform the ESA, initially enacted in 1973. Although the timber industry sought reform because more areas were being designated as critical habitat for threatened and endangered species, the issue has been coupled with the property rights debate. Opposition to the statute grew with demands that landowners be compensated when federal regulations (like declaring an area a critical habitat for species protection) reduce the value or use of the property owner's land by 10 percent of its value, an issue discussed in depth in Chapter 10. The provision stems from the Job Creation and Wage Enhancement Act portion of the "Contract with America," a section termed by the Sierra Club as "the bad neighbor bill."[43] One victory for the environmental opposition came with the passage of a supplemental spending bill that included a provision that banned any new listings of endangered species for the remainder of fiscal 1995, although the order was subsequently lifted.

Since the issue of air quality had already been addressed with passage of the 1990 Clean Air Act Amendments, the 104th Congress switched its attention to the issue of surface and drinking water legislation, which affects not only business interests, but also state and local officials who have complained that they are left responsible for picking up the tab for pollution control projects with no financial support from the federal government, creating an unfunded mandate. The clarion call of "No Money, No Mandate" is being echoed across the country with bipartisan state and local support.

Environmental organizations have argued that any tinkering with the laws would be a setback for public health, although they admit there may be some flaws in the existing legislation. One of the frequently cited examples is that of Anchorage, Alaska, where city leaders asked local fish-processing plants to dump fish entrails into the city's sewer system to foul the water because current law required them to remove a certain percentage of contaminants even though the water was already very clean.[44]

Other major legislative proposals, such as revisions in the 1980 Comprehensive Environmental Response, Compensation, and Liability Act (Superfund), expansion of oil exploration and drilling in Alaska's ANWR, and reforms in the operations of the NPS, were put aside in 1996 as members focused on their own reelection bids.

Environmental opposition groups counted as one of their major successes the "salvage rider" to the 1995 Rescissions Bill, which waived existing environmental laws to speed the salvage logging of dead and dying timber in national forests to prevent catastrophic wildfires. The bill also allowed sales to proceed on tracts of old-growth trees that had previously been canceled by the government out of concern for endangered species' habitat. In 1996, federal officials took the position that it must honor the contracts held by timber buyers, and allowed companies to begin cutting live trees. Several environmental organizations, including the Biodiversity Legal Foundation, the Alabama Wilderness Alliance, and the Oregon Natural Resources Council filed suit attempting to block the timber sales on the grounds that the logging would irreparably harm endangered species, while other groups sought a total repeal of the law or provisions that would allow federal agencies to propose substitute sales. President Clinton, who had capitulated to demands by Republicans to sign the bill originally, later admitted that he had made a mistake in doing so and had not realized its impact and lack of a mechanism to allow for sufficient public input into the decisionmaking process. In the meantime, timber companies rushed to cut as many trees as possible before the December 31, 1996, deadline, when the salvage rider expired.

The controversy over the bill and President Clinton's flip-flop on timber policy is exemplary of how the government's inconsistency on resource issues allows policy windows to open, even briefly, providing organized interests with an opportunity to effect change. In April 1993, the timber industry, working hand-in-hand with grassroots environmental opposition groups, took advantage of one of these "openings." They were well-represented at the president's forest conference, designed to bring together environmental group representatives and logging interests to produce a comprehensive timber policy, later referred to as Option 9. Although the plan was harshly criticized by environmental organizations, the timber industry perceived the policy as more balanced because it met legal requirements that would eventually allow timber sales to proceed. The industry's leaders also relied heavily upon their allies in Congress, including Washington senator Slade Gorton, who had vowed to fight any proposed repeal of the legislation.

BUSINESS IN THE LEGISLATIVE ARENA

It is impossible to predict if the 1994 elections and the actions of the 104th Congress mark a watershed in the way industry groups affect environmental legislation, or if a single election or congressional session is the beginning of a longer-term pattern with conservative overtones. The results of the 1996 elections proved inconclusive. With the ample campaign support of business PACs, Republicans retained control of Congress while the Democrats held on to the White House. The ambitious reform agenda set by the 104th Congress will continue to be tempered by public opinion that is more favorable toward environmental regulation. For example, lacking the political clout to dismantle existing environmental laws, western Republicans like Idaho senator Larry Craig and Oregon representative Bob Smith pledged that the 105th Congress would target the appropriations process and operations of key agencies like the USFS.

Researchers believe that Americans have consistently viewed themselves as environmentalists or sympathetic if not active on environmental issues. But studies also show that concern about the environment has become a settled issue in American consciousness, and citizens have turned their attention to other problems. In a 1996 Princeton Survey Research Associates canvass that asked respondents which item on a list of fifteen national problems they considered the most important, the environment ranked fourteenth. When asked about the most important problem facing the country in a 1996 CBS/New York Times survey, the environment did not make the list, ranking far behind issues such as crime. While the environment has declined in intensity as an issue nationally, it has become more politically potent at the state and local level, responsible, at least in part, for the Republican Party's congressional victories in 1994. Survey data show, however, that there has been no significant transformation of environmental attitudes nationally since 1994.[45] But there are several points that can be made about how business operates in this venue, regardless of any electoral changes ahead.

First and foremost, business interests have become more sophisticated in their legislative efforts since the mid-1980s. Although they may have initially underestimated the influence of the environmental movement, they eventually realized the potential impact of the movement's momentum and spent the next twenty-five years playing catch-up. Today, through trade associations and the addition of professional lobbyists to their payrolls, major industry groups can match mainstream environmental groups and even overpower their lobbying efforts, especially when the electoral winds blow more in their favor and a policy window appears to open.

Industry has also learned not to challenge environmental laws as directly as it did in the past but, instead, to portray them as too costly, without sufficient environmental benefit, or as impossible to implement. Sometimes, they may attempt to create a public perception that some laws are just plain needless or silly, placing some environmental laws in the same category as unessential occupational safety and health rules or complicated tax codes.

Many companies have learned from experience the folly of trying to affect legislation single-handedly or the mistakes that can be made by challenging the entire spectrum of environmental policy. Instead, industry efforts now appear to be more focused and, whenever possible, conducted as part of a coalition rather than as a fragmented effort that sometimes pitted one industry against another.

Lastly, while continuing to use such traditional interest group strategies as lobbying and giving contributions to legislators supportive of their views, business groups often dodge the public and media attention of the hearing room and committee meetings for less visible venues. On some occasions, that might mean flying a group of committee staff members to California to see an industry's operations firsthand, rather than making a large contribution directly to a member of Congress. Or it might involve the hiring of technical experts who would work with the staff as they prepare to mark up a bill. But it might also mean bypassing the legislative process altogether and heading for less visible but possibly more productive venues, as the next two chapters will show.

NOTES

1. Quoted in Neil Hamilton, "Open Season on the Environment," *Sierra,* vol. 80, no. 2 (March–April 1995): 13.

2. Quoted in Herbert Buchsbaum, "Has Regulation Run Amok?" *Scholastic Update,* vol. 127, no. 13 (April 7, 1995): 6.

3. U.S. Environmental Protection Agency, *Environmental Investments: The Cost of a Clean Environment,* EPA-230-11-90-083 (Washington, DC: EPA, November 1990), pp. 2–5. See also, Alan Carlin, Paul F. Scodari, and Don H. Garner, "Environmental Investments: The Cost of Cleaning Up," *Environment,* vol. 34, no. 2 (March 1992): 12–20, 38–44.

4. "Where the PAC Money Goes," *Congressional Quarterly Weekly Report,* April 15, 1995.

5. Samuel P. Hays, *Beauty, Health, and Permanence: Environmental Politics in the United States, 1955–1985* (Cambridge, England: Cambridge University Press, 1987), p. 307.

6. Marianne Lavelle, "Environmental Vise: Law, Compliance," *National Law Journal,* August 30, 1993, p. S1.

7. David Corn, "Shilling in the Senate," *The Nation,* vol. 249 (July 17, 1989): 84–87.

8. Richard H. K. Vietor, *Environmental Politics and the Coal Coalition* (College Station: Texas A & M University Press, 1980), pp. 35–36.

9. Ibid., pp. 44–45.

10. Ibid., p. 48.

11. See Bruce A. Ackerman and William T. Hassler, *Clean Coal, Dirty Air* (New Haven, CT: Yale University Press, 1981).

12. Bruce Babbitt, "If All the Trees in the Forest Fall," *Washington Post National Weekly Edition,* October 30, 1995, p. 29.

13. Nuclear Energy Institute, *About the Nuclear Energy Institute* (Washington, DC: Nuclear Energy Institute, n.d.).

14. For a history of the MCA, later called the Chemical Manufacturers Association, see George W. Ingle and Beverly Lehrer, "The Chemical Manufacturers Association," *Chemtech,* vol. 15 (February 1985): 71–73.

15. Hays, *Beauty, Health, and Permanence,* p. 310.

16. Chris Murray, "CMA Charges Ahead Under New Mandate," *Chemical and Engineering News,* August 13, 1979, p. 17.

17. Ibid., p. 17.

18. For an explanation of pesticide exposure limits and government policy, see Travis Wagner, *In Our Backyard: A Guide to Understanding Pollution and Its Effects* (New York: Van Nostrand, 1994), pp. 235–269.

19. Gregg Easterbrook, *A Moment on the Earth: The Coming Age of Environmental Optimism* (New York: Viking, 1995), pp. 641, 531–532.

20. Ann Reilly Dowd, "Environmentalists on the Run," *Fortune,* vol. 130 (September 19, 1994): 95.

21. "Citings," *World Watch* (November–December 1995): 8.

22. Ingle and Lehrer, "The Chemical Manufacturers," p. 73.

23. Richard E. Cohen, *Washington at Work: Back Rooms and Clean Air* (New York: Macmillan, 1992), pp. 15–16. See also Norman Ornstein and Shirley Elder, *Interest Groups, Lobbying, and Policymaking* (Washington, DC: Congressional Quarterly Press, 1978).

24. Gary C. Bryner, *Blue Skies, Green Politics,* 2nd ed. (Washington, DC: Congressional Quarterly Press, 1995), pp. 117–118.

25. Cohen, *Washington at Work,* p. 111.

26. Bob Gottlieb and Peter Wiley, "The New Power Brokers Who Are Carving Up the West," *Straight Creek Journal,* March 20, 1980, p. 1.

27. Ibid.

28. Cohen, *Washington at Work,* pp. 108–109. For another perspective on the dynamics of this bill, see George Hager, "For Industry and Opponents, a Showdown Is in the Air," *Environment '90* (Washington, DC: Congressional Quarterly Press, 1990), p. 10.

29. Carl Deal, *The Greenpeace Guide to Anti-Environmental Organizations* (Berkeley, CA: Odonian Press, 1993), p. 31.

30. "The Alliance for Responsible Atmospheric Policy," brochure, n.d.

31. Testimony of Kevin Fay, Alliance for Responsible Atmospheric Policy, before the House Committee on Science, Subcommittee on Energy and Environment, September 20, 1995.

32. See George D. Carpenter, "Business Joins Ranks of Environmentalists," *Forum for Applied Research and Public Policy,* vol. 9 (summer 1994): 9.

33. Nancy Shute, "Capitol Shakeup," *Amicus Journal,* vol. 6, no. 4 (winter 1995): 23.

34. Richard Lacayo, "This Land Is Whose Land?" *Time*, October 22, 1995, p. 68. See also B. J. Bergman, "Leader of the Pack," *Sierra*, vol. 80, no. 6 (November–December 1995): 51.

35. See B. J. Bergman, "Alaska's Terrible Trio," *Sierra*, vol. 80, no. 6 (November–December 1995): 53.

36. Hanna Rosin, "Invasion of the Church Ladies," *New Republic*, vol. 212 (April 24, 1995): 20–23, 26–27; and "Member Profile: Helen Chenoweth," *Congressional Quarterly Weekly Report*, vol. 53, no. 1 (January 7, 1995): 58–59.

37. For a synopsis of the legislative maneuvering, see John H. Cushman Jr., "Republicans Clear-Cut Regulatory Timberland," *New York Times*, March 5, 1995, sect. 4, p. 16.

38. Guy Gugliotta, "Would This Go in the Elephant Graveyard?" *Washington Post National Weekly Edition*, December 26, 1994, p. 34.

39. See Bruce Bimber, *The Politics of Expertise: The Rise and Fall of the Office of Technology Assessment* (Albany: State University of New York Press, 1996).

40. "GOP Sets the 104th Congress on New Regulatory Course," *Congressional Quarterly Weekly Report*, June 17, 1995, p. 1696.

41. For a discussion of the role of cost-benefit analysis and regulation, see Bruce A. Williams and Albert R. Matheny, *Democracy, Dialogue, and Environmental Disputes: The Contested Languages of Social Regulation* (New Haven, CT: Yale University Press, 1995).

42. Shute, "Capitol Shakeup," p. 22.

43. Ibid., p. 21.

44. Paul Portnoy, "Beware of the Killer Clauses Inside the GOP's 'Contract,'" *Washington Post National Weekly Edition*, January 23–29, 1995, p. 21.

45. Everett Carll Ladd, and Karlyn Bowman, "Public Opinion on the Environment," *Resources*, Summer 1996, pp. 5–7.

5

The PR Campaigns

SIGN OF THE TIMES: A partial publications list of PERC (Political Economy Research Center: "A Research Center Providing Market Solutions to Environmental Problems"), a think tank based in Bozeman, Montana:

- *Multiple Conflicts over Multiple Use*
- *Enviro-Capitalists*
- *Doomsday Kids: Scaring Children Green*
- *Superfund: Environmental Justice for All*
- *Reinventing Environmentalism in the New Era*
- *The Endangered Species Act: Making Innocent Species the Enemy*
- *Turning a Profit on Public Forests*
- *Property Rights Legislation in the States: A Review*

Organized interests have a broad arsenal of weapons available in their attempts to secure benefits for their members, as we have already begun to discover. In the case of most groups, some of the most critical forces are the strategies used to shape public opinion.

This chapter examines four tactics used primarily by the business segment of the environmental opposition to advocate its cause: the development of public relations campaigns, the sponsorship of initiative campaigns, the practice that environmental groups derogatorily refer to as "greenwashing," and the use of studies and reports promulgated by think tanks and research institutes. Few of the grassroots organizations profiled in this book have the resources necessary to engage in any of the public relations campaigns or strategies identified in this chapter, so the majority of the examples used pertain instead to industry interests.[1]

The use of public relations to shape public opinion about a company or product is a time-honored business strategy,[2] but the practice gained momentum as the environmental movement grew and became more critical of industry in the 1960s and 1970s. As polls indicated the public's support for environmental issues and products, business in many ways capitulated to the environmental movement. While business continued to rely upon the legislative tactics described in Chapter 4, it also moved toward a more conciliatory strategy in an attempt to recast its image before the American public. Rather than fighting the environmental agenda, it used the same imagery and language used by environmental organizations. General Motors Corporation (GMC), for example, photographed its Sonoma-model truck in a stand of what appears to be old-growth redwoods, with sunlight gently filtering through the trees to the ferns below, in a full-page, color advertisement on the back page of the Audubon Society's magazine. The tag line for the ad reads, "Our respect for nature goes beyond just giving you an excellent view of it," and the copy goes on to explain how GMC has made "a sizeable contribution to The Nature Conservancy." While the automaker still attempts to reduce its environmental compliance costs through legislative means, it also tries to soften potential opposition to its policies through the manipulation of its image. By making a financial contribution directly to the organization, it reminds potential customers that its environmental efforts (or at least its donations) are more substantive, and more important, purely voluntary and undertaken without the threat of government-imposed sanctions and regulations.

Why have public relations campaigns become such an important tool for industry? When the strategy works, public opinion about a company is more positive, and potentially, an environmental organization that accepted either the donation or the advertising revenue looks more favorably on the donor. The efforts may also defuse potential opposition by an environmental group, such as a boycott of a company's goods, or may serve to encourage a consumer to choose one company's products or services over another's. Marketing researchers may be able to convince a manufacturer that by, for example, including more recycled content in its products, it will attract buyers for whom recycling is an important component in making a decision about which paper-towel brand to purchase. In some cases, businesses are hoping to influence public opinion so that the public will be more supportive of the industry position when it comes to legislation and enforcement. In that sense, the public relations campaign becomes one way to influence policy outcomes.

Industry appears to be trying a number of strategies in response to environmentalism: on the one hand, continuing to resist legislative and regulatory initiatives, and on the other, acknowledging public attitudes that favor increased environmental protection.

PUBLIC RELATIONS CAMPAIGNS

Much of the public policy debate over the environment is not fought directly in the legislative arena, but in the court of public opinion. Even before the vanguard environmental groups coalesced into an active movement, business interests bore the brunt of the public's criticism for environmental degradation, from urban air pollution to waste dumping, even though there was minimal public attention paid to such problems. Much of the condemnation has been justified; until the period after World War II, neither the government nor industry paid much attention to common practices like dumping effluent directly into streams, or whether the emissions rising from a factory smokestack were potentially harmful to human health. There was a dearth of scientific knowledge about environmental hazards, and in some cases, the government encouraged industry to adopt procedures now considered damaging, exemplified by the slogan "The Solution to Pollution is Dilution" and the belief that potentially harmful emissions or waste would be naturally absorbed in the vast expanse of the atmosphere or oceans. The public often considered the smoggy skies over Los Angeles or the sewage in a local river as part of the cost of progress and economic growth.

As the level of awareness about the effects of pollution grew, environmental groups became more vocal in their criticism of industrial practices. In an effort to defend themselves against what they considered unfair media reporting, businesses became active in their efforts to publicize environmental successes. Industry counterefforts have ranged from the production of well-crafted annual report–type documents outlining a firm's environmental accomplishments to editorial-type advertisements in major news magazines. Business interests also responded by creating the Public Environmental Reporting Initiative (PERI) in 1993, a voluntary effort by major firms to promote what its members consider more balanced and meaningful environmental reporting. To many in business, environmental groups have captured the media, which are no longer capable of reporting their activities objectively.

One of the founding sponsors of PERI, Phillips Petroleum Company, began producing its own report in 1993 and made a commitment "to be the safest company in the petroleum industry and a leader in meeting health and environmental challenges."[3] Trade associations have made similar pledges: CMA's Responsible Care Initiative, the American Petroleum Institute's STEP (Strategies for Today's Environmental Partnership) program, the National Petroleum Refiners Association's BEST (Building Environmental Stewardship Tools) program, and the International Chamber of Commerce's Business Charter for Sustainable Development.

One typical type of public relations campaign has been carried out by individual companies that have used internal (in-house) firms and resources to paint their businesses with a green brush. Dow Chemical, for example, published its own magazine, *Down to Earth,* and sponsored Earth Day activities in the company's hometown of Midland, Michigan, in 1990.[4] Mobil Oil Corporation has become well known for its paid advertisements that appear as columns on the environment and government regulation in mainstream magazines, and individual firms like Canon Film have used environmental themes (photos of endangered species) as a part of their regular advertising campaigns.

A second public relations effort involves the hiring of outside public relations firms to handle special cases and crises. In such instances, crisis management becomes industry's only effective way of trying to make the best of an awful situation. The firm of Burson-Marstellar, for example, has been heavily criticized by Greenpeace for its role in assisting both Exxon and Union Carbide after incidents involving the two firms made headlines around the world (the *Exxon Valdez* oil spill and a toxic gas leak in Bhopal, India, respectively). Burson-Marsteller was also hired by a consortium of Canadian timber companies in 1990 to help cleanse their image after environmentalists began referring to the country as the "Brazil of the North," as a parallel to the policy of some Latin American governments to allow the destruction of rain forests. With a $1 million budget, the public relations firm set up a group it called Forest Alliance and began issuing press releases and airing television infomercials. Public opinion polls showed that the effort significantly improved the public's image of the timber industry within less than three years.[5]

Criticism has been levied by environmental groups against two other well-known public relations firms, Hill and Knowlton and E. Bruce Harrison and Company, for representing firms like Monsanto and groups like the CMA.[6] In his book *The War Against the Greens,* David Helvarg accused Hill and Knowlton of reproducing fake copies of Earth First! fliers during the Redwood Summer demonstrations on behalf of its client, Pacific Lumber. The fliers called for violence during the demonstrations, and there were allegations that the timber company was aware the fliers were not genuine when they were distributed to the media.[7] Hill and Knowlton also represented the tobacco industry until the 1960s. "We couldn't do anything for them because they wouldn't take our advice," says former Hill and Knowlton president Loet Velmans.[8]

Some petroleum companies have understandably chosen to take a more active stance, hiring public affairs professionals to assist them before opposition develops. In the case of Trans Mountain Pipe Line Company, for example, which proposed a $600 million oil tanker terminal on the Olympic Peninsula off Port Angeles, Washington, a public relations team commissioned an opinion poll that indicated which concerns were foremost in the public's mind. To identify those who supported the project, the company sent more than 200,000 issue-oriented brochures to registered voters adjacent to the project, which helped the firm identify supporters. The company then used that database to mobilize supporters for community meetings and to neutralize the few but vocal environmental activists who opposed the project. The group's grassroots efforts redefined the debate from "people vs. big oil" to one of "opponents vs. supporters" of the pipeline.[9] That industry would seek outside counsel is not unusual: In fact, it is considered a preferred strategy by those within the profession who believe an immediate, neutral-appearing response is not only appropriate but necessary.

Nor is the environmental movement exempt from the practice itself. As discussed in Chapter 3, Washington, D.C.–based Fenton Communications was hired by the NRDC to orchestrate the organization's controversial campaign against the chemical Alar in 1989, based on an EPA Science Advisory Board designation that Alar was a probable human carcinogen. The firm also put together a May 1995 press campaign that attempted to link property rights groups, the militia movement, and the bombing of the federal building in Oklahoma City the previous month. Fenton Communications did not identify who had paid the company for its public relations services, or the cost. But one wise use group alleged that the environmental movement staged the event, including a press conference the primary participants of which included author David Helvarg, whose book *The War Against the Greens* was published by the Sierra Club; former BLM director Jim Baca, who resigned over disagreements on the Clinton administration's weak environmental policies; and Jeff DeBonis, who left the USFS in 1989 to found a nonprofit environmental group called the Association of Forest Service Employees for Environmental Ethics.[10]

Jim Bernfield, a communications consultant for the American Resources Information Network, has even provided environmental activists with a "how-to" manual on use of the media and news events as "an opportunity to discredit and marginalize Wise Use. An indictment of the Wise Use movement—sharp at certain times, subtle at other times—should be woven into every speech, interview, and news release." Bernfield suggests that environmental groups should design a media campaign that defines a message and then stick to it, but he also recommends building a relationship of trust with the media and providing a reporter attending a wise use press conference with "penetrating questions" to ask from an environmental perspective. In his words, the place to wage the brunt of the battle against wise use is "at the grass roots, with local issues and local heroes."[11]

THE INITIATIVE CAMPAIGNS

Another public relations strategy used by business involves efforts to shape public opinion through the political process. One reason elections and especially citizen initiatives have become a business target has been the tremendous increase in environmental issues finding their way onto the ballot. From the early 1970s to 1986, for instance, citizens confirmed only eighteen environmental ballot measures in the United States. Yet in the single election of November 1988, American voters approved at least seventeen environmentally related propositions, including measures dealing with recycling, water quality, natural resources, and funding for environmental programs.[12] Moreover, the measures have not been limited to statewide issues. Mobil Oil, for instance, spent $650,000 in 1990 to defeat a local election effort that would have banned the use of hydrogen fluoride at one of its refineries in Torrance, California.[13]

California business exemplifies the power of an effective, allied public relations effort marshalled against the citizen initiative. In November 1990, environmental organizations gathered sufficient signatures to place Proposition 128, the Environmental Protection Act of 1990 known as "Big Green," on the ballot. The 16,000-word list of thirty different measures would have banned a variety of cancer-causing pesticides, prohibited new offshore drilling, stopped the cutting of virgin redwood forests, created an oil spill cleanup fund, and mandated major reductions in carbon dioxide emissions from utility plants. A second environmental measure, Forests Forever, would have banned clear-cutting and would have set aside old-growth forests and redwoods.

Industry opposition took two forms. Because "Big Green" covered such a wide spectrum of environmental issues, it almost automatically brought together a similarly broad coalition of interests to oppose it. Led by timber, chemical, and utility interests, the alliance spent an estimated $16 million to defeat Proposition 128 by a two-to-one margin; the Forests Forever measure lost by a narrower vote.[14]

In addition, the industry public relations effort was taken a step further when another coalition of business interests, led by the timber industry, gathered sufficient signatures to place two competing measures on a ballot that was already overwhelmed with twenty-eight separate initiatives for voters to sort through. The Global Warming and Clear-Cutting Reduction, Wildlife Protection, and Reforestation Act (derided by environmental groups as "Big Stump") and the Consumer Pesticide Enforcement Act (sponsored by the chemical industry and known as "Big Brown") had the dual purpose of confusing voters because of their ballot titles and making it seem as if the state were being overcome with environmental legislation. In addition, "Big Brown" contained a provision that made it and "Big Green" mutually exclusive; only the bill receiving the most votes would become law.[15]

The controversy over wording has become a traditional element of the initiative process and group advocates in California. In March

1996, the ballot contained a highly contentious measure dealing with the hunting of mountain lions. Californians for Balanced Wildlife Management was comprised primarily of hunters who sought to be allowed to kill the animals; the California Wildlife Protection Coalition sought a hunting ban. Both sides produced advertising and promotional materials that did more to confuse voters than to educate them about the issue.

In one sense, the abundance of environmentally related ballot measures may have been a part of the green backlash that was beginning to form in California and Oregon in the late 1980s, buoyed by a business lobby that repeatedly warned that the environmental movement had gone too far in appealing to voters directly at the cost of jobs and lifestyle change. The Sierra Club referred to the industry attack as "Trojan-horse initiatives," which have the effect of disarming the citizen initiative process. Even industry officials, like Kevin Eckery of the Timber Association of California, admit that neither side really wins: "It's a lousy way to make law. Debate gets reduced to 30-second sound bites and road signs containing at most six words, usually beginning with 'No.'"[16]

GREENWASHING

One of the public relations strategies used by businesses attempting to influence public opinion is what environmental groups derogatorily refer to as "greenwashing."[17] The practice is commonly used by public relations firms that specialize in damage control for clients whose reputations have been sullied by poor environmental practices.[18] But it is also used by firms making a legitimate effort to improve their operations, packaging, or overall sense of corporate responsibility toward the environment. There are two ways industry has attempted to market itself and appear more "green" to the public. One strategy is to emphasize the positive steps a company has taken to help the environment. Using this strategy allows a company to point to its efforts that are totally separate from its primary business activities. Like public relations campaigns, however, these efforts still may result in a no-win situation for the firms that engage in touting their record. By appearing "green" on one very visible aspect of a company's operation, attention may be less likely to be raised about another, more fundamental, and more environmentally damaging practice. To the more radical or ideological members of the environmental movement, all corporate interests are suspect, regardless of what they say or do. The tactic also fails if a company attempts to highlight its record when, in fact, close attention reveals that it is not as environmentally responsible as it has portrayed itself.

Despite the image problem businesses continue to face, there are numerous examples where a company has gone out of its way to inform the public of its corporate environmental awareness. Nature product purveyor Smith and Hawken, for example, reminds its customers that it uses shredded paper rather than plastic "peanuts" for its shipping materials and provides a forum for the Rainforest Action Network in its mailings, including petitions in support of the group's efforts to gain a worldwide ban on logging in ancient forests. Grocery retailer Safeway Stores developed an Environmental Options program by alerting shoppers to products on its shelves that are less harmful to the environment and provided customers with a cash credit for bringing their own paper bags for their grocery purchases. In recognition of the impact of environmental issues on children, retailer Dayton Hudson Corporation initiated a major marketing campaign at its Target stores by becoming the international sponsor of a group called Kids for Saving Earth, while Amway Products began running advertisements in national publications as part of a series called "Local Heroes" spotlighting environmental groups like Los Angeles–based TreePeople. Whether or not such public relations efforts pay off in a more positive public image for their sponsors is questionable. Certainly there is enough of a perception by industry that the practice is worthwhile that dozens of firms have jumped on the bandwagon, each trying to "outgreen" one another.

A second strategy is to retool, repackage, or even relabel a company's products. Perhaps the most dramatic example of a business preemptive strike took place in November 1990 when McDonald's announced it was phasing out foam packaging and switching to a new, paper-based packaging that is lighter and thinner than foam. The new packaging reduces the volume of McDonald's product packaging by 90 percent, contains no CFCs, is partially degradable, and may be recyclable as well as compostable. In April 1991, the company went a step further by announcing a plan that would eliminate 80 percent or more of the garbage created by its fast-food restaurants across the United States.

Although these not inconsequential actions by McDonald's to reduce waste won praise from some groups, such as the Sierra Club and the Environmental Defense Fund, their public relations campaigns have also been met with skepticism. When McDonald's teamed up with the World Wildlife Fund to produce and distribute a "Save the Rain Forest" poster, consumer environmental activists characterized the action as a superficial public relations effort to divert attention from environmentally questionable corporate practices. Still, many businesses followed McDonald's lead. Procter and Gamble, for example, began eliminating the 80 million outer cartons used each year for its deodorant products and switched to a different container for its fabric softener container made from 100 percent postconsumer material. The company also reformulated its liquid detergent, changing from a 64-ounce bottle to a 50-ounce concentrated formula that can be refilled from another container made from 50 percent postconsumer recycled plastic. After the refill container was introduced in fall 1990, about 30 percent of the purchasers of its Downy fabric softener switched to the refill instead of purchasing an additional bottle.[19]

Manufacturers of products that have traditionally been targeted by the environmental movement for their poor environmental record have had to be even more creative. The oil companies, for example, can do little to gain environmentalists' favor with an industry whose only products are based on nonrenewable energy sources. So instead, they have tried to reformulate their products and sell "cleaner" gasoline. In August 1989, Atlantic Richfield Company (ARCO) announced it was introducing "an environmental gasoline" called EC-1 to replace leaded regular at more than 700 stations throughout southern California. The lead-free fuel is designed for vehicles not equipped with catalytic converters, and company tests showed that if all users of leaded regular gasoline in the region switched to the reformulated ARCO fuel, the pollution reduction would be equal to removing 240,000 cars off the road, or neutralizing more than 6 percent of the area's automobile-generated air pollution.

ARCO then spent $10 million on an advertising campaign to market EC-1, which garnered the firm front-page coverage in the *Wall Street Journal* and the *New York Times,* as well as prime-time notice on every local television station. Positive endorsements by environmental groups like the NRDC gave ARCO the confidence it needed to become the first oil company to invest in television advertising in Alaska since the *Valdez* accident.[20]

Labeling and public relations campaigns have not always been successful, however. In the early 1990s, two rival firms, the Green Cross Certification Company and Green Seal, began charging companies fees for an "evaluation" and an eventual stamp of environmental approval for their products, based on factors such as biodegradability and the percentage of recycled fibers used. But the certification process never really seemed to capture the public's interest, despite environmental groups' hopes that consumers would switch to the "approved" products and services.

Even those firms that have attempted to build a reputation for their corporate environmentalism have occasionally been targeted for using marketing hype. Anita Roddick, whose Body Shop line of cosmetics had been heralded for setting the standard for other environmentally supportive businesses to follow, was the subject of a highly critical article in *Business Ethics* magazine that alleged that the company's "natural" products were not so natural after all and that the Body Shop's highly publicized contributions to environmental charities were actually less than the industry average. Roddick fought back legally and publicly, even sending out a ten-page refutation of the article to the magazine's subscribers and convincing *Vanity Fair* not to publish a similar story. Still, a 1994 report by the Boston-based investment firm Franklin Research and Development supported many of the charges against the company. The editor of *Business Ethics* scheduled the article for publication despite "strongly worded legal threats" from the Body Shop's lawyers "because I knew that what we printed was true."[21]

Not unexpectedly, the government has intervened in the labeling controversy. The Federal Trade Commission (FTC) has gone after companies for making dubious environmental claims. In 1993, for example, Year Round Lawn Care, a California company later purchased by Orkin Exterminating Company, claimed in its company brochures that the pesticides it used were "practically non-toxic" and safer than "many common household products like suntan lotion or shaving cream." The FTC cited the firm because the company did not have "competent and reliable scientific evidence that substantiates these claims."[22]

Although it is less publicized, industry has also attempted to divert negative attention from its activities by buying its way into environmentalists' hearts, but not without cost. Shaklee Companies, for example, was criticized by environmental groups when the company donated $50,000 to become the first official corporate sponsor of Earth Day '90. Apple Computers and Hewlett-Packard faced similar complaints when they donated equipment to Earth Day organizers, with critics disapproving the concept of any kind of corporate involvement.

New York Times reporter Keith Schneider compares corporate donations and sponsorship of wise use groups to the funding given by industry to environmental groups:

> I find it almost laughable that in the environmental press—*Audubon* magazine, *Sierra Club* magazine, I've read some others—that the rap on the Wise Use movement is that it's corporate funded. Well, the largest corporate donation that I know of in the environmental movement is the million dollars that General Electric gives the Audubon Society to support their Audubon Society specials. Now, General Electric's environmental record has a lot to be desired. They have more toxic waste sites, Superfund sites, than any industrial corporation in the country. I've covered General Electric messes from Hanford to Schenectady, New York. For the Audubon Society magazine to be criticizing the Wise Use movement for corporate funding seems to be the height of hypocrisy.[23]

More skeptical members of the environmental movement have also criticized environmental organizations that have allowed corporations to join as donors or as members of their boards of directors. One researcher noted, for example, that the World Wildlife Fund/Conservation Foundation listed among its major donors Chevron Oil and Exxon, as well as Philip Morris, Mobil Oil, and Morgan Guaranty Trust—companies criticized by other environmental organizations for their poor record of corporate environmentalism.[24] Eric Mann, director of the Labor/Community Strategy Center in Los Angeles, sees such attempts by industry to participate in environmental organizations' decisionmaking processes very cynically:

> The trouble with the "greening of the boardroom" is that since boards of directors are specifically charged with maximizing the profits of their corporations, the corporate environmentalists will comprise nothing more than a new layer of corporate apologists to attack grassroots environmental movements.[25]

The company most often criticized by environmental groups for using environmental groups for its own agenda may be Waste Management, Inc. (WMI), which is the nation's largest operator of toxic waste dumps. Its CEO, Dean Buntrock, was elected to the NWF's governing board after the firm gave thousands of dollars in contributions to the organization. Allegations have also been made that WMI benefited from its affiliation with the environmental group when the NWF met with EPA administrator William Reilly to discuss waste disposal policies that WMI supported.[26]

Other complaints have been levied against the Environmental Grantmakers Association (EGA), which plays an important role in the movement through its coordination of grants to environmental groups. EGA admitted WMI as a funding corporation and then later expelled the corporation "for a pattern of abusive corporate conduct" and for "endangering and degrading the environment." In 1990, EGA admitted Chevron Oil, and later decided to admit another oil company, ARCO.[27]

The no-win nature of industry philanthropy toward environmental organizations is illustrated by the fact that such efforts may arouse hostility from the other end of the political spectrum as well. The Oregon Lands Coalition, for example, which represents timber interests, accused Mattel Toys of exposing "vulnerable" children to the "preservationists' radical agenda" with a Barbie doll television commercial supportive of forest protection. The organization has also protested the sale of specific products, including K-Mart's Save the Trees T-shirts, and has targeted firms such as Canon Copiers, American Greeting Cards, Cotler

Manufacturing, Ralston Purina, and Shearson Lehman Hutton, whose products or services were considered to be proenvironmental.

Similarly, the logging industry was highly critical of General Mills, maker of Lucky Charms cereal, when the company developed an advertising campaign in which the product's leprechaun mascot goes into the forest and finds only tree stumps. In response to industry criticism, General Mills offered consumers free tree seedlings and planting instructions, mentioning in the new advertising campaign that trees are also an important source of lumber for homes.

RESEARCH INSTITUTES AND THINK TANKS

As Chapter 4 showed, industry officials were not particularly active when the first round of environmental statutes was enacted in the late 1960s and early 1970s. But as the legislation became more intrusive and the compliance costs multiplied, the business sector developed other ways of coping with negative publicity.

One strategy was for industry to counter the research findings being promulgated by environmental groups and by government scientific bodies with research of their own. For many corporations, this meant setting up their own internal environmental affairs divisions or making grants to individual scientists who would repudiate the work of other researchers. In some cases, coalitions of industry groups began to pool their industry expertise. Some of those that did so were industry-specific, such as the Edison Electric Institute, which brought together a wide range of utility researchers. Environmentalists castigated several scientists for their mercenary approach to research funding, arguing that they had sold out their neutrality when federal funding became more and more scarce. The Tobacco Institute, for example, has been widely criticized for its funding of university research to show that there is no linkage between smoking and lung cancer. In 1988, the Business Roundtable produced its own economic analysis of the impact of the proposed Clean Air Act Amendments as a way of countering the projected benefits cited by environmental organizations.[28]

Another strategy involves the use of think tanks—privately funded (and tax-exempt) centers of research that produce policy papers or studies on behalf of their clientele, most of whom are ideologically connected rather than linked by type of business. These research institutes exist at both ends of the political spectrum, from the liberal Brookings Institution to the conservative American Enterprise Institute. The environmental opposition has relied upon a host of more conservative think tanks, primarily at the national level, but increasingly at the state level as well. This linkage to conservative think tanks is often cited by environmental groups as evidence that the environmental opposition is really a facade for a broader, more encompassing conservative agenda.

The majority of these policy centers have been created only since the 1970s, with the most comprehensive think tanks represented by the Heritage Foundation (1973) and the Cato Institute (1977). The Heritage Foundation's $23 million budget and 160 employees make it among the most formidable of the conservative think tanks, especially because of its ability to capture media attention. It does so by its frequent publication of position papers on a topic, each of which is estimated to generate 200 or more media articles.[29] The Heritage Foundation is widely credited with being the organization responsible for drawing up the blueprint for President Reagan's environmental policy after his election in 1980 and for suggesting names of prominent conservatives as key appointees during the president's transition period.

Liberal organizations have criticized the Heritage Foundation for its ability to produce massive amounts of public relations materials with a decidedly partisan theme while retaining its tax-exempt status. A number of critics point to the fact that many Heritage mailings include the disclaimer "Nothing written here is to be construed . . . as an attempt to aid or hinder the passage of any bill before Congress," despite the fact that the foundation's materials refer to specific legislation. Internal Revenue commissioner Sheldon Cohen admits the foundation is probably within the law as interpreted by IRS regulations, although "they're standing there with their shoes touching the line."[30]

The Cato Institute, originally based in San Francisco before it moved to Washington, D.C., was dismissed early on as nothing more than a mouthpiece for the Libertarian Party. Like the Heritage Foundation, Cato publishes policy papers on subjects from national defense to tax reform, all with the general theme of reducing government intrusion and overregulation. In recent years, it has created an environmental arm that has focused on hazardous waste, the abolition of the federal Department of Energy and the EPA, and private property rights.[31]

While the Heritage Foundation and the Cato Institute deal with a variety of policies, several smaller groups are focusing more specifically on environmental issues. From Bozeman, Montana, PERC generates news releases on the role of the USFS, studies on state property rights legislation, and policy recommendations on topics ranging from legislation like Superfund, the Clean Water Act, and the Endangered Species Act, to water and fisheries management. Many of its associates and policy studies contributors are scholars with impressive credentials and institutional affiliations including the University of Nevada, Brigham Young University, the University of Arizona, and Clemson

University. Another group, the Competitive Enterprise Institute (CEI) in Washington, D.C., urges "private conservation" rather than government management and control.

A smaller but prolific think tank, the Pacific Research Institute for Public Policy in San Francisco, is perhaps best known for its book *Environmental Gore,* the title of which indicates its conservative parallel to Vice President Al Gore's best-selling book *Earth in the Balance.* The institute attempts to dispel the environmental movement's doomsday predictions about running out of resources and argues instead that many of the pollution problems of the past have been resolved. Similar philosophical studies have been produced by the Foundation for Research on Economics and the Environment (Seattle), the Independence Institute (Golden, Colorado), and the Commonwealth Foundation for Public Policy Alternatives (Pennsylvania). Over thirty-five conservative state-based think tanks are tied together through the State Policy Network.[32]

Other conservative and libertarian think tanks have jumped on the environmental bandwagon even though their primary focus in the past has not been in this policy area. The Reason Foundation, for example, was founded in 1978 and is based in Los Angeles. The group, which bills itself as "a national public-policy research organization with a practical, market-based approach and an outside-Washington perspective," has historically concentrated on economic research. Its Privatization Center publishes *Privatization Watch* to track trends across the country, focusing on airports, education, and transportation. Because of its West Coast focus, most of its environmental research has dealt with urban issues, many in response to legislation and regulations enacted by California's legislature, the California Air Resources Board (CARB), and the South Coast Air Quality Management District.

Somewhat in between on the political spectrum are groups like Resources for the Future, which publishes its own analysis of environmental policy issues and whose advisory council includes both industry and environmental group representatives. The think tank also funds the Center for Risk Management, which has investigated issues such as the safety of electromagnetic fields, the use of science in environmental policymaking, and Superfund and toxic waste cleanup programs. Funding for RFF comes from a variety of sources, including cooperative agreements with the EPA and the U.S. Department of Energy and various academic supporters. While the organization receives more traditional philanthropic support from charities like the Pew Charitable Trusts and the Andrew W. Mellon Foundation, which fund a number of environmental organizations and projects,[33] it also has strong industry backing. Major corporate supporters include the AT&T Foundation, Browning-Ferris Industries, Monsanto Company, and E. I.

Du Pont de Nemours and Company.[34] Some projects that benefit a specific industry group have been funded directly by that industry. For example, the American Forest Foundation asked the Center for Risk Management to develop an interdisciplinary high school curriculum on environmental cost-benefit analysis and risk assessment, although the program is co-sponsored by the Western Regional Environmental Education Council.

Critics also note that foundations with conservative leanings have actively supported the environmental opposition with direct financial support. Cited most often are the Adolph Coors Foundation—which funded a documentary on manufactured chemicals entitled *Big Fears . . . Little Risks*—and the foundations known as the "four sisters": the John M. Olin, Sarah Scaufe, Smith-Richardson, and Lynde and Harry Bradley foundations.[35]

Those criticisms are countered, in turn, by the environmental opposition, which argues that environmental groups receive an even bigger slice of their incomes from private foundations, government grants, and tax subsidies. One opposition umbrella group, the Center for the Defense of Free Enterprise, cited the National Fish and Wildlife Foundation (NFWF) as an example of how environmental groups have taken advantage of public monies in the guise of foundation dollars. In its 1995 report, *Feeding at the Trough,* the group noted that the NFWF, which was created as a charitable and nonprofit corporation by Congress in 1984, now relies upon federal appropriations that it then funnels to environmental organizations, rather than private-sector support, as the legislation initially intended. Funding from one federal agency, the National Oceanographic and Atmospheric Administration, which was designed to support outreach for the Florida Keys National Marine Sanctuary, actually went to the Nature Conservancy for political activities, according to the center.[36]

There are several tactics that are common to most of the think tanks and foundations profiled here. Although most operate with a paid administrative staff, they also employ adjunct scholars and researchers who are responsible for churning out the studies and position papers that become the basis for the groups' media and legislative activities. As a part of that function, many produce their own journals (e.g., Heritage publishes the scholarly *Policy Review,* which named the environmental movement as "the greatest single threat to the American economy"), books (e.g., the Heartland Institute's *Eco-Sanity: A Common Sense Guide to Environmentalism*), and briefing papers (e.g., CEI developed a seventy-page "Environmental Briefing Book" for congressional candidates in 1994).[37]

Some of the think tanks' efforts are specifically designed to counter the environmental movement, such as the Heartland Institute's publication of its own *Free Guide to Saving the Planet*, timed to coincide with Earth Day in 1996. The organization's thirty-six-page tabloid newspaper was targeted for distribution on college campuses, and from its cover, which featured nature photographs, it could easily have been mistaken for a mainstream environmental group publication. Inside, the publisher noted that the articles were representative of "commonsense environmentalism, not the kind of environmentalism that relies on scare tactics or hides a not-so-secret political agenda. . . . We think you will find it a welcome antidote to the shrill and reckless rhetoric that so often appears in Earth Day papers produced by other groups."[38] The publication featured articles urging readers to "rethink recycling," how environmental groups had falsely predicted the exhaustion of the world's petroleum supplies, and "the cold facts on global warming."

The think tanks also distribute their materials through respected external publishers. Rowman and Littlefield, for example, has published several books by Terry Anderson, a professor of economics at Montana State University who is also a senior associate at PERC, and by PERC contributing author Bruce Yandle (*Taking the Environment Seriously* and *The Land Rights Rebellion*). By using traditional publishing outlets to distribute their materials, the members of the environmental opposition can secure a much broader audience for their perspectives than if the materials were to be internally distributed or published by obviously partisan sources.

IMAGEMAKING

One of the most difficult aspects of researching the environmental opposition lies in deciphering its goals on the basis of the names of the organizations, which explain little about who the groups represent or which side of the environmental debate they are on. For that reason, environmental organizations are critical of industry and the environmental opposition either creating front groups that hide their political agenda behind a vague or misleading organizational name, or creating "astroturf" (phony grassroots) groups closely allied with industry.[39]

Called "greenscamming" by some observers, the intent is to soften a group's image by adopting a name similar to that of an environmental organization, that is familiar sounding, or that obscures its actual goals. A spokesperson for the Wilderness Society notes, "No one wants to dance with the devil, so they try to come up with a name that's not too devilish." Northwesterners for More Fish, for instance, is not a sportfishing group as might be expected, but rather a coalition of utilities, aluminum companies, timber firms, and other interests under fire for depleting the fish population. The group had a first-year $2.6 million budget to establish itself "as a credible group supporting positive solutions to enhancing fish populations." Similarly, Friends of Eagle Mountain in Riverside, California, is not a grassroots environmental effort but a public relations firm's creation on behalf of a mining company that seeks to build the world's largest landfill in an abandoned iron ore pit.[40]

Another example is the Washington, D.C.–based National Wilderness Institute (NWI), which is classified as a nonpartisan, educational organization under Section 501(c)(3) by the Internal Revenue Service. The organization's name might conjure up images of an environmental group dedicated to some sort of wilderness protection or training—an impression reinforced by the group's membership brochure that shows photos of its members sitting alongside a stream and placing nesting boxes near a Virginia wetland. The group, however, is a wise use movement organization highly critical of "bureaucracy, red tape and extremism" whose members are "environmentalists who believe in science, technology, private property, economic progress and common sense." NWI has actively sought to eliminate wetlands regulations in the Endangered Species Act and clearly aligns itself with the environmental opposition through a well-crafted mission statement:

> NWI is dedicated to using sound, objective science for the wise management of natural resources. NWI recognizes that renewable resources such as wildlife, fish, wetlands, wilderness, forest, range, air, water, and soil are dynamic, resilient, and respond positively to wise management.
>   NWI recognizes the direct, positive relationship between progress and environmental quality and champions private sector stewardship which enhances the resource base without unnecessarily inhibiting economic growth. NWI supports environmentally sound, site and situation specific practices which harness the creative forces of the private sector, protect or extend private property rights, and reduce the regulatory burden of government.[41]

It is difficult, however, to differentiate among the groups in order to identify those that legitimately represent the interests of business through trade associations and other industry groups that are very explicit about their mission and membership, and those whose intentions are more duplicitous. Sometimes a green-sounding name and efforts to create a positive public image hide a company that continues to behave irresponsibly toward the environment. This makes it especially hard for those firms that do show a measure of corporate responsibility to extol their virtues without facing criticism from environmental groups one way or the other.

EFFECTIVENESS OF PR EFFORTS

How effective have these public relations efforts been? The answer is perhaps a mixed review.[42] If the goal of the public relations campaigns is to deflect the wrath of organized environmental protesters and negative public opinion, some firms have definitely been successful. Companies that have switched product packaging, for example, have found that they are less likely to be targeted and can retain a low, if not altogether positive, profile. Many of the nation's fast-food companies, for example, took McDonald's lead to avoid highly visible negative public exposure by taking action before they became targets for environmental groups.

For the more radical environmental organizations, no amount of corporate environmentalism is sufficient. No matter which way a targeted company turns, an environmental group will be critical. In those cases, industry efforts to do the right thing are perceived as transparent and insincere, even when the company does everything possible to meet a group's demands. Companies that have made substantial contributions to environmental organizations as a way of gaining their favor (or at least diverting attention from their activities) find they make enemies on both sides of the environmental debate. They are castigated by some groups who feel their brethren have been "captured" or co-opted by the very companies they love to hate. Similarly, smaller grassroots organizations, like those profiled in Chapter 10, complain that business contributions (which they feel should more rightfully be directed toward them) are propping up the environmental movement and keeping it alive as membership levels drop.

If there is one change that can be directly attributed to the impact of the environmental movement on business it is the creation of an awareness about corporate environmentalism.[43] That awareness is reflected in two ways. A firm's environmental standing is now a consideration in its operations. After the Bhopal disaster, for example, Union Carbide hired the consulting firm of Arthur D. Little to develop a four-part program of monitoring, liability-containment measures, and audits that are designed to provide quality control and executive reassurance that the company's practices are environmentally sound. The company's actions even moved the entire chemical industry into a more proactive mode with the creation of CMA's Responsible Care Initiative, which includes a shared code of environmental management behavior.[44]

CMA has not had total success with the initiative, however, despite a five-year, $50 million public relations effort. In national magazines, the group pledged in its ads to "open lines of communication" because "our industry hasn't been noted for open doors, much less open dialogue." The ads also provided the public with a toll-free hotline to call to "find out what your local chemical company is making" and to "look at the way we make, handle, and dispose of chemicals." One reporter called Dow Chemical and received several company brochures, but when the reporter asked about the toxic chemical production and waste records at several of the company's facilities, the response was, "I'm curious. Why do you want to know?"[45]

Businesses that do make a conscious effort to improve their environmental practices and record trumpet those efforts, especially when an award is involved. The Council on Economic Priorities, a nonprofit public interest research organization founded in 1969, produces the America's Corporate Conscience Awards for social responsibility. Kellogg officials point proudly to the fact that the company was named one of the top five companies in the environmental stewardship category in 1990 and included the honor in their brochures. In another attempt at self-congratulation, Amway Products' ads have noted the company's recognition as the 1989 recipient of the United Nations Environment Programme Award for Achievement. Similarly, in 1989, when CERES drafted the "Valdez Principles," several companies immediately jumped on board as signatories to prove just how "green" they were.

Although the think tanks and research arms of industry interests do not appear to have had a major impact on policy, they more likely have had an influence on the shaping of public opinion. Congressional staff members who are in a position to measure the think tanks' influence on legislation give them only lukewarm ratings. Their major contribution appears to be that the largest of them, the Heritage Foundation and the Cato Institute, generate substantial media coverage for their positions.[46] Information supportive of the environmental opposition, usually presented at a press conference to report a study's latest findings or through a conservative group's publications that are then recycled through the opposition's extensive electronic information networks, becomes a powerful tool. It may make consumers feel supportive enough to purchase a company's product or less inclined to feel negatively toward an entire industry if the public relations efforts work the way they are supposed to work. Despite many success stories, however, industry groups have realized that if they cannot win in the legislative arena or in the court of public opinion, they must use another route—the bureaucratic end run discussed in the next chapter.

NOTES

1. Grassroots groups are, however, beginning to develop an awareness of the importance of public relations campaigns. The December 1994 "Taking Back America" seminar in Reno, Nevada, sponsored by the group Stewards of the Range, included a presentation by Tracy Mitchell, former press secretary to the campaign for Congressmember Helen Chenoweth. President of Patriot Communications, Mitchell's seminar materials on getting media attention about the war on property rights advised grassroots groups to profile the attacker ("college students who want to save the world, academic, ivory-tower types, and wealthy elitists") and to "stay pro-active, even after the immediate problems are resolved."

2. For a summary of the strategies used by the nation's largest public relations firms, see Alicia Mundy, "Is the Press Any Match for Powerhouse P.R.?" *Columbia Journalism Review*, vol. 31 (September–October 1992): 27–34.

3. *1994 Health, Environmental, and Safety Report* (Bartlesville, OK: Phillips Petroleum Company, 1994), p. 2.

4. See Art Kleiner, "The Three Faces of Dow," *Garbage* (July–August 1991): 52–58.

5. Kim Goldberg, "Logging On," *Columbia Journalism Review*, vol. 32 (November–December 1993): 19–20.

6. See Carl Deal, *The Greenpeace Guide to Anti-Environmental Organizations* (Berkeley, CA: Odonian Press, 1993), pp. 15–16.

7. David Helvarg, *The War Against the Greens: The "Wise Use" Movement, the New Right, and Anti-Environmental Violence* (San Francisco: Sierra Club Books, 1994), p. 4.

8. Mundy, "Is the Press Any Match," p. 34.

9. Chris Crowley, "With Environmental Opposition to Projects, Fight Fire with Fire," *Oil and Gas Journal*, vol. 90, no. 31 (August 31, 1992): 30–31.

10. On the Alar incident, see Ronald Gots, *Toxic Risks: Science, Regulation, and Perception* (Boca Raton, FL: Lewis Publishers, 1993); and Ann Reilly Dowd, "Environmentalists on the Run," *Fortune*, vol. 130 (September 19, 1994): 93. On the company's involvement in the 1995 militia tie-in, see "Greens Blame Wise Use Groups for Oklahoma City Bombing," *The People's Agenda* (spring 1995): 1.

11. Jim Bernfield, "Working with the Media," in John Echeverria and Raymond Booth Eby, eds., *Let the People Judge: Wise Use and the Private Property Rights Movement* (Washington, DC: Island Press, 1995), pp. 327–338.

12. John Mark Johnson, "Citizens Initiate Ballot Measures," *Environment*, vol. 32, no. 7 (September 1990): 4–5, 43–45.

13. Mark Ivey, "The Oil Industry Races to Refine Its Image," *Business Week*, April 23, 1990, p. 98.

14. See Bradley Johnson, "Big Business Attacks Big Green," *Advertising Age*, vol. 61 (October 22, 1990): 4; "Black Day for California's 'Big Green,'" *New Scientist*, November 17, 1990, p. 20; Richard Lacayo, "No Lack of Initiatives," *Time*, September 3, 1990, p. 52; and Elizabeth Schaefer, "A Daunting Proposition," *Nature*, vol. 347 (September 27, 1990): 323.

15. Seth Zuckerman, "Flying False Colors," *Sierra*, vol. 75, no. 5 (September–October 1990): 20–24.

16. Ibid., pp. 21–22.

17. For a perspective on greenwashing, see Tom Athanasiou, *Divided Planet: The Ecology of Rich and Poor* (Boston: Little, Brown, 1996).

18. See, for example, Marion K. Pinsdorf, *Communicating When Your Company Is Under Siege* (Lexington, MA: Lexington Books, 1987); and L. L. Golden, *Only by Public Consent* (New York: Hawthorn Books, 1968).

19. See Laurie Friedman, "Procter and Gamble Zeroes In on Green," *American Demographics*, vol. 13 (July 1991): 16.

20. Bruce Piasecki, "Corporate World Shows More Care for Environment," *Forum for Applied Research and Public Policy*, vol. 9 (summer 1994): 6–11.

21. Maureen Clark, "Socially Responsible Business Brawl," *The Progressive*, vol. 59 (March 1995): 14.

22. Ethan Seidman, "We're Environmentally Friendly!" *Garbage*, vol. 5 (June–July 1993): 66.

23. Keith Schneider, "Working Journalists Speak Out on Wise Use," in Echeverria and Eby, eds., *Let the People Judge*, p. 352.

24. Eve Pell, "Buying In: How Corporations Keep an Eye on Environmental Groups That Oppose Them," *Mother Jones*, vol. 15 (April–May 1990): 23–26.

25. Eric Mann, "Environmentalism in the Corporate Climate," *Tikkun*, vol. 5 (March–April 1990): 61.

26. Eve Pell, "Stop the Greens: Business Fights Back by Hook or by Crook," in Echeverria and Eby, eds., *Let the People Judge*, p. 22.

27. Ibid., pp. 22–23.

28. See Gary C. Bryner, *Blue Skies, Green Politics*, 2nd ed. (Washington, DC: Congressional Quarterly Press, 1995); Richard E. Cohen, *Washington at Work: Back Rooms and Clean Air* (New York: Macmillan, 1992); and D. Kirk Davidson, "Straws in the Wind: The Nature of Corporate Commitment to Environmental Issues," in W. Mitchell Hoffman, ed., *The Corporation, Ethics, and the Environment* (New York: Quorum Books, 1990).

29. Barbara Ruben, "Getting the Wrong Ideas," *Environmental Action* (spring 1995): 25.

30. Michael Kinsley, "The Envelope, Please," *New Republic*, September 20 and 27, 1993, p. 6.

31. See Colleen O'Connor and Bob Cohn, "A Baby Boomer's Think Tank," *Newsweek*, September 1, 1986.

32. Ruben, "Getting the Wrong Ideas," p. 25.

33. In 1994, for example, the Pew Charitable Trusts gave $100,000 to the American Oceans Campaign in support of a campaign to educate the public and policymakers on the need to strengthen the National Estuary Program. The charity also provided $140,000 for the Environmental Defense Fund's efforts to strengthen the provisions of the Montreal Protocol and $175,000 to the Nature Conservancy to fund a feasibility study to develop a network of conservation lodges. The Andrew W. Mellon Foundation gave $750,000 in general support funds to the Center for Plant Conservation in 1993, as well as $600,000 for the Marine Biological Laboratory at Woods Hole, Massachusetts, for ecological research and training. Data on these grants and others like them can be found in *Environmental Grantmaking Foundations, 1995 Directory* (Rochester, NY: Environmental Data Research Institute, 1995).

34. Many industry foundations have been criticized for their efforts to fund environmental projects. The AT&T Foundation, for example, gave Clean Dallas, Inc., $30,000 in 1993 to fund a multiyear project to increase the region's use of recycled and secondary materials. It also gave E-Call of Boston $25,000 to support the setup of a twenty-four-hour Ecology Hotline.

35. Chip Berlet and William K. Burke, "Corporate Fronts: Inside the Anti-Environmental Movement," *Greenpeace* (January–March 1991): 8–12.

36. *Feeding at the Trough* (Bellevue, WA: Center for the Defense of Free Enterprise, 1995).

37. Ruben, "Getting the Wrong Ideas," pp. 22–23.

38. Joseph Bast, "A Fable for Today," *Earth Day '96: A Free Guide to Saving the Planet* (Palatine, IL: Heartland Institute, April 22, 1996), p. 3.

39. Phil Brick, "Determined Opposition: The Wise Use Movement Challenges Environmentalism," *Environment,* vol. 37, no. 8 (October 1995): 38.

40. Jane Fritsch, "Friend or Foe? Nature Groups Say Names Lie," *New York Times,* March 25, 1996, pp. A1, A8.

41. "NWI: Voice of Reason on the Environment," brochure, n.d.

42. See, for example, David B. Sachsman, "Public Relations Influence on Coverage of the Environment in San Francisco Area," *Journalism Quarterly,* vol. 53 (spring 1976): 54–60.

43. See, for example, Thomas F. P. Sullivan, *The Greening of American Business: Making Bottom-Line Sense of Environmental Responsibility* (Rockville, MD: Government Institutes, 1992); E. Bruce Harrison, *Going Green: How to Communicate Your Company's Environmental Commitment* (Homewood, IL: Business One Irwin, 1993); and L. R. Jones, *Corporate Environmental Policy and Government Regulation* (Greenwich, CN: JAI Press, 1994).

44. Piasecki, "Corporate World," p. 8.

45. "Why Do You Want to Know?" *Mother Jones,* vol. 17 (March–April 1992): 18.

46. Ruben, "Getting the Wrong Ideas," p. 25.

6

End Run:
The Bureaucratic Arena

SIGN OF THE TIMES: Strategists considering which agency in the state or regional bureaucratic arena would best serve their interests might look to California, which provides numerous access points at which to oppose environmental policy, including:

- *The California Environmental Protection Agency*
- *The California Air Resources Board*
- *The California Department of Water Resources*
- *The California Coastal Commission*
- *The Waste Management Board*
- *The California Department of Fish and Game*
- *The California Occupational Safety and Health Administration*
- *The South Coast Air Quality Management District (and its regional cousins)*

Beginning around 1965, government regulation exploded on the American political scene. New agencies were created at the federal level: From 1960 to 1980, the number of federal regulatory agencies increased from twenty-eight to fifty-six. Among the new sections of the bureaucracy were the Equal Employment Opportunity Commission, the Environmental Protection Agency, the Occupational Safety and Health Administration, the Consumer Product Safety Commission, the Commodities Futures Trading Commission, and the National Highway Traffic Safety Commission, to name just a few. Older, existing agencies found their authority expanded, and state and local governments established their own regulatory mechanisms, from agencies that oversee cable television franchises to those that regulate utilities.[1]

Although no new regulatory agencies were created under the administration of Ronald Reagan, and regulatory staff and budgets began to be reduced during the 1980s, the lack of growth did not equate to significant cutbacks in regulatory structure. However, under

Reagan, it became clear that regulatory agencies, especially the EPA, were highly responsive to the pressures of the political system and, therefore, ripe for influence by organized interests.

Political scientists and journalists usually focus their research on the ways organized interests affect the legislative process in the form of detailed case studies, like the bill creating the national health care service,[2] a law increasing user fees on inland waterways,[3] the adoption of the federal budget,[4] or the passage of the 1986 Tax Reform Act.[5] Various incarnations of the Clean Air Act have been the focus of the majority of the environmental legislative case studies, from the 1970 amendments,[6] the 1977 version sponsored by Maine senator Edmund Muskie,[7] and, most recently, the 1990 Clean Air Act Amendments.[8] Other case studies of the development of environmental legislation include those describing the Hazardous and Solid Waste Amendments of 1984 and the Superfund Amendments and Reauthorization Act of 1986.[9]

There is a general acceptance among researchers that the traditional analysis that focuses on the legislative process from a purely structural perspective is inaccurate and incomplete. As *National Journal* reporter Richard Cohen, himself the author of several case studies, notes:

> Generations of students have learned about the legislative process from publications like "How Our Laws Are Made," a Government Printing Office document available in most congressional offices. But the formal description in this primer has become so irrelevant that it verges on the ludicrous.[10]

Although legislation is clearly one expression of public policy, the agencies and individuals who implement legislative intent play what many observers consider to be an even more influential role in the policymaking process. Research is now beginning to focus on the increasing importance of the implementation phase of the process and the reliance upon administrative rulemaking.[11] As policymaking relies more and more on professionals with specialized technical expertise and less on legislative initiative, the entire decisionmaking process changes. Where policy was once made in public in committee hearings, it has now become more secretive and conducted in closed administrative sessions. A number of scholars have argued that some components of the administrative branch have actually been "captured" by those they regulate,[12] while others believe that the pressures of organized interests like industry on an agency are mitigated by other external and internal forces.[13]

> For some reason, however, analytical literature on American public policy most often disregards the bureaucrats' influence on interpreting and implementing the law. Nevertheless, quite real people do

make and carry out policy. They staff congressional committees, regulatory agencies like the Environmental Protection Agency, and administrative departments like Interior. Only to a limited extent does the written law of congressional mandate constrain their decisions.[14]

What factors determine the effectiveness of organized interests (in this case, the environmental opposition) in influencing the bureaucracy? The resources available to groups include size (measured as membership or budget), ability to mobilize resources, the dispersion of members, cohesiveness, intensity of commitment, prestige, the number of groups represented and coalition breadth, and, occasionally, legal standing.[15]

This chapter examines the ways in which the environmental opposition has edged further away from attempting to influence policy within the legislative arena and, instead, used its leverage and power to affect the bureaucracy, the courts, and the unelected sector of the policy process—the end run process. While industry in general continues to expend its resources attempting to influence legislation, it now has increased its expenditures to influence public opinion and to monitor and attempt to influence the bureaucratic arena. Although this strategy is not new and has in fact been historically used by groups like the coal industry in its efforts to deflect the impact of clean air laws,[16] it is being used increasingly by a number of business interests. Indirectly, it examines the resources available to industry groups outlined above and how they have been used to influence environmental policy-making in the bureaucratic arena.

AVOIDING THE PUBLIC LIMELIGHT

One of the many reasons why industry representatives and occasionally other segments of the environmental opposition have chosen to fight the regulatory battle in the bureaucratic arena rather than in Congress was touched upon briefly in the previous chapter: Many industries simply cannot afford to publicize their environmental shortcomings in the glow of the legislative spotlight.

The media and representatives of environmental organizations are much more likely to attend a congressional hearing in Washington, D.C., than they are to peruse the *Federal Register* for notice of an obscure agency workshop. In fact, some regulatory agencies are more likely to use an internally created mailing list to notify interested parties of a rulemaking workshop than to make a concerted attempt to broaden their outreach. Only when legislation specifically requires that particular parties be notified of an agency's intended action is it likely that there will be significant input from anyone outside a relatively small circle of interests. Industry trade associations also use a variety of communication channels, such as facsimile machines, association newsletters, and magazines, to alert their members to important workshops. Only the most diligent of advocates can be expected to tap into the myriad of sources of information on the rulemaking process to track and keep up with the implementation of federal rules. For the most part, citizens seldom participate because these meetings and workshops are not well publicized.

The visibility of the rulemaking process is also affected by the timing in which it is conducted. An incumbent president, for example, might avoid announcing a controversial proposal on wetlands designations until after an election cycle has been completed. Similarly, the media and environmental organizations are usually preoccupied with holiday activities during the week between Christmas and New Year's Day—a period notorious for last-minute bureaucratic maneuvering. Just before President Reagan's second term was about to end in 1988, the administration published an announcement in the *Federal Register* that proposed to change policies regarding the strip mining of coal in national parks and wildlife refuges. The proposal appeared December 27—two days after Christmas—when only the most assiduous of observers would have paid much attention to it.

By removing an environmental issue from the legislative arena to the less visible and more difficult to track bureaucratic arena, organized interests can better control the debate. With its more extensive resources, industry has been able to do just that, employing policy analysts whose sole mission is to track rulemakings, hearings, and opportunities for public comment. Although the larger mainstream environmental organizations have begun to develop those capabilities, most grassroots groups do not have them and are reliant upon Washington, D.C.–based groups to do the tracking for them.

TAKING ADVANTAGE OF VAGUENESS

Although the practice is not unique to environmental policy, Congress often resorts to the strategy of intentionally making legislation vague. Conventional wisdom says that the more vague the legislative expression of goals, the greater the agency's ability to set regulatory policy. In addition, vagueness allows the environmental opposition to take advantage of delays and administrative discretion while regulators attempt to figure out what the statute means. By the time the definitions are sorted out, a developer or company or farmer may have already completed a project with little government interference.

There are several reasons why legislation is written in vague terms. Sometimes, the subject matter of the legislation is so technically sophisticated that the members of Congress themselves have little choice but to leave the fine-tuning of the wording of a statute or regulation up to scientists and researchers more familiar with the subject matter. On other occasions, Congress has preferred to state its intentions in the form of goals rather than specifics. In the Clean Air Act Amendments of 1970, for example, the law simply mandated that the nation's air quality be improved to a condition not detrimental to human health—an admirable, if ambiguous, mandate. Other times, legislation is hurried through the procedural maze of lawmaking for purely political reasons, such as to meet a self-imposed deadline, a criticism voiced against some of the legislation that was produced as a result of the "Contract with America" in 1995–1996.

When Congress finds itself embroiled in a number of competing and overlapping legislative battles, one unfortunate consequence may be that a bill does not receive sufficient legislative scrutiny. For example, in 1976, Congress enacted the Resource Conservation and Recovery Act, giving the EPA substantial discretion and failing even to define "hazardous waste," in large part due to legislators' preoccupation with the Toxic Substances Control Act.[17] And sometimes, after especially contentious, time-consuming debate or markup sessions, legislators simply give in to the process, voting to enact a bill that in reality could have benefited from further debate and deliberation, as some believe happened with the 1990 Clean Air Act Amendments. President Bush's insistence that Congress come through with a bill as the keystone of his environmental program may have worn down members of Congress who had been grappling with reauthorization since 1977.[18]

One of the continuing battles over statutory vagueness involves the nation's wetlands. In the Federal Water Pollution Control Act Amendments of 1972, Congress included provisions that required anyone who altered the landscape of a wetland to first obtain a permit from the Army Corps of Engineers as a way of protecting ecologically sensitive areas. The key component of the measure was Section 404, which makes it unlawful to put dredged or fill material into navigable waters—the term "wetlands" was never actually used.

That changed in 1975 when a court ruled that the statute applied not only to rivers but also to wetlands that drain into rivers, so the race to define what Congress had intended began. Four agencies—the EPA, the Department of the Interior, the Department of Agriculture, and the Army Corps of Engineers—developed their own regulations and wetlands designations guides. The definitions also affected other laws, such as the 1985 food security bill known as "Swampbuster," which made farmers ineligible for federal assistance if they drained existing wetlands on their property.

An environmental opposition group called the National Wetlands Coalition (made up of real estate interests) brought the issue to the attention of President Bush, who asked his vice president, Dan Quayle, to study the definition problem under the aegis of the White House Council on Competitiveness. In August 1991, the group issued the *Federal Manual for Identifying and Delineating Jurisdictional Wetlands*. The proposal was met with heavy criticism by business and farm interests in the form of more than 80,000 formal comments. While Congress continued hearings on the definition, agencies charged with implementing the law continued trying to interpret what the statute meant. The Army Corps of Engineers used a 1987 version of a wetlands manual, the EPA and the USFWS used another developed in 1989, the Soil Conservation Service had its own slightly different criteria, and other federal agencies adopted the 1991 manual's proposed rules.[19]

The Clinton administration's struggle with the wetlands statute has continued to allow for wide discretionary interpretation, in part due to uncertainties that were never cleared up during the Bush administration. In 1992, a circuit court ruled in favor of a developer who had been fined $55,000 by the EPA because he had failed to obtain a permit from the Army Corps of Engineers to fill a small pond. The court ruled that the EPA did not have the authority to impose the fine because the pond was isolated and not interdependent with any other body of water. By 1993, the Army Corps of Engineers had gone back to using its 1987 wetlands delineation manual.

The 104th Congress used its Republican majority to take another stab at the wetlands issue in 1995. This time, the National Academy of Scientists was brought in to present the results of its two-year study that Congress had requested to help it understand the wetlands delineation controversy. But the new Republican leadership made it clear that the decision on how to interpret congressional intent would eventually be a political, rather than a scientific, decision.[20]

As a result, the environmental opposition has been able to sit back and watch while government agencies fight internal battles over intent and definition. Such strategies seldom require an industry to play the "bad guy" role because the turf struggles and politics of the bureaucracy make it easy for those opposed to environmental regulations to just sit back and watch the problem resolve itself. During the interim, life goes on.

PLAYING THE "ADVISORY" ROLE

Industry influence on the executive branch has frequently come in the form of its role as an informal or formal adviser to the president and the agencies under his direction.

President Reagan, for example, relied heavily upon a "kitchen cabinet" of business leaders for advice, especially Coloradan Joseph Coors, who provided input not only on environmental policy but on the president's appointments, including the controversial selection of James Watt as secretary of the interior.

But the president also has the power to establish ad hoc advisory committees to assist him in policy development. One of the first advisory groups, the National Petroleum Council, was established in 1946 to advise the Department of the Interior on oil and gas policies, and in subsequent years, on all aspects of energy policy. In 1971 and 1972, a task force of twenty-seven corporate representatives prepared a massive report on the relationship of environmental conservation to national energy needs, concluding that although the nation faced serious environmental problems, government should not go overboard and should consider the cost benefit to society and the impact of that factor upon the economy. A subsequent fourteen-volume report, *U.S. Energy Outlook,* was published in 1972 and served as the definitive source of information and policy recommendations for the next several years. More than 500 energy industry experts contributed to the document.[21]

In 1970, President Richard Nixon established the National Industrial Pollution Control Council (NIPCC) in Executive Order 11523 as a way of assisting business interests in coping with the onslaught of federal environmental laws typified by the National Environmental Policy Act. The group's purpose was to "advise on plans and actions of Federal, State, and local agencies involving environmental policy quality policies affecting industry which are referred to it by the Secretary [of Commerce] or by the Chairman of the Council on Environmental Quality."[22]

The NIPCC consisted of thirty subcouncils representing almost every segment of the polluting spectrum, from coal to poultry-rendering to steel manufacturers. In conjunction with the AMC, the Edison Electric Institute, and other trade associations, the NIPCC provided support for research on the economic impact of new pollution control legislation and developed a series of cost-impact studies that were widely circulated among government agencies, including the EPA. The NIPCC operated in secrecy, even though the media and environmental organizations pressured Commerce Secretary Maurice Stans to open up the group's meetings, which he refused to do.[23]

The group was disbanded in 1973 when environmental groups pressured Congress to rescind budget authority for the NIPCC, but during its brief tenure, its members paid a price to have access to the policy process. Federal Elections Commission and public interest group campaign reports found that NIPCC members had contributed

nearly three-quarters of a million dollars to President Nixon's reelection campaign in 1972; five NIPCC members were eventually investigated for their contributions, and four were convicted of violations of federal campaign contribution law. One of those contributors,
Orin Atkins, chairman of the board of Ashland Oil, explained:

> There was a good business reason for making the contribution and,
> although illegal in nature, I am confident that it distinctly benefit-
> ted the corporation . . . its intention was to give us a means of ac-
> cess to present our point of view to the executive branch of the
> Government.[24]

In their advisory capacity, business interests have a direct line of
access to decisionmakers, often at the very highest level. Although
some ad hoc advisory committees may also include representatives of
environmental organizations, their effectiveness in influencing policy
seldom matches that of industry. Because access can often be enhanced
in the form of campaign contributions from well-funded industry
PACs, individual contributors, and their families, business interests
may have a more impressive voice than environmental groups.

PROVIDING ORCHESTRATED COMMENTARY

As a part of the implementation process, virtually all environmental
statutes go through some form of public comment period. Proposed
changes in water quality standards, for example, are initially published in the *Federal Register,* with an announcement that includes the
specific dates of the comment period. Scheduling requirements to meet
legislative mandates often require short comment periods, and tight
deadlines may mean that the agency has likely already made up its
mind. The comment period, in such instances, may have little influence or may not lead to any change in direction.[25]

    This phase allows interested parties, environmental groups and in-
dustry alike, to provide the administering agency with feedback on the
regulatory mechanism and standards. As a general rule, the public
comment period is dominated by industry interests, whose influence is
measured in not only quality but quantity.

    In preparing the first round of its guidelines for the national am-
bient air quality standards called for in the 1970 Clean Air Act
Amendments, for example, the EPA allowed for an unusually short
ninety-day comment period, with fifty-one environmental and civic
interest groups submitting comments, while only thirty-eight commercial and industrial organizations submitted comments, indi-

cating, as one EPA official noted, that industry "hardly knew the Clean Air Act existed."[26]

Months later, when the EPA promulgated its implementation plan guidelines for the states, the situation had changed considerably. A total of 458 groups submitted comments, 400 of them representing industrial firms and trade associations. Many of the submissions were highly technical, ranging up to 250 pages in length. This time, the NIPCC had orchestrated the comment effort, guaranteeing that the submissions represented a broad spectrum of interests.[27]

Although environmental groups often complain that such orchestrations are undemocratic because they rarely represent grassroots public opinion, the tactic is available to anyone who chooses to use it. Today, specialized computer software and the services of a lobbying firm can allow an organized interest to make its voice heard as never before. An individual can call an 800 telephone number, give her or his name, address, and zip code to a recorded voice, and in less than a minute at no cost, a letter will be sent to the individual's congressional representative or senator, or to an agency dealing with an issue or regulation.[28]

Members of Congress or agencies that are truly interested in obtaining public input on an issue do not necessarily rely upon form letters or comments submitted at rulemakings that are identically worded, but the sheer quantity of commentary may indicate the strength of a group's efforts to influence the implementation of a statute or the intensity of feelings about it.

BRINGING IN THE EXPERTS

Another of the ways in which business interests affect the implementation phase of environmental legislation is through their use of technical expertise. During the early history of the new regulatory agencies, administrators realized that they needed their own in-house teams to evaluate environmental problems and to provide the agency with independent, neutral information. At the EPA, this meant the creation of a separate research arm for the agency.[29]

But as mentioned previously, political pressures often affect an agency's operations, and during the Reagan administration's process of limiting regulatory impacts on businesses, research budgets were often the first to be reduced. At the EPA, for example, the agency's overall operating budget was cut by 29 percent from 1981 to 1983, with its research budget cut by 46 percent, forcing the agency staff to become more reliant upon industry for information.[30] At the same time, the administration coupled the budget cuts with a federal hiring

160

BUSINESS GETS ORGANIZED

freeze, making it difficult to recruit or replace critical personnel. The position of assistant administrator for research and development, for instance, went unfilled on a permanent basis during this period.

In setting the new source performance standards as part of the 1970 Clean Air Act Amendments, the EPA faced the task of setting regulations for five industrial categories, a responsibility that placed the policy debate in the hands of industrial engineers. As a result, only five environmental groups participated in the process, with only the Sierra Club and the Natural Resources Defense Council providing any technical recommendations, which one observer termed "relatively simplistic." The Conservation Foundation called for tough standards but admitted, "We do not possess the technical competence to discuss in detail the standards themselves or the specified testing procedures: we therefore confine our comments chiefly to administrative procedures and to the general principles."[31]

At other times, industry has been able to capitalize on the lack of scientific consensus on an issue to promote its own agenda. When the EPA first promulgated its six National Ambient Air Quality Standards in 1971, for instance, there was little scientific knowledge about the effects of long-term exposure to low levels of pollution. Most of the research up until that time had been conducted in a laboratory setting, and generally with animals rather than people as the subjects of the experimentation. Thus, when industry researchers presented what appeared to be scientifically valid reasons for lowering the exposure standards in light of inconsistent scientific data, they were successful. Similar controversies have erupted over the issues of pesticide exposure, hazardous waste, and global climate change.

ALTERING THE ARENA

One way in which business interests have been able to manipulate the policy process using the bureaucracy stems from the very nature of the executive branch. The fragmentation of responsibility for environmental problem solving provides numerous contact points where organized interests can attempt to influence policy outcomes.

More than twenty federal agencies have some measure of control or jurisdiction over environmental policy within the fourteen cabinet-level departments, from the Agriculture Stabilization and Conservation Service within the Department of Agriculture, to the Federal Aviation Administration within the Department of Transportation. Various commissions and independent regulatory agencies also make environmental rules, such as the Nuclear Regulatory Commission and the Federal Trade Commission. The powers of those agencies and commissions are widely dispersed from a geographical standpoint. At the federal level, for example, the more than 3 million employees who work for the government are not concentrated in Washington, D.C.; seven out of every eight work outside the capital.[32]

One of the classic examples of how industry has chosen to attack environmental legislation from another access point is through relatively obscure bodies created by executive order. In 1981, President Reagan established the Task Force on Regulatory Relief to provide industry interests with a way to circumvent laws and regulations perceived as being too intrusive or costly to business. President Bush appointed a similar group in 1989, with Vice President Dan Quayle heading the Council on Competitiveness, also known as the Quayle Council. The group, which operated in secret, began reviewing dozens of environmental statutes that had been approved by Congress or the EPA and, in an effort "to reduce the regulatory burden on the free enterprise system," quashed their implementation. It rejected one EPA rule that would have required that recyclable items be separated from trash before burning and another that would have prohibited the incineration of lead batteries. Congressional representative Henry Waxman of California once accused the members of "helping polluters block EPA's efforts," and the Sierra Club called the council (disbanded by President Clinton when he took office) "a pipeline into the federal regulatory apparatus for corporate interests."[33]

The Department of the Interior and the Environmental Protection Agency play the key roles in the policy process, and certainly those two bureaus are the traditional focus of most of the attempts to influence the implementation of environmental regulations. However, much of the policymaking process involving the EPA is made even more complex because it usually issues regulations and then looks to the states for the implementation of its rules. In the case of hazardous waste, for example, states have considerable discretion in their site cleanup activities, and this allows industry another contact point in deciding where to fight the bureaucratic battle.

Because the states have their own layers of bureaucracy—usually specific to individual issues like air or water quality—there are hundreds more access points or arenas in which to pursue or oppose environmental policymaking. The end run can continue even further down the political pyramid as well. State agencies work with a variety of city and regional bodies that also administer and regulate environmental laws.

In California, for example, the implementation of federal clean air act laws is split between CARB, which regulates mobile sources like trucks and automobiles, and a host of regional air quality agencies, which regulate stationary sources like utilities and dry cleaners. The regional agencies (which exist in those areas of the state that are not in compliance with federal ambient air quality standards) draw up half of the state's implementation plan (SIP), which shows how it will attempt to comply with the federal law; CARB draws up and eventually approves the SIP in conjunction with applicable state agencies. In order to coordinate the various resource and pollution agencies, the state was forced to create the California Environmental Protection Agency in 1991.

This allows an opponent of a particular portion of the SIP, such as regulations on the amount of volatile organic compounds used in paints and other solvents, to attack through the regional air quality agencies. At some point in time, the opponent might argue that it is necessary, from an economic standpoint (like production costs to comply), for the state to insist upon some form of consistency or standardization of the rules.

An example of the way in which industry takes advantage of the end run strategy occurred in 1996, when CARB repealed a state legislative mandate that had required automakers to make available for sale 160,000 zero emission (exhaust-free) cars through the year 2002, starting with 20,000 in the 1998 model year. The law had originally been intended to force the "Big Seven" automotive companies (GMC, Ford, Chrysler, Toyota, Honda, Mazda, and Nissan) to step up design and production of electric vehicles as one solution to the state's smog problem.

But industry lobbyists conducted a uniform, cohesive, and well-funded campaign against the quota system, arguing that current technology would make the price of cars too expensive and that existing battery ranges would limit the electric cars' utility for most Californians. Eventually, they agreed to a plan whereby the companies would have 14,000 electric cars available by 1998, although they are free to set the actual volume of electric cars they produce each year and those plans can be kept secret. The only part of the original legislation left intact after the CARB negotiations was a requirement that by 2003, 10 percent of all vehicles offered for sale, or about 100,000 cars, must produce zero emissions.

Environmental organizations criticized not only the orchestrated lobbying effort itself, but also the result: a voluntary production agreement between automakers and state air quality officials that observers complain has no penalties if quotas are not met and that they fear will result in a request for another reprieve by automakers as the 2003 deadline approaches. But the industry was successful in convincing the board's members that the legislation was ill conceived, marking the first time in three decades that an air quality regulation had been rescinded. Automakers were effective not by appealing to the highly partisan and contentious state legislature, but by working closely with the more technically inclined staff and board members of CARB—a classic bureaucratic end run.

The beneficiary of this complicated network of agencies and rule-making bodies is usually industry rather than environmental groups. Most companies are accomplished, either through their own resources or through trade associations to which they belong, at monitoring administrative law. Those that cannot do so find themselves playing catch-up as the bureaucratic wheels turn with or without them.

DELAY AND SUE

When these previously mentioned strategies appear to be failing, industry and environmental groups alike proceed to two more tactics: taking advantage of the slow nature of the bureaucracy to delay implementation, or filing suit against the agency to force compliance or to gain exemptions.

Sometimes the delays inherent in implementation are not intentional or controlled by organized interests. In the case of the 700-page-long 1990 Clean Air Act Amendments, for example, the EPA was given only two years to complete 150 regulatory activities, including 100 rulemakings—an unheard of time frame for any agency. To place that task in perspective, consider that, in the past, the EPA issued seven or eight major regulations *per year* on all phases of environmental law—from pesticide rules to water pollution.[34]

In the case of the Resource Conservation and Recovery Act, enacted in 1976, the EPA took four years to implement the first set of rules under the legislation. State governments were concurrently holding their own rulemaking sessions, or waited until federal funds for implementation of the law were made available.[35] This lengthy rulemaking period gives industry sufficient time to muster its defenses, do the necessary research, and present a unified front in its efforts to derail the implementation of the law.

Prior to the passage of NEPA in 1969, the courts were most often used to adjudicate disputes between a single polluting company and an affected citizenry. But as the regulatory framework expanded under new legislation, the courts became more likely to review agency rules, and industry found it necessary to fight back in a more cohesive and activist manner.[36] As a result, most companies now maintain their own internal legal staffs, in addition to hiring outside firms to litigate specific cases.

Along with the scientific and policy expertise business interests needed to counter environmental groups, they somewhat belatedly realized the need for legal assistance that transcended a particular segment of industry. These legal support groups have assisted industry attorneys in fighting the regulatory battles and, more recently, in handling individual citizen suits against the government in the form of conservative public interest law firms. Today, more than twenty-five of the firms are actively pursuing litigation under the umbrella group the National Legal Center for the Public Interest. Most of them are regionally based, such as the Mid-Atlantic Legal Foundation and the Mid-America Legal Foundation, and each functions independently. Generally, they operate with a small staff of a dozen or so attorneys, leveraging their influence with large, for-profit firms.

The legal support groups did not start out as the litigation arm of industry or the property rights movement. They have been described as the ideological mates of the conservative Republicans who took over in the 1994 congressional elections, on the side of whites, men, and property owners who they say are victims of liberal orthodoxy. They have been modeled after the National Association for the Advancement of Colored People's Legal Defense Fund and the American Civil Liberties Union, although those organizations cringe at the comparison. As an attorney for one of the conservative public interest firms characterized his role, "I look upon us as bearers of the torch of the civil rights movement. I see us as successors to Martin Luther King and Thurgood Marshall."[37]

The first legal support group to be established was the Pacific Legal Foundation (PLF) in 1973, headquartered in Sacramento, California, but with branch offices in other states. Founded as part of a direct assault on the growing number of public interest law firms, PLF began its efforts by challenging the legality of environmental impact reports and the use of the chemical DDT. The foundation was organized by the California Chamber of Commerce and became the model for similar efforts throughout the country.

Although it was founded three years after the PLF, the Mountain States Legal Foundation (MSLF) became a well-established fixture during the Reagan administration because of the influence of Colorado brewer Joseph Coors, who served as a member of the president's "kitchen cabinet" of advisers. The MSLF is distinguished by a long line of conservative leaders, many of whom went on to serve in various agencies within the Reagan and Bush administrations. Its founding president, James Watt, was named secretary of the interior under Reagan, and its officers have included former governor of Washington Dixie Lee Ray and former U.S. senator James McClure. Watt's tenure as president came about because of his affiliation with Coors, who knew him from conservative political circles. MSLF president William Perry Pendley served under Watt as assistant secretary for energy and minerals.

The foundation's first case involved Ferrol G. Barlow of Pocatello, Idaho, who refused to allow health and safety inspectors into his small plumbing business without a search warrant. The case eventually wound its way through the legal system to the U.S. Supreme Court, where Barlow won on a 5:3 decision that became a symbolic victory against federal regulation. Although MSLF's participation had involved only filing an amicus brief with the Court, Watt used the case to exemplify the foundation's motto, "In the Courts for Good, Defending Individual Rights and Sound Economic Growth."[38]

The environmental movement's chief criticism of these legal foundations has been their nonprofit status. Tulane University law professor Oliver Houck studied the charitable activities of the law firms in 1984 and reported that many of the legal cases filed by groups like the PLF and the MSLF did not meet IRS criteria for nonprofit status.[39]

The resurgence of the property rights movement has rekindled interest in the legal support groups because many of those fighting government regulations are truly unable to afford assistance with their litigation. The complexity of property rights law and takings clauses outlined later in this book limits their access to only a few practitioners and firms.

One of the newer litigation and legal studies groups is the Constitutional Law Center (CLC), established in 1994 as an expansion of the wise use group Stewards of the Range. Unlike many of the other legal support groups, the CLC has primarily focused its efforts thus far on a single case, that of rancher Wayne Hage, the plaintiff in the property rights case *Hage v. United States*. Attorney Mark Pollot, a former Reagan administration official, is the lead attorney on the case and director of the CLC, which also hopes to train attorneys in property and constitutional rights and carry out public information and media education programs.

WHERE NEXT?

There is an ongoing debate among researchers who study environmental politics as to which arena best serves the interests of the public in making environmental policy. Recently, they have focused attention on the states.[40] The argument is that the states represent the single most important access point for both those supporting and those opposing environmental policy because it is the state agencies that decide how many resources to devote to the implementation of the law.[41] A state, for example, that is unwilling to spend money on enforcement of federal Clean Water Act regulations simply declines to do so, and there is often little that federal regulators can do about the situation. As a result, the commitment of various states to environmental protection varies considerably.

Some businesses argue that they use the bureaucracy to their advantage in this way, locating their factories in those states with poor reputations for environmental regulation. Others note that states like California, which is infamous for establishing air quality standards that are more strict than those at the federal level, have developed an antibusiness reputation that has hurt potential economic development.

Certainly there are costs and benefits to consider regardless of what venue an interest chooses. Lobbying against the implementation of quotas for electric cars in California, for example, certainly was cheaper from a financial standpoint for the automotive industry than fighting a citizen initiative developed by environmental organizations might have been. In the California situation, the auto manufacturers chose to bring in technical experts who were able to work closely with and convince a small number of individuals, rather than attempting to implement a public relations effort to fight for electoral success, or to mediate partisan differences in the state's legislature. Since CARB's members are nonpartisan and not elected, however, there was no opportunity to try to influence their decision by making political campaign contributions to them. The board's decision to accept the automakers' claims would have to be made on the merits of their case and other political influences, not on the basis of money funneled into an election effort.

But in many cases, by waiting until the implementation phase of the policy process, groups also take the chance that this last-resort venue may work against their interests. Had the automakers been unsuccessful before CARB, they might have been forced to return to the legislative arena to convince the members of that body that their original statute had been written too vaguely or that it was unfeasible to comply with during a period of economic stress on the state. That strategy would have taken longer, would have probably forced the companies to contribute heavily to political campaigns as a way of gaining access to individual legislators, and would have been much more visible an effort than CARB's relatively insulated hearings and meetings. To resort to legal action would have been extremely time consuming (although it might have stalled the proposed quotas), expensive to litigate, and still might not have provided the hoped-for result.

These are the factors that make the bureaucratic end run so attractive to the environmental opposition, especially to the industry segment that has the technical expertise to go one-on-one with administrative specialists. It is a tactic that many environmental groups are now learning to exploit as well, but it is in this political venue that they are playing catch-up to industry interests.

NOTES

1. For an overview of the regulatory explosion, see Kenneth J. Meier, *Regulation: Politics, Bureaucracy, and Economics* (New York, St. Martin's, 1985).

2. Eric Redman, *The Dance of Legislation* (New York: Simon and Schuster, 1973).

3. T. R. Reid, *Congressional Odyssey* (New York: W. H. Freeman Co., 1980).

4. Daniel P. Franklin, *Making Ends Meet* (Washington, DC: Congressional Quarterly Press, 1992).

5. Jeffrey Birnbaum and Alan Murray, *Showdown at Gucci Gulch* (New York: Random House, 1987).

6. Charles O. Jones, *Clean Air: The Policies and Politics of Pollution Control* (Pittsburgh, PA: University of Pittsburgh Press, 1975).

7. Bernard Asbell, *The Senate Nobody Knows* (New York: Doubleday, 1978).

8. See Richard E. Cohen, *Washington at Work: Back Rooms and Clean Air* (New York: Macmillan, 1992); and Gary C. Bryner, *Blue Skies, Green Politics*, 2nd ed. (Washington, DC: Congressional Quarterly Press, 1996).

9. See Charles E. Davis, *The Politics of Hazardous Waste* (Englewood Cliffs, NJ: Prentice Hall, 1993).

10. Cohen, *Washington at Work*, p. 7.

11. The seminal work on the subject is Jeffrey Pressman and Aaron Wildavsky, *Implementation* (Berkeley: University of California Press, 1984).

12. See, for example, Samuel P. Huntington, "The Marasmus of the ICC," *Yale Law Journal*, vol. 61 (April 1952): 467–509; and Marver H. Bernstein, *Regulating Business by Independent Commission* (Princeton, NJ: Princeton University Press, 1955).

13. See Paul Quirk, *Industry Influence in Federal Regulatory Agencies* (Princeton, NJ: Princeton University Press, 1981).

14. Richard H. K. Vietor, *Environmental Politics and the Coal Coalition* (College Station, TX: Texas A & M University Press, 1980), p. 10.

15. Meier, *Regulation*, pp. 19–22.

16. See Vietor's description of the coal lobby's efforts to influence the implementation of the Clean Air Act Amendments of 1970 (in *Environmental Politics*).

17. Charles E. Davis, *The Politics of Hazardous Waste* (Englewood Cliffs, NJ: Prentice Hall, 1993), p. 77.

18. For a more detailed analysis of how legislators approached the 1990 law, see the perspectives of both Bryner (*Blue Skies*) and Cohen (*Washington at Work*).

19. See Jon Kusler, "Wetlands Delineation: An Issue of Science or Politics?" *Environment*, vol. 34, no. 2 (March 1992): 7–11, 29–37. See also Stephen M. Johnson, "Federal Regulation of Isolated Wetlands," *Environmental Law*, vol. 23, no. 1 (1993): 1; and John G. Miniter, "Muddy Waters: The Quagmire of Wetlands Regulation," *Policy Review*, vol. 56 (spring 1991): 75–76.

20. John H. Cushman Jr., "House and Science Panels Clash on Wetlands' Fate," *New York Times*, April 7, 1995, p. A30.

21. Vietor, *Environmental Politics*, pp. 55–56.

22. Executive Order 11523, Senate Subcommittee on Intergovernmental Relations, *Hearings on Advisory Committees*, 91st Cong., 2nd sess., December 1970, pp. 501–502.

23. Vietor, *Environmental Politics*, pp. 51–54.

24. Ibid., pp. 54–55.

25. Henry V. Nickel, "Now, the Rush to Regulate," *Environmental Forum*, vol. 8, no. 1 (January–February 1991): 19.

26. Vietor, *Environmental Politics*, pp. 161–165.

27. Ibid., pp. 169–170.

28. Jane Fritsch, "A Free Phone Call Away," *New York Times*, June 23, 1995, p. A1.

29. See J. Clarence Davies and Barbara S. Davies, *The Politics of Pollution*, 2nd ed. (Indianapolis, IN: Pegasus, 1975).

30. Dick Kirschten, "Ruckelshaus May Find EPA's Problems Are Budgetary as Much as Political," *National Journal*, March 26, 1983, pp. 659–660.

31. Vietor, *Environmental Politics*, pp. 179–180.

32. For an overview of the fragmentation of the executive branch, see Kenneth J. Meier, *Politics and Bureaucracy: Policymaking in the Fourth Branch of Government*, 2nd ed. (Monterey, CA: Brooks/Cole, 1987).

33. "Industry's Friend in High Places," *Sierra*, vol. 76, no. 5 (September–October, 1991): 42. See also "Quailing over Clean Air," *Environment*, vol. 33, no. 2 (July–August 1991): 24.

34. Jacqueline Vaughn Switzer, *Environmental Politics: Domestic and Global Dimensions* (New York: St. Martin's, 1994), p. 55.

35. See Joseph Petulla, *Environmental Protection in the United States* (San Francisco: San Francisco Study Center, 1987), pp. 98–99.

36. See Frederick R. Anderson, *NEPA in the Courts* (Baltimore, MD: Johns Hopkins University Press, 1973); Werner F. Grunbaum, *Judicial Policymaking: The Supreme Court and Environmental Quality* (Morristown, NJ: General Learning Press, 1976); Lettie M. Wenner, *The Environmental Decade in Court* (Bloomington: Indiana University Press, 1982), and R. Shep Melnick, *Regulation and the Courts: The Case of the Clean Air Act* (Washington, DC: Brookings Institution, 1983).

37. Richard Perez-Pena, "A Rights Movement That Emerges from the Right," *New York Times*, December 30, 1994, p. B6.

38. Ron Wolf, "New Voice in the Wilderness," *Rocky Mountain Magazine* (March–April 1981): 33.

39. Oliver A. Houck, "With Charity for All," *Yale Law Journal* (July 1984): 1419–1563.

40. See, for example, Barry G. Rabe, *Fragmentation and Integration in State Environmental Management* (Washington, DC: Conservation Foundation, 1986); Elizabeth Haskell, "State Governments Tackle Pollution," in *Managing the Environment* (Washington, DC: U.S. Environmental Protection Agency, 1973); James P. Lester, "A New Federalism?" in Norman J. Vig and Michael E. Kraft, eds., *Environmental Policy in the 1990s* (Washington, DC: Congressional Quarterly Press, 1990), pp. 59–79; and Edward Laverty, "Legacy of the 1980s in State Environmental Administration," in Michael S. Hamilton, ed., *Regulatory Federalism, Natural Resources, and Environmental Management* (Washington, DC: American Society for Public Administration, 1990), pp. 68–70.

41. See, for example, Christopher Duerksen, *Environmental Regulation of Industrial Plant Siting* (Washington, DC: Conservation Foundation, 1983).

PART III

THE WAR AT
THE GRASSROOTS

7

The Sagebrush Rebellion

SIGN OF THE TIMES: In 1979, the Nevada state legislature enacted A.B. 413, the first of several state and federal legislative efforts that became the basis for the Sagebrush Rebellion. Among the provisions of the bill were the following:

Section 2. The legislature finds that . . .

4. *The intent of the framers of the Constitution of the United States was to guarantee to each of the states sovereignty over all matters within its boundaries except for those powers specifically granted to the United States as agent of the states.*
5. *The attempted imposition upon the State of Nevada by the Congress of the United States of a requirement in the enabling act that Nevada "disclaim all right and title to the unappropriated public lands lying within said territory," as a condition precedent to acceptance of Nevada into the Union, was an act beyond the power of the Congress of the United States and is thus void.*
6. *The purported right of ownership and control of the public lands within the State of Nevada by the United States is without foundation and violates the clear intent of the Constitution of the United States.*
7. *The exercise of such dominion and control of the public lands within the State of Nevada by the United States works a severe, continuous and debilitating hardship upon the people of the State of Nevada.*

Although it has been argued that there have been several "Sagebrush Rebellions" in U.S. history,[1] the term, coined by Nevada journalist John Rice, is now usually applied to the organized opposition to federal lands policies that took place from 1978 to 1981. What makes this period in the evolution of environmental opposition so fascinating is that it mirrors so closely the issues and rhetoric of similar land use battles in the 1800s and late 1940s outlined in Chapter 1. The Sagebrush Rebellion also set the stage for the wise use, county supremacy, and property rights segments of the environmental opposition that formed in the following decade. This chapter examines the effectiveness of using state legislatures as venues for promoting the environmental opposition's policy agenda and how, in conjunction with congressional leaders, the Sagebrush rebels attempted to turn an essentially regional controversy into a national one.

The word "rebellion" may be somewhat misleading. The opposition to federal policies and to segments of the environmental movement developed over a period of about three years and to a large extent involved more political posturing and legislative declarations than the term might otherwise imply. The contemporary Sagebrush Rebellion resulted from a number of factors that occurred the 1960s and 1970s, including the growth of a well-organized and increasingly well-funded environmental movement, public sentiment that encouraged federal involvement in wilderness preservation, and a concerted effort by Congress to enact sweeping environmental legislation.

Against this backdrop was the deeper and recurring question of the overall role of the federal government in managing natural resources. Why it erupted again in the form of the Sagebrush Rebellion is the focus of this chapter, which outlines the issues and interests involved. The chapter concludes with an analysis of the reasons why the Sagebrush rebels failed to gain support for their proposals, and how their activism provided direction for the environmental opposition a decade later.

A QUESTION OF FEDERALISM

To what extent should decisions about the nation's natural resources be made at the federal level, or should those issues be decided exclusively at the state and local levels? This issue is but one of many that eventually ignited the first flames of the Sagebrush Rebellion in 1978. Three underlying questions are central to an understanding of the federal role in natural resource management: How much control over resource use decisions should be assigned to residents of the areas where the resource is located? What mix of environmental and developmental values should be used in making those decisions? To what degree should those decisions be made in the public or the private sector?[2]

During the Sagebrush Rebellion, the opponents of federal control focused their efforts on two specific legislative mandates, the 1964 Wilderness Act and the 1976 Federal Land Policy and Management Act. The Wilderness Act had been enacted as a part of the Kennedy administration's efforts to bolster its record on the environment, while the FLPMA's passage represented the unified force of the environmental lobby. The Wilderness Act designated lands to be set aside primarily for aesthetic and recreational use, and the FLPMA specified that the public lands were to be retained in federal ownership and gave the federal government the authority to administer the public lands in perpetuity. Together, the two bills effectively locked up the public lands from most extractive uses.

The environmental opposition also used constitutional interpretation as one of the foundations for the Sagebrush Rebellion. Although there is no basis for the argument within the Constitution itself, the Rebels relied upon what is known as the "equal footing" doctrine, which was first advanced in 1845 in the Alabama case *Pollard's Lessee v. Hagan*.[3] As was discussed in Chapter 1, for new states to be admitted to the Union, they had to renounce claims over public domain land within their territory, and agree to what would become known as the disclaimer clause: the preeminence of Congress that prohibited states from imposing taxes on federal property or interfering with the disposal of public lands. However, the rebels argued that the conditions that had been set up to govern the admission of new states were inherently unfair, and that the states were no longer equal as long as the federal government maintained dominant control over the land.[4] The rebels maintained that public lands must be "returned" to the states because when the thirteen original colonies were admitted to the Union, all the land within their borders belonged to the states because no federal estate had been created. Similar claims had been made during the early 1800s by Alabama, Indiana, Louisiana, and Missouri. As new states were admitted to the Union, the question of how much land would belong to the federal government and how much would be given to the states became highly politicized.

For example, Congress supported Nevada's statehood in 1864 under generous terms, initially granting the state nearly 4 million of its current total of 12 million state-owned acres even though it had a population of only 7,000 residents, much smaller than any other state admitted previously. Congressional Republicans, fearing that the presidential election that year might be decided in the House, added Nevada as an antislavery state to improve President Lincoln's chances of reelection. Today, the federal government manages nearly 54 million acres of Nevada's land, more than three quarters of the state. Arizona and New Mexico, admitted in 1912, received 12.8 and 10.5 million acres, respectively, while Alaska, admitted in 1959, received 103 million acres. In 1996, 35 percent of Arizona's 73 million acres was federally managed, 29 percent of New Mexico's 78 million acres, and 68 percent of Alaska's 365 million acres.[5]

The contemporary Sagebrush rebels argued that western states were not being treated equally because large portions of their lands were still under federal jurisdiction, thus redefining the dispute as a "states' rights" issue.[6] The debate was both legal and political, based on what supporters believed was solid constitutional ground and on the clearly partisan interests of livestock owners who wanted to maximize their control of the land. The distinction between ownership and sovereignty is crucial. The issue was centered on how lands should be managed; management is a prerogative attached to ownership. The states clearly have sovereignty over the people on the federal lands, but lacking ownership, it is argued, they cannot manage the lands.

A second legal issue that served as the basis for the rebellion was that the federal government was placed in a position of implied trust over the public lands, predicated on the property clause of the U.S. Constitution. The trust argument was interpreted to mean that those lands held in the public domain ought to be disposed of in an expeditious fashion, as the government had done during the nineteenth century with the Homestead Act and other similar legislative initiatives. This "public trust" theory, which had a somewhat stronger basis in the opinion of legal scholars than did the equal footing doctrine, was one of the rationales for the rebels' argument that the federal government return all lands to the states.

This reliance upon constitutional issues was a key element of the Sagebrush rebels' strategy and would continue to be used by other segments of the environmental opposition—especially the property rights and county supremacy movements—as a way of framing the debate over land use. This helped the rebels to take what some observers considered to be a political issue colored by self-interests into a different and less partisan venue of judicial and legal interpretation.

THE CARTER CONNECTION

Some observers believe that attempts were made in the late 1970s to reignite the debate over ownership and management of the federal lands that had last surfaced in the 1940s in part because of the federal government's attitudes toward the West under the administration of President Jimmy Carter. During his four years in office, Carter showed little interest in the environment and even less interest in the land west of the Rocky Mountains. He made only four trips to the region during his tenure and showed "the provincial ignorance of a southern man who never knew the West—ignorance of western concerns and western people, of the West itself."[7] This perception that the West was being ignored may have been responsible for the opening of a policy window because considerable attention had been paid to environmental issues under Presidents Nixon and Ford. After their administrations, both the public's attention and that of President Carter turned to other policy problems, such as the energy crisis and the taking of U.S. hostages in Iran. With Carter preoccupied with other issues, policy entrepreneurs within the Sagebrush Rebellion had an opportunity to advance their agenda in the region.

There were mixed feelings among westerners over Carter's unsuccessful proposal to construct 200 MX missiles by 1984 and to deploy them across the western desert. The MX was designed to replace the Minuteman missile as an important weapon in the nation's arsenal against Soviet attack. The project involved a complex system of nearly 5,000 horizontal shelters deployed throughout the Nevada-Utah basin, with the missiles constantly being shifted from one site to another to avoid detection. The project was estimated to cost between $33–$100 billion to build and a half billion to operate each year—three times greater than the cost of the Alaska pipeline.

The project would have radically changed the face of the western landscape. One part of the proposal called for deep basing the missile silos—a strategy that would have had an unknown impact on the region's environment. The need for skilled labor for such a massive program would have had other social consequences, as small western towns were tapped for the construction of the project. In the environmental impact statement for the project, Air Force Undersecretary Antonia Chayes said, "While the impacts may appear severe when viewed from the perspective of a little-developed area of the country, from a national perspective—and the MX is a national program—the impacts are not that large."[8]

Whereas some critics of the MX program were concerned about potential environmental impacts, there were also those whose interests were more focused on the benefits that massive federal defense expenditures would bring. Cecil Andrus, who served as secretary of the interior under Carter, was an Idahoan and clearly saw the potential economic value of the program. He would later serve as governor of Idaho—evidence that his association with Carter's policies and the MX program was not politically fatal.

The Carter administration's perceived indifference to western interests appears to have ignored the forces of public opinion. In a September 1981 poll taken just before President Reagan announced the missiles would not be deployed in the desert, 58 percent of the respondents interviewed in eight western states opposed the MX program being based in their backyards.[9] Those kinds of statistics explain why Jimmy Carter can accurately be described as one of the catalysts behind the Sagebrush Rebellion. The outpouring of sentiment was even more graphically demonstrated with the outcome of the 1980 election between Carter and Reagan. Reagan won twelve of the thirteen western states, losing only Hawaii.

ORGANIZING A REBELLION

By the late 1970s, the emotional energy that had powered previous rebellions had matured to the point where it coalesced into several well-
organized interest groups. Unlike prior efforts that had opposed federal land use policies against a somewhat undefined public interest
and disorganized environmental movement, this Sagebrush Rebellion
faced off against well-funded groups and the public opinion that supported them legislatively.

The unifying issue that would tie the rebels together was their previously articulated goal of having the remaining public lands under
federal control transferred to the states and, eventually, to private citizens. The Nevada legislature paved the way for the creation of the rebellion's major organizations after several committees and commissions studied the potential legal problems involved with the land
transfer in the 1960s and early 1970s. This led to an informal meeting in
1978 between conservative Arizona senator Barry Goldwater and former California attorney general John L. Harmer. Together they established the League for the Advancement of States Equal Rights (LASER).
The organization was designed to publicize the perceived excesses of
wilderness preservation groups seeking to tie up valuable grazing land
and mismanagement within the BLM.

The organization was formally incorporated in Utah in 1979 as a
tax-exempt organization whose stated aims were "charitable, educational, scientific, and the analyses of economic, social, environmental,
and legal problems relating to the western states." Individuals and
businesses were invited to join LASER if they were dedicated to the di-
vestiture of federal public lands, although it appears many of the
group's expenses were picked up by three large mining interests rather
than supplied through individual contributions.[10]

LASER had the advantage of bringing together not only the opposition leaders from each state, but also representatives of various commodity groups. At the organization's 1980 meeting in Salt Lake City,
Nevada representative James Santini held a formal hearing of his
House Subcommittee on Mines and Mining, bringing the group additional media coverage that it otherwise might not have been able to
generate on its own. But the organization faded from the political
scene soon after the Salt Lake City meeting, and LASER appeared to
have been abandoned by its political and financial backers.

At the regional level, efforts to unify rebellion sentiment behind a
common agenda frequently broke down because the coalitions represented so many different interests. For example, at its September 1979
meeting, the Western Coalition of Public Lands passed a resolution reaf-

firming strong support for the multiple use of public lands and pledged
to endorse federal Sagebrush Rebellion legislation only if it was amended
to ensure equitable treatment for county governments. That issue perme-
ated the group's regional meeting in Reno, along with issues like wilderness designations and withdrawals of public land.[11] Another regional
group, the Western Association of Land Users, targeted the BLM directly,
accusing the agency of "wiping us out. There isn't one thing that any of
us here uses that doesn't come from the land. We play on it, hunt deer,
fish, get lumber. They're denying us the right of our lifestyle."[12]

Instead of relying upon a national or regional lobbying strategy,
other organizations began forming to urge individual state legislators
to enact land transfer measures. In Nevada, the Public Lands Council,
comprised primarily of BLM grazing permit holders, convinced the
state legislature to appropriate $250,000 for a legal challenge to the fed-
eral government's jurisdiction over BLM lands. Support also came
from development interests that were convinced Nevada would suffer
economically if the land were not freed up. Regional organizations,
such as the Western Conference of the Council of State Governments
and the Association of Western State Land Commissioners, joined in to
endorse the legislative efforts.

The extractive resource industries supported the rebellion with
resolutions and moral support. In Utah, for example, former state legislator Calvin Black used his influence with the Utah Mining Association to convince the organization to pass a resolution in support of
the goals of the movement; he would later rely upon development and
grazing interests for further backing. But the rebels had considerable
difficulty in building cross-state coalitions because of the multiplicity
of players involved, many of which were more interested in their own
state's problems than in seeking a regional or national remedy.

The rebellion also received the support of the MSLF, which had
been created as part of a legal network designed to counter similar organizations within the environmental movement. The MSLF had the
support of Clifford Rock, a consultant for Joseph Coors of Colorado,
who had used his family's brewing company interests to form the National Center for the Public Interest. The foundation became a critical
link in the rebellion and in later property rights battles that followed
because it could litigate on behalf of its members, bringing the rebellion back into the judicial arena.

The MSLF started with a small budget (estimated at $194,000 in its
first year of operation) but grew substantially over the next five years
to $1.2 million in 1980. One of the reasons for the foundation's success
was its president, James Watt, who would later be named secretary of
the interior in the Reagan administration.[13]

THE REBELS AT THE STATEHOUSE

Following a traditional strategy in which organized interests will choose a political decisionmaking arena based on their perceptions of how successful they will be in that arena, the Sagebrush rebels began their attack on land use at the statehouse level.[14] The legal basis for their claim to the federal lands had been repudiated in 1976 in *Kleppe v. New Mexico,* and there appeared to be insufficient congressional interest to mount a purely political campaign in Washington, D.C. Many eastern members of Congress wondered what all the fuss was about and moved forward on their policy agenda to fight a battle oriented toward urban, rather than Sagebrush, issues.

Between 1979 and 1981, fifteen western states debated Sagebrush legislation that challenged the federal government's control over the public lands. Despite agreement on the states' goal, each state legislature appeared to have a different perspective on how to proceed. One reason why there were so many differences in approach was that the targets of anger varied from state to state. Similarly, there were profound differences on how each state's leaders approached the legislature, their resources, and the outcome of their efforts.

There was some sense of political unity at the statehouse level through the Western Governors Policy Office in Denver, which conducted several studies of the rebels' grievances. Director Philip Burgess argued that "wilderness designation and wildlife protection should not be accomplished at the cost of livestock and agricultural production, the traditional backbone of our western economy."[15] But Burgess's views and his desire to present a united western front were lost among state leaders whose grievances against the federal government reflected decades of unresolved hostility and bitterness. Not surprisingly, the most thinly populated states were at the forefront of the rebellion, indicating that the movement was strongest in areas where a limited number of individuals had the most to gain. The Sagebrush Rebellion was also the most organized in states where the federal government managed large tracts of land (Nevada, Utah, and Idaho) and where a less urban and diversified economy depended largely upon politically powerful livestock interests.

In comparing how the states approached Sagebrush legislation, Nevada has the longest history of efforts to secure federal lands, and that issue, more than any other, was the target of the rebels. In the 1960s, Nevada's legislature had agreed to request the federal Public Land Law Review Commission to consider federal land grants to the state. In the early 1970s, it set up a commission to consider means of deriving additional benefits for the state from the land; and in 1979, the legislature claimed BLM lands as state property. Between 1979 and

1981, the Nevada legislature passed seven Sagebrush Rebellion bills; the most prominent of the bills was passed in 1979 on a vote of 38:1 in the lower house and 17:3 in the upper house, evidence of a political cohesiveness unmatched anywhere else in the country.[16]

Under the leadership of Nevada assembly member Dean Rhoads, the coalition of support brought together urban Las Vegas and Reno interests with residents concerned about a federal proposal to place MX missile sites in the state. In 1979, the state took on the BLM, filing suit to force the agency to remove the increasingly destructive wild horses from valuable cattle rangeland. Other conservatives simply sought more autonomy over land use decisions, especially intensified development in a state that had few other resources to draw upon in comparison to its western neighbors.

Although the state legislature was almost unanimous in its support for the rebellion, among the four legislators who voted against the bill was state senator Clifton Young, who argued that the state would forfeit $20 million annually in federal grants. He dismissed the Sagebrush Rebellion as "a combination of demagoguery, avarice and animosity and a handy way of venting spleen against the hated Feds."[17]

The majority of the other states that supported bills similar to Nevada's were those wherein the opposition could count on the support of citizens angered by almost every federal regulation in existence. Wyoming's state legislature got the ball rolling by defying the federal 55-mile-per-hour speed limit that had been implemented as a result of the Arab oil embargo. The state legislature had long accused the federal government of land-grabbing, and the state's citizens had a formidable ally in the National Inholders Association, a segment of the property rights movement that became an influential segment of the environmental opposition. Private citizens who owned property in Grand Teton National Park accused the NPS, the USFWS, and the USFS of restricting their ability to improve their lands. The property owners were joined by representatives of the coal industry, who were engaged in a protracted battle against the Office of Surface Management (OSM). The state's coal miners argued that OSM's complex regulations were designed for the industry's operations in Appalachia, not the West, and that its unreasonable limitations and exclusions were driving smaller operators out of business.

Idaho's Sagebrush rebels saw the BLM's restrictions on grazing lands as the key issue in their battle with the federal government. In one instance, the BLM took two years to prepare an environmental impact statement for the state's Magic Valley area and then gave the public only forty-five days to respond, which ranchers perceived as a continuation of the government's cavalier attitude toward time. In the meantime, ranchers were in limbo over whether or not their grazing rights would be further limited. In comparison, Montana had the potential of becoming one of the states leading the rebellion in 1979 over the issue of states' rights and the siting of a Montana Power line route. But there was insufficient legislative support, and the issue disappeared.

The Utah statehouse chose to focus its battle with the federal government on efforts by the USFWS to set aside 35 square miles of grazing lands as protected habitat for the desert tortoise, an endangered species, with 62 acres for each of the 400 reptiles remaining. The BLM ordered grazing to be reduced in the area, where one rancher bitterly complained, "Cattle have brought a lot more money into the county than tortoises ever have."[18] Utah's legislature was among those of three states that passed one of the original rebellion bills in 1980 during a time when the movement had its most successful legislative momentum. The measure, similar to Nevada's bill, was evidence of state-level support for similar legislation introduced by the state's congressional delegation. The Utah legislature also increased its appropriation to the state attorney general's office to handle public land litigation.

Colorado's expression of Sagebrush angst came from several sources. Unlike many of the other areas in the rural West where air pollution was not a major issue, the city of Denver failed to meet federal air quality standards in 1979. The Environmental Protection Agency threatened to withhold $300 million in federal highway and sewage treatment funds from the state if Colorado failed to come up with an adequate pollution control plan. The sanctions—included as a part of the federal Clean Air Act—raised the ire of the state legislature, whose members denounced the federal government's threats. Robert Burford, who served as speaker of the Colorado house before becoming head of the BLM and marrying EPA administrator Anne Gorsuch, said, "The real issue is not just the imposition of sanctions . . . the real issue is the right of the people of Colorado to live under the laws they want to live under."[19]

On the issue of turning over federal lands to the states, one of the few governors to openly oppose the Sagebrush Rebellion, Governor Richard Lamm of Colorado, questioned whether his state had the resources necessary to manage 14 million acres of national forests and 8 million acres of land controlled by the BLM. Despite these concerns, the state filed an administrative claim to 10,000 acres of oil-rich BLM land in 1979, arguing that the state had the right to choose which land it would receive under inaccurate conveyances when Colorado was admitted as a state.[20] The state legislature passed a Nevada-style bill in 1981, but Lamm later vetoed his state's Sagebrush legislation, virtually ending further support for the Sagebrush rebels in Colorado.

In several other states, Sagebrush legislation had public backing but little or no political support from elected officials. For example,

New Mexico's 1980 Sagebrush legislation had support from both houses of its legislature, but not from the state's governor. In California, supporters called for further study of the state's BLM lands by the State Land Commission. The measure was highly partisan, and although it passed both houses in 1981, its fate was sealed when nearly 70 percent of the legislature's Democrats voted in opposition and it was vetoed by the state's Democratic governor, Jerry Brown.

Washington State initially had the strongest bipartisan support for a rebellion bill of any of those considering such measures, enacting a bill that called for the transfer of BLM lands (which made up only 1 percent of the state's land) to the state. Yet despite the bill's passage by a vote of 90:7 in the lower house and 42:1 in the upper house, the measure was later overturned by a 60 percent no vote in a statewide referendum. One reason may have been that Washington State did not have large areas of unappropriated public lands managed by the Department of the Interior.

A similar situation existed in Arizona. Governor Bruce Babbitt's was among the more moderate voices raised in the rebellion, and his animosity was directed not so much at the issue of property rights as it was toward his resentment of the Washington, D.C., bureaucracy he would later come to lead as secretary of the interior in the Clinton administration. He argued against federal control and deplored the fact that "land use for 70 percent of Arizona's surface area is planned on C Street in Washington."[21] When the state legislature passed a rebellion bill in 1980 patterned after the Nevada law, it was vetoed by the governor, so the legislature passed a second bill overriding the governor's veto—a measure later sustained in a voter referendum.

Support for the Sagebrush Rebellion was much more limited in the remaining states that were counted on as part of the rebellion. In Oregon in 1979, Sagebrush bills that would have declared title to all public lands to be vested in and managed by the state were introduced into the state's part-time biennial legislature but died in committee. Another measure was introduced in 1981 as the movement's momentum was fading, which would have established a commission to consider reduction of federal landholdings within the state. The measure failed in the state's lower house and was never even considered in the state senate. Although Alaska, Hawaii, and North Dakota considered themselves part of the West, their physical distance from the Sagebrush rebels limited their participation. All three states' legislatures managed to enact resolutions of support for the movement, but they added little else to the effort.

Alaska was a somewhat reluctant participant in the Sagebrush Rebellion, even though President Carter had used the Antiquities Act of 1906 to reserve more than 56 million acres of public domain for national

monuments within the state. One bill, H.B. 53, appropriated $2 million
to the governor's office to finance the state's lobbying efforts in Washington, D.C., to undo federal withdrawal of Alaska lands. In 1982, after
most of the Sagebrush rebels had folded up their tents, Alaska voters
overwhelmingly passed their own "Tundra Rebellion" legislation that
asserted a claim to portions of BLM land in their state, but it had little
impact on a movement that had already passed them by.

One report on Alaska's role may have overestimated the state's
clout:

> Alaska can mortally injure the Sagebrush movement if it chooses not
> to participate. Alaska's problems with federal land management poli-
> cies are far more serious than those of most western states and in fact,
> may be the most serious of all. If Alaska chooses to sit on the side-
> lines, it will set a precedent that fence-straddling western legislatures
> may follow, thus leaving Nevada and perhaps one or two others car-
> rying the fray alone.[22]

Why were the states unable to unite behind a single front, since so
many of these issues appear to have overlapped? One comparison of the
Sagebrush legislation found marked differences between supporters
and opponents on various issues within each state. Republicans overwhelmingly supported land transfers to the states, although there was
some support among rural Democrats. Legislators who were ranchers or
farmers were supportive; Sagebrush legislation was opposed by representatives whose districts included Native Americans or concentrations
of urban minorities.[23] Another study found support strongest in those
states with strong grazing lobbies and large concentrations of BLM land,
with less apparent support in states with mostly USFS land.[24]

In an early version of what would later become the fight over unfunded mandates, unexpected opposition came from those governors
who were farsighted enough to realize that land transfers would increase
the cost of land management. Rural westerners began to wonder if there
was any benefit in exchanging a federal landlord for a state or local one,
with little support for corporate ownership that might lock up the land
even more.[25] As a result, there was insufficient agreement among the
states to keep the rebellion going for very long. A single battle in one state
like Nevada could not sustain the momentum the movement needed.

THE SAGEBRUSH REBELLION GOES TO WASHINGTON

Once the rebels transferred their efforts from the state legislatures to
Washington, D.C., their lobbying efforts seemed like Sagebrush Rebellion déjà vu. As Chapter 1 noted, the strategies used by the various or-

ganizations duplicated what they had tried to do in the 1940s, with only the names of the players changing.

The western members of the Senate Appropriations Committee and the Committee on Energy and Natural Resources attempted to do in 1979 what Senator McCarran and his allies in Congress had tried to do in 1947: take the issue to the public in hopes of building a groundswell of support for the transfer of public lands.

Six senators led the charge in their own states: Harrison Schmitt and Pete Domenici of New Mexico, Jake Garn and Orrin Hatch of Utah, Paul Laxalt of Nevada, and James McClure of Idaho. Orrin Hatch introduced the first federal Sagebrush legislation in 1979, becoming the de facto national spokesperson for the rebellion. Two bills (S. 1680 and H.R. 5436), entitled the Western Lands Distribution and Regional Equalization Act and referred to as the Western Lands Act, proposed the transfer of 544 million acres of national forest and BLM lands to state ownership in thirteen states west of the 100th meridian within five years of passage. A commission in each state would be set up to administer the transfer program.

Hatch was joined by other senators who shared his desire to return the lands to the state legislatures and, eventually, to private citizens. Utah's other senator, Jake Garn, shared Hatch's religious beliefs and political conservatism. They both espoused the belief (sometimes attributed to Mormon conservatism) in antifederalism and the concept of using the land's resources for economic benefit. They were joined by Paul Laxalt, who had served as Nevada's governor and as manager of Ronald Reagan's presidential campaigns in 1976 and 1980. Schmitt had previously criticized the BLM; McClure was responding to a sizable livestock constituency in his state.

In addition to the three primary land use bills, several others were introduced that potentially would have moved the Sagebrush rebels closer to their political goals. Senator Laxalt sponsored S. 739, which would have amended the venue provisions of federal procedural law, which would then have given landowners more choice in deciding where to file a civil action. Two other bills, H.R. 463 and H.R. 2764, would have required the federal government to pay state and local governments an amount equivalent to the property taxes generated by federally owned land if it were privately owned.

The bills gave western members of Congress a potent political issue to take home to their constituents; hearings were held in Albuquerque, Las Cruces, and Farmington, New Mexico; in Cedar City, Utah; Reno, Nevada; and Hailey, Idaho. As had been the case in 1947, carefully orchestrated testimony at the hearings was provided by representatives of groups like the National Cattlemen's Association and the National Wool Growers Association.

The NPCA claimed that environmental organizations were not notified of the hearings and that many of their members learned about them only by accident. At the Albuquerque hearing, for example, five members of environmental organizations were recognized for testimony in comparison to twenty representatives of the livestock industry. At Senator Garn's hearing in Utah, of forty-three witnesses, only three represented environmental groups, and they were chided by the senator for their "erroneous views."[26]

But the senators were unable to convince enough of their colleagues to take up the issue. They were preaching to the choir at home, but no one else in Washington seemed to want to listen. The bill stalled in the Senate Energy and Natural Resources Committee despite support from powerful western senators who felt the legislation was, if nothing else, symbolic of the anger of their western constituents.

One of the other issues that the Sagebrush rebels brought to Washington was the addition of more public lands to the areas already designated as federal wilderness. In 1973, for example, more than 33 million acres of public lands had been included in the federal wilderness reserves—38 percent of the nation's total wilderness designations were in the West. In January 1980, the USFS recommended annexation of 15 million more acres, and in 1982, another 36 million acres. From the perspective of those who lived in the West, "zealous conservationists will pursue land acquisition virtually forever, using every legal tactic at their command, whether or not the government can afford it, whether or not the people want it."[27] In that sense, the Sagebrush Rebellion was as much a backlash to the environmental legislation enacted during the early 1970s as it was a specific reaction to President Carter's alleged antiwestern attitudes.

To counter the wilderness acquisition process, a different approach was taken by California's controversial senator S. I. Hayakawa. His bill, the RARE Review Act of 1981, would have forced the federal government to make brisk decisions on areas designated for wilderness; failure to make those designations would have automatically restored them to recreational use or further development. The bill was heavily supported by the mining and energy industries, along with the National Association of Manufacturers, the American Cattlemen's Association, and the Federal Timber Purchasers Association—all of whom saw the proposal as an expedient way of reopening lands that had been placed in reserve under previous administrations since the turn of the century.

OUT WITH A WHIMPER

Despite the limited success of the state legislation, the Sagebrush rebels managed to attract a considerable amount of media attention and perpetuated the idea that this was a nationwide movement rather than an isolated regional issue.

But by mid-1981, the Sagebrush Rebellion had become a subdued outcry against federal intrusion instead of an organized insurrection. The election of Ronald Reagan muted the anger of many who believed his conservative political philosophy and western background would make him their ally. By naming James Watt as his interior secretary, Reagan undertook the task of bringing the West firmly into the Republican fold.[28]

Watt, who had earned his anti-environmental credentials at the MSLF, appeared to relish the prospect of dueling with the Sierra Club, the Wilderness Society, and other national environmental groups. One by one, he brought an end to what he perceived as the environmental excesses of previous administrations, placing a moratorium on the addition of new parklands, proposing to turn wildlife refuges over to the states, and supporting the exploration of oil, gas, and mineral resources in wilderness areas throughout the West. His "good neighbor policy" allowed state and local officials to petition the federal government for lands designated as "surplus" using an extremely broad definition of the term.

The Reagan administration also made it clear that it was interested in divesting itself of public lands through what it termed an "asset management program." In order to reduce the burgeoning national debt, several senators courted budget director Richard Darman with a plan that would allow the federal government to sell "excess" lands—perhaps as many as 100 million acres under one proposal. The policy was made a part of the administration's 1983 budget and coincided with a general public mistrust of the government's ability to manage its own affairs.[29] Environmental organizations argued that what the Sagebrush rebels really wanted was not better management of the public lands (a goal both sides supported) but, rather, privatization under the guise of fiscal responsibility.[30]

The asset management program was unsuccessful, primarily because there was little demand for the surplus land that was actually made available for purchase. After two years of operation, the government sold less than 20,000 acres, most of it in the East or in urban areas. Federal agencies were slow in designating land to be offered under the program, and state and local governments were too cash-strapped to justify buying more land than they already owned. The economic downturn in the extractive resource industries produced few buyers, especially when most western users could already lease the land at low cost.[31]

But several other factors were responsible for closing the door on the remnants of the rebellion by the mid-1980s. One of the two primary targets of the environmental movement, Anne Gorsuch Burford, resigned amid controversy in March 1983 and was replaced by former EPA administrator William Ruckelshaus, appeasing many environmental leaders. Watt resigned seven months later after the press reported indiscreet remarks he had made before a group of lobbyists. Watt's resignation removed an even more visible target, leaving the Sagebrush rebels with fewer allies in the executive branch.

Many of the Sagebrush rebels also got a reality slap from LASER leader Dean Rhoads, who had already concluded that the land issue was not likely to be settled in the courts. He presumed the rebels would lose at the Supreme Court level in a 5:4 split, and he held out hope that the Reagan election and potential appointments held more promise than continued efforts at litigation. The future of the Sagebrush Rebellion, Rhoads said, lay in the direction of "piece-meal legislation, administrative actions, executive orders, and revamping of regulations."[32]

THE RESURGENCE OF
ENVIRONMENTAL ORGANIZATIONS

At the same time as the Reagan administration was giving the rebels less of a reason for rebelling, they also faced environmental organizations that had been revived with the administration's antipreservation policies. Although the actions and policies of the Reagan administration provided the raison d'être for environmental organizations to regroup, the groups were successful because of three factors: a new professionalism within the organizations, a broadened and larger membership base, and a shift in tactics.

In 1981, leaders of the nation's largest environmental organizations (later called the Group of Ten) met to forge an alliance against the Reagan administration and to coordinate their lobbying activities. The environmental organizations were also becoming more professionalized. Mainstream groups like the Audubon Society, the Sierra Club, and the Environmental Defense Fund depended upon revolving-door "envirocrats" with broad organizational or legal expertise, rather than grassroots supporters who had a soft spot in their hearts for birds and bunnies.[33]

Membership in the groups had skyrocketed with the appointments of Watt and Gorsuch, with some arguing that Reagan was the best thing that could ever have happened to the environmental movement. For example, the Sierra Club's "Dump Watt" campaign collected over a million signatures in an attempt to convince Reagan to relieve the secretary of the interior of his duties. The Audubon Society used its direct attacks on the Reagan administration in direct-mail campaigns that raised more than ten times its largest previous total. Its director, Russell Peterson, reported that prior to 1981, the group had never netted more than $84,000 on a single mailing, but a 1981 Reagan attack piece generated $985,000 and more than 30,000 responses.[34] With a broadened membership base and a growing financial war chest, the environmental lobby could not only go toe-to-toe with the grazing, timber, and mining interests, they could win against them in Congress and in the state legislatures.

In fact, much of these groups' efforts shifted away from mobilizing local-level followers and toward what they did best: challenging the political system in the legislative and judicial arenas. That effort was made easier by the development of the environmental movement's legal expertise through such groups as the Natural Resources Defense Council, which was formed in 1970. NRDC and two other legal arms of the movement, the Environmental Defense Fund and the Sierra Club Legal Defense Fund, later added scientific and economic expertise to their organizations to provide independent analyses and research to their arsenal of resources.

The departure of Gorsuch and Watt also gave the environmental movement a political push as its members looked toward the 1984 presidential campaign. To many, the only way the environmental policy agenda could be turned around and the momentum represented by the Sagebrush Rebellion stopped completely was to defeat Ronald Reagan. In February 1984, key environmental leaders announced the formation of an independent organization, Environmentalists for Mondale, supporting the man who appeared to be the only Democratic candidate capable of defeating the incumbent president. In September 1984, the Sierra Club broke its long-held position of not endorsing candidates and joined another environmental group, Friends of the Earth, in formally endorsing Mondale. Although the environmental movement had enhanced its clout by rebuilding its membership base and professionalizing its operations, it did not have enough support, nor was the environment a salient enough political issue with the voting public, to have much of an impact on the outcome of the presidential election. Reagan won every electoral vote except those of Mondale's home state of Minnesota and the District of Columbia in the November general election.[35]

THE AFTERMATH OF THE REBELLION

Three states attempted to keep the spirit of the Sagebrush Rebellion alive throughout the early years of the Reagan administration. By a margin of 57 to 42 percent, Arizona voters turned down a 1982 ballot

initiative that would have repealed their state's Sagebrush statute, although they also reelected Governor Bruce Babbitt by a two-to-one
majority. Nevada's legislature memorialized Congress to transfer federal lands to the state in 1983, and Utah's "Project Bold" sought to consolidate the state's checkerboard landholdings for future exchange
with the federal government.[36]

Overall, the Sagebrush rebels were not successful in maintaining
their limited momentum for a variety of reasons. Their early attempts
to influence policy during the Carter administration were thwarted by
a president who had little interest in their region or their issues. When
they chose the statehouse as their next political venue, their efforts
were largely unsuccessful because each state's grievances against the
federal government were different. They also found that although they
had some measure of public, and in some cases legislative, support,
they were still in the minority, often against governors or voters who
were openly hostile to their cause. When they transferred their efforts
back to Washington, D.C., they found that the support of a few western
members of Congress was insufficient to garner the kind of national interest they needed. It has also been argued that the Sagebrush Rebellion lacked an authoritative spokesperson or leader, although there
was some continuity and similarities in statements made by various individuals perceived as leaders. The opposition never really achieved
what they had hoped to from President Reagan, either. Rather than
convincing the president that the transfer of public lands was not only
legally justified but politically appealing, they only managed to
achieve some loosening of the grip of federal regulatory control. For
some, that achievement was enough. For others, the ideological war
over who owns the public lands would continue.

Arizona State University law professor John D. Leshy has observed,

> I believe that the Sagebrush Rebellion will ultimately be viewed as
> representing not the beginnings of a second American Revolution,
> but instead as a last gasp of a passing era, a poignant effort to turn
> back the clock to the days when competition among uses of federal
> lands was rare, when resources seemed inexhaustible, and when a
> consensus existed for exploitation.
>
> Those calling for state or private ownership will, I would sug-
> gest, ultimately find that they are a minority—that the public lands
> have friends and supporters in numbers greater than the rebels
> imagined.[37]

Leshy's dismissal of the rebels may have been premature, as the
next three chapters will show. Although the Sagebrush Rebellion may
not have been successful in its ultimate goal of forcing the federal government to dispose of the public domain lands, the issues it raised re-

main unresolved. This brief political rebellion did provide one valuable lesson for future strategists: It displayed the saliency of focusing the public's attention on federal regulations. It was the one issue that seemed to bring state leaders together, although their targets of animosity were different from state to state. The environmental opposition would eventually be able to capitalize on the discontent over the federal government's resource management policies and also over its overall regulatory role. Key environmental opposition strategists and supporters simply had to wait until the next policy window opened so they could try again.

NOTES

1. Various authors have numbered these battles for the public lands as a common thread in U.S. history. See, for example, William L. Graf, *Wilderness Preservation and the Sagebrush Rebellions* (Savage, MD: Rowman and Littlefield, 1990); and Dyan Zaslowsky, "Does the West Have a Death Wish?" *American Heritage*, vol. 33, no. 4 (1982): 26–37.

2. See John G. Francis and Richard Ganzel, eds., *Western Public Lands: The Management of Natural Resources in a Time of Declining Federalism* (Totowa, NJ: Rowman and Allanheld, 1984), p. 2.

3. *Pollard's Lessee v. Hagan*, 44 U.S. (3 How.) 212 (1845). See also *Coyle v. Smith*, 221 U.S. 559 (1911) for a distinction between quid pro quo (such as the retention of public lands) and the issue of the political equality of states within the Union. Note also Article 4, Section 3, of the U.S. Constitution.

4. See John D. Leshy, "Unraveling the Sagebrush Rebellion: Law, Politics, and Federal Lands," *University of California, Davis, Law Review*, vol. 14 (1990): 319–320.

5. Ibid., p. 323, nn. 18, 19. Data on the amount of federally managed land is compiled by the U.S. General Services Administration, Interior Department, and the U.S. Department of Agriculture.

6. Graf, *Wilderness Preservation*, p. 228.

7. Richard D. Lamm and Michael McCarthy, *The Angry West: A Vulnerable Land and Its Future* (Boston: Houghton Mifflin, 1982), p. 239.

8. Ibid., p. 158.

9. Ibid., pp. 139–140.

10. Graf, *Wilderness Preservation*, pp. 242–243.

11. Resolution, Western Coalition on Public Lands, Regional Meeting, Reno, Nevada, September 5–7, 1979.

12. Margot Hornblower, "The Sagebrush Revolution," *Washington Post*, November 11, 1979, p. B3.

13. Graf, *Wilderness Preservation*, pp. 243–244.

14. For an explanation of the theory behind this strategy, see E. E. Schattschneider, *The Semisovereign People* (New York: Holt, Rinehart, and Winston, 1960); and Manfred Kochen and Karl Deutsch, *Decentralization: Sketches Toward a Rational Theory* (Cambridge, MA: Oelggsschlager, Gunn, and Hain, 1980).

15. Lamm and McCarthy, *The Angry West*, p. 266.

16. Francis and Ganzel, eds., *Western Public Lands*, pp. 31, 37.

17. Quoted in Melinda Beck and Michael Reese, "Sagebrush Revolt," *Newsweek*, September 17, 1979, p. 39.

18. Lamm and McCarthy, *The Angry West*, p. 258.

19. Ibid., pp. 248–249.

20. Kenneth T. Walsh, "Colorado Moves to Claim 10,000 Acres of U.S. Land," *Denver Post*, September 4, 1979, p. 1.

21. Lamm and McCarthy, *The Angry West*, p. 254.

22. Joseph M. Chomski and Constance E. Brooks, *The Sagebrush Rebellion: A Concise Analysis of the History, the Law, and Politics of Public Land in the United States* (Alaska: Legislative Affairs Agency, 1980), p. 130.

23. John G. Francis, "Environmental Values, Intergovernmental Politics, and the Sagebrush Rebellion," in Francis and Ganzel, eds., *Western Public Lands*, pp. 29–46.

24. Graf, *Wilderness Preservation*, p. 230.

25. See Frank J. Popper, "The Timely End of the Sagebrush Rebellion," *Public Interest*, vol. 76 (1984): 61–73.

26. Charles Callison, "'Sagebrush Rebellion' Is Just Another Name for a Public Lands Heist," *National Parks and Conservation Magazine*, vol. 54 (March 1980): 10.

27. Lamm and McCarthy, *The Angry West*, pp. 262–263.

28. For an overview of the Reagan administration's environmental policies, see Jonathan Lash, Katherine Gilman, and David Sheridan, *A Season of Spoils: The Reagan Administration's Attack on the Environment* (New York: Random House, 1984); and C. Brant Short, *Ronald Reagan and the Public Lands* (College Station: Texas A & M University Press, 1989).

29. See Barney Dowdle, "Perspectives on the Sagebrush Rebellion," *Policy Studies Journal*, vol. 12, no. 3 (1984): 473–482.

30. George Reiger, "Sagebrush Rebellion III," *Field and Stream*, vol. 90, no. 3 (July 1985): 29–30.

31. Popper, "The Timely End," p. 69.

32. R. McGreggor Cawley, *Federal Land, Western Anger* (Lawrence: University Press of Kansas, 1993), p. 111.

33. Robert Gottlieb, *Forcing the Spring: The Transformation of the American Environmental Movement* (Washington, DC: Island Press, 1993), p. 130.

34. Ibid., p. 123.

35. Cawley, *Federal Land*, pp. 149–150.

36. Francis, "Environmental Values," p. 44.

37. Leshy, "Unraveling the Sagebrush Rebellion," pp. 349–350.

8

The Wise Use Movement

SIGN OF THE TIMES: Advertisement placed by the Yellow Ribbon Coalition in the magazine American Timberman and Trucker *in 1989:*

> A Call to Arms: *Our timber communities are under siege. If we do not unite we will perish, the victims of the radical preservationist movement that is destroying our communities and timber industry. Mills are closing. Hard-working men and women—family people— are losing their jobs, the direct result of preservationist lawsuits and timber sale appeals that are locking up our forests. We must unite in our common defense.*[1]

In his 1947 biography, *Breaking New Ground,* conservationist and forester Gifford Pinchot coined a phrase that would reappear more than thirty years later as symbolic of a new effort to oppose the environmental movement. Pinchot wrote, "Conservation means the wise use of the earth and its resources for the lasting good of men."[2]

The phrase "wise use" was later picked up by individuals who believed and supported Pinchot's philosophy of sustainable management and the multiple use of natural resources. But the phrase has also been used by members of environmental organizations and others who have lumped together a wide-ranging spectrum of groups in the contemporary environmental opposition and called them collectively (and often derogatorily) "the so-called wise use movement."

This chapter begins by discarding the "so-called" label to refer to the organizations and individuals profiled here as adherents to parts of the wise use movement's goals. It makes no claims about whether or not the positions advocated by the movement's adherents are in fact "wise," but instead adopts a neutral position that is more descriptive than judgmental. It includes information about several groups profiled in earlier chapters, some of which preceded the actual development of the movement but later came under its "umbrella" of organizations. What the wise use policy entrepreneurs have done is bring together these disparate organizations to create the perception that it is, in fact, a much more focused and numerically more powerful movement than it may actually be. While one observer estimates that there are probably fewer than 100,000 activists involved in the wise use movement itself,[3] others include in their calculations institutional backers from other organizations such as the National Rifle Association and the American Farm Bureau Federation. With the members of these groups added in, the "membership" of the wise use movement figures into the millions.

The chapter also makes a distinction that is critical from a nomenclature perspective. Although one researcher has defined the wise use movement as "a coalition of industrial, agricultural, and conservative political interest groups organized to capitalize on a relatively narrow, but committed, support base,"[4] such an amalgamation ignores clearcut differences in both the style and the substance of the groups involved. It hints that the coalition is ideologically cohesive and that its members are all consistently active participants, unified in their strategies or motivations. A more accurate representation of the wise use movement, however, is that it consists of several umbrella organizations to which a diverse subset of interest groups loosely belong (such as timber organizations, livestock associations, snowmobile enthusiasts, farmers, hunting clubs). Some individuals may be called "members" of the wise use movement when, in actuality, their level of participation stems only from the fact that their parent group belongs to one of the umbrella organizations or that they are on a publication's mailing list. Condensing the diverse groups into a single entity may be easier for those attempting to simplify the political landscape into an "us-vs.-them" debate, but it is not wholly accurate and tends to overstate the size and clout of wise use.

One of the key issues raised by environmental organizations is whether or not the wise use movement is really composed of grassroots groups or if it is industry sponsored and financed. There are some examples—although they tend to be the exception rather than the rule—where a particular mobilization effort is not totally the work of local groups. In Questa, New Mexico, for example, the owners of the mining firm MolyCorp/UNOCAL gave its employees paid time off and brought them to Santa Fe to attend congressional hearings to protest proposed changes in the 1872 Mining Law.[5] Environmental groups have charged that the companies bused in schoolchildren to wave placards that proclaimed the mining law changes would destroy their families and communities.[6] Industry is not alone in its role as accomplice to the grassroots efforts. In 1995, congressional hearings in Medford, Oregon, on the federal salvage timber program (usually scheduled Monday through Friday to accommodate members of Congress and their staffs' travel schedule) were held on a Saturday morning so that hundreds of timber workers and their families would be able to attend and rally in support of the legislation without losing time off from work.

But a nationwide study commissioned by the Wilderness Society concluded that "wise use is a local movement driven primarily by local concerns, not national issues." In reviewing wise use groups in all fifty states, the study found the movement's members

> are apparently genuinely grassroots. That is, they are local individuals addressing local concerns who joined with other individuals, groups and funders as a matter of common concern. It is true that special interests have in many cases fostered local wise use groups to further their own agenda, but it is foolish to lay this movement solely at the doorstep of Exxon, Georgia-Pacific, or Kawasaki. Real people have perceived a real threat. The national wise use movement is attempting to give these grassroots groups coherence, it did not give them life.[7]

The general assessment of the study was that

> nationally, at this time, the movement is more smoke than fire. We believe the true strength . . . lies at the local level, where it is fully engaged in scores of resource issues. . . . Environmentalists, who focus on wise use's conspiracy and vanguard messages and say the movement is too extreme to become a major force in America, overlook the power of the mainstream message. They also fail to see that the underside of the mainstream message paints a convincing portrait of environmentalists as the extremists in the debate over striking a balance between man and nature.[8]

This chapter is designed to illustrate the differences among the interests by providing a brief background on the development of the wise use movement and the policy entrepreneurs who have been the driving force behind it. The chapter continues with an explanation of the key issues that have been the target of wise use advocates and an overview of the major umbrella groups within the movement. To further distinguish between the wise use movement and other segments of the environmental opposition, the chapter discusses some of the movement's strategies, with particular attention to the perception that there is a growing militancy in some of the wise use groups and the movement's expansion into other issue areas with new adherents and supporters. Also noteworthy is the fact that the tactics employed by wise use organizations are often the same ones used successfully by environmental groups. Both sides have attempted to lay claim to representing mainstream America's values and views about the environment, and the chapter concludes with an overview of the more moderate mainstream message now being used by wise use leaders.

BACKGROUND AND DEVELOPMENT OF THE MOVEMENT

In most social movements, there is often a galvanizing event or crisis that brings together like-minded individuals who consolidate their grievances and begin to take organized action. With wise use, although no singular incident was responsible for the movement as a whole, the activists did start coming together at roughly the same time the Sagebrush Rebellion was gaining momentum in the West. But 1976 marked a key year in which environmental opposition activism moved from a purely industry-related level to one involving grassroots alliances.

One of the primary organizations that pursued a common agenda with other activists was the Associated California Loggers (ACL). The organization led a convoy of 100 logging trucks to tie up early-morning, rush-hour traffic on the Golden Gate Bridge in opposition to a proposed logging buffer zone around California's Redwood National Park. That rally, which garnered national media attention, led to a second convoy of more than two dozen logging trucks that made their way to Washington, D.C., where they were joined by 300 timber workers opposed to the logging ban. The two events encouraged other interests, like log truck owners, to join forces with the ACL.

ACL executive director David Snodderly had spent nearly two years attempting to find a way to involve the wives of his members in some form of activism, sensing that the women might have more time than their husbands to do grassroots lobbying and meet with legislators on a one-on-one basis. He also hoped the women would help communicate with his predominantly male membership on timber issues based on their own perspectives of what was happening in Sacramento and Washington, D.C. After the two ACL rallies in 1976, he met with a small group, most of whom were wives of the group's board members, and presented a proposal for a new organization, eventually named Women in Timber—California. The group's leaders began working with other logging interests in the West, forming other state-level affiliates and, eventually, a national organization.

According to Snodderly, the original purpose was somewhat introspective—to focus on interests of loggers—and it was not until much later in the organization's development that the membership base expanded and both the ACL and the women's groups began tackling a wider range of environmental issues. But during the next twenty years, Women in Timber would become one of the most well-organized and powerful voices in the environmental opposition, combining grassroots activism and a strong ideological partnership with industry organizations.[9]

Almost concurrently, a group of property owners in Yosemite were being organized by Chuck Cushman to protest the federal government's policies on landholding in and near the nation's national parks—the formation of what would later become the property rights faction of the environmental opposition. Both segments were alike in their antipathy toward President Jimmy Carter's inattention to issues that affected them, such as logging restrictions or wilderness designations, and they considered the president, who was a peanut farmer prior to becoming governor of Georgia, more concerned about peanuts than trees. Snodderly says the timber industry had tried unsuccessfully to convince Carter "that logging is still farming" but that the president seemed uninterested in the problems of the West. This hostility would later grow into support for Carter's opponent in the 1980 presidential election, Ronald Reagan.

The timber workers appear to have been among the first of those employed in the extractive resource industries to perceive that environmental legislation and regulation were a threat to their livelihoods. In the early 1980s, their legislative focus was on logging restrictions, but they later became more concerned about the implementation of the Endangered Species Act. When the USFWS began taking the initial steps to list the Northern spotted owl as a threatened species in the late 1980s, the level of grassroots timber activism increased tremendously. The bird's habitat ranges along the Pacific coast from Canada to the San Francisco Bay Area, and the proposed listing affected potential timber sales and jobs throughout the Northwest.

Other timber worker–led opposition groups began to form in response to the owl controversy, and it became clear that their interests would be better served by the development of an umbrella group that could bring the grassroots organizations together to plan strategy and lobby more effectively. Key to the grassroots effort was the need for communication and development of the ability to monitor the legislative and regulatory activities of government agencies. Few of the newly emerging local organizations had such resources, so some turned to preexisting trade associations like the California Forestry Association; others believed a more grassroots activist group was needed to counter the environmental movement, which was perceived to be the driving force behind the antilogging efforts.

The publicity over the spotted owl controversy in the late 1980s and early 1990s marked the opening of a policy window—a specific political opportunity for those with grievances against the government and the leaders of the environmental movement. The policy entrepreneurs perceived that the public might side with the loggers whose jobs appeared to be threatened, rather than an obscure bird, and capitalized on grievances that gave them the opportunity to appear as compassionate and reasonable. The window opened long enough for a small group of individuals to build umbrella organizations that would eventually bring a broad spectrum of concerns together under the banner of wise use.

The Wise Use Policy Entrepreneurs

The two individuals most closely identified as founding leaders in the wise use movement are Ron Arnold and Alan Gottlieb. Together, the men have become policy entrepreneurs, putting together an organizational infrastructure that not only grew rapidly in a short period of time, but that sustains itself and continues to gain momentum and power nationwide.

Ron Arnold is a former Sierra Club member who enjoys hiking and assisted the group by putting together slide shows in the mid-1960s while he was working as a graphics designer and illustrator at the Boeing plant in Seattle. He later worked with the Alpine Lakes Protection Society on another slide-show presentation until he resigned; Arnold says he grew disenchanted with the Sierra Club over the issues of private property rights and the use of natural resources. He cites, for example, his frustration over the organization's use of photographs of timber in a stream by a Weyerhaeuser logging operation near Mt. Hood, Oregon. Arnold knew the logging manager and believed the logs had accidentally slid down into the stream, while the group's members claimed the company had intentionally dumped them. The photographs were released to the press, and Arnold later resigned, because in his words, "I felt alone and betrayed." Others believe he faded from the environmental group when he quit Boeing and started his own graphics company in 1971, and one observer commented that Arnold had never been in step with the Sierra Club philosophically.[10]

For the next several years, Arnold produced slide shows and films for various timber firms and industrial clients, and also began writing articles and giving lectures as a part of his consulting business. He fought the expansion of Redwood National Park on behalf of three timber companies in 1977, and in 1979, he wrote a series of articles for the magazine *Logging Management* in which he proposed the need for an activist movement to defeat the efforts of the environmental movement. His writing efforts later expanded into several books, including *Ecology Wars* and *Trashing the Economy,* and a biography of James Watt written for the conservative group Committee for a Free Congress.[11]

In 1984, Gottlieb was a direct-mail fund-raiser who at the time was raising money for Ronald Reagan's reelection campaign; he contacted Arnold after reading the Watt biography. Gottlieb had been a student conservative leader while in college and later worked for several political candidates and ballot measures, including serving as national director of Youth Against McGovern (the 1972 Democratic presidential candidate) and as a board member of the conservative organization Young Americans for Freedom. Those efforts led him to establish several groups representing his clients' interests, including the Center for the Defense of Free Enterprise, the Citizens Committee for the Right to Keep and Bear Arms, and the Second Amendment Foundation. The groups are housed in an office complex in Bellevue, Washington—also home to Ron Arnold, who joined Gottlieb at CFDFE in 1984.

Gottlieb's critics have disparaged his credibility, noting that he was convicted in 1984 of filing a fraudulent tax return. Gottlieb himself calls the conviction "a badge of honor" and considers himself an anti-tax hero, part of his activities as a board member of the American Conservative Union. Others have called him a profiteer whose main goal is making money from his wise use and Second Amendment groups.[12]

Although other individuals have emerged as leaders of competing groups within the wise use movement, none are as visible or sought after for expertise or as media contacts as are Arnold and Gottlieb. Neither of the two men fits the common stereotype that portrays the opposition leadership as ill informed or on the political fringe. Arnold has a powerful command of western history and has carefully researched both the environmental movement and the political and regulatory process; Gottlieb's background in marketing meshes well with Arnold's ability to serve as a spokesperson for the media. As policy entrepreneurs, they are savvy, sophisticated, and extremely aware of the impact of their commentary and rhetoric. This allows both individuals to become a lightning rod for the movement, and they have managed to capitalize on their visibility to make flamboyant statements to the press that are immediately treated as wise use dogma.

Several environmental journalists have recounted the story that when Arnold appeared on the television program *Nightline* in 1992, he told the reporter, "We intend to destroy the environmental movement once and for all by offering a better alternative, the wise use movement." Later in the program, which included a studio segment contrasting Vice President Al Gore and conservative commentator Rush Limbaugh, Arnold was said to have noted, "The environmental movement is the establishment now, and now we are the rebels coming to tear them down. Now they're Goliath and we're David, and we intend to put the stone in their head."[13] The sound bites appeal to the media and provide fodder for environmental organizations, but they have also led some wise use advocates to disassociate themselves from CFDFE and its leaders because they feel the two men are doing more harm than good by making comments that are not only outrageous, but embarrassing to the more moderate members of the movement.

Arnold and Gottlieb nevertheless remain in a position of authority within the movement because few challenge them or their organizational resources, and no one matches their expertise in the field. A woman from one wise use organization commented:

> I don't mind the fact that Alan and Ron are out there making all the noise and getting all the attention. Although it sometimes makes them look like loonies, it makes the rest of us look normal in comparison. Every movement needs a foil to make the rest of us seem reasonable, and that's what they do best.

Movement Diversity

Despite the antagonism between members of environmental groups and their opposition, the two in fact have several similar characteristics. One of the attributes of the wise use movement that is similar to the environmental movement is the diversity of the issues it has targeted. Although it could be said that, overall, the environmental opposition has an antigovernment regulatory agenda and lobbies against many of the policies advocated by the majority of environmental groups, it is also splintered and in the process of expanding and diversifying its issues and its base of membership organizations.

Both the environmental and the wise use movement are also characterized by the strong role played by women at the grassroots level. Within the wise use movement, women became early activists through their membership in groups like Women in Timber, Women in Mining, and American Agri-Women. In the environmental movement, women like Love Canal community organizer Lois Gibbs and *Silent Spring* author Rachel Carson were at the forefront of an activist grassroots movement that has grown to include such issues as nuclear power and lead poisoning. Social movement researchers believe women's activism is a response to a perception of a grievance that affects the individual and/or her family. Both women who are members of environmental groups and those associated with wise use often respond that their activism is based on a desire to protect their children's futures. In the words of one Arizona woman who is an adherent to the wise use movement's goals, "My children are the most important thing in my life. I will do whatever it takes to make sure no one does anything to harm them." Environmental leader Cora Tucker, who first became an activist through her efforts to stop a uranium project near her home in rural Virginia, expressed a similar philosophy. In commenting on the role of women in dealing with toxic waste sites, she noted, "We become fighters when something threatens our home."[14] Such sentiments have been associated with the philosophical roots of ecofeminism, a synthesis of feminist, ecological, and antimilitarist themes.[15]

The majority of the wise use movement's issue targets have dealt with the management of natural resources and the use of public lands.

That becomes a very broad base from which to organize disparate interests, but those interests do not always pursue the same goals for the same reasons. For example, the public lands debate brings together those who seek access for recreational use and want less acreage designated as federal wilderness areas as well as those who believe that more federal preserves within the state of Alaska should be opened up for sport hunting. On the periphery of that same debate are those who have targeted the expansion of the national parks system and others who are opposed to the way the parks are currently managed. Members of extractive resource industries seek more secure access to public lands for timber, grazing, and mining.

More recently, the wise use movement has attempted to expand its reach to become more inclusive by inviting in representatives of hunting groups, labor organizations, and other resource industries such as tuna fleet owners and shrimpers. As one observer has noted, this makes the groups appear to represent a broad-based coalition of populists and "little guys." At the same time, wise use groups characterize the environmental movement as "elitist," representing special interest groups.[16]

Whether that characterization is accurate or not, the environmental movement has lost the membership momentum that began in the mid-1980s, when membership in the ten largest environmental organizations was estimated at about 4 million members. That figure doubled by 1990, when it began a gradual decline.[17] This appears to represent a pattern of sorts: When Congress is considering a weakening of environmental statutes or when agency budgets are being reduced, as was the case during the Reagan and Bush administrations, membership in mainstream environmental groups increases. When a more environmentally friendly president is elected, as was the case with Clinton in 1992, membership begins to slowly decline.

There may be a correlation with economic prosperity as well. In one report, the American Association of Fund-Raising Counsel noted that charitable donations overall jumped 11 percent in 1995, the biggest increase since 1986, with environmental and wildlife groups showing strong gains for the second year in a row. Donations in 1995 increased to $4 billion, a 13 percent increase. A spokesperson for the study, consultant Nancy Raybin, identified two reasons why groups fared better than in previous years: a perception of a stronger economy that provided donors the wherewithal to give, and the fact that organizations worked harder to raise funds in the face of threatened government budget cuts. Nonprofit groups, she said, "made a major effort to communicate with their donors, and tried to distinguish themselves from other nonprofit organizations to protect their own images."[18] But even when the economy was in recession during the Reagan administration, environmental groups benefited financially when their membership grew because they publicly targeted the ouster of controversial interior secretary James Watt.

The specter of wise use has given environmental groups an opportunity to initiate new membership and fund-raising efforts, urging supporters to challenge attempts to reduce the government's regulatory control over environmental protection. The Wilderness Society, for example, has called for a "reaffirmation of old connections" to its grassroots membership as a way of fighting "bigness with bigness" and the disaffection of those "struggling to survive in the very heat and smoke of local battlefields."[19]

THE UMBRELLA ORGANIZATIONS

Perhaps the best way to identify the wise use movement's primary issues is to rely upon Ron Arnold and Alan Gottlieb's original 1989 mission statement, *The Wise Use Agenda*—twenty-five goals for its supporters to work toward. The targets included major alterations in the ESA, such as excluding "non-adaptive species such as the California condor and endemic species lacking the vigor to spread in range"; the opening up of most public lands for mineral and energy production and off-road vehicle use; giving the job of providing concessions in the national parks to private firms with "expertise in people moving such as Walt Disney"; and making it a felony for any national forester to let a natural forest fire burn usable timber. Under the agenda, old-growth timber would immediately be subject to logging, and private property rights would be protected by eliminating restrictions on development.[20]

This broad agenda has allowed wise use leaders to attract a diverse constituency of interests, some of whom are in agreement with the majority of the movement's goals, others who have limited themselves to specific issues. To keep the movement alive and growing, the leadership is constantly looking for new issue targets—adding to its list of members those who support the use of animals in medical experimentation, for example, who then begin to absorb some wise use issues such as revisions in the ESA.

As is the case with any group of individuals who share a common grievance, organized interests differ over time in their cohesiveness and the extent of their resources. This is especially true in the wise use movement, which sprang from perceived economic threats directed at the timber industry and expanded to other sectors of the economy. That explains in part why it is so difficult for researchers to track and identify the groups—they come and go, changing names, post office boxes, meeting times and places, and even their goals and mission as a group. Many of the supporters of the movement are not "members" in the traditional sense and are perhaps better classified as "adherents" to the issues that are the focus of the major umbrella groups.

In addition to the CFDFE, some of the other major umbrella groups associated with wise use are the Alliance for America, the Blue Ribbon Coalition, and the Western States Public Lands Coalition. There is a considerable overlap in membership among the groups, although each appeals to a slightly different constituency and performs a different function. Although CFDFE has been referred to as a conservative think tank by its critics, it is not nearly as prestigious or scholarly as institutions like the Heritage Foundation or the Cato Institute. CFDFE fills a niche as the ideological source for many of the wise use movement's manifestos, which it publishes itself. The organization in fact refers to itself in its literature as having been founded as "a tax-exempt education foundation . . . to underwrite educational projects oriented to the average American." The center was established "so that Americans who understood and valued the free enterprise system could contribute to the defense and promotion of the economic system that made America a prosperous nation."[21]

In contrast, the Alliance for America represents a much broader coalition of small, mostly local groups, who regard the alliance as a clearinghouse for information and as a focal point for their lobbying efforts in Washington, D.C. The group is perhaps best known for its annual "Fly In for Freedom," which brings several hundred local activists to the capital to lobby Congress one-on-one. During the event, the activists also plan various rallies that receive prominent media coverage and further advance their agenda before the public. Organizers are said to have told participants at one fly-in event, "Wear workclothes with special attention to gloves, boots, hard hats, bandannas."[22]

The BRC is comprised almost exclusively of outdoor recreationists, and its monthly magazine notes its dedication "to the preservation of all forms of Off-Road Recreation in an environmentally responsible manner." As outlined in Chapter 3, this umbrella group's effectiveness can be attributed to its attempts to bring together a broad core of recreational users, although some refuse to associate with the organization in any way. The BRC is also known as one of the most legislatively active of the wise use organizations, using its monthly *Blue Ribbon Magazine* as a way of coordinating its lobbying efforts by calling subscribers' attention to key bills and regulations that affect its members at the state and federal levels.

Another umbrella group, People for the West!, was established by the Western States Public Lands Coalition in 1989 to represent the mining industry's interests, especially attempts by some Democratic and Republican members of Congress to revise the 1872 Mining Law.[23] Many of the group's tactics have been typical of other organized interests. For example, People for the West! played a key role in efforts to alter plans to create an ecosystem plan for Yellowstone National Park by sending thousands of "I oppose the 'Yellowstone Vision for the Future'" letters to affected federal agencies.[24]

One leader of the Greater Yellowstone Coalition, which supported the plan, admitted that its members were simply outorganized. Others argue that the plan was defeated because of rumors the park was to be expanded fivefold and that hunting, fishing, mining, and logging would be banned. "Pre-hearing rallies whipped the crowd into near hysteria," wrote one observer. "There were 700 people in there. You can't imagine the virulence of the outcry."[25]

Wise use publications frequently proclaim that they have the support of organized labor, citing the backing of timber workers and their opposition to President Clinton's forest plan as evidence. Groups like the Oregon Lands Coalition (an offshoot of the Association of Oregon Industries) have estimated that the president's proposal would lead to the loss of 85,000 jobs—a rallying cry for the industry if ever there was one. Although some unions, such as the AFL-CIO of Montana, have refused to support the wise use movement, one union official notes,

> As mills continue to close each year at a historic rate that exceeds the rate of the year before, it is probably a rational fear. Once you have folks that are scared, then you have folks that are receptive or vulnerable to any kind of solution. At that point, the wise use groups speak to the woodworkers' fears better than most of the locally based and certainly better than the nationally based environmental groups.[26]

THE GRASSROOTS GROUPS

The umbrella groups serve as a clearinghouse for hundreds of smaller regional, statewide, or local organizations that adhere to the wise use philosophy to one degree or another, but that may have virtually no interaction with the national movement except to receive the umbrella group's publications. These smaller groups often seek political support from public officials as a way of establishing their identity and credibility. For example, six Republican senators asked former interior secretary Manuel Lujan to serve in a supporting capacity for Our Land Society of Idaho, noting, "Advocates of environmental paranoia, locked-up resources, costly regulation have never lacked a forum for their views . . . and this imbalance must be corrected."[27] Similarly, a photograph of President George Bush and Alan Gottlieb appears on the back cover of *The Wise Use Agenda* and the president's symbolic greeting by telegram to the group appears in several media accounts, lending further credence to the movement's claims that it developed support at the highest level of the White House.

One of the factors that has enhanced the wise use movement's effectiveness is that the smaller organizations that cleave to one or more of its principles actually do represent a diverse spectrum of interests— some of them grassroots, some of them not. The Washington, D.C.– based Committee for a Constructive Tomorrow, for example, has on its board of academic/scientific advisers a panel of researchers representing distinguished institutions like the New York University Medical Center, the Brookhaven National Laboratory, and Rutgers University. In contrast, Citizens for Total Energy (CITE), which is a pronuclear power group, operates out of the residence of a homemaker in rural California. Its purpose is "to promote a balanced energy policy between environmental protection and economic growth," and it is truly a grassroots effort. Unlike the nuclear power industry itself, which is noted for its slick promotional materials, CITE's logo was designed by high school students.

While the umbrella groups serve as the foundation for the wise use movement, its heart can be found in the hundreds of state- and local-level groups like the California Desert Coalition (CDC) and the Shasta Alliance for Resources and Environment (SHARE), which are representative of similar organizations throughout the United States. Despite the common allegation that wise use serves as a front for industry interests, many of these smaller groups have little if any source of revenue outside their own individual membership dues and direct-mail appeals.

The CDC was organized in 1986 around a specific issue—the proposed California Desert Protection Act. The law, which was heavily supported by the Sierra Club and introduced by California senator Alan Cranston, would have placed 8 million acres of desert lands in the National Wilderness Preservation System, including 1.5 million acres considered by CDC members as essential recreational and resource lands. The CDC embarked on traditional organized interest group tactics to try to defeat the bill, including testifying before Congress, giving key legislative staff members tours of the proposed area, and providing policymakers with CDC's perceptions of the impact of the legislation. The group also gained the support of a member of Congress who represented the affected region, thus this member's staff assisted CDC in gaining media coverage for its efforts.

Although conservatives were successful in stalling action on the legislation for nearly ten years, California senators Diane Feinstein and Barbara Boxer conducted a major lobbying effort that resulted in the bill's passage and President Clinton's signature in 1994. The passage of the measure did not bring an end to the group's existence; rather, in some ways it revitalized it after the lengthy legislative struggle. The CDC later exhorted its members:

> The Coalition is not made of quitters, losers, soreheads or pessimists. During the last nine years, we have become experienced in the game of politics. We overcame incredible odds to mount a surprisingly effective campaign against a piece of legislation that was expected to pass quickly and without difficulty. This was one of the most hard-fought battles in recent Congressional history, and with your help, we almost succeeded against the enormously wealthy national environmental movement.[28]

With the change in leadership brought on by the 1994 congressional elections, the CDC regrouped and changed its tactics to support measures that would repeal the California Desert Protection Act and another bill that would block funding for the new Mojave National Preserve. The group, like many others in the wise use movement, has also broadened its base of support by lending its name and resources to private property groups fighting measures in the California state legislature, national park reform, and the Endangered Species Act. Even though the initial goal of its legislative efforts was not achieved, the CDC, by adapting to change, not only maintains its presence but expands its potential membership base and funding sources.

In contrast, SHARE is an autonomous committee of the Greater Redding, California, Chamber of Commerce, established in 1986 "as leaders of the community became aware of the threat to our way of life evolving from changes in land and resource management policies being dictated by people and organizations with no connection to nor responsibility for those resources."[29]

As a small, local organization, its goals are more focused on regional interests—in this case, resource management policies in northern California—but its newsletters cover a much broader range of traditional wise use issues. Like many other local groups, SHARE could not exist as an effective organized interest if it were forced to rely upon a purely local source of funding. Instead, as an outgrowth of the Chamber of Commerce, it has access to the chamber's administrative services, including office space and legislative expertise. Like other local wise use groups, SHARE uses its facsimile machines to bring a one-page summary of fast-breaking legislative events or issues to the attention of its members. Although SHARE might not be able to survive without the Chamber of Commerce's resources, it is hardly exemplary of the supposed big business connection alluded to by critics in the environmental movement.

Both CDC and SHARE are typical of the wise use movement's grassroots organizations, although they vary in their membership base, strategies, and overall policy success. Individually, they have little clout, but as part of a coalition that is becoming more and more organized, they are being taken seriously as players by decisionmakers, the media, and the environmental movement.

MOVEMENT STRATEGIES

There is little difference between the strategies members of the wise use movement employ and those employed by members of most environmental groups. Both sides have used the traditional tactics of organized interests, such as lobbying members of Congress directly or conducting rallies and demonstrations in support of or in opposition to a legislative proposal. There are three strategies, however, that appear to have been especially useful for wise use leaders: the creation of a tightly connected network of members and organizations that can be quickly and effectively mobilized, the development of a counter–public relations effort, and the use of rhetoric and imagery to delegitimize the environmental movement.

The Network

Some observers believe the wise use movement has no peer when it comes to its ability to link its far-flung members together and mobilize them. Using tactics initially credited to organizations like the National Rifle Association and groups within the religious right, the wise use movement has developed an impressive ability to mass-market itself and communicate its agenda.

Policy entrepreneurs like Ron Arnold and Alan Gottlieb have managed to create the perception of a network of adherents using what one consulting firm commissioned by the Wilderness Society characterizes as an increasingly mainstream message by using both technology and articulate leadership. The CFDFE, for example, uses its massive computer capabilities to manage a mailing list with an estimated 5 million names of sympathetic supporters. Those supporters are also linked through a nationwide network of fax machines, Internet sites, e-mail, and other technology that is the envy of most of the smaller environmental groups. Those living in rural areas appear to make considerable use of the Internet as a way of staying in touch with other supporters, and even the smallest of the groups have established home pages on the World Wide Web. The network allows groups to communicate rapidly and effectively and to respond cohesively to issues where public input is permitted. For example, during the public comment period on the seventy-six-page plan for the expansion of the Yellowstone National Park ecosystem, 5,625 letters of the total 8,690 commenting on the plan were form letters opposing any limitations on industry.[30]

In interviews conducted during the research for this book, members of the wise use movement repeatedly expressed the utility of facsimile machines, either ones they owned themselves or to which they had access. One woman said she keeps her fax machine on automatic twenty-four hours a day, receiving as many as eighty faxes a day from the various groups with which she communicates. More common were those who said they receive an average of two or three per day. Many of those interviewed cited the convenience of being able to send messages to multiple recipients and at lower cost by using off-peak transmission hours. Others mentioned the instantaneous nature of the communication, even when the person on the receiving end is not available. One organization's executive director routinely sends copies of her group's legal filings to her counterparts in half a dozen states—a process that is faster and less expensive than the normal legal courier service. Faxes are often used to spread the word about upcoming conferences, rallies, and legislative alerts, which is especially useful for the majority of wise use adherents who live in the rural West and do not have access to other information sources. One Washington, D.C.–based group's lobbyist boasted that she could "get the word out about what just took place in the Endangered Species Act hearing faster than the members of Congress could get the story out to their own constituents." The opposition groups have also found a place on the information superhighway, with both the large umbrella groups like the Alliance for America as well as small, local groups like the Coquille, Oregon, chapter of Timber Resources Equal Economic Stability (TREES) constructing home pages on the World Wide Web.

One feature common to most of the local organizations in the wise use movement is the overlapping of information sources. A story that reported that a Washington, D.C., public relations firm was behind the alleged linkage of the environmental opposition to militias and the 1995 Oklahoma City bombing appeared in dozens of wise use group publications, in some cases, almost word for word. Groups rely upon their network for this type of information since they do not have the resources to do the investigations or writing themselves.

The Public Relations Connection

Wise use advocates are hungry for publicity, eager to agree to interviews in order to get their views in front of the American public. They couple that willingness to share their positions on various issues with an efficient internal public relations network.

Ron Arnold and Alan Gottlieb have managed to promote their version of the wise use agenda by creating their own publishing and distribution company that operates out of the CFDFE headquarters in Belle-vue, Washington. The press operation is centered on what it calls the "Battle Book" concept: "Where free enterprise is in danger, we select talented, informed and involved authors who show what the average American can do to solve real problems." The titles in its series include books on regulation, private property rights, anti-industry activism, taxation, and free enterprise versus communism.

This internal publishing network has provided the leadership and supporters of the movement with a readily available, legitimized rallying point and revenue source. Its books are likely to be prominently displayed at any wise use group rally or workshop. Wayne Hage, author of one of the Free Enterprise Press titles, *Storm over Rangelands*, notes, however, that most of the books are being read by people who are already supporters of wise use:

> We are having a hard time getting the mainstream press to pay much attention to these books, though. We don't get a lot of reviews in newspapers or magazines, and we have a hard time getting them placed in public libraries where other people can see them. Even if we do get them into a public library, someone checks it out and never returns the book. They simply disappear and never get replaced.[31]

The CFDFE also operates a nationwide newspaper syndicate that distributes columns and commentary to more than 400 newspapers, reaching an estimated 8 million readers in the United States. In addition, CFDFE literature touts its American Broadcasting Network of radio stations that produces public affairs programs and documentaries; Gottlieb reportedly served as president of Westnet Broadcasting, Inc., which filed with the Federal Communications Commission as an affiliate of an AM radio station in Portland, KBNP.[32] Other wise use groups are similarly entrepreneurial, churning out dozens of think pieces, position papers, and newsletters.

Another major public relations tool utilized by wise use groups is a somewhat indirect one. As a counter to the Times-Mirror Corporation's environmentally supportive television programming on the Outdoor Life Channel, wise use organizations asked their members to support an alternative but similarly named network called the Outdoor Channel, which is available to satellite television owners and full-power broadcast stations:

> This network represents traditional American outdoorsmen and women and traditional American values. The Outdoor Channel does not "preach to the choir." Through its entertaining and informative outdoor programming, featuring everything from hunting and fishing to prospecting and treasure hunting, the Outdoor Channel at-

tracts the mainstream American audience. The audience also views issue-oriented programs that, through truth and common sense, bring balanced solutions to the debate.[33]

Many of the leaders within the movement feel they have been ignored by the media or, worse yet, that their positions are being misrepresented. That sentiment is expressed by a staff member of the CDC:

> Our organization is not anti-environmental. I stress this because, typically, so-called environmental groups discount any opposition to their agenda as "anti-environmental." This is so untrue. Our organization represents people and organizations who truly care about our resources and their wise use. Unfortunately the mainstream media is not offering the public a true representation of us and similar organizations. Clearly, our work as educators is far from being done.[34]

To combat what they perceive as misrepresentation, the major umbrella groups have mounted a strong public relations campaign designed to counter negative publicity originating with the environmental movement or directly from the media itself. Wise use leaders have not sat idly by taking hits in the press; each time they have had their agenda attacked or questioned, they have responded with a campaign of their own. They have also not been content to remain in a defensive posture and have attempted to try to shape public opinion by using whatever forums they can access to get their message out. By readily agreeing to interviews with the press and making appearances on television and radio programs, movement leaders find themselves the subject of articles in the mainstream media, further establishing their credibility. The groups then widely distribute copies of the articles about themselves, further broadening their audience and potential for public support.

Environmental groups, in turn, respond with a countercampaign to that mounted by wise use. Jim Bernfield, who has served as a communications consultant for the American Resources Information Network, which supports the environmental movement, has provided recommendations on how to use the media "to discredit and marginalize Wise Use. An indictment of the Wise Use movement—sharp at certain times, subtle at other times—should be woven into every speech, interview, and news release," he counsels. "If the Wise Use movement seems to be dictating the agenda of a news source, a strong and swift response of calls and letters must be orchestrated showing the station or paper that you are a force to be considered."[35]

The two sides then play off each other in the press, trading allegations and accusing the other of misrepresenting the facts or attempting to manipulate public opinion by exploiting the media. The strategy is time-honored and effective, regardless of who uses it.

Delegitimization

The term "delegitimization" is used to describe the strategy employed to reduce a group's authenticity or the validity of its arguments, isolating its members and their grievances from the mainstream. This process is accomplished in a number of ways. Many groups rely upon powerful visual imagery and incendiary rhetoric to characterize the opposition, denying them a familiar, human face by depersonalizing them and portraying them as alien and irrational. Those with a different ideological perspective are portrayed as "demons" whose sole purpose is to destroy the society, literally and figuratively, pitting "good" against "evil," or as a struggle of David versus Goliath in a battle for the hearts, minds, and souls of the group. It assumes that there is a shared public interest that must be preserved against those who seek to destroy it.

By depersonalizing the opposition, it becomes easier to see them as threatening and evil and, eventually, to legitimize misrepresentations of their motivations. One of the ways the wise use movement has attempted to use this strategy against members of environmental groups is by linking them to communism by using what has been called the "watermelon theme"—"green on the outside but red on the inside." The strategy was effective during the Reagan administration when the Soviet Union was depicted by the president as an evil empire intent on destroying the United States—a philosophy recycled from previous generations that had already grown weary of admonitions about the communist menace. Wise use leader Ron Arnold is said to have used this strategy of linking environmentalism and communism in a 1984 presentation to a pesticide trade group in Canada:

> The Soviet Union would never allow such a thing as a wilderness area in which valuable resources of petroleum or timber or nonfuel minerals could never be extracted, yet they encourage the Free World to voluntarily lock up more and more of their natural resources from economic production. . . . Environmentalism is an already existing vehicle by which the Soviet Union can encourage the Free World to voluntarily cripple its own economy.[36]

The use of inflammatory rhetoric is a tool used by many organized interests, and wise use speakers have an uncanny tool for picking hot-button topics and crafting language designed to push those buttons in sympathetic crowds. Environmental movement supporters have been branded with a wide variety of labels and as advocates of various causes, from the more benign "tree huggers" and "bunny lovers" to champions for the United Nations, one-world government, and the repeal of the Second Amendment provisions regarding the right to bear arms. At the very least, they are accused of being "environmental extremists" who have pushed the regulatory and legislative barriers too far.

In Montana, for example, community organizer Dennis Winters reportedly told a rally of timber workers to oppose a compromise agreement reached by organized labor and environmental leaders because the proposal would lock up the land for "goddamn forever," causing a 30 percent unemployment rate. "And along with that comes wife batterment, child molestation, and the rest of it. . . . Now do you think the environmentalists give a damn about the fact that kids are going to be molested as a result of this?"[37]

A similar effort during the winter of 1990–1991 was used to thwart the Yellowstone Vision for the Future. Supporters of wise use like People for the West! and the Wyoming Heritage Society came to Montana State University in mining industry–chartered buses and were asked to attend rallies wearing yellow armbands just prior to attending a public hearing on the document. "One lady got up there, jaw quivering, used her time to say the Pledge of Allegiance, then looked at me and called me a Nazi," remembers Yellowstone Park superintendent Robert Barbee. "I was Saddam Hussein, a Communist, a Fascist, everything else you could think of."[38]

The Yellowstone controversy was fueled by another tactic of delegitimization: simply outhustling the opposition by providing decisionmakers with more information on one side of the issue than the other. Roger Ekey, communications director for the environmental group Greater Yellowstone Coalition, believes the proposal by the USFWS and the NPS to improve coordination and management of public lands in the region was defeated because most of those who attended the public hearing had never read the official documents for the plan. Instead, their opinions were shaped by "fact sheets" prepared and distributed by wise use groups. Ekey now says the environmental movement should plan a more aggressive counterattack, researching wise use groups before an issue arises to develop a rapid response approach to their claims.[39]

Delegitimization of another sort involves the use of misinformation, often deliberate and calculated, perhaps occasionally used as hyperbole. In 1993, a Los Angeles religious radio station played host to the late Dixie Lee Ray, whose credentials included serving as a member of the zoology faculty at the University of Washington and public service as the former governor of the state of Washington and as chair of the Atomic Energy Commission. During the broadcast, Ray asked listeners whether they approved of $2.6 million being spent to protect the cockroach or the American dung beetle, which she claimed were on the ESA list. The story has been oft-repeated by conservative media as indicative of how the environmental movement has sought protection for various species at huge cost to taxpayers.

Ray brought a credibility to wise use that came under fire when some of her statements were more closely scrutinized. The cockroach example stems from a paragraph in her 1993 book, *Environmental Overkill: Whatever Happened to Common Sense?*, in which she notes that interfering with the habitat of the Puerto Rican cave cockroach invited "heavy fines and jail sentences. Penalties are far more likely to be imposed for 'environmental crimes' even when committed unknowingly than for unlawful acts like burglary or aggravated assault in the criminal justice system."[40] But one investigative report on wise use found that the endangered species list contained neither the cockroach nor the dung beetle and that Ray had made similar misstatements throughout her public appearances and in her book.[41]

Another way wise use groups have distinguished their perspective from that of the environmental movement is by delegitimizing environmental group members as neopaganists, part of a New Age Eastern religion and movement. The linkage is alleged to stem from the reference to environmentalists as nature worshipers and ancient druids (Celtic priests) who were said to sacrifice human beings under trees. The theme was introduced by a popular 1971 book by John McPhee about former Sierra Club executive director David Brower, *Encounters with the Archdruid*, in which a property developer negatively characterized Brower as a modern druid.

THE ENVIRONMENTAL MOVEMENT'S
RESPONSE TO WISE USE

For their part, environmental organizations have attempted to delegitimize the wise use movement and its leaders as well, often by drawing linkages to a wide range of conservative causes and interests. One of the most persistent criticisms is that the wise use movement is actually one of the political arms of the Reverend Sun Myung Moon and the Unification Church. The connection comes from a number of allegations about wise use leaders, the most direct of which appears to be the fact that both Ron Arnold and Alan Gottlieb were said to have served on advisory boards of the American Freedom Coalition (AFC). The AFC is a nationwide conservative organization, and reporters allege that one-third of the group's assets have come from Unification Church "business interests."[42]

Environmental groups have been equally critical of authors who have tried to link the environmental movement with Eastern religions as a way of attacking their credibility. In her book *Under the Spell of*

Mother Earth, Fundamentalist author Berit Kjos writes of a parable in which Satan uses twentieth-century nature worship as a way of over-throwing God's rule on earth. Environmental groups have criticized Kjos as a supporter of the wise use group Committee for a Construc-tive Tomorrow and the conservative Carthage Foundation.[43]

One of the environmental movement's watchdog groups, the Western States Center in Portland, Oregon, argues that there are also close connections between wise use and the religious right, especially at the local government level. One of the center's publications exam-ined the 1992 election in which the Oregon Citizens Alliance (OCA)—a New Right grassroots organization that chose homosexuality as its major campaign issue—gained a widespread following in the state. Be-cause the OCA has attempted to use direct democracy strategies like the citizen initiative and recalls of local government officials, there is an alleged linkage to wise use groups (especially in Washington State) that have also used these strategies.

The linkage ignores the fact that environmental organizations have also used citizen initiatives as a way of advancing their political agenda. Still, groups like the Western States Center argue that because "goals such as privatization and reduced government regulation fit neatly under the roof of several existing groups [like the OCA]," the re-ligious right, wise use, industry, and other forces are tapping the same population pool and thus creating ties among the factions at the grass-roots level.[44]

Another report produced for the Canadian government alleges that the movement has a connection to the right-wing regimes in Latin America and the contras in Nicaragua.[45] Still another linkage has been alleged to connect wise use advocates and former presidential candi-date/convicted felon Lyndon LaRouche. A LaRouche associate, Roge-lio Maduro, was alleged to be the leader of a campaign to oppose the U.S. ratification of the Convention on Biological Diversity, which was a product of the 1992 Earth Summit.[46]

THE MILITANCY/WISE USE LINKAGE

Environmental organizations have become alarmed at what they per-ceive to be a darker side to the debate over the management of natural resources. The NPCA, for example, began publishing a "Wise Use Watch" column in its monthly magazine as a way of tracking groups and alerting its members to their activities.[47] Other organizations, many of which grew out of such liberal organizations as People for the American Way that observe the activities of the political far right, began monitoring wise use groups as they became more visible in the early 1990s.[48] Their publications regularly include exposés on the right-wing connection and related human rights issues.[49] Their primary concern has been whether or not wise use groups are becoming more militant in the level of their opposition to the environmental movement and the increasing potential for confrontation with the more radical elements of both wise use and environmental groups like Earth First!

The Role of the Radicals

Protest can take a variety of forms, but the more radical forms of violent protests are usually the result of actions by individuals who become dissatisfied with the pace of issue resolution. They are desperate to "move things along" and seldom represent the majority of a group's members or the movement as a whole.

The environmental movement's leaders have documented what they believe to be an increasing number of threats directed at their members, with many of the cases involving harassing phone calls, death threats, and vandalism. The incidents are often reported to police or uncovered by investigative journalists, who often attribute the activities, accurately or not, to members of the wise use movement. The result is a growing perception that wise use is synonymous with violent protest.

More common are incidents involving some form of disruption of an environmental group's activities, or, as wise use groups refer to them, "acts of civil disobedience." In the summer of 1977, for example, opponents of the RARE wilderness designation hearings packed and disrupted a series of local meetings. A hearing in Bonners Ferry, Idaho, was disrupted by a fleet of roaring logging trucks, so the meeting was moved to a local football field. Shortly thereafter, lumber company helicopters buzzed about the hearing until organizers were forced to discontinue the meeting altogether.[50] In 1996, disruption was the tactic of choice when hundreds of angry loggers, miners, and ranchers in Jacksonville, Oregon, demonstrated outside a concert whose proceeds benefited six environmental organizations. Using chain saws, air horns, firecrackers, and synthetic skunk aroma, the protesters vented their frustration at singer Bonnie Raitt, who recently had been arrested at an antilogging demonstration in California. One demonstrator said he was discouraged by what he called the "hypocrisy" of environmental group members who use forest products. "They want to have their cake and eat it, too," he said, while another noted, "If they stop using our product, we'll stop cutting."

Cataloging incidents of violence against members of environmental organizations is another common interest group tactic and part of the strategy of delegitimization mentioned previously. Often the alleged linkage with a radical fringe is tied to a key incident that may or may not be directly related to current events. Some environmental group members, for example, begin the militancy chronology with the 1974 death of antinuclear activist Karen Silkwood as evidence that those who oppose the environmental movement are engaged in a war against its members. Nearly a third of David Helvarg's book *The War Against the Greens* is filled with stories of environmentalists who have been threatened or had their property damaged, allegedly by anti-environmental radicals. In each instance, leaders of the environmental movement have pointed an accusing finger at loggers, miners, hunters, and virtually anyone who does not share their goals as the parties responsible for the escalation of actions.

After the highly publicized sinking of the Greenpeace vessel *The Rainbow Warrior* in a New Zealand harbor in 1985, later discovered to be part of the French government's effort to thwart the group's antinuclear activism, environmental groups were on the alert expecting similar terrorism. The most often cited of the incidents involved two members of the radical environmental organization Earth First!, Judi Bari and Daryl Cherney, who were injured in a 1990 car bombing in Oakland, California. The two activists had been organizing the ten-week-long Redwood Summer protests against the logging of forests in northern California and had received death threats over their involvement.[51] Both Bari and Cherney were later arrested on charges of possession and transportation of an explosive device—a pipe bomb that exploded beneath the seat of Bari's car. The charges were later dropped by the district attorney's office for lack of evidence, although there was considerable speculation that the two activists had manufactured the bomb themselves. Others disbelieved that theory, maintaining that the bomb was intended to, if not kill, at least intimidate Bari and Cherney.

The incident became even more puzzling when local newspapers began receiving communications from individuals claiming credit for the bombing. One individual, the "Lord's Avenger," contacted the media and outlined details about not only the bomb that injured Bari and Cherney, but also a second bomb that had been left outside a Louisiana Pacific mill, which was to be blamed on Bari. Several suspects were investigated by the Federal Bureau of Investigation, but Judi Bari personally believes the timber industry was responsible. She believes the FBI never followed up on leads, including a written death threat she received before the bombing. The two activists later filed suit against the government because they believed the FBI had never fully investigated the incident.[52]

There is little disagreement as to whether or not this incident of violence and intimidation took place. The facts themselves are not in dispute. But despite the thousands of hours spent by local, state, and federal law enforcement agencies (along with private investigators hired by environmental organizations), no one has ever been arrested in connection with the Bari case.

"Death threats come with the territory these days," notes Andy Kerr, former executive director of the Oregon Natural Resources Council.[53] Kerr has been hanged in effigy and is a frequent and visible target of the environmental opposition in the Pacific Northwest. Kerr has gone nose to nose with county officials seeking to preserve what they see as the traditional economic base of their communities. To them, Kerr truly is the enemy.

It is important, however, to try to determine whether any of the incidents can be directly linked to organized militancy within the environmental opposition, or if they stem from individuals who decide to act independently on the basis of a personal grievance or perspective. For example, one widely reported case involved a Sierra Club member in Alabama who reported to police that he and a friend had been confronted in the woods by a drunken hunter.

It's the worst thing that ever happened to me in the woods, having a man with a gun pointed at my chest with his finger on the trigger calling me an environmentalist and saying I'm stealing his forest and he's not going to take it anymore.[54]

The man was later released after being questioned by police because he was not considered dangerous. He later committed suicide, and the Sierra Club member says that he was subsequently subject to threats and vilification by local residents who are also part of the environmental opposition.

Does this incident represent a form of anti-environmental conspiracy, as some believe, or does the fact that the individual was intoxicated, owned a gun, and was angry at environmental groups represent an isolated case of a mentally disturbed individual who took out his frustrations on the first two men he happened to encounter that day? Or, is it the logical consequence of the delegitimizing and dehumanizing rhetorical strategies employed by wise use groups? Although the confrontation could be seen as evidence of the potential for violence over deeply held beliefs, it is difficult to trace individual incidents to specific organizations or to identify them as part of the wise use movement's strategy against environmental groups.

In another case sometimes attributed to the new militancy, Native American environmental leader Leroy Jackson was found dead in his car just before he was scheduled to go to Washington, D.C., to testify against a proposal to cut old-growth trees on the Navajo reservation.

As in the case of the Oakland bombing, speculation about the cause of Jackson's death has been widespread. He was considered a healthy, forty-seven-year-old runner who never drank or smoked when his body was found in the back of his Dodge van by New Mexico state police at a rest stop. His death was later ruled to have been the result of methadone intoxication, with traces of Valium and marijuana in his body.

Jackson was the founder of Dine Citizens Against Ruining the Environment and had been an active opponent of the tribal-owned Navajo Forest Products Industry. His death, under what friends consider questionable circumstances and the state police declared as accidental, further fueled conjecture over whether the environmental opposition had taken a new, more violent turn.[55]

Government officials, especially those associated with the BLM and the USFS, believe they, too, are targets of wise use militancy. One rancher was alleged to have warned a BLM official "that if he had only two bullets left, he would save one of them for him." USFS workers report a pattern of intimidation and confrontations with citizens who believe the federal government has no right to enforce federal laws on private property. Without referring to any specific linkage between militias and wise use, one observer has commented that the two groups have redirected hatred into an "acceptable" target in the form of disagreement with the government. "When that type of hatred is made acceptable by being transferred to our public servants— such as those who used to work in the Murrah [Federal Office] Building—a new strain of bigotry has the chance to thrive in the American mainstream."[56]

Some leaders of the wise use movement have made an attempt to defuse criticism over their tactics and to disclaim any linkages to militant activists. In 1994, the CFDFE developed the "Reno Declaration of Non-Violence," which states:

> Two vital causes have come into conflict. In pursuing divergent views of nature and humanity's place in that nature, the environmental movement and the wise use movement confront each other daily. Their differences are the subject of widespread political debate, of pressure to change law and policy, of appeals to public opinion.
>
> But while responsible leaders of both movements embrace political advocacy and non-violent protest, some have escalated non-violent political confrontation into violence. By this declaration we absolutely and unconditionally reject and denounce the use of weapons or personal violence against our opponents or vandalism against their property.
>
> We absolutely and unconditionally accept the power of unarmed non-violent moral conviction as the only standard of behavior in confrontations between our two movements. We call upon all leaders of

the environmental movement and the wise use movement to join with us in refusing to countenance any use of weapons, personal violence upon our opponents, or vandalism against their property.

By this declaration we agree and bind ourselves to take positive actions designed to prevent personal violence between supporters of our respective movements. We will provide written statements to our supporters declaring the peaceful intent of our organizations and explaining detailed non-violent procedures in all confrontations where emotions are likely to become engaged.

In the event these positive actions fail, we agree and bind ourselves to mutually aid victims of relevant violence and vandalism as possible, to assist law enforcement agencies in prosecuting violators, and to seek civil sanctions against violators where appropriate.

This is a legally binding document to which we voluntarily consent. Nothing in this declaration is intended to limit the right of self defense by any legal means in the event that another initiates personal violence. State laws on self defense remain the moral, ethical, and legal standard for proper behavior when under physical attack.

Nothing in this declaration is intended to limit the vigorous advocacy of our causes. The mutual rejection of personal violence and vandalism against property in no way lessens our sharp disagreement on issues, our wholehearted devotion to our movement, or our will to prevail. We surrender nothing by renouncing violence. We give away nothing by upholding fundamental human decency.

Whether the document is sufficient to convince environmental group members that wise use leaders are committed to more traditional strategies remains to be seen. For their part, some members of the environmental movement are doing little to ease tensions, seeking to exploit perceptions that there are connections between wise use political activism and right-wing violence.

ForestVoice, a quarterly publication of the Eugene, Oregon–based Native Forest Council, published a *Time* magazine photo taken of the April 1995 bombing of the Alfred Murrah Federal Office Building in Oklahoma City, which shows a medic attempting to assist a severely injured victim of the blast. The accompanying article includes the following paragraph:

> Wise use organizers who whip rural crowds into hateful frenzies against environmentalists and against government employees charged with enforcing the laws on public lands, also bear responsibility for creating a climate that encourages violence. When they accuse environmentalists and the government of conspiring to take away their rights and property, then invite angry rural people to strike out against their "oppressors," they plant the seeds that erupt as threats, intimidation, and ultimately violence.[57]

Although considerably less publicized, there is a parallel concern about violence among members of the environmental opposition. A

1995 survey found that 34 percent of those responding indicated they had been threatened or harmed, or felt their personal safety was at risk, because of their wise use activism. Most incidents involved threatening or hateful letters or telephone calls, especially after a letter they had written to a newspaper had been published, or after they had spoken at a hearing or other public meeting also attended by members of environmental groups. When the most activist members of wise use groups spoke at public forums, they noted they had been the target of bomb threats; and one highly visible national leader said she had spoken to the FBI about threats she had received. Others detailed acts of deliberate sabotage, ranging from one person who had found fences on her ranch property torn down to a snowmobile user whose equipment had been vandalized.[58]

Just as the incident in Oakland lent credence to the allegations that the environmental opposition was becoming more violent, the 1995 mail bomb murder of Gil Murray, executive director of the California Forestry Association, convinced many of those in wise use groups that radical environmentalists were responsible for terrorism. With the 1996 arrest of Theodore Kaczynski, the man suspected of Murray's death and other violence attributed to an individual known as the Unabomber, there was increasing concern among environmental opposition groups that their lives were in danger. Interestingly, both members of the environmental movement and those within wise use share a distrust of the government's ability to protect them or their property. Some wise use activists believe that government agencies like the BLM have, in fact, been responsible for property damage or conspired with environmental groups against them.

The Sahara Club

Ask a member of the environmental movement who they suspect is behind much of the threats and violence in the West and they are likely to mention the name Rick Sieman and the southern California–based Sahara Club. The organization was founded in 1989 by Sieman and Louis McKey, both off-road motorcycle racers who named their group as a foil to the Sierra Club and as a counterpoint to Earth First! Sieman and McKey were among the 3,000 participants in the Barstow (California) to Las Vegas motorcycle race across the desert, which had been criticized by numerous environmental organizations. The environmental groups criticized the BLM for granting permits for the event because they believed the race did irreparable damage to the fragile desert ecosystem, including habitat for an endangered tortoise. Earth First! members had been accused of sabotaging the race on several occasions in order to intimidate the riders. In 1989, the BLM canceled the race permits.

Sieman has boasted that his organization includes a special division called the "Sahara Clubbers" and is quoted as saying, "I'm the smallest at 220 pounds. Our biggest are ugly, 300-pound desert riders. If indeed we find Earth First!ers setting traps, we're going to take care of them with baseball bats. If the police can't take care of business, we're going to take care of business for them."[59]

He has also boasted that his favored tactic is crude harassment, such as disruption of environmental meetings and protests. The organization has its own computer bulletin board on which it lists the names, addresses, telephone numbers, and license plate numbers of environmental group members. In 1990, he conducted a "Dirty Tricks Workshop" for northern California timber activists who had organized against the Redwood Summer protests and claims he has conducted dozens more workshops across the country. The club's newsletter has advised its members, "You have to do whatever you feel is necessary to fight our enemy and fight for our freedom. We don't want to know who you are, or what you're doing, but get the job done!"[60]

The group's newsletter often features "suggestions" by its members on how to disrupt environmental group meetings, although the Sahara Club has frequently targeted government agencies as well. One member advised his colleagues, "I have stocked up on Superglue and find it works best in the door locks of BLM vehicles. One little squirt in each lock and they have to break the window to get in. If I have time, it's also fun to let the air out of the tires, then Superglue the valve caps back on so they can't be refilled."[61]

As a result of the motorcycle race issue, the Sahara Club targeted California senator Alan Cranston, who sought for years to have that portion of the Mojave Desert designated as a national park. When Cranston left the Senate, the group changed the object of their disaffection to California senators Barbara Boxer and Diane Feinstein, who continued to shepherd the bill through Congress, referring to the women as "ultra-liberal bitches." In congressional hearings on the legislation in 1992 in Beverly Hills, Sahara Club members allegedly physically harassed several female members of the Sierra Club attempting to testify.[62] Whereas the Sahara Club might take responsibility for the initial salvo in the legislative battle, less radical groups within the environmental opposition kept the fight going using more traditional interest group strategies like letter-writing campaigns to Congress.

Most political movements historically have included a radical fringe, and the zeal of these members draws public attention to the cause and promotes public awareness of grievances. Just as the group Earth First! has provided a radical foil for the environmental movement, the Sahara Club has served a similar purpose for the environmental opposition, even though its activities have not been as widely publicized as those of Earth First! But as the Reno declaration suggests, the presence of a radical element within a movement allows the rest of the group to not only look more moderate, but to disavow the militancy of the radical fringe. Virtually every wise use group has publicly distanced itself from violence, but in private, leaders admit that the presence of groups like the Sahara Club has allowed them to try to appeal to the public with what then seems like a more moderate agenda. But that strategy also creates in the public's mind the perception that the radical elements of a movement (especially those associated with antigovernment groups like the Freemen and the Branch Davidians) are more likely to be guilty of criminal behavior than to be ideologically committed to a particular cause.

WISE USE AND ENVIRONMENTAL POLICYMAKING

The wise use movement can point to a smattering of policy victories during its short life, most of them based on the traditional strategies used by organized interests. Most of its efforts have been focused on regional battles, such as the Yellowstone ecosystem plan. By forming an alliance with other organizations and industries, for example, under the banner Yellowstone Regional Citizens Coalition, the members of diverse groups have developed considerable power in stopping or delaying projects that were considered critical to environmental groups.

The movement has also claimed some public relations–related successes by using its clout to influence media sponsors over programming its members consider biased. For example, in 1989, the wise use network embarked upon a massive fax and letter-writing campaign to sponsors and to the Turner Broadcasting System protesting the showing of the film *Rage over Trees.* The Ford Motor Company pulled its ads from the program after receiving urgent requests from dealer associates in the Pacific Northwest who told corporate officials the airing "would really hurt their business."[63] Other efforts convinced General Electric and Stroh's Brewery not to renew funding for the television program *World of Audubon* after wise use groups threatened the companies with a boycott over segments dealing with ranching, logging, and the film *The New Range Wars,* which dealt with cattle grazing on public lands. Although the Turner system aired *Rage over Trees* anyway, the company reportedly lost $100,000 in advertising revenues in doing so.[64]

The three major legislative targets of the movement—the Endangered Species Act, the Clean Water Act, and the 1872 Mining Law— were bottled up in the 104th Congress, which, despite its conservative leadership, became less willing to gut legislation than it was to incrementally change it or put it on hold until after the 1996 elections. Instead, wise use groups joined a coalition of other conservative organizations and their followers who managed to place a temporary moratorium on the listing of new endangered species and advocated cuts in environmental regulatory agency support during the battle over the federal budget in 1996.

Wise use leaders continue to try to win over additional supporters by what appears to be a rational appeal to a middle ground on the environment, often using their knowledge of legislative history and judicial interpretation to bolster their arguments. Just as the environmental movement capitalizes on its war stories about wise use advocates, wise use leaders fault both the government and environmental organizations for failing to adhere to the original intent of the law. Ron Arnold, for example, cites the 1916 National Park Service Act, which states that the purpose of a national park is to conserve the scenery, natural and historic objects, and wildlife, as well as to provide for the enjoyment of the parks. Although both environmental organizations and wise use groups would agree to the first part of the law's intent, they differ in interpretation over what the use and enjoyment aspect of the legislation means.

Preservation-oriented environmental groups note that the law also intends for the parks to remain unimpaired for the enjoyment of future generations, a goal they believe is incompatible with increased access. On Memorial Day weekend in 1996, for example, they note that thousands of visitors were turned away from Yosemite National Park between 11:00 A.M. and 4:00 P.M. because park officials could not handle the human and automobile congestion. Without usage restrictions, they believe, vital ecosystems would have been trampled, pollution from vehicles would have impaired air quality, and the overall park experience would have been diminished for everyone. The tug-of-war between the two sides is exemplified by this difference in interpretation of the law and how it ought to be implemented, and neither side seems willing to compromise on its perspective.

In light of the allegations about militancy and corporate sponsorship, the wise use movement today is attempting to recast its image by using what one group calls a "mainstream message that is geared for common consumption and persuasion." By moving away from the earlier vanguard message that appealed more to right-wing activists (such as tying the environmental movement to Marxism) or the conspiracy message (which polarized the debate by playing on emotions and fears), the wise use movement now has a more positive rhetoric that taps into basic American values. The core arguments of the mainstream wise use message have been identified as:

> *Balance:* Humans and nature can exist in productive harmony. Nature
> can be properly protected by the use management of economic activity.
> *People Come First:* Humans are the preeminent species. Nature exists
> for humans, whose needs come first.
> *Can-Do Attitude:* Science, technology and our own ingenuity can solve
> our environmental problems.
> *Freedom of Choice Is Our Individual Right:* The best government is the
> government that governs the least. Individual freedom, individual
> choice must be predominant.[65]

There is, of course, a flip side to this message that paints environmental groups as extremists who do not seek a balance between jobs
and nature, who consider humans less important than protecting insects, who believe science cannot solve environmental problems, and
who support the rights of the majority over the rights of the individual. This mainstream message is full of powerful imagery that harkens
back to a time when humans could conquer any problem before them,
to basic values and ideas that resonate with many citizens who may
have already developed the perception that environmental groups had
gone just a little too far in their zeal. It is a message that can also be
readily accepted by those who believe that government has become
too big and too bureaucratic and by those who have a basic distrust in
political leaders or the process by which they are elected. In short, the
wise use movement calls for change in a way that they hope many
Americans will find easy to support, especially those in the middle
class who have already developed an inexplicable disenchantment for
the direction in which the country is heading.

The people who are generally assumed to be adherents of wise use
issues are neither the demons environmental group members would
like to believe they are, nor are they part of a conspiratorial movement
financed by industry interests. As several studies have found, the majority of these individuals are not actively involved in or even aware of
the national movement. Instead, they have been subsumed under a
label that has then been appropriated by the movement's policy entrepreneurs to exaggerate their numbers and, eventually, to give them
political clout at a time when the policy window has made it possible
for their grievances to gain a favorable public audience.

> The national wise use movement's strategy is a classic one. With a
> finely-honed, persuasive message, their smoke and mirrors gambit
> can be used quite effectively to lobby Congress, impress the media
> and, given the right circumstances, the lack of an organized counter-
> vailing force and time, create a tangible national movement.[66]

There is little doubt that the wise use movement's umbrella groups
have put pressure on both legislators and groups within the environ-

mental movement. Their presence may not yet have had a serious impact on the output of the environmental debate, but in concert with the county supremacy and private property rights groups, they have forced their way into being given a place at the table, as the next two chapters will show even more clearly.

NOTES

1. In Thomas Harding, "Mocking the Turtle," *New Statesman and Society*, vol. 6, no. 271 (September 24, 1993): 45.

2. Gifford Pinchot, *Breaking New Ground* (New York: Harcourt, Brace, 1947), p. 505.

3. David Helvarg, "Anti-Enviros Are Getting Uglier," *The Nation*, vol. 259 (November 28, 1994): 649.

4. Phil Brick, "Determined Opposition: The Wise Use Movement Challenges Environmentalism," *Environment*, vol. 37, no. 8 (October 1995): 19.

5. Kate O'Callaghan, "Whose Agenda for America?" *Audubon* (September–October 1992): 85.

6. Richard M. Stapleton, "Greed vs. Green," *National Parks* (November–December 1992): 36.

7. MacWilliams Cosgrove Snider *The Wise Use Movement: Strategic Analysis and the Fifty State Review* (Washington, D.C.: Environmental Working Group, March 1993), pp. 1, 27.

8. Ibid., pp. 2–4.

9. Author interview with David Snodderly, April 1996.

10. Ron Arnold's biographical sketch draws from a variety of sources, many of them contradictory. See, for example, David Helvarg, *The War Against the Greens: The "Wise Use" Movement, the New Right, and Anti-Environmental Violence* (San Francisco: Sierra Club Books, 1994), pp. 130–140. For a different perspective that is more sympathetic to Arnold, see William Perry Pendley, *It Takes a Hero* (Bellevue, WA: Free Enterprise Press, 1994), pp. 267–269.

11. Ron Arnold, *Ecology Wars* (Bellevue, WA: Free Enterprise Press, 1987); with Alan Gottlieb, *Trashing the Economy: How Runaway Environmentalism Is Wrecking America*, 2nd ed. (Bellevue, WA: Free Enterprise Press, 1994); and *At the Eye of the Storm: James Watt and the Environmentalists* (Chicago: Regnery Gateway, 1982).

12. As in the case of Ron Arnold, the biographical material on Gottlieb is contradictory. See Helvarg (*The War Against the Greens*, pp. 126–130) and Pendley (*It Takes a Hero*, p. 271). See also Margaret Knox, "Meet the Anti-Greens," *The Progressive*, vol. 55, no. 10 (October 1991): 21–23.

13. Helvarg, *The War Against the Greens*, pp. 269–270.

14. Robert Gottlieb, *Forcing the Spring: The Transformation of the American Environmental Movement* (Washington, DC: Island Press, 1993), p. 209.

15. There is considerable debate over the definition of "ecofeminism" and a substantial literature on the role of women in grassroots environmental organizations. On ecofeminism, see, for example, Janet Biehl, *Rethinking Ecofeminist Politics* (Boston: South End Press, 1991); and Irene Diamond and G. F. Orenstein, *Reweaving the World: The Emergence of Ecofeminism* (San Francisco: Sierra Club Books, 1991). For studies of women in grassroots environmental groups, see, for example, Sherry Cable, "Women's Social Movement Involvement: The Role of

Structural Availability in Recruitment and Participation Processes," *Sociological Quarterly*, vol. 33 (1992): 34–50; and Dorothy Nelkin, "Nuclear Power as a Feminist Issue," *Environment*, vol. 23 (1989): 14–39. For a comparison of women in wise use, see Jacqueline Vaughn Switzer, "Women and Wise Use: The Other Side of Environmental Activism," paper presented at the Western Political Science Association annual meeting, San Francisco, March 14–16, 1996.

16. Brick, "Determined Opposition," p. 19.

17. "Membership of the Ten Largest Environmental Groups," *USA Today*, October 19, 1994, p. A8.

18. Karen W. Arenson, "Donations to Charities Rose 11% Last Year, Report Says," *New York Times*, May 13, 1996, p. A9.

19. T. H. Watkins, "Fat Cats and New Voices," *Wilderness*, vol. 56, no. 198 (fall 1992): 8.

20. Alan Gottlieb, ed., *The Wise Use Agenda* (Bellevue, WA: Free Enterprise Press, 1989).

21. Center for the Defense of Free Enterprise, membership brochure, n.d.

22. Stapleton, "Greed vs. Green," p. 35.

23. See Patricia Byrnes, "The Counterfeit Crusade," *Wilderness*, Vol. 55, no. 197 (summer 1992): 29–31.

24. For more on what happened with this proposal, see Robert Ekey, "Wise Use and the Greater Yellowstone Vision Document," in John Echeverria and Raymond Booth Eby, eds., *Let the People Judge: Wise Use and the Private Property Rights Movement* (Washington, DC: Island Press, 1995), pp. 339–347.

25. Stapleton, "Greed vs. Green," p. 35. For additional information on the Yellowstone document, see Richard M. Stapleton, "On the Western Front," *National Parks* (January–February 1993): 32–36.

26. David Lapp, "Wise Use's Labor Ruse," *Environmental Action*, vol. 25, no. 3 (fall 1993): 24.

27. Margaret Knox, "Wise Guys," *Mother Jones* (January–February 1991): 16.

28. "The War Is Not Yet Over," *Desert News Letter*, vol. 8, no. 1 (1995): 1.

29. Letter from R. K. Kelly, SHARE executive secretary, to author, October 13, 1995.

30. Thomas A. Lewis, "Cloaked in a Wise Disguise," in Echeverria and Eby, eds., *Let the People Judge*, p. 13.

31. Interview with Wayne Hage by author, August 26, 1995.

32. MacWilliams Cosgrove Snider, *The Wise Use Movement*, p. 61.

33. Jake Hartwick, "The Battle for the Hearts and Minds of the American Public Is upon Us!" *Desert News Letter*, vol. 8, no. 1 (1995): 7.

34. Letter from Carol Parks, California Desert Coalition, to author, October 2, 1995.

35. Jim Bernfield, "Working with the Media," in Echeverria and Eby, eds., *Let the People Judge*, pp. 327–338.

36. Helvarg, *The War Against the Greens*, p. 139.

37. Lapp, "Wise Use's Labor Ruse," p. 25.

38. Stapleton, "On the Western Front," p. 34.

39. Ekey, "Wise Use," pp. 339–343.

40. Dixie Lee Ray, with Lou Guzzo, *Environmental Overkill: Whatever Happened to Common Sense?* (Washington, DC: Regnery Gateway, 1993), p. 89.

41. Tim Callahan, "Environmentalists Cause Malaria! (and Other Myths of the 'Wise Use' Movement," *The Humanist*, vol. 55 (January–February 1995): 10.

42. Margaret Knox, "The Grass-Roots Anti-Environmental Movement," *Utne Reader* (July–August 1992): 108–109.

43. Callahan, "Environmentalists Cause Malaria!" p. 14.

44. Dave Mazza, *God, Land, and Politics: The Wise Use and Christian Right Connection in 1992 Oregon Politics* (Portland, OR: Western States Center, 1993).

45. Lapp, "Wise Use's Labor Ruse," pp. 24–25.

46. Michael W. Robbins, "Biodiversity and Strange Bedfellows," *Audubon*, vol. 97 (January–February 1995): 4.

47. See, for example, "Wise Use Watch," *National Parks* (May–June 1995): 16.

48. Among the organizations that have been closely monitoring wise use groups (and their alleged connection to the militia movement) are the Clearinghouse on Environmental Advocacy and Research, the Western States Center, and Political Research Associates.

49. See, for example, William K. Burke, "The Wise Use Movement: Right-Wing Anti-Environmentalism," *Public Eye*, vol. 7, no. 2 (June 1993). *Public Eye* has been published by a number of organizations since its inception, including the Repression Information Project, the National Lawyers Guild Civil Liberties Committee, and Political Research Associates.

50. Richard D. Lamm and Michael McCarthy, *The Angry West: A Vulnerable Land and Its Future* (Boston: Houghton Mifflin, 1982), p. 232.

51. For a summary of the Redwood Summer radicalism, see Betsy Carpenter, "Redwood Radicals," *U.S. News and World Report*, September 17, 1990, pp. 50–51.

52. Helvarg, *The War Against the Greens*, pp. 330–339. Bari's views of the incident and its aftermath can be found in her article "Fighting an FBI Frame-Up," *Earth Island Journal* (summer 1994): 40–41.

53. Helvarg, "Anti-Enviros Are Getting Uglier," p. 651.

54. Ibid., p. 646.

55. For a more complete description of the Jackson incident, see Helvarg, *The War Against the Greens*, pp. 385–389.

56. Kenneth S. Stern, *A Force upon the Plain: The American Militia Movement and the Politics of Hate* (New York: Simon and Schuster, 1996), pp. 131 132.

57. Victor Rozek, "Speak No Evil," *ForestVoice*, vol. 8, no. 2 (March–June 1995): 8.

58. Switzer, "Women and Wise Use," p. 29.

59. Paul Rauber, "Ugly Guys with Baseball Bats," *Sierra*, vol. 76 (May–June 1991): 73.

60. Ibid.

61. Paul Rauber, "Wit and Wisdom of the Wise Users," *Sierra*, vol. 80 (November–December 1995): 33.

62. Helvarg, *The War Against the Greens*, p. 249.

63. Knox, "Meet the Anti-Greens," p. 23.

64. Stapleton, "Greed vs. Green," p. 34; and Knox, ibid., p. 23.

65. MacWilliams Cosgrove Snider, *The Wise Use Movement*, pp. 12–20.

66. Ibid., p. 2.

9

County Supremacy and the War on the West

SIGN OF THE TIMES: In May 1995, a group of ranchers met at the Knights of Columbus Hall in Sierra Vista, Arizona, just weeks after the bombing of the Alfred Murrah Federal Building in Oklahoma City. The invocation they offered at the beginning of the meeting of the Coalition of Arizona/New Mexico Counties for Stable Economic Growth included the following entreaty: "May we realize that actions have consequences. . . . May the federal departments make decisions that bless the lives of the people. May we find no room for those things that are destructive and bad."[1]

The original "War on the West," many observers believe, began with the conflict between conservationists and preservationists at the turn of the century. Likening the tug-of-war to a national morality play, former Colorado governor Richard Lamm described the two sides' differences in perceptions and values.

> In the eastern mind, savers held the earth; takers destroyed it. And easterners were the savers. The tragedy was that the East never understood the desperation of western life, the quiet panic that underlay the living of each day. Conservationists, disciples of Thoreau and Muir, fought for the lockup and nonuse of the wilderness without any thought of western consequences; cloaked in moralism and self-righteousness, they branded dissenters "vandals" and "destroying angels." Even moderates—Pinchot and his apostles of efficiency—understood little more. Men of science and technology, they knew nothing of the West, nothing of the fierce economic faith that drove it and its people, nothing of the relentless compulsion of little men to settle and build.
>
> A chasm separated East and West that could not and would not be bridged. Eastern technocrats spoke of "integrated planning" and "central direction"— all of it from federal bureaus and all of it circumventing, or trampling, local people and local jurisdictions. . . . Trapped between the wilderness on one side and the wilderness cult on the other, the West raged at "forest enthusiasts" and "cranks," at "college professors and landscape gardeners," "dreamers," and "mad

theorists who sit in their marble halls and theorize," who held that "trees are more important than human beings."[2]

Lamm's description of the "chasm" between East and West remains accurate today. Today's War on the West, at least as far as westerners perceive it, still pits easterners (environmental organizations and the federal bureaucracy) against westerners who consider the resources and even land within the public domain to be theirs.

The phrase "War on the West" became widely used after the 1992 presidential campaign, when Democrats dominated western states' elections and took the victory as a mandate to phase out government subsidies that had been in place since the nineteenth century. After the election, the Democratic leadership announced it was taking aim at two specific programs: grazing fees and the Mining Law of 1872. Environmental groups, sensing the opening of the policy window with Al Gore, a committed movement supporter, as Bill Clinton's vice president, fully expected the administration to move swiftly to revise grazing fees and mining and timber laws, which they believed amounted to a giveaway of valuable public resources.

The Republican Party, however, was prepared to fight the policy shift, and the slogan "War on the West" started appearing on bumper stickers in rural areas and in campaign speeches as the 1994 electoral cycle began. The imagery harkened politicians back to the sectional disputes of the Sagebrush Rebellion, and it became easy for candidates to warn their constituents that the battle was raging once again. In New Mexico, for example, Republican senatorial candidate Colin McMillan, a rancher and oil executive, expressed his view in noting, "This campaign is about the attack on the Western way of life"; while in Idaho, Republican challenger Helen Chenoweth unseated Congressmember Larry LaRocco with similar comments. "It's the white, Anglo-Saxon male that's endangered today," she said, a remark that hit home in a district that is about 95 percent white.[3]

The slogan was also used by Republican leaders who sent out a strongly worded "Dear Colleague" letter in early 1995. The letter went out after the National Taxpayers Union and Citizens Against Government Waste joined with more than twenty environmental organizations to produce the *Green Scissors Report* outlining recommended cuts and reforms in federal programs. Among the items listed in the report were the elimination of some western public works projects and proposed increases in fees paid by industries to use federal lands. According to the letter, the groups were accused of betrayal. "Although NTU and CAGW ride under the flag of fiscal conservatism, these groups are merely two more regiments in Clinton's 'War on the West.'"[4] The letter epitomizes the ambivalent and sometimes contradictory attitude of environmental opposition groups that profess an antifederal message when they perceive the government is being excessively intrusive, but who support traditional "pork barrel" projects in their region when they stand to benefit.

After the victories of conservative Republicans in the 1994 midterm elections proved that many voters accepted the idea that the West was at war over natural resource policies, there was an implicit understanding that the soldiers in that battle would need more than just a slogan to keep their interests in the media spotlight. The focus of the war became known as the "county supremacy movement."

This chapter examines the movement and its parallels to the wise use movement and the efforts of property rights activists, which will be discussed in the chapter that follows. Indeed, there is considerable overlap in terms of the movements' organizational structure, tactics, and, in some cases, leadership. But there are distinct differences among these three segments of the grassroots opposition, especially the policy success that they have had, as will be explored in the conclusion of the chapter.

COUNTY SUPREMACY GROUPS AND LEADERSHIP

Like the wise use and property rights movements, the county supremacy movement has at its core a small number of individual leaders and grassroots organizations. Unlike the other two, however, county supremacy groups operate almost exclusively at the county level, and the majority of them have been established in the rural West. The groups are coordinated through one or two umbrella-like clearinghouses that provide both technical assistance and a sense of cohesiveness for what is more properly described as a regional, rather than a national, campaign.

The Utah-based National Federal Lands Conference (NFLC) is the primary umbrella organization, spearheading the efforts of counties to pass ordinances that supersede or void federal regulations they find objectionable. The group's motto, borrowed from John Adams, is "Property Must Be Sacred or Liberty Cannot Exist." The NFLC was founded by four ranchers in 1989 and is incorporated as a tax-exempt, charitable organization. The group's brochure notes that its purpose is threefold: education, legislation, and litigation. Among its founders were grazing litigant Wayne Hage and outspoken New Mexico rancher and miner Dick Manning. The group operates with an advisory council that has included numerous members with ties to the wise use movement, including Ron Arnold of the CFDFE and Mark Pollot, attorney for the property rights group Stewards of the Range.

As an umbrella group, the NFLC's primary activity is the dissemi-
nation of information. In that capacity, it is perhaps best known for
sponsoring workshops throughout the West in which local resource
users and public officials are invited to hear about how their county
can become part of the movement. Although it also has an unknown
number of dues-paying members and sponsors, it appears to obtain
the bulk of its funding from the receipts from its "how-to" conferences
and the accompanying videos, audio tapes, and books.[5]

Ruth Kaiser, who moved to Utah in 1986, is the group's executive
director and has a background in constitutional history. The ranchers
asked her to serve in an administrative capacity for the group, although
it is clear that she has deep ideological sympathies to what the NFLC is
trying to do. She notes, "I ain't a hero. This is my job. It's what I do. I believe all of us, working together, networking with other organizations,
are going to run the other side off the map, or die in the effort."[6]

A second umbrella group (although smaller and more regionally
focused than the NFLC), the Coalition of Arizona/New Mexico
Counties for Stable Economic Growth, was founded in Catron County,
New Mexico, in 1989. It was established through the effort of Dick
Manning of the NFLC, who convinced the county to join the coalition
in 1990 and who became one of its charter members. Initially, the
group coalesced around the issue of grazing on public lands in the Gila
National Forest, where ranchers claimed elk were eating valuable forage. Unlike the NFLC, which has more individual members, the coalition is made up primarily of representatives of various counties, who
pay an annual membership fee to participate. Other memberships are
held by major corporations, livestock groups, and small businesses.[7]

The coalition has been less visible in promoting county supremacy
ordinances than in litigating other issues on behalf of its members; its
primary target has been the Endangered Species Act. It also provides
some technical assistance to counties and individuals seeking status reports on proposed federal ESA legislation in their areas and on how
those listings might affect them economically.

Another small group, the Nevada-based County Alliance to Restore the Economy and Environment, has urged its members to look
closely at the Constitution, meticulously researching complex legal
theories in the state's law library to back up their claims. Local groups
like these have little difficulty in convincing their members that they
need no longer pay federal grazing fees, or that it is perfectly legal to
divert water in defiance of federal prohibitions.[8]

Although the membership of these groups may be local, some of
their resources are more likely to be national. County supremacy
groups rarely can obtain the level of legal and organizational expertise
they need from within their own ranks. For the most part, they have
become dependent upon national groups that share their political phi-

losophy. Conservative think tanks like the Cato Institute, the Los Angeles–based Individual Rights Foundation, the New Mexico–based consulting group the Land Center, or well-established conservative legal assistance groups like the Pacific Legal Foundation and the Mountain States Legal Foundation are working side by side with county activists. Other legal assistance programs work on wise use as well as county supremacy issues. The Federal Lands Legal Foundation, for instance, was created in 1991 in Roswell, New Mexico, to assist livestock owners in their efforts to litigate grazing allotments and ESA designations, but it also has represented the coalition in its efforts to retain county sovereignty.

One of the most prominent figures in the county supremacy movement's legal efforts is Karen Budd-Falen, the daughter of a Wyoming ranching family whose legal expertise has given the movement much of its clout. Budd-Falen has written extensively on what she believes is the legal basis for the county supremacy movement and has provided her services in representing counties in several cases. She is also one of the promoters of the theory that federal laws should take into account the "custom and culture" of the local area, and she developed the Catron County ordinance described later in this chapter.

The Land Center has generated the most controversy of the groups listed above, primarily because of its role in drawing up a 200-page "free market land use plan" for Catron County. The firm is reported to have received $25,000 for its services, but dissatisfaction with the plan (allegedly over its failure to address the issue of private property rights) was sufficient to cause county officials not to release it to the public. The firm also allegedly lost a $750,000 contract with the Utah Association of Counties to draw up similar land use plans for that state after the association heard about Catron County officials' dissatisfaction with its efforts. The group has moved on to assisting counties in other states.[9]

Generally, however, the county supremacy movement can be characterized as considerably smaller than the wise use and property rights movements, with power centered in a small handful of individuals and groups. Because it is almost entirely dependent on membership dues, it does not have the financial resources of other grassroots groups, and it certainly does not appear to have attracted the corporate backing that is alleged to be behind wise use organizations. It relies upon the legal resources of other conservative causes rather than foundations dedicated to the county issue per se.

BATTLE STRATEGIES AND ISSUES

Although there is considerable overlap between what the county supremacy groups have attempted to accomplish and the goals of the wise use and property rights movements, there are some subtle differences in strategy and issues that make a distinction among the three important.

The Legal Theories

The county supremacy groups rely upon three complex legal theories to bolster their case, each of which has been challenged by scholars and through litigation.[10] This section briefly describes the theories but does not attempt to assess their validity. The first theory stems from the Constitution and uses the argument that the federal government's authority extends only to those lands that it legally owns as outlined in Article 1, Section 8. Those lands include

> such District (not exceeding ten Miles square) as may, by Cession of particular States, and the acceptance of Congress, become the Seat of the Government of the United States, and to exercise like Authority over all Places purchased by consent of the Legislature of the State in which the Same shall be, for the Erection of Forts, Magazines, Arsenals, dock-Yards, and other needful Buildings.[11]

According to this strict constructionist view of the Constitution, the federal government's authority is limited to the lands within the District of Columbia, defense facilities, and "needful buildings" that would ostensibly be considered post offices and other sites that serve the remaining enumerated powers. If this legal position is accepted, the role of the federal government is virtually nil, since it has but minimal lands to regulate or control.

A second legal theory is based on the "equal footing" doctrine explored in other chapters. Under this premise, the federal government historically and contractually held the land in the new territories in trust until they could be fully established, with the understanding that at some point in time, the government would divest itself of its interests and return the land to the states to manage as they saw fit. Advocates of this view believe the federal government has broken its contractual agreement by refusing to release lands now held as national parks, national forests, and wilderness preserves. The argument carries the most weight in states in the West where the federal government retains control over a significant percentage of the land.

Lastly, a final theory rests on the National Environmental Policy Act, enacted in 1970, which county supremacy advocates believe was intended to encourage local governments to establish their own environmental protections. The language in NEPA calls for the federal government to cooperate with state and local governments to "preserve important historic, cultural, and natural aspects of our natural heritage"—referred to by adherents as the "custom and culture" concept.

The county supremacy movement's legal advisers, such as Karen Budd-Falen, argue that it is important for each county to first identify and then codify what its custom and culture is so that the federal government can defer to the counties and allow them to make policy according to that definition.[12]

The extension of the custom and culture argument is that a county has the right under NEPA to do whatever might be necessary to restore or maintain its unique character, whether that character be as a grazing community or as one devoted exclusively to mining. County supremacy groups rely almost exclusively on a predominating culture that favors extractive resource industries over any other use.[13] As one critical environmental publication puts it, "Upon this scant foundation they cobbled together the theory that if counties define their 'custom and culture' as, say, overgrazing public lands or leveling national forests, federal agencies are obliged to preserve that way of life."[14] Another critic noted, "The custom of our past is to seize land by force from the natives, plunder the resources using slave and child labor, wash away land with hydraulic mining and clear-cut virgin forests."[15]

It is the custom and culture theory that has led dozens of counties throughout the United States to consider or establish local ordinances that require the federal government to consult with them on any major federal action within their borders.

The County Ordinances

Going beyond the construct of states' rights, the ordinances that are a part of the county supremacy movement take the federalism framework down a notch to the local level. The foremost example has occurred in Catron County, New Mexico, which legitimately holds title as the capital of the county supremacy movement. Catron County has a population of less than 3,000 people within its nearly 7,000 square miles of high desert in the southwestern part of the state. It has been dominated by ranching interests ever since it was named after political power broker Thomas B. Catron, a former U.S. district attorney; a descendant, James W. Catron, has served as the attorney for Catron County and is active in several of the county supremacy organizations. As is the case in many of these regions, most political decisions are dominated by longtime ranching interests at the county level.

In 1991, Catron County adopted its Interim Land Use Policy Plan Concerning the Use of Public Lands and Public Resources and Protection of the Rights of Private Property.[16] As the title clearly indicates, the ordinance is a major assertion of the county's power to control state and federal lands within its geographical boundaries. It places all decisionmaking powers about the use of the county's lands and resources within the hands of its elected county commissioners. Even more important, the ordinance requires the federal government to consult with the commissioners about any plans to acquire or dispose of county land, or to change any existing management procedures without their approval. The county is made the designated planning agency and thus gives itself the lead role in any decisions about wilderness designations, wildlife recovery plans, road closures, changes in grazing permits, or other duties and responsibilities that are the traditional responsibility of federal and state governments. It nullifies any legislation or regulations that the county's political leaders find objectionable.

At its core, the Catron County ordinance is indicative of the antifederalist mood of the West based on mythical visions of a time long since past;[17] others perceive it as a thinly veiled usurpation of power to allow local interests to run roughshod over existing environmental regulations. The tone of its proponents is, however, clearly stated in the introduction to the 1992 "Catron County Comprehensive Plan": "Federal and state agents threaten the life, liberty, and happiness of the people of Catron County. They present a clear and present danger to the land and livelihood of every man, woman and child. A state of emergency prevails that calls for devotion and sacrifice."[18]

Estimates of the number of counties across the country that have considered or adopted Catron County–like ordinances vary from as few as 35 to as many as 500, with the vast majority of them located in the West. One study of four western states shows some commonalities among the counties that have successfully passed county supremacy ordinances. They are almost exclusively rural, with a higher percentage of federal land, a higher percentage of their budget derived from federal resource payments, and lower spending on the environment than among non–county supremacy counties. The study also found a higher level of conflict over the environment, and their elected officials perceived a poorer relationship with both the state and the federal government than did their urban counterparts. Not surprisingly, these rural counties also have higher levels of families in poverty, lower per capita incomes, and lower rates of housing growth than do urban counties.[19]

Not all of the ordinances have focused on western grazing interests. In Ontonagon County, Michigan, for example, the county's ordinance sought to restrict federal acquisition of private lands, prevent the designation of new wild and scenic rivers, maintain timber cutting "at levels consistent with custom and culture," and retain the 1872 Mining Law. The ordinance included an ideology, as well as implementation rules, requiring that "all natural resource decisions affecting Ontonagon County [shall] be guided by principles of protecting private property rights, protecting local custom and culture, maintaining traditional economic structures through self-determination, and opening new economic opportunities through reliance on free markets."[20]

For the most part, though, the development of county supremacy ordinances is still in its infancy, with many local officials studying the legal ramifications and no doubt waiting for additional court clarification before attempting to move further with this strategy. It is a costly approach for a county to take, both financially and politically. Some counties have slowed down the pace of what appeared at least initially to be a rush to follow Catron County's lead. Out of fourteen counties that had indicated they were considering county supremacy ordinances in the summer of 1995, six had decided against it by December 1995.[21]

The Litigation Route

Some individuals within the county supremacy movement have turned to the courts to litigate what they believe to be their right to self-government, realizing in many cases that their efforts are more symbolic than substantive. In doing so, they have copied a strategy that has been used frequently by environmental groups, as one activist notes: "The best approach is what the American left did so well in the 1970s and 1980s with the environment—procedural lawsuits. [Federal officials] cannot humanly comply with every rule and regulation they have. Find the bureaucratic slip-up."[22]

For example, the Coalition of Arizona/New Mexico Counties filed suit in the U.S. District Court in Albuquerque to block the USFWS from listing the Mexican spotted owl as an endangered species. The group feared that the listing, which followed by several years the widely publicized designation of the Northern spotted owl as a threatened species in the Pacific Northwest, would lead to severe restrictions on logging, grazing, and mining in an owl habitat. Rather than resorting to protests or more traditional grassroots strategies like letter-writing campaigns, the coalition used a legal microscope to find errors in the government's public notice and planning documents. "This is all working within the system," one activist notes. "We're not talking bomb-throwing. We're not advocating violence. We're making them obey the federal law."[23]

It is important to draw a further distinction between the county supremacy activists' litigation and that of groups that have been broadly labeled as part of the "patriot movement." In 1994, for example, an organization alleged to have ties to various militia groups, the Republic of Texas, began filing petitions with various courts, including the International Court of Justice at The Hague, seeking to overturn the federal government's 1845 annexation of Texas after President Andrew Jackson recognized the independence of the Texas Republic. The organization sent a letter to each of the state's 254 counties ordering them to swear allegiance to the republic or risk being replaced. These groups reject not only federal and state environmental laws but virtually all traditional legal systems, relying instead on their own interpretations of common law.[24]

Many of the county supremacy movement's litigation efforts have been unsuccessful. In New Mexico's Lincoln County, for example, the county adopted a Catron-style land use plan in January 1992, including a requirement that the existing ratio between private and public lands in the county be maintained in order to preserve the county's tax base. The county brought suit in December 1992 against the Bureau of Land Management when the agency attempted to trade land with a private property owner, which would have had the effect of reducing the ratio of private property in the county. The suit was dropped by the county in April 1993 after it conceded that its legal position was not tenable. As county commissioner Wilton Howell admitted, "This was a common sense approach. We weren't going to win."[25]

Although Catron County was the initial leader in adopting a county supremacy ordinance, officials in Nye County, Nevada, led the fight to test their legal theories in the courts. Dick Carver, a Nye County commissioner, became the county's chief activist in 1993 when he wrote Interior Secretary Bruce Babbitt to protest the administration's proposed Rangeland Reform '94. He recalls that he asked himself at the time, Why am I responding to Bruce Babbitt on Rangeland Reform when in fact the state of Nevada owns the land? He convinced his fellow commissioners to pass their own version of the Catron County ordinance, and then moved to petition the USFS to open up a former stagecoach road as a way of exerting the county's authority to control land within its boundaries. Carver took the battle a step further in 1994 by using a county-owned bulldozer to open up the road himself in the presence of USFS officials and a crowd of supporters. Although no violence occurred, the federal government filed suit against Nye County because "Nye was actively defying federal authority and creating potentially violent situations, sending letters to arrest federal employees who were simply doing their jobs. We didn't pick Nye. Nye picked us."[26]

Nye County is typical of the battleground over county supremacy. As the third largest county in the United States, its 18,155 square miles are about equal in size to the combined land of Vermont and New Hampshire. It has a population of less than 20,000 (less than one person per square mile), with 93 percent of its lands owned by the federal government—either the BLM, the USFS, or the Department of Defense, which operates the Nevada Test Site and the Tonopah Test Range. The county is also home to a proposed Yucca Mountain nuclear waste site, one of the most controversial environmental issues in the region. Even more telling is the growing hostility of local officials toward what they perceive to be federal intrusion, the result of rising tensions over everything from perceived protocol faux pas to bureaucratic paperwork foul-ups.[27]

The government's suit against Nye County, filed in federal district court, pitted county supremacy activists against U.S. Department of Justice officials who were receiving complaints from federal employees who said they could no longer do their jobs. Rangers working for the USFS, the BLM, and the NPS sought federal help, claiming they had been harassed and intimidated by county officials who argued that under county supremacy ordinances, federal laws regulating grazing or mining were no longer applicable. Roger Marzulla, a former assistant U.S. attorney general who later joined the environmental opposition group Defenders of Property Rights, represented Nye County. Deputy Assistant U.S. Attorney General Mike Coppelman, who handled the case for the federal government, was quoted as saying, "The United States has a multi-step strategy for dealing with threats and with these county ordinances, and the first step was to knock out the legal basis" for such measures.[28]

In a March 14, 1996 decision, Federal District Court Judge Lloyd D. George ruled the Nye County ordinance illegal. He noted that as far back as the administration of Abraham Lincoln and the 1846 treaty in which Mexico gave the Southwest to the United States, there was sufficient historical precedent to establish that the federal government owned the public domain. In this case, land not specifically claimed by Nevada when it became a state in 1864 had come under the control of the federal government, which now manages nearly 87 percent of the state's lands. "It is declared that, as set forth in this decision, the United States owns and has the power and authority to manage and administer the unappropriated public lands and National Forest System Lands within Nye County," Judge George concluded.

Judge George dealt Nevada officials another blow in an August 28, 1996, ruling that invalidated as "unenforceable" a state statute enacted during the Sagebrush Rebellion. Nevada's legislature had argued that the federal government had inequitably denied the state its claims to unappropriated land when Nevada became a state by failing to give it any land grants, violating the intent of the Constitution and placing a hardship on the state's residents. The judge declared the state statutes unconstitutional and in violation of the Constitution's supremacy clause, further eroding any hope that county supremacy ordinances would find support in the federal courts.[29]

Militancy

Another difference that distinguishes these activists is that, of the three contemporary grassroots movements in the environmental opposition—wise use, county supremacy, and property rights—those engaged in the War on the West are perhaps the most militant and radical in their attitudes.

Some of the opposition has been sanctioned, if not directly organized, by local governments. Near Moab, Utah, in 1979, Grand County commissioners defied a BLM order that required closure of a nearby canyon; the county sheriff ordered the arrest of any BLM employee who attempted to enforce the closure.[30]

Although there have been numerous reports of confrontations between ranchers and state, local, and federal officials, many believe it is the threat of confrontation that lies at the heart of the uproar over county supremacy. Besides the problems posed by outright defiance of the law, some federal employees, like Ann Morgan, state director of the Bureau of Land Management in Nevada, are clearly concerned for their safety. "We can't protect the resource because we are afraid our employees will be shot," she says. "It's not worth that."[31] Others, like Jeff Ruch, counsel for Public Employees for Environmental Responsibility, the group that represents hundreds of federal natural resource agency workers, believes the judge's decision in the Nye County case was insufficient. "While this case is a good and modest first step, in our view the underlying problem of intimidation and threats to Forest Service employees has not been addressed." The supervisor of the Toiyabe National Forest, which covers Nye County, commented further, "This stuff has scared the hell out of me."[32]

Environmental groups have led the effort to tie in county supremacy activists with the militia movement, with some success. The Oklahoma City bombing, perhaps more than any other single event in recent history, focused the public's attention on domestic terrorism. Initially thought to be the work of Middle Eastern extremists, the federal government's investigation soon shifted to a small group of homegrown terrorists accused of having ties to a number of paramilitary organizations. Timothy McVeigh, one of the suspects arrested in the bombing, was alleged to have been connected to the Michigan Militia. By a somewhat circuitous route, those paramilitary ties were then connected to property rights groups and characterized as evidence of a growing anti-environmental conspiracy. Recognizing the potential public relations damage of such a linkage, several organizations took immediate action to disassociate themselves from violent tactics altogether, as evidenced by the "Reno Declaration of Non-Violence" outlined in the previous chapter.

The tie-in with property rights groups came in part through the actions of Idaho congressmember Helen Chenoweth, who has been an outspoken supporter of wise use issues and whose comments were included in a tape sold by the Militia of Montana. Chenoweth has also spoken out against the "unwarranted invasion of private land," allegedly by armed wildlife agents in helicopters enforcing the Endangered Species Act—a charge repeatedly denied by federal authorities. Republican senators Larry Craig of Idaho and Lauch Faircloth of North Carolina, and Representative Steve Stockman of Texas asked the U.S. Department of Justice for clarification about similar reports of federal action brought to their attention by constituents.[33]

The militia/property rights connection has also been applied in the cases of radical attacks on federal and state officials who have attempted to enforce federal land use laws. Law enforcement agencies have still not solved the October 1993 bombing of an empty BLM office in Reno, Nevada, nor have they discovered the identity of the persons responsible for the March 1995 bomb explosion outside the office of a USFS district ranger in Nevada. The USFS is engaged in a long-running property rights dispute involving members of the Nye County commission, who have disavowed any connection with the bombing and originally offered a $100,000 reward for information leading to a conviction, although the reward offer was later withdrawn. The ranger's supervisor was threatened with a follow-up call that warned, "You're next," and several months later, another bomb exploded outside the ranger's home.

Another target has been former BLM director Jim Baca, who resigned from his post in the Clinton administration to take a position as a consultant with the Wilderness Society. After the Reno BLM bombing, Baca received a threatening letter warning him that there would be more to come. The letter was signed the "Tom Horn Society," referring to a nineteenth-century gunman hired by cattle ranchers to shoot settlers and Mexican sheepherders on public lands the cattlemen claimed as their own.[34]

To date, no arrests have been made in any of the explosions, which have caused property damage but no injuries. Senator Harry Reid of Nevada attributed the bombings to the "underbelly" of the county supremacy movement, but there is little doubt in the minds of many federal employees and environmental group members that the underbelly includes a number of very committed individuals who support a more militant approach to dealing with a federal government they no longer accept and now openly disregard.

WHO'S WINNING THE WAR?

Unlike the wise use or property rights movements, there are two unique features of the county supremacy movement. Because it is organized almost exclusively at the county level, it is less well integrated into the environmental opposition than are other groups and interests. The county supremacists are among the newest and, therefore, the least entrenched of the opposition forces, despite efforts to expand their message outside the West. At the same time, the county activists can make a compelling case in their favor by arguing that decisions over land use ought to be made at the local level rather than from the bureaucratic distance of Washington, D.C. The movement also allows its supporters to argue for the multiple use of lands (one of the themes of the wise use movement) as long as they are under local control. This perspective is becoming more common among those who fear the loss of local control over policies that directly affect them, whether the issue is the environment, crime, or education.

A second difference among the three segments of the grassroots opposition is that county supremacy represents a large number of elected officials, rather than disgruntled citizen activists. This factor provides some credibility, if not a political base, for their actions.

Despite those factors, the movement appears to be spreading less quickly (or at least it may have fewer adherents as a result of Judge George's two federal court rulings) because there are real concerns about both the constitutionality of the premises upon which county supremacy is built and the accompanying perceived linkage with militancy. Nonetheless, the movement has been most successful in those rural counties where there is a strong civic network that allows activists to work together with little chance for dissenting opinions and views. Politically influential ranchers and miners have managed to control much of the process because they have traditionally done so. This time, they have a focused target (the federal government) and have used the tools of other organized interests (such as litigation) to get what they want from the political system.

Environmental organizations have only infrequently attempted to challenge NEPA-style ordinances. The New Mexico–based Southwest Environmental Center has become one of the environmental movement's watchdogs on county supremacy, due especially to its proximity to the controversy in Catron County. It takes the movement very seriously, calling it

> a virus [that] cannot stand alone but depends for its survival upon being able to infect and take control of local governments. County governments provide a ready-made structure for the rapid dissemination of the Movement's views. In addition, the involvement of elected officials gives the Movement a legitimacy not available to other "Wise Use" groups. To the outside world, it appears that ordinances and land use plans reflect the will of local electorates, when, in fact, dissenting voices in the local community have been carefully excluded or ignored.[35]

The center goes on to offer a series of recommendations on how best to counter the county supremacy movement, including investigations of possible misconduct by public officials, addressing legitimate economic concerns and economic misinformation, participating in county planning and policymaking, and building coalitions with hunters and natural resource agencies.

The major legal challenge from the environmental community has been led by Scott W. Reed, a Stanford Law School–trained attorney in private practice in Coeur d'Alene, Idaho, who filed suit against a Boundary County, Idaho, ordinance, which was almost identically worded to the one in Catron County.[36] Sparsely populated, Boundary County is located in the heavily forested northern tip of Idaho along the Canadian border, both geographically and ideologically distant from federal regulators in Washington, D.C. Three-quarters of the land is owned by the federal government, and the county's economic base is heavily tied to extractive resource industries, especially timber.

The suit, filed by a group of local environmentalists in Bonners Ferry, Idaho, represented by Reed, met with a considerable amount of opposition from local residents. Over 800 registered voters (out of almost 5,000 voters registered in Boundary County) signed a petition in support of the county's land use plan, evidence of considerable popular support for the county supremacy movement there. But the state court struck down the county's ordinance in 1994, lending some credence to the argument that continued losses in the judicial arena are dampening support for the county supremacy movement.[37]

Implications

It is too simplistic to refer to the current War on the West as a new version or continuing round of the Sagebrush Rebellion for a number of reasons. The county supremacy movement is not as well organized nor is it as widespread as were the activities of organized interests in the late 1970s and early 1980s. County supremacy lacks the elements of organizational structure and resources of the more enduring interests of the wise use and property rights movements, as well. It is more accurate to see the three grassroots movements as overlapping in some of their goals, types of leadership, and strategies, but unequal in terms of their likelihood of success or extent of resources.

In addition, although at least one goal among the movements may be similar (gaining additional control over lands now part of the public domain), advocates of county supremacy really show little interest in taking over full administrative (and therefore financial) control of the federal lands. The costs of full county control are prohibitive in those rural counties that are already experiencing great difficulty in meeting their residents' needs.

Under existing laws, federal land management agencies insulate local communities from the liabilities and costs of complying with environmental regulations. In the case of wildfires, for example, the Department of the Interior, the United States Forest Service, and the Bureau of Land Management spent an estimated $900 million in the western states in 1994—costs that would have to be assumed by counties under the proposed ordinances. Another $95 million is estimated to be spent annually to administer and improve public range-lands, $300 million is spent to maintain and improve facilities on public lands, and millions more go to protect critical habitats for endangered species and to maintain roads. In addition, states (and, indirectly, counties and municipal governments) would forgo the revenues they receive now from mineral, oil, and gas leases on the lands—half of which currently go to the state and counties of origin. Other revenues that stem from federally funded and maintained irrigation, energy, and flood control projects would be lost. Eventually, that revenue loss would be felt in a reduction of county and state services.[38]

The legal basis for the movement alone is likely to lead toward its demise. Most legal scholars believe that when challenges like the *Boundary Backpackers v. Boundary County* case or a potential appeal of the Nye County suit finally reach the U.S. Supreme Court, county supremacy ordinances will be ruled unconstitutional under Article 4 of the U.S. Constitution, which gives Congress the power to "dispose of and make all needful rules and regulations respecting the territory or other property belonging to the United States."[39] The U.S. Supreme Court has already ruled against the states in cases like *Kleppe v. New Mexico*,[40] in which New Mexico officials attempted to retain control over wild horses on federal lands despite passage of the federal Wild, Free-Roaming Horses and Burros Act.

The Supreme Court might also rely upon the supremacy clause, as has been the case with similar attempts by the states to exert their authority. In a Kentucky case, *Hancock v. Train*, the Court ruled that the state could not require federal installations to obtain state air contaminant permits even though the federal Clean Air Act intended for states and the federal government to coordinate their efforts in implementing the regulations. The Court allowed Congress exclusive legislative authority over federal property, in effect preempting state law.[41]

More recent attempts by states to impose their will in federal land matters have met with a similar outcome. In *California Coastal Commission v. Granite Rock Company*, for instance, the U.S. Supreme Court ruled (albeit in a 5:4 decision) that the state's coastal commission requirement that a mining company obtain a state permit to work its unpatented mining claims in a national forest was unconstitutional. The Court attempted to draw a distinction between land use planning and state environmental regulation, leaving only a narrow band of state authority intact.[42]

Similar attempts by counties to force the government to accept their version of constitutional intent are likely to meet with a similar fate, no matter what the composition of the Court is from a partisan standpoint. Legal commentators believe that the Catron County ordinance "would under any interpretation be 'state land use planning' which all nine justices in *Granite Rock Company* would agree was pre-empted by federal law."[43] As attorney Scott Reed puts it, "The county supremacy ordinances have the durability of cow chips. County supremacy is a gaseous myth. The methane falls mainly on the plain."[44]

County supremacy activists have not totally given up, despite the Nye County ruling. In Elko, Nevada, a group of citizens made plans in 1996 to convene a grand jury to try officials who they believed were guilty of crimes for attempting to enforce USFS regulations in their county. Dick Carver, who refuses to recognize any federal land management agency, was not disappointed with the judge's decision in the Nye County case: "We made our point. We got what we wanted. We had to take an aggressive stance in order to get our seat at the table. We did that. And now, they are listening to us." In that sense, Carver is correct. After the Nye County ruling, federal officials called for conciliation and a search for common ground, with Attorney General Janet Reno asking the parties "to come together and address our differences."[45] The county supremacy activists, although they may be less organized and fewer in number than those of the wise use or property rights movements, may have convinced the federal government to listen to their concerns. The momentum of the movement may have been diffused by the Court's decision, but its leaders have positioned themselves to at least have their grievances heard at the highest levels of government. Their greatest challenge may be to distance themselves from the "militant underbelly" to make their arguments warrant being given a seat at the table while this particular policy window remains open.

NOTES

1. Marianne Lavelle, "Activist Counties Battle the Federal Government over Land-Use Controls," *National Law Journal,* vol. 17, no. 40 (June 5, 1995): A1.

2. Richard D. Lamm and Michael McCarthy, *The Angry West: A Vulnerable Land and Its Future* (Boston: Houghton Mifflin, 1982), pp. 224–225.

3. Timothy Egan, "Campaigns Focus on Two Views of West," *New York Times,* November 4, 1994, p. A29.

4. Note, *National Review,* May 29, 1995, p. 14.

5. Kevin Bixby, *A Report on the County Movement* (Las Cruces, NM: Southwest Environmental Center, 1992), p. 8.

6. William Pendley Perry, *It Takes a Hero* (Bellevue, WA: Free Enterprise Press, 1994), pp. 142–143.

7. Bixby, *A Report,* p. 9.

8. Tom Kenworthy, "Dueling with the Forest Service," *Washington Post National Weekly Edition,* February 27–March 5, 1995, p. 31.

9. Bixby, *A Report,* p. 13.

10. Lavelle, "Activist Counties," p. A22.

11. U.S. Constitution, Article 1, Section 8. This section enumerates the powers of Congress; the cited section is the last of those powers and is followed by the "elastic clause," which gives Congress power to make laws necessary and proper to carry out the preceding powers.

12. See Florence Williams, "Sagebrush Rebellion II," *High County News*, vol. 11 (February 24, 1992): 1. See also Andrea Hungerford, "Custom and Culture Ordinances: Not a Wise Move for the Wise Use Movement," *Tulane Environmental Law Review*, vol. 8, no. 2 (summer 1995): 457–504.

13. See Scott Reed, "The County Supremacy Movement: Mendacious Myth Marketing," *Idaho Law Review*, vol. 30 (1993–1994): 525–553.

14. "Wishful Thinking," *Sierra* (January–February 1994): 40.

15. Constance Mathiessen, "Weaverville, No Place Like Home," *California Lawyer* (August 1993): 33.

16. Catron County, New Mexico, Ordinance 004-91 (May 21, 1991).

17. Reed, "The County Supremacy Movement," pp. 525–553.

18. Barry Sims, "Private Rights in Public Lands?" *Workbook*, vol. 18, no. 2 (summer 1993): 55.

19. See Stephanie L. Witt and Leslie R. Alm, "County Government and the Public Lands: A Review of the County Supremacy Movement in Four Western States," in Brent S. Steel, ed., *Public Lands Management in the West: Citizens, Interest Groups, and Values* (Westport, CT: Greenwood, forthcoming).

20. "Wishful Thinking," p. 40.

21. Witt and Alm, "County Government."

22. Lavelle, "Activist Counties," p. A22.

23. Ibid.

24. Gwen Florio, "Fed-Up Sheriff Declares He's Law of Land in 'Fredonia,'" *The Oregonian*, June 2, 1996, p. A24.

25. Sims, "Private Rights," p. 57.

26. Erik Larson, "Unrest in the West," *Time*, October 23, 1995, p. 66. See also Ronald J. Ostrow, "U.S. Sues County to Halt Seizure of Federal Land," *Los Angeles Times*, March 9, 1995, p. A3.

27. Larson, "Unrest in the West," pp. 55–56.

28. Timothy Egan, "Court Puts Down Rebellion over Control of Federal Land," *New York Times*, March 16, 1996, p. 1.

29. Ibid., p. 9.

30. Lamm and McCarthy, *The Angry West*, p. 276.

31. Kenworthy, "Dueling with the Forest Service," p. 31.

32. Egan, "Court Puts Down Rebellion," p. 9.

33. Timothy Egan, "Terror in Oklahoma: In Congress: Trying to Explain Contacts with Paramilitary Groups," *New York Times*, May 2, 1995, p. A19.

34. David Helvarg, "Anti-Enviros Are Getting Uglier," *The Nation*, vol. 259 (November 28, 1994): 651.

35. Bixby, *A Report*, pp. 3–4.

36. *Boundary Backpackers v. Boundary County*, No. CV93–9955 (Idaho 1st Jud. Dist. Ct.) January 27, 1994.

37. Reed, "The County Supremacy Movement," pp. 552–553.

38. Christopher A. Wood, "All Uneasy on the Western Front," *Washington Post National Weekly Edition*, May 15–21, 1995, p. 24.

39. See, for example, Albert W. Brodie, "A Question of Enumerated Powers: Constitutional Issues Surrounding Federal Ownership of the Public Lands," *Pacific Law Journal*, vol. 12 (1981): 715–725; and Rene Erm II, "The 'Wise

Use' Movement: The Constitutionality of Local Action on Federal Lands Under the Preemption Doctrine," *Idaho Law Review,* vol. 30 (1993–1994): 631–670.

40. 426 U.S. 529 (1976).
41. 426 U.S. 167 (1975).
42. 480 U.S. 572 (1987).
43. Reed, "The County Supremacy Movement," p. 548.
44. Ibid., p. 527.
45. Egan, "Court Puts Down Rebellion," p. 9.

10

The Property
Rights Movement

SIGN OF THE TIMES: Peggy Reigle worked for the New York Daily News *as its vice president of finance before she retired to Maryland's eastern shore and bought an abandoned 138-acre farm. In 1990, she became a property rights activist when her neighbors complained to her about inconsistencies in federal wetlands regulations. Recent interpretations of the law had made the land they had purchased fall under the federal definition of a wetland, meaning they would be unable to build on their own property, wiping out the savings that she and others had invested in their land. Her activism led her to become chairman of the Fairness to Land Owners Committee (FLOC), a group that now claims over 15,000 members in forty-five states, 90 percent of whom she says are victims of "wetlands abuse."[1] Reigle says she works twelve hours a day, seven days a week for FLOC, whose members commonly post signs on their property like this one:*

PRIVATE PROPERTY

No Trespassing

Without the written permission of the owner
who tends the land and
pays the mortgage and taxes.

IF YOU WORK FOR FEDERAL, STATE, OR LOCAL GOVERNMENT
Don't waste your time asking.

If you are a member of, or agree with, any
Radical Environmental Groups—
The National Wildlife Federation,
The National Audubon Society,
Sierra Club, etc.—
Don't Even Watch My Birds.

Member of The Fairness to Land Owners Committee[2]

Although many of the land use battles outlined in previous chapters have focused on the vast expanses of landholdings in the West, there is an equally bitter property rights battle being waged by individuals throughout the United States. To an even greater extent than with the wise use and county supremacy movements, these conflicts with the government are likely to be personal and local, rather than regional or national. A report sponsored by the W. Alton Jones Foundation concluded that the property rights movement was not allied with wise use and its members were not foot soldiers for corporations. In fact, the report's author noted, the roots and diversity of the groups qualified property rights advocates as a grassroots movement of modest means.[3]

One of the reasons why the property rights movement has developed some level of credibility and visibility is that individual disputes and grievances are often repeatedly recounted and circulated by the media, with a different spin put on each retelling of the story. For example, a story from the FLOC newsletter told of two Florida men who went to prison for failing to comply with environmental regulations when they dumped sand in a ditch on their property that the federal government had declared to be a wetland. This single anecdotal example was later cited in the conservative publication the *American Spectator* to support the allegation that "the increasing extremism of environmental regulation has caused the de facto seizure of a great deal of property all over the country, forestalling billions of dollars worth of economic activity."[4] The stories are then cited by movement leaders or the conservative press, who use them as exemplary of a much more serious problem of government intrusion into the lives of ordinary, law-abiding citizens.

The stories of property rights movement activists typically begin with an attempt to develop a piece of property, either by building a home, clearing land, or draining a marsh. In many cases, they encounter federal regulations for the first time at that point and are genuinely bewildered at the bureaucratic response to what they have done. In other instances, a routine application for a building permit may trigger an outcry by a local environmental organization that files an injunction against the landowners.

The resulting backlash against both the government and its regulatory supporters leads some landowners to seek assistance from national property rights umbrella groups like the ALRA or Stewards of the Range, which then use the cases to illustrate the excesses of the system. Other landowners will attempt to gather small groups of their neighbors together in what they perceive to be a David-vs.-Goliath struggle. But for the most part, much of the property rights battle is fought by individuals who later become members of the disenchanted class who feel the government's red tape and impersonality has turned against them.

This chapter begins by examining the various perspectives that are common to those within the property rights movement, followed by profiles of the primary umbrella organizations and their leadership. Included in the discussion is a brief overview of the debate over the legal issue of "regulatory takings": the belief that if a property owner loses the right to use the land because of a federal regulation, then the landowner should be appropriately compensated for that loss. This is followed by a description of the groups' tactics and strategies, especially the litigation that has become characteristic of the property rights movement. Then the chapter goes back to explore where the legal challenges fit into the efforts of the environmental opposition to control the debate over environmental policymaking. Finally, the chapter reviews the allegation that the various grassroots movements in recent decades have been closely associated with industry and with the broader, sometimes militant, conservative and antigovernment agenda.

PERSPECTIVES ON THE LEGAL AND HISTORICAL ISSUES

The perspective of those involved in issues related to private property rights can be seen from three somewhat related views about the role of the government.[5] The first perspective comes from those landowners who have held title to their property, perhaps for generations, and who do not accept any effort by a government bureaucracy or by the courts to tell them what they can or cannot do with their land. This perspective is simplistic but widely held, and it is equally accepted in the East and South where property has been under the control of a family for perhaps 200 years compared to the more recently homesteaded West.

A second perspective holds that although there may be some valid reasons why a government agency ought to be able to designate land use for the common good (such as to provide an easement for fire protection or to preserve a historic site), that designation ought to carry with it compensation for the landowner. Supporters of this view accept zoning regulations as a form of protection for their neighborhood and its property values, but also feel that they are entitled to fair and equitable financial recompense if their investment is lost or diminished. The U.S. Supreme Court raised this concept in 1922 when it ruled, "While property may be regulated to a certain extent, if the regulation goes too far it will be recognized as a taking."[6]

A third perspective, held more often by corporate interests than by individual landowners, sees property as part of a more complex element of a capitalist economy. If property is not valued highly by society, then they believe the entire economic framework of the nation is at risk. Their stake in the property rights debate is more an aggregation of interests than one based on personal grievances.

All three perspectives, to some extent or another, rely upon history—from the interpretation of common law to current cases before the U.S. Supreme Court. The subtle language of property rights, as it applies to both land and water, rests on a series of principles that are reflected in both English and American property laws. Controversies in the West, where many of the natural resource issues were initially focused, colored the debate that continues today as part of the property rights movement.

One of the underlying legal principles that have become the basis for those holding the first perspective is the doctrine of prior appropriation, *"Qui prior est in tempore, potior est in jure,"* or he who is first in time is first in right. When used in the context of water, for example, the first person who comes upon a stream and claims its water, or a part of it, acquires the right to exploit and use it as if it were personal property. Under this doctrine, the right is derived regardless of how far away the person lives from the water source. From a practical standpoint, the "finder" has the right to divert the water for agricultural use or irrigation, or can, in fact, drain the stream completely.

Under English common law, a contrasting legal approach is the riparian principle, which holds that only those who actually live on the banks of a river can lay claim to its flow, but that, in actuality, no one actually "owns" the water. Those living adjacent to the water could use it for natural purposes like drinking and washing, but a stream could not be diverted for personal use or diminished in any way at the exclusion of others' uses.[7]

Westerners were much more likely to subscribe to the doctrine of prior appropriation—a sort of "finders keepers" approach to the vast resources of the American frontier. Those who "discovered" land or water naturally assumed that it was theirs to use and was an essential element of economic growth and development. In an arid environment, it seemed logical that someone who discovered a source of water ought to be able to dam the flow or divert it to water crops, feed livestock, or process mineral ore.

The courts strengthened the doctrine of prior appropriation through a series of rulings that added the idea of "reasonable use." Under this concept, no one could appropriate more than could be reasonably used, and what was reasonable was in large part what was the most economically productive. The concept later became known as the "Colorado doctrine" because residents insisted that diversion was necessary in order to facilitate development in their state. As historian Donald Worster notes, "It seemed to be natural and reasonable to a group of people who were intent on conquering, expanding, accumulating, and getting ahead."[8]

In an ideal world, the doctrine of prior appropriation would work smoothly, and one need only appeal to a neighbor's goodwill to acquire water; in reality, the doctrine jammed the courts with litigation. During the late nineteenth century, irrigation rights became the subject of numerous conferences and, eventually, constitutional debates over whether or not the rivers and streams of the West constituted public property and ought to be managed by some form of governmental administration.

In contemporary jurisprudence, the issue has been expanded to include an assumed right to use even publicly held lands as one sees fit—the basis of one of the more lengthy and controversial property rights cases involving cattle rancher Wayne Hage. Hage, who owned a grazing permit for his ranch near Pine Creek, Nevada, filed suit against the federal government in 1991 following the events that ensued after he refused to take his cattle off federal lands and relocate them as part of the permit's requirements that the land not be overgrazed. He argues in his suit that he should be compensated for losses he has sustained due to the introduction of elk into the region by the Nevada Department of Wildlife; the elk, Hage contends, eat grass that his cattle might otherwise eat.[9] Hage filed suit when USFS officials confiscated his cattle, sold them, and kept the proceeds. Hage claimed judicial support for his position when, in a March 1996 interim opinion, the chief justice of the U.S. Court of Federal Claims, Judge Loren Smith, wrote, "While it is true that the judiciary has a particularly focused mission in protecting the liberties of the citizen, it is no less true that members of the legislative and executive branches have an equally heavy responsibility for guarding those same precious liberties."[10] *Hage v. United States* is likely to be one of the most important legal challenges to property rights legislation in the 1990s, with an outcome that will influence the legal issues outlined in this chapter for thousands of other property rights activists.

The common denominator that ties these cases and principles together is that property rights jurisprudence is still under development. Despite precedents that go back to the Magna Carta, changes in the political environment have provided property rights groups with the critical mass they need to begin to influence the policy process, as the following overview of the groups indicates.

THE PROPERTY RIGHTS GROUPS

Although the legal issues regarding prior appropriation have been around for centuries, the movement that stemmed from them is a more recent phenomenon, tied to the Carter administration and the late

1970s. Under the leadership of Interior Secretary Cecil Andrus, the president made an intense effort to convert millions of acres of BLM lands into federal wilderness areas, national parks, and wildlife refuges. In 1965, slightly more than 50 million acres of land were designated as federal parks, refuges, or wilderness preserves; by 1980, that number approached nearly 225 million acres, rising to nearly 260 million acres as the decade of the 1990s began.

The president's efforts occurred at the same time the leaders of the Sagebrush Rebellion were beginning to organize and attempts were being made to force the government to sell off public lands to private owners or give them back to the states. Thus, there was a collision between efforts on the part of the executive branch to increase federal control of the lands at the same time western interests were seeking to reduce that control.

It is more difficult to trace the historical antecedents of the property rights movement than the other two segments of the grassroots environmental opposition. Rather than coalescing as a result of a single incident, the movement sprouted in various regions of the county during the late 1970s, often paralleling other events but without a unifying force. For example, in 1981, at the "Colonies in Revolt" conference in Sun Valley, Idaho, sponsored by the Institute of the American West, speakers called for "an assertion of individual rights." Property rights were an inherent element of the Sagebrush Rebellion, whose leaders relied upon Interior Secretary James Watt to support their cause during the Reagan administration.[11] But generally, property rights battles were fought on a personal level by individuals who had personal grievances against the government and who somewhat belatedly discovered there were organizations at the national level that shared their interests.

As is the case with the wise use and county supremacy movements, the battle over property rights is led by a handful of umbrella groups that provide information and support. What makes the property rights movement somewhat different from the other two, however, is that it is less a grassroots "membership" movement than it is a "group" with shared but individualized grievances. The "group" is more accurately characterized as families or individuals fighting their own private war against the government bureaucracy rather than card-carrying, dues-paying members who have a sense of belonging to any real organization.

Chuck Cushman, profiled earlier as the leader of the nonprofit group American Land Rights Association, is one of several policy entrepreneurs who lead the property rights movement. He calls himself "a tank commander in the war against environmentalists" and insists it is not merely a war but "a holy war between fundamentally different religions. The preservationists are like a new pagan religion, worshiping trees and animals and sacrificing people."[12] As one observer notes, "For twenty years, Cushman has made a living putting a name to the vague fears of small-town, recession-bound America. The name is the federal government, whose different land-managing agencies are 'all the same.'"[13] He has targeted Washington State as one of the most important battlegrounds for the environmental opposition in the 1990s and uses his extensive mailing list capabilities and fund-raising efforts in concert with genuine skills in community organizing. Like wise use groups, Cushman's organizations depend heavily on computers, faxes, and direct mail. As he asked one audience rhetorically, "What are the three most important words in political action? List, list, list. If you don't have a list you're not in the game. . . . The next most important words are network, network, network."[14]

Cushman's organizational skills not only brought together the first of the property rights coalition groups, but they have placed him in the forefront of a movement that is beginning to swell with competing and not always complementary groups. While the majority of the property rights groups focus on serving as a clearinghouse for information, only a handful provide direct legal assistance, such as the Defenders of Property Rights, founded in 1991. The group was created with the express purpose of filing strategically identified litigation and lobbying for land use legislation that would benefit its members. Other conservative legal foundations also provide support, although they spread their expertise around a broader spectrum of political and social issues.

Several of the national property rights organizations were formed in the early 1990s at the same time the more resource-oriented wise use groups were being founded. Like the wise use groups, many began as local or regional organizations and then expanded their base, becoming national clearinghouses for information and publications. Carol LaGrasse, for instance, started the Property Rights Foundation of America in November 1993 after she had spent four years working on the issue in New York. The group publishes a quarterly journal, *Positions on Property*, and a bimonthly newsletter, *New York Property Rights Clearinghouse*, and offers its free services to groups needing organizational consulting. It is one of the primary bases for activists in the East, unlike wise use groups that are usually headquartered in western states.

Another major group, Stewards of the Range, was established as a result of the filing of Wayne Hage's case in 1991, initially existing as part of the wise use group Center for the Defense of Free Enterprise. It became a separate entity in August 1994 and has subsequently expanded into a constitutional rights advocacy group with over 4,000 members. From its Boise headquarters, Stewards of the Range publishes a national property rights newspaper, *Cornerstone*, and operates the Constitutional Law Center, which serves as a resource and training base for those litigating property rights cases. One of its major functions remains fund-raising to support the Hage litigation, although its members pay dues to belong to the organization.

Like many of the property rights organizations, Stewards of the Range is dominated by charismatic leadership (in this case, attorney Mark Pollot and plaintiff Wayne Hage). Although the group operates with a board of directors, it is Pollot and Hage who take their case to the public, generate the bulk of the publicity, and push their agenda forward. The cost of membership in Stewards, like other grassroots groups, is low ($25), allowing individuals to receive the benefits of group membership without the costs of being a part of the organization's day-to-day administration.

Stewards of the Range fills an important niche in the communications linkage among property rights advocates through its National Rights Library. Its catalog features a variety of property rights books as well as general works on economics (such as Adam Smith's *The Wealth of Nations*) and the environment (such as Dixie Lee Ray's books). Pollot and Hage also sell their books at Stewards' events and other environmental opposition workshops as a way of reaching supporters. This is an often overlooked aspect of grassroots group activities: keeping members who are geographically dispersed connected not only through newsletters, but also through educating them on the group's mission and beliefs. It is this function that helps group members develop a common perspective, based on having read the same books and articles that repeat the common message.

The property rights movement also includes groups that are organized on the state level, such as Virginians for Property Rights, the Maine Freedom Fighters, and Oregonians in Action. Many of the smaller groups are unable to provide their members with much more than moral support, since they seldom develop any corporate backing. Some sponsor workshops where potential litigants are instructed in the intricacies of working with the Freedom of Information Act; others simply lend their names to the cause.

Some of the smaller grassroots groups have been born as a result of an individual landowner's efforts and frustrations in dealing with the federal government. The Council on Property Rights, for example, grew out of the response David Lucas received from property rights owners after the U.S. Supreme Court ruled in his case. The Environmental Conservation Organization grew into a sizable coalition of interests after a contractor, Henry Lamb, read an article about restrictions on farming because of conflicts with the Endangered Species Act. While the Alliance for America is now considered more aligned with wise use issues than with property rights specifically, the group's first president, David Howard, became involved because he lived within the boundaries of a state preserve, New York's Adirondack Park. In researching development proposals for the region, he formed the Adirondacks Blueline Confederation and later the *Land Rights Letter* as a way of monitoring attempts to restrict development in his own backyard.

The property rights movement in New York State is different from that of western grazing interests, although it, too, stems from disputes that are a century in the making. In 1894, the state enacted a constitutional amendment that declared the Adirondack Mountains "forever wild," but a subsequent timber boom denuded much of the region's forests. During the early part of the twentieth century, the state began to provide protection for the area, with the intention of buying up privately owned property within the proposed boundaries of the park. In 1968, disputes over a lack of zoning and land use restrictions and increased tourism led Governor Nelson Rockefeller to appoint a commission to study the park's future and, in 1971, to create the Adirondack Park Agency. During the 1970s (when wise use and the Sagebrush Rebellion were comparable movements in the West), New York's property rights activists began to organize, although they were not especially successful in changing the state's intention on preservation of the land. Their interests were countered by a propreservation group of environmental activists, the Adirondack Council.[15]

The Adirondack Park example is also typical of how property rights activists coalesce around a purely local issue but are less likely to participate when the political agenda is broadened. In April 1990, a commission appointed by New York governor Mario Cuomo made 245 recommendations to protect the region, including stronger land use controls. A dissenting report by a member of the commission, Robert Flacke, helped mobilize a number of small opposition groups, such as the Adirondack Solidarity Alliance, the Adirondack Conservation Council, Citizens Council of the Adirondacks, and the Adirondack Fairness Council. Despite their common interest in property rights, the groups were unsuccessful in persuading their members to expand their activism when the political issue was broadened outside Adirondack Park concerns. In 1992, sixteen of the property rights groups called upon their members to join in a rally at the state capital of Albany to protest proposed legislation that would protect more of the state's shorelines and wilderness areas. Promoters were alleged to have claimed that the rally would attract 5,000 supporters, but only 200 actually attended.[16] Many of the smaller local groups faded from the scene when the New York State legislature began to implement some of Governor Cuomo's commission's recommendations, and the momentum that fueled the initial local debate is now focused instead on umbrella groups like the Property Rights Foundation of America.

Like wise use organizations, some of the umbrella property rights groups have turned to the World Wide Web as a way of providing their supporters with information that might otherwise be difficult to track down. Dick Welsh, the executive director of the National Association of Reversionary Property Owners (NARPO), developed a web page site devoted to assisting "property owners in maintaining their complete land ownership and resisting government confiscation." NARPO's web page provides information on recent court cases and journal articles, explains how a property owner can find a federal regulation, allows the browser to send a message directly to the White House, and has Internet links to other property rights groups around the country. Technology like this web site thus gives activists access to information and research tools, along with an electronic "relationship" to an unknown number of other groups and supporters. Browsers can easily perceive that they are part of a nationwide movement of similarly disposed believers, and there are few ways of quantifying how broad that support base might be. Even the web site's on-line visitor counter can be misleading, since this site, and others like it, are routinely "visited" and monitored by environmental groups as well as property rights supporters.

Environmental organizations have done their best to discredit the property rights movement, just as they have done with wise use groups. The San Francisco–based Media Alliance links property rights groups to the right-wing John Birch Society, noting that society members turned out protesters against the Northern Forest Lands study, a joint effort by the federal and state governments to plan the future of development in New England. The organization also has tried to draw a connection between the Maine Conservation Rights Institute and Christian Fundamentalism, simply because the two organizations are based in that state.[17]

Environmental groups have been joined by dozens of nonenvironmental organizations that oppose the property rights movement for a variety of reasons specific to their own political needs. They range from the U.S. League of Cities and the National Council of Senior Citizens to the United Mine Workers of America. In addition, thirty-three state attorneys general signed a letter to members of Congress in 1995 arguing that takings bills would greatly increase the cost of government. Thus property rights activists have been targeted by a broad spectrum of stakeholders with a common belief that is the antithesis of their perspective.

REGULATORY TAKINGS

Whereas the first perspective on property rights has a strong basis in historical appropriation of land, the second perspective relies more on the Constitution by calling for compensation for the loss of the right to use the land. This section does not attempt to provide an in-depth analysis of the legal controversies that surround the takings issue; both the legal and political literature are overwhelmed with commentary on this issue.[18] Instead, the goal here is to provide a brief overview of the basis for regulatory takings and how the property rights movement has capitalized on it.

The keystone of regulatory takings is the concept of federalism or, more specifically, the Fifth Amendment to the U.S. Constitution, which attempts to balance out the protection of individual rights with those needs of the majority. The takings clause in the amendment states, "nor shall private property be taken for public use, without just compensation." At face value, the argument is simple enough: If you want to use my land, just pay me the fair market value for it and it's yours.

The takings issue is not new; for years the courts have made interpretations on the amendment, primarily when controversies arose over the government's powers of condemnation and eminent domain. In instances where land was needed for public use, such as the construction of a new freeway, houses were commonly condemned and the owners were paid damages, usually in the form of payment of the fair market value of the dwelling.

But the issue gained additional exposure in 1985 with the publication of a book by University of Chicago law professor Richard Epstein,[19] which placed the takings controversy in the context of government regulation and created an intellectual basis for the movement. Epstein's views were echoed by the Cato Institute and the Federalist Society, and later by conservative organizations that latched onto property rights as another reason to reduce government intervention. Since that time, regulatory takings have expanded to a broad range of environmental issues including wetlands, endangered species, and wilderness designations.

Wetlands Preservation

It has been argued that the difficulty faced by the bureaucracy in defining wetlands identified in Chapter 6 is at the heart of the property rights movement, but, in fact, it is but one of several issues that have galvanized property owners. One reason for this is that wetlands issues affect a different clientele group than many of the other property rights issues. Most of those affected are small landowners, often farmers or rural interests, who have generally been less involved in dealing with the bureaucracy than their counterparts in other segments of the environmental opposition. Many of them encounter federal rules for the first time and have little knowledge of the ecological value of their property.

On the other end of the clientele spectrum are members of environmental organizations whose perspective places a higher premium on wetlands as an important ecosystem resource. As scientific expertise has expanded our knowledge of the critical value of wetlands, environmental groups have called upon government to maintain them in their natural state and to use public resources to acquire them when necessary.

Theoretically, there are two ways in which wetlands could be protected and regulated. One way would be for those who recognize the value of wetlands as a resource to buy them from the owners, a tactic used commonly by environmental groups like the Nature Conservancy. This option involves a monetary cost, depending upon the group's ability to negotiate an agreement and the landowners' willingness to sell. This also requires groups to convince others of the value of wetlands as a resource and to raise the funds privately to purchase the land. A second tactic, advocated by some environmental groups, is to place pressure on government to enact regulations that designate sensitive areas and restrict their use and development, avoiding purchase costs.

> Taking the moral highground, the environmental lobby can demand that "greedy" (or ignorant) landowners be instructed (via regulation) to change their land-use plans. Land rights formerly held by landowners, such as rights to farm or build homes, are taken by the government at zero price by regulating the use of property. For those seeking control of a resource, gaining such control without paying for it is a preferred arrangement.[20]

To date, the federal government has chosen the second of the two alternatives to lessen the fiscal impact of its policies, which has resulted in pledges like that made by President George Bush that there would be "no net loss" of wetlands. Rather than buying the land directly from the property owner, or providing compensation when taking the land through eminent domain actions, federal regulations have moved toward regulatory fiat, such as simply passing rules that prohibit a farmer from dredging a pond or building a house.

Environmental organizations have been relatively successful in convincing the government to adopt the regulatory/no cost option. Organizations like the Wilderness Society and the Sierra Club have done a superior job in lobbying Congress on the merits of wetlands preservation than have individual property owners, who lack the cohesiveness and political resources of the mainstream environmental groups. Property owners lack political organization, are geographically dispersed, and are therefore politically ineffective in convincing policymakers of the soundness of their arguments, or in their clout as a voting bloc. As one author notes:

Wetlands owners seeking to organize for political action encounter substantial problems—identifying other wetlands owners, gaining consensus on what should be done, and avoiding free rider problems that arise when the benefits of lobbying accrue to one and all, even those who did not join the rally. The rent-seeking theory tells us that politicians respond to what (and who) they hear and see, which means they assign less importance to the desire of private property owners. Faced with competition from well-organized interest groups, private property owners lose out in the race for political rents.[21]

The Criminalization of Property Rights Activism

Another factor that distinguishes those property owners fighting regulation of wetlands from other issues is the fact that many of the plaintiffs have been charged with criminal offenses for their actions. Although the majority of the cases have involved civil prosecutions, there has been an increasing reliance on the part of federal agencies to enforce the law criminally. The result has been a series of highly publicized cases that have given property rights groups their own horror stories about federal intrusion along with a unique and diverse assortment of issue martyrs.

Criminal sanctions are available when the prosecution proves to the court that the individual knowingly violated the clean water statutes by discharging a pollutant or violating the terms of a permit. A felony conviction carries with it a sentence of no more than three years in prison and/or a fine of $5,000–$50,000 per day of violation. Repeat offenders are subject to more severe punishments, while those convicted on misdemeanor discharges may be subject to lesser misdemeanor penalties.

One of the first criminal cases involved the owner of a Florida construction company who pled guilty to eight counts of illegally filling in and dredging wetlands in 1984. He agreed to do large-scale restoration work in exchange for a suspended sentence and probation, which were revoked when officials later discovered he had illegally destroyed a mangrove swamp, for which he was sentenced to six months in prison and a $10,000 fine.[22] Other cases over the next several years resulted in similar fines and penalties but little publicity for the participants.

But in 1990, the cases of *United States v. Jones* and *United States v. Ellen* gave the property rights movement its first two media stars. In the *Jones* case,[23] Paul Jones had purchased land in Maryland to create a private wildlife preserve and duck haven, and was charged with negligently filling in wetlands in violation of federal statutes. Jones later admitted he had violated the law, and he pled guilty to avoid trial. The court sentenced him to eighteen months' probation, $1 million in fines, and $1 million in restitution that was made to the Conservation Fund of Arlington, Virginia, to expand the Blackwater Wildlife Refuge.

In the companion case *United States v. Ellen*,[24] William Ellen (a conservation biologist who had been Paul Jones's project manager) was charged in U.S. District Court in Baltimore with six felony counts of knowingly filling in wetlands as the wildlife preserve was being built. According to prosecutors, Ellen had challenged the officials' interpretation of the wetlands designation and allowed his construction crews to dump two truckloads of dirt on the property before the issue had been settled. As one Army Corps of Engineers official later stated, "It's a matter of a person flaunting the federal government. Forget the wetlands issue." The prosecution argued that Ellen's twenty years of experience as an environmental consultant should have provided him with the expertise needed to determine which acreage was wetlands (and therefore protected) and which was not. Ellen attempted to argue that even the Army Corps of Engineers, the Soil Conservation Service, and state officials had difficulty with the wetlands designations on the property. Ellen also argued that he had in fact *created* 45 acres of wetlands through his design of the project. The government countered that the duck ponds he had built would cause harm because ducks and geese would defecate in the water, so officials used dynamite to create a 400-yard channel connecting them to salt water.[25]

A jury found Ellen guilty on five of the six counts of wetlands violations, with the prosecution asking for a sentence from twenty-seven to thirty-three months in prison; the judge sentenced him to the lowest possible penalty—six months in prison, four months of home detention, one year of supervised release, $250 in special assessment, and sixty hours of community service.[26]

Ellen became a martyr in the eyes of property rights activists, with groups like FLOC unsuccessfully petitioning the Bush administration for a pardon. His name became a rallying point for the movement, which depends upon such incidents to fuel the emotional fires that keep it going.[27]

A third key figure often cited by property rights supporters is mechanic John Pozsgai, the defendant in *United States v. Pozsgai*.[28] The Pennsylvania man was charged with forty-one counts of knowingly filling in wetlands without a permit, even though he had been warned to obtain one by the Army Corps of Engineers. A Hungarian refugee, Pozsgai argued that the land he had purchased had formerly been a dump filled with 7,000 old tires and that he had actually improved it from an environmental standpoint. The courts rejected his claims, sentencing him to concurrent three-year prison sentences, $200,000 in fines, and an order to restore the wetlands.

At times, even environmental organizations have seemed somewhat alarmed at the bureaucracy's urge to enforce. In Pozsgai's case, the Audubon Society noted that although Pozsgai could not be considered blameless, he did appear to have been singled out for punishment by the U.S. Department of Justice while corporate polluters have rarely faced such stiff penalties.[29]

Cases like these have given the environmental opposition not only the Davids they need to enhance the perception that government regulation has become a David-vs.-Goliath struggle, but also rallying points for the overall reform of federal environmental laws.[30] Property rights groups use these criminal prosecutions as a way of arguing that federal resources are poorly prioritized and that the real victims are landowners who are at the mercy of government bureaucrats. It is a compelling case, reiterated and reinforced by the conservative media that regale their listeners and readers with horror stories to prove the point that government regulation is out of control.

Endangered Species Protection

Similar arguments about property rights exist as a result of the implementation of the ESA. The law gives the USFWS the authority to prevent landowners from altering their property in any way if it threatens a species that has been designated as threatened or endangered, or its habitat. As biologists have better understood the relationship of a species with its environment, they have increasingly seen the protection of habitat rather than that of individual plants and animals as being what is most essential to prevent the extinction of a species. Protecting an animal or plant, if it does not have a sufficient range of land for its nutritional and reproductive needs, is useless. From a legal perspective, the protection of species (the common good or public interest) is seen as outweighing the interest of the individual property owner.

As was outlined in Chapter 2, the protection of wildlife has led to a number of clashes between the federal government and individuals. And as is the case with wetlands preservation cases, several ESA claims have been used by the environmental opposition to make its case before the public. Property rights groups see ESA provisions as another case of the federal government's penchant for taking land without compensation.

Somewhat ironically, the government cannot only "take," but it can also "give" if it chooses to do so. In 1965, Congress passed the Land and Water Conservation Fund Act and created the Land and Water Conservation Fund (LWCF) with the express intention of giving the Department of the Interior funds and authority to purchase habitats for endangered species. From 1965 to 1994, approximately $3.6 billion was made available to federal agencies for land acquisition, along with $3.2 billion as matching funds for states to purchase species habitats. From 1965 to 1979, the total purchases under the fund increased from an average of 729 acres per year to 258,270 acres per year. An additional 12 million acres were added under President Carter's executive order in 1978, and 42.9 million acres of Alaska territory through the 1980 Alaska National Interest Lands Conservation Act.[31]

When the Reagan administration took over in 1981, Congress cut appropriations to the LWCF, and land purchases fell to an average 145,000 acres per year. Reagan sought to have all funding for the program eliminated, although funding was restored during the Bush administration ($365 million for fiscal year 1993) and, to the disappointment of environmental groups who hoped a Democratic president would be more supportive of the program, reduced again under President Clinton ($209 million for fiscal year 1994).[32] Property rights advocates believe that such programs are a better way of dealing with ESA implementation—buying the land directly.

Section 9 of the ESA prohibits the taking or harming of an endangered species, which has led to confrontations with property owners whose land includes ESA habitats. If landowners do something to their property that destroys a habitat, they are subject to criminal sanctions. Like wetlands owners, those with lands on which endangered species live have sought to challenge the law or have sought compensation for the taking of their land when the government refuses to allow them to use it as they want, which they believe diminishes its value.

The result has been still another set of cases, many of them highly publicized, in which property owners have been told they cannot use their land. One family in California's San Joaquin valley faced criminal charges when they plowed up portions of their farm to plant barley for cattle feed. The USFWS charged them with destroying the habitat for the endangered blunt-nosed lizard, even though officials could not find any evidence of the lizards on their property. To avoid an expensive legal battle, they ended up giving 60 acres of their land to the USFWS. Another family argued that land use restrictions on the 500 acres they purchased in Utah cost them $2.5 million in diminished property value when the Kanab ambersnail was found on their land.[33]

Perhaps the most publicized case (and one that conservative radio talk show hosts cited for months as an example of what is wrong with federal ESA regulations) involved a Taiwanese immigrant, farmer Taung Ming-lin, who was accused of plowing under critical habitat for the Tipton kangaroo rat, and was charged with three violations of the ESA for killing five of the protected rodents. Federal prosecutors said that Ming-lin had been repeatedly sent registered letters warning him that the land was critical habitat, but that he ignored them. After a year of controversy capitalized on by property rights groups, the federal government agreed not to prosecute Ming-lin if he waited six months, obtained the proper permits, and donated $5,000 toward endangered species protection. Property rights advocates use this case in their literature as an example of the kind of federal intrusion they believe needs to be stopped.

Wilderness and Park Expansion

Although Americans have always prided themselves on the legacy they have created in the form of the national park system, wildlife refuges, and wilderness areas, many property rights groups believe the government has gone too far. Unlike wise use groups that advocate opening up more of the land for general public usage, property rights groups look at park expansions as personal attacks if their property gets included when park boundaries are redrawn and they find themselves subject to new federal statutes.

Environmental groups point to what they believe to be a more disturbing trend among property rights activists. Private interests are now lobbying members of Congress to revamp the entire NPS by trimming away "questionable units" throughout the country, leading NPCA president Paul Pritchard to comment, "The dismantling is being done in every conceivable fashion." In Ann Arbor, Michigan, for example, developer Bob Kuras hoped to trade 161 acres of land he had originally envisioned as a golf resort to the federal government after he became involved in a dispute over the property's status as a wetland in 1996. The NPS often negotiates land exchanges and boundary adjustments, with the caveat that any deal benefit the park system. But Kuras wanted to swap his 161 acres for 204 acres with a view of Lake Michigan that are part of the Sleeping Bear Dunes National Seashore. Kuras gained the support of Michigan's lieutenant governor and several members of the Michigan congressional delegation, who included Kuras's proposal as part of other lands' legislation. The NPS, which manages the property, protested any federal legislation that would allow the swap to take place, arguing the land swap would "create a visual intrusion . . . and significantly detract from the pastoral scene." Similar efforts have been made to give control of federally owned lands to groups in Alaska, Minnesota, Utah, and California.[34]

Much of the organizational credit for uniting property owners to fight this issue goes to Chuck Cushman's initial group, the National Inholders Association, which began with a lawsuit against the NPS by neighbors in and around Yosemite National Park in the late 1970s. One of Cushman's more publicized victories involved the proposed 20,000-acre Stone Lakes National Wildlife Refuge near Sacramento, California, which was designed to be a resting place on the Pacific flyway for migratory birds. Builders and local chambers of commerce initially supported the refuge, but changed their minds after Cushman helped organize local residents who called themselves the North Delta Conservancy. Despite its environmentally correct–sounding name, the organization opposed creation of the refuge, and area residents received a nine-page warning that disease-carrying mosquitoes would breed in the refuge and kill children in neighboring subdivisions. The refuge was eventually created in 1992 after delays and a reduction in both its size and its mission, but it faces dwindling operating resources as a result of continuing efforts by property rights activists to thwart the government's efforts.[35]

THE STRATEGIES

Unlike other segments of the environmental opposition, property owners have relied primarily upon the judicial arena to seek redress for their grievances, virtually ignoring the legislative and executive branches. Although some property owners have received legal assistance from groups like the Pacific Legal Foundation, the majority have initiated litigation on their own, or with the assistance of private counsel. With the multitude of property owners seeking legal aid, there are insufficient resources to spread around, and as a result, many of the cases never get past the filing stage or are quickly dismissed by the court. This section begins with a summary of those court cases that have gained some degree of public notoriety and press exposure, and then goes on to explain why litigation alone has not provided property rights advocates with the results they had hoped for.[36] It continues with an examination of the other strategies used by property rights advocates to advance their cause.

The Court Cases

For years, frustrated landowners have attempted to air their grievances before both the U.S. Supreme Court and the U.S. Court of Federal Claims to seek redress. Although regulatory takings jurisprudence can be traced back to several early cases from the 1920s, the U.S. Supreme Court renewed its contemporary expansion of takings law during its 1987 term. The Court's interest was in part due to the appointment of Justices Sandra Day O'Connor and Antonin Scalia and the elevation of William Rehnquist as chief justice. Initially, the Court's desire to revisit takings laws was embodied through three key cases: *Keystone Bituminous Coal Association v. DeBenedictus,*[37] *First English*

Evangelical Church v. County of Los Angeles,[38] and *Nollan v. California Coastal Commission*.[39] Two of the three cases gave supporters the ammunition they needed to put more pressure on legislators to look more closely at the takings principle, although the rulings themselves benefited just a small handful of property owners directly.

In *Keystone*, the government's arguments won out over those of the property owner, but the Court ruled favorably for the property rights movement in the *First English* decision, which involved a church that had been barred from rebuilding a summer camp on land it owned after a 1978 flood because the buildings would have violated a county flood control ordinance. An amicus curiae brief filed with the Court on behalf of twenty-four states claimed that "adoption of appellant's radical reformulation of takings jurisprudence would cripple amici's ability to perform regulatory functions upon which their citizens' health, safety, and welfare quite literally depend."[40] Despite the states' plea, the Court held the county was required to compensate the church for taking its use of the property without compensation.

The *Nollan* case involved a family that had decided to replace their small oceanfront bungalow with a single-family permanent home. The owner sought a permit from the California Coastal Commission, which agreed to grant the permit but only if the family agreed to donate a portion of their land to the state as a permanent right of easement to the public to pass along the beach. The Court ruled in favor of the property owner and ordered the commission to compensate the family.

But the most highly publicized case that brought the takings issue into the mainstream press was the eagerly anticipated 1992 U.S. Supreme Court decision in *Lucas v. South Carolina Coastal Council*.[41] The plaintiff, David Lucas, had purchased two beachfront lots outside Charleston, South Carolina, in 1986 and planned to develop them by building a single-family home on each one. Subsequently, the state enacted the Beachfront Management Act, which precluded construction in "critical areas," which now included Lucas's property, rendering the land "valueless." He challenged the statute, arguing that it constituted an unconstitutional taking of his property without compensation. The state argued that no compensation was required even if the statute did constitute a taking because the law was reasonably necessary.

The U.S. Supreme Court ruled that regulations that deny the property owner economically viable use of his or her land required compensation, but it left several legal loopholes with regard to how the loss of value of the land is to be determined.[42] Still, the case gained such exposure in the media as an example of federal bureaucrats meddling with small landowners that the case was portrayed as not only a symbolic, but also a material, victory. The state was ordered to pay Lucas $1.5 million for his property.

Environmental organizations and most legal scholars viewed the
Lucas decision with alarm, arguing that it represented an expansion of
the takings clause on political rather than legal grounds.[43] Certainly
the legacy of conservative Reagan appointees to the U.S. Supreme
Court cleared the way for more victories for property rights advocates,
although the rulings have been inconsistent.

In 1994, the Court ruled 5:4 in its decision in *Florence Dolan v. City
of Tigard*,[44] an Oregon case in which a property owner had been ordered to give up a 15-foot strip of her land to the city, which was
building a network of bike paths and a greenway. What made the case
somewhat unusual was that Dolan had applied to the city for a permit
to enlarge her plumbing supply business, and the agreement to donate
the land was one of the conditions of getting her permit. The Court
ruled that the city had an obligation to demonstrate a relationship of
"rough proportionality" for requiring the donation and sent the case
back to the city for further proceedings.

Another strategy of the environmental opposition has been to pursue cases in the U.S. Court of Federal Claims, which hears claims
against the U.S. Treasury involving $10,000 or more. Its decisions are
reviewed by the U.S. Court of Appeals for the Federal Circuit and, occasionally, by the U.S. Supreme Court. In 1990, the court ruled in favor
of the plaintiff in two cases: *Loveladies Harbor, Inc. v. United States*[45] and
Florida Rock Industries, Inc. v. United States.[46] These two cases seemed to
indicate the court's willingness to expand the compensation to property owners concept when all, or virtually all, viable economic use of
the land is removed through federal regulation, such as that of the
Clean Water Act permit requirements. Those who purchased property
before the 1972 legislation was enacted and were unaware of the need
to obtain the appropriate permits appear to be more likely to receive
compensation from the court.[47] The appeals court subsequently af-
firmed the trial court's ruling in the *Loveladies* case but reversed the
lower court's decision in *Florida Rock Industries*.

This strategic arena is important for property rights advocates because the Federal Court of Claims has been significantly more sympathetic to their interests, in part due to the influence of Reagan appointee and chief judge Loren Smith, a self-described libertarian/
conservative. Prior to 1990, cases involving the allegation of a property
taking were rare; in 1991, fifty-two cases were filed, the most in a
decade. Now, hundreds of cases are pending before the Federal Court
of Claims and the appellate court, which are dominated by conservatives appointed during the Reagan and Bush administrations.

One of the biggest victories for the property rights movement in
the Federal Court of Claims was a 1992 decision[48] in which the federal government was ordered to pay a Wyoming coal company,

Whitney Benefits, $150 million because the Department of the Interior had barred mining in a protected area, which the company said rendered its coal holdings worthless. The U.S. Supreme Court upheld the lower courts' rulings.[49] By appealing to the Federal Court of Claims, property rights groups have learned to move their disputes to a more supportive arena with judges who clearly identify with their cause.

The Executive Order

President Reagan responded to the 1987 cases with a statement about "getting the government off the back of business" and with Executive Order 12630, "Governmental Actions and Interference with Constitutionally Protected Property Rights."[50] The order and the subsequent June 1988 guidelines promulgated by Attorney General Edwin Meese for the evaluation of risk and avoidance of unanticipated takings are considered by property rights advocates virtually equal in importance to the Fifth Amendment in providing a legal basis for their perspective.

The document requires the government to budget funds for compensation to property owners if a "Takings Impact Analysis" (TIA) (similar to that called for under NEPA's environmental impact analyses) shows a government regulation will deprive the owner of the use of the land. Despite its lofty-sounding language, the impact of the executive order is not that monumental. It does not impede existing environmental laws and regulations, but it does require that the takings concept be evaluated before a proposed act triggers Fifth Amendment provisions.

Some legal scholars have argued that the TIA was advanced by the Reagan administration as a way of introducing additional delays into the regulatory process. They note that rather than serving the interests of property rights owners who saw the executive order as a mechanism for further protecting their constitutional rights under the Fifth Amendment, the TIA simply fostered deregulation.[51]

Although property rights organizations have rallied around the executive order as an example of what ought to be done by the federal government, in reality the measure has been all but ignored by subsequent administrations. Because it has had so little impact on zoning and other regulatory actions, property rights advocates have also attempted to advance their cause in two other policy arenas—state legislatures and Congress.

State Legislative Efforts

While litigation remains the number one tool of the property rights movement, it has been partnered with efforts to gain protection for private property at the state level. The groups' supporters are aiming to influence state legislation on two issues: bills that require greater attention to the impact on property owners' concerns when projects are still in the planning stage (often referred to as "look before you leap" legislation), and bills that would trigger compensation when a property's value is diminished by a specific percentage as a result of government regulation.

The reason for the expansion of the battleground to the state legislatures, supporters say, is the increasing emphasis of the federal government on regulation and enforcement of environmental laws. Even though mechanisms exist for the government to provide compensation to landowners when their land must be purchased to provide sensitive habitats or to meet other environmental goals, regulatory takings became the rule rather than the exception.

Only three states—Washington, Arizona, and Delaware—had passed property rights laws prior to 1993, but by August 1994, more than a hundred related bills had been introduced in forty-four states to uphold the counterpart of the Fifth Amendment at the state level. Laws had been enacted in twelve states, with the debate continuing throughout state legislatures.[52]

The focus of property rights activists has been Washington State, home to Chuck Cushman's ALRA, Alan Gottlieb and Ron Arnold's CFDFE, and other private property rights groups. In 1992, the state enacted an amendment to its 1991 Growth Management Act, a state land use planning law that required the state's attorney general to establish a checklist enabling agencies to evaluate the impact of proposed regulatory or administrative actions. In April 1995, the state went a step further when the legislature passed Initiative 164, which considered private property to be "taken" if a regulation limited development for any reason other than preventing a public nuisance. The measure provided no lower limit for compensation, so even a small loss of value became grounds for a property owner to sue.

Frustrated environmental groups took action a day later, launching a new initiative campaign that was designed to block the legislature's action. A spokesperson for the No on 164 Coalition said the law would create "regulatory chaos and a fiscal and state nightmare" for local and state governments. "They could go broke or lose the quality of life in their communities. All it takes is one ornery, selfish property owner to put up a gas station in a residential neighborhood, or to be paid off not to."[53]

The state's voters sent the legislature a strong message when supporters of the campaign to repeal the compensation measure gathered more than twice the number of signatures needed to put the issue on the state ballot in November 1995. Referendum 48 would have required an economic impact analysis and consideration of alternative measures before the state could regulate or restrict the use of private property, and it would have required the state to provide compensation to property owners who had their property taken for general public use. Despite the fact that takings bill supporters outspent opponents by a two-to-one margin, the measure was overwhelmingly defeated by 60:40 percent. Property rights supporters argued that voters were influenced by a University of Washington study that showed that implementation would cost between $4 billion and $11 billion. As the conservative publication *National Review* commented, "The anti-referendum forces framed the issue in terms of efficiency, never confronting the moral component of what Thomas Jefferson called 'the first principle of association, the guarantee to everyone of his industry and the fruits acquired by it.'"[54]

Arizona's 1992 law was a stand-alone property rights bill that had the full support of the state's governor, Fife Symington, who stated:

> Private property rights lie near the source of liberty under which Americans are free to enjoy the God-given beauty of the Earth. It is the nature of government constantly to close in on that liberty, to diminish it, to consume it. It is no coincidence, I think, that the most filthy environmental conditions in the history of the world are found today in the former Soviet Union and in Eastern Europe. A clean environment is a commodity like any other, and it cannot be had without cost. Paying that cost requires capital; accumulation of capital requires markets; and markets require eternal vigilance in the protection of private property.[55]

Although the bill was initially supported by a wide range of interests, from the Arizona Association of Realtors to local union leaders, environmental groups immediately went on the offensive and gathered sufficient signatures to successfully repeal the bill on the November 1994 ballot. There, too, antitakings bill groups were outspent nearly two-to-one.

The third initially successful measure, Delaware's 1992 "look before you leap" legislation, also required a full analysis of rules and regulations by the attorney general to determine the potential impact on private property rights. The bill was heavily supported by agricultural interests in the state, as well as Delaware's governor and attorney general.

After these three state measures had been enacted, other states began examining the property rights issue as groups formed coalitions to try to increase their chances of success. In Idaho, for example, sixteen organizations formed the Idaho Private Property Coalition in 1992, including the Idaho Wool Growers Association, the state's Cattle and Dairymen's Associations, and the Idaho Farm Bureau Federation.

At the urging of a coalition of property rights groups, Oregon's legislature passed two property rights measures in 1995, but the governor later vetoed both bills, one of which would have provided compensation if state or local environmental rules reduced property value by $10,000 or 10 percent. In some states, even more so than at the national level, coalition building became the strategy of choice, uniting commodity organizations, wise use groups, and property owners behind a unified goal of securing some form of takings bill.

The coalitions were not always successful, and they often led to contentious debates among the members of the groups involved. In West Virginia, for instance, the property rights issue was hotly debated by the West Virginia Farm Bureau Federation, which found itself facing opposition from unions and environmental organizations. "These groups waged absolute war on the West Virginia Farm Bureau and supporters of the Private Property Protection Act utilizing gross intellectual dishonesty and alleging the bill would create a variety of ills to the state," wrote one farm bureau official.[56]

Gradually, state legislatures appear to have backed away from takings bills. They recognize the difficulties of trying to develop a coherent framework for their courts to work with, especially since most of the rulings at the federal level have been made on an ad hoc basis. They also recognize that the TIAs required under most state statutes open up the doors of potential litigation because the information prepared in the documents becomes public information and thus discoverable. Even the threat of litigation might lead state or local officials to kill any environmental regulation that they believe might be construed as a taking.[57]

The Federal Legislation

For the past several sessions, property rights advocates have waged a parallel, if less successful, effort at persuading Congress to enact a national version of the laws under consideration at the state level. The Congressional Property Rights Task Force has held hearings and drafted numerous bills, all designed to assess the impact of either proposed regulations or payment bills that would compensate owners if their land loses value due to government regulations. Most have incorporated some form of TIA that would be required before a federal agency could issue "any policy, regulation, proposal, recommendation or related agency action which could result in a taking or dimunition [in the] use or value of private property." This language, from the Private Property Rights Act of 1994 introduced by former Kansas senator Bob Dole, has been repeated in similar TIA bills at the state level. Other efforts have been aimed at codifying Executive Order 12630.

The payment-oriented bills introduced thus far have differed primarily in how much of a reduction in land value is caused by a regulation, triggering the compensation payout. Several have focused on a 50 percent reduction in value; others have used a dollar figure (such as a $10,000 reduction in the property's fair market value). Even the Republican "Contract with America" included a compensation provision as a part of its reform package.

Even with the changeover from a Democratic-controlled Congress to a Republican one, federal TIA or compensation legislation was unsuccessful. Environmental groups like the Wilderness Society and the National Wildlife Federation warned of the potential impact of such laws, arguing that the legislation could even affect civil rights and drunk-driving laws if a regulation reduced a company's business and thus constituted a "taking."[58] They point to a Wyoming case in which a group of ranchers sued the state, claiming that bag limits on deer and other wildlife constituted a "taking" because the owner of the land could no longer manage the land as she or he saw fit. Although the case lost initially in federal court, it is on appeal and could have far-reaching implications for state wildlife management laws.[59] Others have warned that the TIA process itself would slow down the wheels of government regulation and impede the government's ability to protect the public's interest by having a chilling effect on efforts by governments to enact more strict environmental legislation.[60]

Still other arguments have been made that takings bills strike at the very heart of environmental protection laws. As Glenn P. Sugameli, counsel to the NWF, noted:

> The property rights and values of American citizens are protected by environmental laws that prevent pollution, flooding and other threats to their health, homes and businesses. Proposed federal "takings" bills would overturn the Constitutional balance and radically redefine property rights in a way that threatens fundamental protections for people, neighboring homes and communities.[61]

The more obvious reason federal takings legislation is unlikely to pass is economic: The concept would cost too much. Those bills that focus on compensation would—as their sponsors are free to admit—bankrupt the government. The fiscal impacts of an expanded definition of regulatory takings should not be underestimated. Before the *Nollan* and *First English* decisions were handed down, the federal government had "takings awards" figures of $23.1 million in 1985, $5.5 million in 1986, and $20.2 million in 1987. A year after the two decisions, the federal government had more than $1 billion in takings claims pending against it.[62] This gives lawmakers only one other option: water down existing environmental laws, like the ESA, so that fewer takings will occur.

PROPERTY RIGHTS AND THE
ENVIRONMENTAL OPPOSITION

Property rights advocates are fond of providing journalists with cases like those cited here, each one sounding, at least at face value, like a regulatory nightmare that has engulfed a hardworking farmer or landowner. But what is important about the cases is that while individually, they may not represent a national uproar over the ESA or wetlands regulations, collectively, they become repeated as exemplary of what property rights activists perceive as the government's callous attitude toward property and individual rights. Just as easily, they can be used by issue entrepreneurs like Chuck Cushman to whip a crowd into a frenzy by regaling it with war stories from the property rights front. More so than with any other segment of the environmental opposition, property rights advocates seem especially sensitive to the efforts of issue entrepreneurs to capitalize on their fears about the government.

But like some of the examples used by members of the environmental opposition, not all of the stories are true, regardless of how often they get repeated and retold. Louisiana congressmember Billy Tauzin, for instance, used an incident from his state to illustrate his position during House debates on a proposed federal property rights bill. In his telling of the story, the Gautreau family had gotten permission from the Army Corps of Engineers to dig a pond and use the fill as a foundation. Then they built another home on their property and sold it to another family, the Chaconas. According to Tauzin, the Corps told the Gautreaus that the dirt road they used as access to their homes was on a wetland and could not be used, and that the Chaconas family might have to forfeit their house, evidence, Tauzin said, of the government's arrogance in enforcing wetlands regulations. But according to John Chaconas, the real problem was that the Gautreaus had failed to obtain a dredging permit even though the Soil Conservation Service had advised the family they needed to so. Chaconas, who filed suit against Gautreau, was invited to Washington, D.C., to testify before a House task force on wetlands, but when he showed up, was told he would not be appearing. Despite disclaimers from Tauzin's staff, Chaconas believes his appearance was canceled because he would have contradicted a wetlands horror story frequently recounted by Tauzin.[63]

Somewhat belatedly, environmental groups have recognized the potential impact of the expansion of property rights jurisprudence.[64] Much of their prior lethargy about takings and other issues may have been because the debate was being carried out primarily in the courts. Since judicial wheels move so slowly and the courts are generally reluctant to make sweeping new judicial interpretations, there may have been a sense that the issue was under control. But highly publicized cases like *Lucas,* the flurry of state initiatives, and the 1994 congressional elections made it clear that property rights advocates were becoming better organized and were actively seeking out more sympathetic ears in statehouses and in the Capitol. Despite their efforts, nonenvironmental groups ranging from the National Governors Association to the American Federation of Labor and Congress of Industrial Organizations now oppose the state and federal proposals. In vetoing Idaho's takings measure in 1993, Governor Cecil Andrus made clear the reasons for his opposition to the legislation:

> This bill is not concerned with the protection of property owners and the promotion of the social welfare of Idaho citizens. Instead, its central focus is the protection of select property owners (developers, polluters, etc.) to do what they want regardless of [the effects of] their actions on their communities and their neighbors.[65]

By successfully mobilizing their efforts in Washington State against the proposed compensation legislation, environmental groups realized that there was still a strong public commitment to environmental protection. Had environmental groups not dedicated themselves to the signature-gathering efforts and grassroots opposition efforts that worked so well in similar campaigns in the past, the property rights movement might have used Washington State as an example of broad support for takings compensation. Although the state's property rights activists vowed to return to the voters with similar measures in subsequent elections, the 1995 referendum's defeat may lead property rights activists in other states (who are not as well organized) to return to the courts, arguing individual cases on an ad hoc basis. This strategy is time consuming and expensive, and only the most ardent of activists are likely to remain committed under those circumstances, potentially reducing the property rights movement's momentum even further. It is appropriate to conclude that as long as environmental organizations continue to monitor state and federal legislative efforts and repeat the type of grassroots mobilization campaign they organized in Washington State, they can attempt to confine property rights issues to the judicial arena where policymaking is more likely to be incremental and limited.

THE GRASSROOTS MOVEMENTS IN PERSPECTIVE: LINKAGES TO INDUSTRY AND THE ANTIGOVERNMENT AGENDA

The one issue that seems to permeate every discussion about the environmental opposition, including the property rights movement, is whether or not there is a linkage between industry interests that front for grassroots groups and a more sinister connection between grassroots organizations (wise use, property rights, and county supremacy) and a libertarian, antigovernment agenda. At its extreme, the critics go further to forge the linkage with particular groups like the John Birch Society and the organized militia and patriot movements.

From all indications, the power of the environmental opposition stems from one of two sources: the personal aggrandizement of the policy entrepreneurs who head up the umbrella organizations, or a broader, antigovernment intrusion agenda that appeals to a totally different group of adherents with only a marginal interest in the environment.

Among the policy entrepreneurs, the linkage with conservatism may be ideological but it is also a matter of practical concern. Libertarian or conservative think tanks and legal foundations provide some capital and credibility that make the umbrella groups seem larger and more powerful than their policy success rate would indicate. It becomes a marriage of convenience, with the policy entrepreneurs gaining resources (membership dues, book and newsletter sales, workshop fees, media visibility) that keep their organizations going, their leaders paid, and the right-wing groups benefiting by creating the perception that a whole new cadre of adherents has accepted their political perspective. The conservative right, in effect, benefits from the "spillover effects" of green backlash.

But there is also a genuine linkage between antigovernment groups and some of the more militant or philosophically radical individuals within the environmental opposition, which allows the use of the environment to camouflage a more conservative political agenda. An example might be that of Tule Lake, California, resident David Porter Misso. Misso, a former antiwar activist who refers to himself as "an older radical hippie," twice staged what he termed the Lava Beds National Park Federal Fee Freedom Convoy. The object of the protest was the collection of a $4.00 park entrance fee to travel through the park to access a lake within the park or to harvest firewood on park property. The fee is collected from visitors by the National Park Service; Misso believes the fee should not apply to local residents.

Despite the fact that one publication referred to the incident as "David Misso's War," this term exaggerates both the circumstances and the clout of similar isolated protests. The "convoy" consisted of three vehicles in its first attempt and fines of $50; on his second attempt, Misso contacted media from both Oregon and California to garner publicity—only six cars showed up to participate in the convoy. After receiving a second citation, Misso eventually represented himself in federal district court where a judge found him guilty of not paying the user fee and fined him $60.

Like many of those opposed to the federal government, Misso is not part of a mammoth organized effort to restructure environmental policy, nor have his efforts had any impact on the bureaucracy and the implementation of federal regulations. By publicizing Misso's case and portraying him as a soldier in a larger war, both the media and interest groups have given him a visibility and stature that are inappropriate to his real standing.

The fact remains that despite the attempts by journalists and environmental group leaders to portray the environmental opposition in the most negative of possible lights, the "enemy" is not nearly as powerful or monolithic a foe as they would like the public to believe. The environmental opposition suffers from a lack of cohesiveness among its myriad groups, a lack of resources with which to mobilize its members or influence policy, the absence of an articulated policy program, and the countervailing forces of public opinion. Like the seeds of discontent that have sprung briefly to life in other eras of American political history, wise use groups and their related advocates have relied upon a window of opportunity that is rapidly closing. The other segment of the opposition—business interests—is shifting strategy and is much more likely to be successful in influencing environmental policy, albeit in multiple political arenas as the forces of electoral change ebb and flow.

Those who have sounded a warning that environmental protection is under siege may be misreading a historical pattern that indicates otherwise. Although it is true that more Americans are becoming skeptical and distrustful of government, and that there is sincere disillusionment about the way the bureaucracy operates, those feelings do not equate with acceptance of a philosophy that is in total contradiction to the environmental ethic that remains a core value in America. As we enter the next millennium, historians, political scientists, and sociologists who look back on the 1990s are more likely to view this period as simply another short phase in the evolution of the environmental opposition, but they are not likely to see a major shift in values based primarily on environmental protection. If the antigovernment forces grow in power and visibility, as some observers believe has already begun to happen, that power will only nominally be linked to issues and individuals related to environmental protection.

A more accurate linkage would be one profiled by Kenneth Stern in his book *A Force upon the Plain: The American Militia Movement and the Politics of Hate*. In describing the land use battles that he says "were made for militias," Stern concludes that those involved are part of a hatred of government transferred to a hatred of federal employees. But he also notes that the new militancy might just as easily be driven by such varied motivations as white supremacy, anti-Semitism, or the anti-abortion movement. The county supremacy movement, for example, is more likely a cover for bigotry, Stern argues, that resulted from a post-Soviet world where there was no longer an evil empire on which to focus Americans' hatred.

> This new form of prejudice has co-opted the dehumanizing and stereotyping attributes of gutter bigotry and turned them on our public servants, who are seen not as doing the work of America—delivering the mail, clearing Forest Service roads, protecting the environment and wildlife, maintaining the interstate highway system, helping lost campers—but as doing the work of "the beast."[66]

It would be erroneous to classify the entire spectrum of those considered part of the environmental opposition into Stern's mosaic of bigotry. It has been the intent to this book to show that many of those who oppose environmental regulations promulgated by local, state, and federal agencies, and even those who oppose particular environmental groups or the movement itself, are not part of a monolithic antigovernment conspiracy. Many who have been labeled "anti-enviros" wear that title unjustly. It may be just as convenient for the policy entrepreneurs to lump them together to inflate their membership figures as it is for the media and environmental groups to have a new enemy to challenge, but in either case, the characterization is inaccurate and misleading.

NOTES

1. Tom Bethell, "Property and Tyranny," *American Spectator,* vol. 27, no. 8 (August 1994): 16–17. Reigle's involvement in the development of FLOC is also outlined in Ron Arnold and Alan Gottlieb, *Trashing the Economy,* 2nd ed. (Bellevue, WA: Free Enterprise Press, 1994), pp. 19–20.
2. Wallace Kaufman, "The Cost of Saving," *American Forests,* vol. 99, nos. 11–12 (November–December 1993): 17–19, 58–59.
3. Ibid., p. 19.
4. Bethell, "Property and Tyranny," p. 16.
5. Bruce Yandle, ed., *Land Rights: The 1990s' Property Rights Rebellion* (Lanham, MD: Rowman and Littlefield, 1995), pp. ix–x.
6. *Pennsylvania Coal Co. v. Mahon,* 260 U.S. 393, 415 (1922).
7. Donald Worster, *Rivers of Empire* (New York: Pantheon, 1985), p. 88.
8. Ibid., pp. 91–92.
9. For an environmental group's perspective on the Hage case, see Ted Williams, "Taking Back the Range," *Audubon,* vol. 95, no. 1 (January–February 1993): 28–33. For Hage's perspective, see Wayne Hage, *Storm over Rangelands,* 3rd ed. (Bellevue, WA: Free Enterprise Press, 1994).
10. Quoted in letter from Margaret H. Gabbard, executive director of Stewards of the Range, n.d.

11. Nancie G. Marzulla, "The Property Rights Movement: How It Began and Where It Is Headed," in Yandle, ed., *Land Rights,* p. 13.

12. Thomas A. Lewis, "Cloaked in a Wise Disguise," in John D. Echeverria and Raymond Booth Eby, eds., *Let the People Judge: Wise Use and the Private Property Rights Movement* (Washington, DC: Island Press, 1995), p. 16.

13. Margaret L. Knox, "The World According to Cushman," *Wilderness,* vol. 56, no. 200 (spring 1993): 28.

14. David Helvarg, "Grassroots for Sale," *Amicus Journal,* vol. 16, no. 3 (fall 1994): 26.

15. The history of the Adirondack controversy is outlined by David Helvarg in *The War Against the Greens: The "Wise-Use" Movement, the New Right, and Anti-Environmental Violence* (San Francisco: Sierra Club Books, 1994), pp. 204–227.

16. MacWilliams Cosgrove Snider, *The Wise Use Movement: Strategic Analysis and Fifty State Review* (Washington, DC: Environmental Working Group, 1993), pp. 206–207.

17. William Kevin Burke, "The Wise Use Movement: Right-Wing Anti-Environmentalism," *Propaganda Review,* no. 11 (1994): 8–9.

18. See, for example, Lawrence Blume, Daniel Rubinfield, and Perry Shapiro, "The Taking of Land: When Should Compensation Be Paid?" *Quarterly Journal of Economics,* vol. 99 (1984): 71; Raymond Coletta, "Reciprocity of Advantage and Regulatory Jurisprudence: Towards a New Theory of Takings Jurisprudence," *American University Law Review,* vol. 40 (1990): 297; Saul Levmore, "Just Compensation and Just Politics," *Virginia Law Review,* vol. 77 (1991): 285; Frank Michelman, "Takings, 1987," *Columbia Law Review,* vol. 88 (1988): 1600; and Joseph Sax, "Takings, Private Property, and Public Rights," *Yale Law Journal,* vol. 81 (1971): 149.

19. Richard Epstein, *Takings: Private Property and the Power of Eminent Domain* (Cambridge, MA: Harvard University Press, 1985). Several authors have attempted to expand on Epstein's premises from an economic standpoint. See, for example, William A. Fischel, *Regulatory Takings: Law, Economics, and Politics* (Cambridge, MA: Harvard University Press, 1995).

20. Karol J. Ceplo, "Land-Rights Conflicts in the Regulation of Wetlands," in Yandle, ed., *Land Rights,* p. 106.

21. Ibid., pp. 107–108.

22. CR 83-891 (S.D. Fla. 1988).

23. S-90-0216 (D Md, May 31, 1990).

24. CR 2-90-02 (D Md) upheld, Nos. 91–5032 (4th Cir. 1992).

25. See "EPA's Most Wanted," *Wall Street Journal,* November 18, 1992, p. A20.

26. Ceplo, "Land-Rights Conflicts," p. 135.

27. Paul Jones, the other party in the case, was severely criticized by property rights groups who believe the wealthy landowner used Bill Ellen as a scapegoat. Jones was appointed by the Clinton administration to serve on the board of directors of the National Fish and Wildlife Foundation, a nonprofit charitable corporation created in 1984 to administer and accept gifts of property that further conservation. Officials of the CFDFE have repeatedly called for Jones's ouster. See *Feeding at the Trough* (Bellevue, WA: Center for the Defense of Free Enterprise, 1995).

28. 947 F.2d 938 (3rd Cir. 1991).

29. John G. Mitchell, "The Fable of Pozsgai's Swamp," *Audubon,* vol. 92 (July 1990): 112–114.

30. See, for example, Michael Blumm and D. Bernard Zaleha, "Federal Wetlands Protection Under the Clean Water Act: Regulatory Ambivalence, Intergovernmental Tension, and a Call for Reform," *University of Colorado Law Review*, vol. 60, no. 4 (1989): 695–772.

31. Lee Ann Welch, "Property Rights Conflicts Under the Endangered Species Act: Protection of the Red-Cockaded Woodpecker," in Yandle, ed., *Land Rights*, p. 154.

32. Ibid., pp. 154–155.

33. Ibid., p. 166.

34. H. Josef Hebert, "Private Interests Pick Away at Parks," *Medford* [Oregon] *Mail Tribune*, July 7, 1996, p. 7A.

35. Knox, "The World According to Cushman," p. 31.

36. For an assessment of the legal aspects of property rights from the perspective of one of the movement's key litigators, see Mark L. Pollot, *Grand Theft and Petit Larceny* (San Francisco: Pacific Research Institute for Public Policy, 1993).

37. 480 U.S. 470 (1987).

38. 482 U.S. 304 (1987).

39. 483 U.S. 825 (1987).

40. Charles R. Wise, "The Changing Doctrine of Regulatory Taking and the Executive Branch," *Administrative Law Review*, vol. 44 (spring 1992): 404.

41. 112 S.Ct. 2886 (1992).

42. See Justice Blackmun's dissent in the *Lucas* case for an explanation of these issues. See also James R. Rinehart and Jeffrey J. Pompe, "The Lucas Case and the Conflict over Property Rights," in Yandle, ed., *Land Rights*, pp. 67–101; and Donald Large, "Lucas: A Flawed Attempt to Redefine the Mahon Analysis," *Environmental Law*, vol. 23, no. 3 (1993): 883–890.

43. See, for example, "Symposium, *Lucas v. South Carolina Coastal Council*," *Stanford Law Review*, vol. 45 (1993): 1369; and "Colloquium on *Lucas*," *Environmental Law*, vol. 23, no. 3 (1993): 869.

44. 129 L Ed 2d 304 (1994).

45. 21 Cl. Ct. 153 (1990).

46. 21 Cl. Ct. 161 (1990).

47. Ceplo, "Land-Rights Conflicts," p. 130. See also Sharon Dennis, "The Takings Debate and Federal Regulatory Programs," in Echeverria and Eby, eds., *Let the People Judge*, pp. 158–168.

48. 25 Cl. Ct. 232 (1992).

49. Keith Schneider, "Environmental Laws Face a Stiff Test from Landowners," *New York Times*, January 20, 1992, p. A1.

50. *Federal Register*, vol. 53, no. 53 (March 15, 1988): 8859.

51. See Wise, "The Changing Doctrine," p. 426.

52. Hertha L. Lund, "The Property Rights Movement and State Legislation," in Yandle, ed., *Land Rights*, pp. 200–231. The states that initially passed measures to ensure private property rights were Arizona, Delaware, Idaho, Indiana, Mississippi, Missouri, North Carolina, Tennessee, Utah, Virginia, Washington, and West Virginia.

53. David Foster, "Ripe for the Taking," *Medford Mail Tribune*, July 30, 1995, p. 3A.

54. "West World," *National Review West*, December 11, 1995, p. 2.

55. Lund, "The Property Rights Movement," p. 203.

56. Ibid., p. 207.

57. See Note, "Recent Legislation," *Harvard Law Review,* vol. 108 (1994): 519–524.

58. Patricia Byrnes, "Are We Being Taken by Takings?" *Wilderness,* vol. 58, no. 208 (spring 1995): 4–5.

59. See John McCoy, "The Takings Issue," *Field and Stream* (April 1995): 26.

60. See Barbara Moulton, "Takings Legislation: Protection of Property Rights or Threat to the Public Interest?" *Environment,* vol 37, no. 2 (March 1995): 44–45.

61. Glenn P. Sugameli, "Takings Bills Would Destroy Protections for Property and People," *The Initiative Press and Seminars* (January 1996): 3.

62. Wise, "The Changing Doctrine," p. 414.

63. Tom Kenworth, "Letting the Truth Fall Where It May," *Washington Post National Weekly Edition,* March 27–April 2, 1995, p. 31.

64. See, for example, William Callaway, "Taking Liberties," *National Parks* (November–December 1994): 24–25.

65. McCoy, "The Takings Issue," p. 27.

66. Kenneth S. Stern, *A Force upon the Plain: The American Militia Movement and the Politics of Hate* (New York: Simon and Schuster, 1996), p. 247.

Conclusion:
Environmentalism
in the Balance

SIGN OF THE TIMES: In 1996, Carl Pope, executive director of the Sierra Club, sent a letter to prospective members with this urgent plea:

> *Dear Friend:*
>
> *As I write you, anti-environmental forces in Congress are escalating their all-out war on America's environment. If they succeed, they will rob us of our natural heritage—pollute our air and water . . . cut down our forests . . . close some of our beloved national parks . . . and threaten the health and quality of life of thousands of American families.*
>
> *What is turning out to be the most anti-environmental Congress in history will—if we let them—literally wipe out some of the most vital protections environmentalists have fought for over the last 100 years! Ardent anti-conservationists are taking full impact of their powerful positions in Congress—from which they are mounting a devastating assault on our nation's air, water, forests, parks and wilderness. Behind them are powerful special interests—big timber, oil, mining and others—who have succeeded in buying their way into the halls of Congress. And now, they are the ones calling the shots on the fate of America's precious natural resources!*

The purpose of this chapter is to summarize the key points that have been made in the preceding sections of the book and, more specifically, to try to place the environmental opposition in context. It examines the effectiveness of the opposition in shaping the policy debate and public opinion and in affecting the outcome of environmental policymaking. It also reviews the ways in which the environmental movement has responded to the opposition's actions and explores whether similar conflict is likely to occur in future debates over the environment.

THE POLICY IMPACT OF THE
ENVIRONMENTAL OPPOSITION

One of the key questions raised by an analysis of any political movement is whether or not its members have actually affected policy. They may do so at various stages of the policymaking process: at the point where the policy agenda is set and decisions are made about what issues will be the subject of discussion; during the formulation and adoption of policies, which usually occurs in legislative bodies; and during the actual implementation of the policy once it has been adopted.[1]

One of the primary themes of this book is that the policy impact of business and industry interests is quite different from that of the grassroots groups, which supports my contention that the grassroots organizations do not pose a substantial threat to the efforts made by environmental organizations to develop a framework of legislative and regulatory programs. There are several reasons that have been identified in support of the conclusion that business has been more effective than the grassroots organizations in influencing environmental policy and its implementation.

First, organized industry opposition is more enduring than that of the grassroots groups, dating back to the mid-twentieth century, while most of the wise use, county supremacy, and property rights groups were established as late as the 1980s. While it has been shown that the sentiments exemplified by the grassroots activists are deeply rooted in U.S. history, only one or two of the umbrella opposition groups pre-date 1980. Even more established groups like the AFBF, which some observers argue is on the periphery of the wise use movement, have not totally adopted an antifederal stance and in many cases have embraced government programs like farm subsidies that serve its members' interests. Thus, although there may have been a continuing philosophical foundation for the environmental opposition throughout much of U.S. history, the organizational basis for the opposition has fluctuated over time. Grassroots opposition groups have come and gone as their leadership and membership have shifted over time. In that sense, the longevity of the business community's organizations and leaders provides them with political clout and credibility the other groups are still attempting to achieve.

Second, business interests have used a wider variety of political tactics than the grassroots groups. Some of those strategies are typical of organized interests (lobbying and contributing to political candidates), while others are more nontraditional, such as the bureaucratic end runs described in Chapter 6. The grassroots groups lack the resources to engage in a similarly broad spectrum of tactics and must

rely instead upon activities that are often less effective, such as spo-
radic letter-writing campaigns and protests. Since the membership of
the grassroots organizations is so geographically dispersed, those efforts often result in less visible action and fewer policy successes than
can be claimed by industry and trade associations. No single grassroots group serves as the focal point for the divergent interests of the
environmental opposition, so group mobilization is often disorganized
and haphazard.

One of the tactics that demonstrates business interests' superior
use of financial resources is contributions to congressional candidates.
Traditionally, business tries to place its money where it is most likely to
make a difference, with incumbents and the majority party, although
some hedge their bets by giving to both parties. When Republicans
gained control of Congress in 1995, political action committees sensed
that the GOP would be more likely to support a probusiness deregulation agenda and dramatically shifted their contribution patterns. In
1993–1994, the top 400 PACs (which are dominated by industry interests) donated 65 percent of their monies to Democrats and 34 percent
to Republicans. But after the 1994 election, the pattern was reversed,
with 53 percent of their contributions targeted toward Republican incumbents and those toward the Democrats dropping to 47 percent
during the first six months of 1995. The ninth-ranked PAC, for example, the National Automobile Dealers Association, increased its contribution to Republicans from 70 percent to 76 percent, while the sev-
enth-ranked PAC, AT&T, reduced Democratic contributions from 61
percent to 42 percent. Realtors, whose environmental concerns are reflected in many of the property rights measures that faced the 104th
Congress, used their position as the fifth-ranked PAC to switch allegiance very dramatically, increasing their Republican giving from 46
percent in 1994 to 72 percent just a year later.[2]

Business has also benefited by contributing "soft money" (virtually unlimited contributions given to political parties that are not subject to federal campaign finance laws) to fund voter registration drives,
get-out-the-vote efforts, and policy initiatives not related to specific
candidates. Republicans in 1995 collected $20 million in soft money—
double their Democratic counterparts—with the tobacco companies
leading the charge. In the first six months of 1995, tobacco interests
gave the Republican Party $1.5 million—tenfold what they gave in
1993—as a way of supporting Republicans who would help protect
their firms against additional regulation by the FDA.[3] Grassroots
groups simply cannot compete at that level and thus lack the access to
legislators that political contributions provide industry interests.

Even with their advantages, however, industry, too, has not been
an implacable foe for the advancement of the environmental move-

ment's objectives, often because businesses' demands are highly individualized and fragmented. While some coalitions have been forged, disputes over clean air or water legislation often pit one industry against another, with little agreement on the appropriate path of redress. As was pointed out in Part II of this book, those factors have kept business and its organized interests from substantive legislative success, forcing industry to accept incremental policy change and to turn to other arenas in seeking its divergent goals.

Both the grassroots groups and business interests vary tremendously in their goals and how they expect to meet them. While one wise use group might seek to open up the Arctic National Wildlife Refuge to mining and oil drilling because its members feel the public lands ought to be accessible to commercial interests, those goals are not likely to be shared by the members of property rights groups seeking exemptions from the ESA for their personal parcels of land. As Part III showed, the majority of the grassroots groups have labor resources (membership), some of whom feel intensely about their goals; but the actual figures on how many individuals can be identified as belonging to or participating in group activities is unknown. Although there is an identifiable core leadership within the grassroots groups, the majority of their supporters appear to be issue sympathizers rather than activists. The grassroots groups have few tangible resources available to them, especially in comparison to the more established and better-funded mainstream environmental groups with which they are in conflict. Similarly, efforts to enact clean air legislation in 1990 split industry into competing interests represented by coal companies, hydroelectric power providers, natural gas firms, automakers, and nuclear power advocates.

Some of the larger environmental organizations are in the process of developing substantive clout over industry when it comes to influencing policy, even at the implementation phase where business has had some notable success. In the mid-1980s, the USFS began to increase allowable timber sales to meet public demand for lumber and worked closely with the timber industry to double the annual harvest. Groups like the Sierra Club and the Natural Resources Defense Council filed hundreds of administrative appeals under the planning and public participation requirements of the National Forest Management Act that delayed or blocked the agency from proceeding with some timber sales for years.

Overall, however, neither the business community nor the grassroots movements that make up the environmental opposition have been able to dramatically change the direction of environmental policy, a topic that is explored in greater detail in the following section.

MEASURING POLICY SUCCESS

Another way of looking at policy success is based on a model developed by political scientists Thomas R. Rochon and Daniel A. Mazmanian. They use three criteria to define "success" for movements like the environmental opposition: whether the protesting group gains new advantages for its members (policy change), whether the group is accepted as a valid representative for newly defined social interests (process change), and the ability of the group to change social values, ultimately redefining the political agenda (value change). They argue that to be completely successful in gaining the legal and behavioral changes sought by movements, all three criteria must be met.[4]

Policy Change

Using those three criteria, the environmental opposition has a low success ratio. On the first, policy change, there is little evidence that grassroots groups or business have thus far been able to rescind any of the major federal legislative proposals enacted since the passage of the NEPA in 1969 or the creation of the EPA in 1970. There is also scant evidence that the opposition has been able to block major policy initiatives that enhance environmental protection or are part of the environmental movement's political agenda, such as the Marine Mammal Protection Act and the Toxic Substances Control Act. Although mainstream environmental groups may be dismayed at the lack of enforcement of various regulations, or by budget cuts within agencies, the statutes themselves remain on the books with only incremental changes in their implementation. Efforts by members of Congress to prevent President Clinton from fulfilling his campaign promise to make the EPA a cabinet-level agency have been successful, but the move would have been largely symbolic and would have made little impact on the agency's day-to day administration. Promises made by Speaker of the House Newt Gingrich to overhaul key statutes like the Clean Water Act, Endangered Species Act, and Superfund legislation were unsuccessful during the 104th Congress, in large part due to sectional cleavages within the legislature. Members of Congress from western states—home to the majority of the grassroots groups—have found few supporters among eastern lawmakers who have prioritized other parts of the Republicans' "Contract with America." In addition, public criticism of what many saw as a wholesale assault on environmental protection (especially water quality and EPA cuts that would affect enforcement) hit hard at moderates within the Republican Party who refused to sign on with their support.

Gingrich himself noted that his party would have to reposition itself toward the center on environmental issues. In an April 1996 speech before business leaders at the National Environmental Policy Institute, Gingrich called for a "new environmentalism" that would operate on a cooperative, rather than confrontational, basis where the parties would seek to work together wherever possible.[5] Such an admission by the House Speaker appears to be further evidence that while the 1994 congressional takeover by Republicans signaled demands for change in some policy areas, the party's leadership eventually realized that environmental protection was an area that still has the support of most voters who are unwilling to accept a massive overhaul of existing legislation.

A typical example of the inability of the environmental opposition to rely upon those members of Congress generally considered supportive of their political agenda was a 1995 bill co-sponsored by Republican senator Conrad Burns of Montana. His proposed legislation would have given states the opportunity to take control of 270 million acres of federal land—one of the major goals of the wise use and county supremacy groups. But Burns ran into the well-organized opposition of a group he thought he could have relied upon—the hunting lobby—which opposed the measure because of fears that sport hunters would lose access they currently have to BLM lands. Their "Keep Public Lands in Public Hands" campaign, timed to coincide with the opening of elk season, urged hunters to contact the senator's office directly. Burns later announced that he would not even vote for the bill he co-sponsored.[6] Neither business interests nor the grassroots groups have been successful in influencing substantive environmental policy change. At best, the environmental opposition might be able to claim credit for slowing down or stalling new initiatives proposed by environmental groups (such as reform of mining laws or grazing fees), but they have not been able to alter the overall momentum toward environmental protection.

Efforts at the state level to force the federal government to give up portions of the federal domain have failed either at the ballot box or on the governor's desk, and court decisions have stalled, if not ended, the efforts of those hoping to give the counties control over their land. In those venues, the grassroots environmental opposition has been unsuccessful as well.

Although it might be argued that business interests have sometimes been able to achieve delays in policy implementation, such as compliance dates for auto emission reductions, the overall direction of policy remains the same, and the federal government and states remain committed to the goal of dramatically reducing the amount of pollutants produced by automobiles. Such delays are best thought of as short-term victories in a longer battle.

Process Change and Value Change

On the second criteria—process change—business and industry groups had already found their way to the decisionmaking table through early environmental legislation that requires public comment periods or consultation. Grassroots group representatives have not been able to expand their involvement in the process beyond what already exists, and they have not been able to force the creation of any new channels or institutional structures to provide them with a voice in policymaking. Federal officials have agreed to meet with some property rights activists, although they appear to have agreed to do so as a way of avoiding more violent confrontations and militancy. But it appears that, except in rare instances, members of the grassroots groups have gained few if any venues or processes to allow them any additional access to channels for pursuing their grievances than those they already possess.

The environmental opposition has also failed in the model's third criteria—value change—as explained in the following overview of public attitudes about the environment.

THE CONTINUING SALIENCE OF ENVIRONMENTALISM

In his analysis of the wise use and property rights advocates' impact on Washington, D.C., policymaking, David Helvarg notes that in the midst of debates over issues like health care reform, NAFTA, and foreign policy, "environmentalism is, if not moving to the front burner, at least heating up the back of the stove." He writes:

> There are stirrings both institutionally and legislatively that have everyone slightly unnerved, a sense of change that justifies both the fears of the present crop of anti-environmentalists and the skepticism of mainstream environmental activists. It is, as the intellectuals like to put it, a transitional period in American history when the dominant paradigm no longer applies and a new way of viewing the world emerges.[7]

There appears to be little evidence that the environmental opposition —whether industry interests or grassroots groups—has managed to diminish the public's enduring support for environmental protection, although surveys show that other issues have historically been of greater concern. When George Gallup asked respondents in his national survey to identify the most important problem facing the nation in 1967, the environment did not even make the list, nor did it appear when the question was asked in three surveys in 1968 or one in 1969. The Vietnam War and the economy overshadowed most Americans' lives during that period. Not until May 1970 (after the first Earth Day) did the issue appear as a concern, when it ranked second and was mentioned by 53 percent of those responding. By June 1970, the environment had dropped off the list, overshadowed by the campus unrest that was sweeping the nation. Pollution and ecology returned to the Gallup list in March 1971 (ranked sixth, with only 7 percent naming these as the most important problems), and by June 1971, the topics ranked tenth. Although the environment was mentioned as an important issue in polls throughout the early 1970s (especially when the energy crisis became the most important problem cited in January 1974), since that time, the environment has been ranked as the most important problem by a steady 4–5 percent of respondents.[8] A 1995 study of public opinion surveys about the environment conducted by political scientist Everett Ladd and former *Public Opinion* managing editor Karlyn Bowman found that the environment has now become a "core value" to most Americans. The study also reported that the majority of citizens believe that a clean environment is not incompatible with economic growth, but that much of the urgency of the 1970s has dissipated as the public has adopted what the study's authors term a "Lite Green" view of environmental issues.[9]

That term reflects the fact that while many individuals feel environmental issues are important, that concern is frequently overwhelmed by other, more pressing issues that take priority. There are overwhelming public opinion survey data from the 1990s that show that the majority of Americans are deeply concerned about the environment and identify themselves as environmentally supportive. A 1994 Roper survey found, for example, that 47 percent of those interviewed rated environmental pollution as a "very serious" threat, similar to the percentages of surveys conducted a decade earlier. Similarly, a Gallup Organization poll that asked Americans, "Do you consider yourself to be an environmentalist or not?" resulted in 73 percent answering affirmatively. A Cambridge Reports study that asked respondents to mark on a numerical scale the extent to which they would identify themselves with the label "environmentalist" found that 58 percent answered on the "do identify" side of the scale.[10]

The Ladd/Bowman report argues that while public opinion polls show agreement that people care about the environment, we have little information about what society is willing to do to advance the environment as a core value, what trade-offs the public is willing to make for it, or what happens when limited resources force clashes between competing values. In their view, the public can agree upon specific goals, such as clean air and continued economic growth, without knowing how to achieve those goals.

There may be a contradiction in support for the environment when it comes down to actual day-to-day choices involving costs. For example, while Americans have indicated a desire for clean air, 1992 presidential candidate Ross Perot found little support for his proposed $0.50 per gallon gasoline tax that would have helped reduce the federal deficit, but also would have been likely to reduce automobile usage and, subsequently, improve air quality. Congress made a similar choice in 1996 when they voted to reduce gasoline taxes because of election-year consumer complaints about high gas prices, even though the result might be an increase in the number of miles driven and, therefore, more air pollution. Often, there is a philosophical level of support for protecting the environment that is not matched by political or pocketbook support.

Saliency is also tempered by the fact that many Americans may believe that most domestic environmental problems like air and water pollution have been "fixed," and it becomes more difficult for them to become concerned about environmental issues that are global or distant. The problems of climate change, desertification, or increases in infectious diseases due to poor sanitation often seem remote and requiring more resources than individuals are willing to muster to deal with them. These attitudes then begin to allow policy entrepreneurs to crack open the policy window just far enough to allow for discussion of problems closer to home that are observable or personal, such as a neighbor's inability to build a vacation retreat on land because it has been declared part of an endangered species' habitat.

Other authors believe that there is adequate evidence that environmentalism is increasing, citing surveys that show that Americans want environmental protection even when asked to make difficult trade-offs. A 1990 *New York Times*/CBS survey, for example, found that 56 percent of the respondents agreed with the statement, "We must protect the environment, even if it means jobs in the local community are lost." Other surveys that have asked how much respondents would pay to help protect the environment have found that 64 percent agreed they would pay as much as 10 percent more a week for grocery items if they were sure the products would not harm the environment. A 1990 Cambridge Reports study that asked for a specific dollar figure as to how much a person would pay for goods and services "if you knew that as a result . . . business and industry would . . . not harm the environment" came up with a median figure of $36.99 monthly, up from a 1984 figure of $10.23 in constant 1990 U.S. dollars.[11]

But Ladd and Bowman respond that such hypothetical questions are of little value because the public does not think hypothetically about policy choices:

> The public points to the ends that policy makers should work to achieve. The public does not think much about the means. These problems are greatly extended when phony trade-offs are offered, when questions are asked in imprecise or misleading manners, or when the context in which the questions are asked is ignored.[12]

They conclude, "But we are now more inclined to think that for most Americans, the urgency has been removed, and the battle to protect the environment is being waged satisfactorily. Despite the many ambiguities in survey findings, impressive evidence of such a shift exists."[13]

SEARCHING FOR ENVIRONMENTAL PERSPECTIVE

One of the reasons why some Americans may embrace the message of the environmental opposition is because they no longer accept the doom-and-gloom prophecies of authors who have made predictions about environmental degradation that have yet to occur. Such authors as Anne Ehrlich and Paul Ehrlich, who in the 1960s predicted impending massive global overpopulation,[14] and Vice President Al Gore, with his book *Earth in the Balance*,[15] exemplify the credibility gap that exists in the minds of those who have lapsed from the flock of environmental believers. Gore's rhetoric, especially, does not match the perspective of those who feel real progress is being made in environmental protection. Gore writes, for instance:

> [Nuclear holocaust] is not unlike the challenge we face today in the global environmental crisis. The true catastrophe lies in the future, but the downslope that pulls us toward it is becoming recognizably steeper with each passing year. What lies ahead is a race against time. Sooner or later the steepness of the slope and our momentum down its curve will take us beyond a point of no return.[16]

Gore's view of a global environmental crisis is being challenged not only by business, industry, and grassroots groups that make up the environmental opposition, but by authors whose views are much more positive and, more important, becoming widely disseminated. A number of writers typify a challenging perspective about the environment that may be reflective of what many Americans believe intuitively is happening to their planet. In his book *No Turning Back: Dismantling the*

Fantasies of Environmental Thinking, former Wilderness Society lobbyist Wallace Kaufman writes that the environment is getting worse but blames environmental organizations for "losing touch with reality" because "differences in how we understand nature and what we should do about environmental problems have created a major split in our political life."[17] That view is echoed by wise use groups that see the environmental movement as the enemy because it relies upon a crusade mentality rather than science.

A second book, the widely reviewed *A Moment on the Earth: The Coming Age of Environmental Optimism,* by reporter Gregg Easterbrook, analyzes virtually every major environmental issue and argues that environmentalists

> are increasingly on the wrong side of the present, risking their credibility by proclaiming emergencies that do not exist. What some doctrinaire environmentalists wish were true for reasons of ideology has begun to obscure the view of what is actually true in "the laboratory of nature." It's time we began reading from a new script, one that reconciles the ideals of environmentalism with the observed facts of the natural world.[18]

Easterbrook argues that several of the key indicators of environmental health need to be viewed in terms of "ecorealism." He notes that several categories of pollution have already ended, that within our lifetimes pollution will end within the Western world, that such environmental catastrophes as runaway global warming are almost certain to be avoided, and that nearly all technical trends are toward new devices and modes of production that are more efficient, use fewer resources, produce less waste, and cause less ecological disruption than technology of the past.[19] These kinds of predictions are what in part have allowed the environmental opposition to develop its message and to relay it to millions of Americans who have begun to question whether or not the environmental movement has gone too far in its protectionist zeal.

In addition, it is difficult for the environmental movement to convince the public of the need for enhanced environmental protection when the problem involves very gradual processes, whose progress and effects are not visible except over decades, such as ozone depletion; when the problem occurs in a distant or unseen location, like a coral reef or Antarctica; or when a concept like species diversity in a tropical rain forest seems too abstract. The public is more likely to be responsive when there is a more visible problem, such as video footage of the efforts made to save dolphins trapped in fishing nets, or images of oil-soaked waterfowl on Alaskan beaches, both of which were widely broadcast by the media.

The challenge for environmental groups is to make such long-term problems as population growth, the spreading of infectious disease, biodiversity loss, or global climate change seem important issues to tackle now. Even though the predictions may not have come true on schedule, the environmental movement must still make the case that unless some preventive measures are taken soon, the problems will grow to the point where they may no longer be solvable.

THE RESPONSE BY ENVIRONMENTAL GROUPS

One of the implications of the rapid rise of attention directed toward the environmental opposition is that its message and popularity caught the environmental movement's leaders off guard, in effect, allowing the opposition to take advantage of a policy window as outlined in the Introduction to this book. That sentiment has been voiced by a number of group leaders, as well as by Yellowstone National Park superintendent Robert Barbee after the National Park Service and the U.S. Forest Service backed down over protests against the expansion of the park's ecosystem in 1990. Even though groups like the NPCA alerted their members about the issue, attended public hearings, and testified, "The environmental community simply was not prepared for the scale of the opposition against the Yellowstone Vision document," one NPCA official said later.[20] After bitter accusations that environmental groups were asleep at the wheel and complacent on the basis of past policy successes, it was only natural that organizations would mount a counterattack. Janet Ellis, president of the Montana Audubon Society, has advised supporters to "take on anti-environmentalists step-by-step" by identifying opponents and potential allies and "working to present our side of issues as 'the voice of reason.'"[21]

Another window for the environmental opposition may have opened because of disarray within the environmental movement itself. The growth of large national organizations centered in Washington, D.C., and New York may have squeezed out the grassroots support, primarily at the local level, which had been the hallmark of the movement during its growth years. Others within the environmental movement believe the answer to combating the environmental opposition can be summed up in signs similar to those that guided the Clinton administration's campaign in 1992, only this type reads, "It's the People, Stupid." As a regional director of the Wilderness Society characterized it, the large national groups let the wise use movement take the high ground. "We failed to communicate that we care about people. We didn't speak . . . about economics."[22]

We have to aggressively involve the public throughout the process: hold community meetings, early on, with anyone affected or interested. We have to do our own organizing. We have to work the grassroots. We have to educate. We have to get people to hearings.[23]

The disarray within the environmental movement is also exemplified by the divisive split within the Sierra Club in 1996 over the issue of commercial logging in national forests. The group's half-million members were asked in a mail-in vote whether they supported a ban on all logging, with the issue pitting the club's first executive director, David Brower, against Earth First! founder Dave Foreman. The highly publicized internal controversy resulted in the Sierra Club adopting the logging ban on a two-to-one vote in part due to the activism of a dissident group, John Muir Sierrans, whose members had supported a strict ban on logging for several years. Many small local Sierra Club chapters were split on the issue, although it did receive the endorsement of most of the club's largest chapters in Los Angeles, San Francisco, and New York City. But the dispute showed that even an environmental group with a lengthy history and significant resources is not always unified in the goals its members seek to pursue.

To counter the impression that there has been an inadequate response to the perceived threat posed by grassroots opposition groups, several have begun to actively mobilize against them. The Wilderness Society, for example, which has been hard hit by wise use groups' attempts to fight wilderness designations, calls its efforts a "reaffirmation" campaign to reconnect itself with its grassroots constituency. In 1992, the group mounted its "New Voices for the American West" campaign with a specially funded outreach campaign, a *New Voices* newsletter, and small grants for local conservation groups to "protect their neighborhoods from poorly managed (and sometimes illegal) mining operations and erosion and streamside degradation from clearcutting and overgrazing."[24]

It would also not be unexpected for some environmental groups to rest on their laurels and to dismiss the grassroots groups as a political nuisance. Although political scientist Phil Brick views the environmental opposition as stronger and better organized than the research for this book would indicate, most in the environmental movement would agree with his statement about the challenges ahead.

It is easy for environmentalists to find solace in polls indicating high levels of support for environmental laws promoting public health, conservation of natural resources, and endangered species. It is much harder to convert that support into effective public policy, especially when an increasingly divided environmental movement must face a well-organized and ideologically energized countermovement. It remains to be seen whether or not environmentalism can recapture the public's imagination and renew a sense of commitment to its causes, especially when other social issues such as welfare, health care, and crime currently loom larger in voters' minds.[25]

THE FUTURE: ACCOMMODATION
AND A SEARCH FOR CONSENSUS

If history is an indication of what lies ahead, the environmental opposition will not simply disappear. Its roots, especially those related to land use, lie deep within the public's attitudes toward environmental protection and property. The policy entrepreneurs may come and go, and the umbrella organizations and their smaller group members may vary in the level of their membership and level of political activity. It is doubtful, given the multiplicity of policy problems facing the public elected officials, that environmental groups will be successful in pushing the environment nearer the top of the policy agenda without the kind of crises that have made it a salient issue in the past. Even today, reports of massive environmental degradation in Eastern Europe or immense oil spills that dwarf that of the *Exxon Valdez* receive little media or public attention. Other problems—the economy, growing health care costs, terrorism—dominate the policy debate and the public's interest.

Environmental organizations will, in the short term, still attempt to capitalize on their delegitimization of the grassroots opposition to bolster their sagging membership and revenues. By creating an "enemy," as they did in the 1980s when the Reagan administration appointed James Watt and Anne Gorsuch Burford to key posts, environmental groups can create a motivational hook that they currently lack. Wise use groups fit that niche nicely, especially when they engage in rhetoric that inflames the passions of those who are truly committed to environmental protection.

Conservative members of Congress who were elected in the 1994 Republican sweep and referred to themselves as "the browns" found that their attempts to dismantle environmental protection laws met with little support, even in their home districts. "The Republicans made a horrible mistake, an abominable error," said one resident of Elko, Nevada, a mining area that is also in the heart of the property rights and county supremacy movements' territory, adding, "They were misled by zealots."[26]

But a second response—and one that is likely to be more enduring and productive—is the realization by many environmental organizations' leaders that the time has come to look for common ground. Michael W. Robbins, editor of *Audubon* magazine, exemplified this attitude in a 1996 editorial when he wrote about "pretty scary" confrontations over wolves in Yellowstone National Park, sugar growing in the Everglades, and salvage logging in the Northwest.

> It may be that determination to make changes in this world must be fueled by such passion. But simply pitting strong feelings against other strong feelings leads nowhere near the territory of resolution— as anyone knows who's witnessed a playground dustup or a marriage. What will point toward resolution is the recognition of common interest—and some understanding of the other's interests and strong feelings. It's easy for loggers and ranchers and commercial fishers to dismiss environmentalists as Druidical wackos who can't grasp the importance of making a living. And it's just as facile for enviros to label as shortsighted greed what others feel is simply making a living. With some mutual appreciation of the strong feelings, then maybe there can be a civil dialogue about common interests like sustainable forestry and fishery—even if that means attending a hostile hearing.[27]

There are beginning to be more indications that participants in the environmental debate are ready to at least sit down together to attempt to work out their differences. In April 1996, for example, nearly 500 individuals from California to Alaska and their Canadian counterparts came together in Victoria, British Columbia, at a conference called "Towards Sustainable Fisheries" to attempt to find ways to slow the dwindling runs of salmon. The five-day meeting brought together representatives from such environmental groups as American Rivers with such public officials as Fran Ulmer, Alaska's lieutenant governor, and Moe Sihota, British Columbia's minister of the environment. Although no substantive agreements were reached at the meeting, the conference was remarkable in that it brought together for the first time people who are most accustomed to yelling at one another across a courtroom.[28]

On a similarly contentious issue—grazing rights—President Clinton's secretary of the interior, Bruce Babbitt, turned to the Colorado Rangeland Reform Working Group, which proposed a less centralized, more collaborative structure for public range management. Working with Colorado governor Roy Romer, the group's negotiations revealed the differing perspectives of the participants: ranchers who argued that humans are part of ecosystems and that grazing policy must support community well-being, and environmental group members who saw the issues simply as a question of how much resource extraction people were willing to forgo to maintain the ecosystem's resources, like songbirds, which might not be obviously or directly seen as beneficial to humans. The key outcome from the group's discussions was that "the warring parties must at least recognize and articulate the abiding

differences in their attitudes towards ecosystem health if a common
sense of 'appropriate' land use is ever to be achieved."[29]

There are dozens of other examples where compromise is becoming more the rule than the exception. In June 1996, after five years of
negotiations, eight governors and four Native American tribal leaders
endorsed a series of recommendations made by the Visibility Trans-
port Commission that will improve the quality of air over the Grand
Canyon. The pact involved often contentious debates among federal,
state, and local officials as well as industry groups like the Nevada
Mining Commission and corporate interests like Southern California
Edison. Similar calls for negotiations have come from the owners of
Jet-Skis, who faced a two-year ban on use of personal recreational watercraft by officials in San Juan County, Washington.

The dispute pits the Personal Watercraft Industry Association
against local residents who raised complaints about personal safety
and harm to the region's eagle population. Now attorneys for the two
sides are speaking of potential time or place restrictions in lieu of a
ban. And there is even evidence of some common ground developing
over the issue of endangered species. Near the Selway-Bitterroot
Wilderness area of Idaho, representatives of the Intermountain Forest
Industry Association, a timber group, agreed with the national environmental group Defenders of Wildlife to create a thirteen-member citizen management committee to deal with the restoration of grizzly
bears to the region.

To many observers, such cooperative efforts are long overdue. The
past twenty-five years of disputes over environmental protection have
done little except to polarize the debate, forcing those with common
goals to choose sides and shout even more loudly to be heard. For
some policy entrepreneurs, continuing the conflict has a very tangible
benefit—the appearance of a holy war that allows groups to recruit
new members and promote their agendas. But for those truly concerned about solving environmental problems, the eventual realization
that neither side is totally "wrong" or "right" will go a long way toward the fulfillment of mutually agreed upon goals. Because much of
the environmental policy debate is based on competing aesthetic and
economic interests, it is unlikely that consensus will ever be complete
and, in fact, highly likely that when the next policy window opens,
new entrepreneurs will step forward to attempt to capitalize on public
disaffection with the pace or direction of environmental policy.

But this book ends with positing the belief that continuing attempts to weaken or dilute environmental policy, by both the industry
segment of the environmental opposition as well as grassroots groups,
will be unsuccessful. The public's support for a mainstream environmental agenda remains strong and has become a core value of Ameri-

can political culture, even though that support is coupled with an over-all distrust of the government's ability to solve environmental problems. Efforts to build consensus and open lines of communication are reflective of the realization that there is little support for a "war" among those who share a common interest in the environment, and that the peace talks have already begun.

NOTES

1. Numerous authors have explored the stages of the policymaking process. This section relies primarily on the work of James Anderson, *Public Policymaking: An Introduction,* 2nd ed. (Boston: Houghton Mifflin, 1994); and Malcolm Goggin, Ann Bowman, James P. Lester, and Laurence J. O'Toole, *Implementation Theory and Practice: Toward a Third Generation* (Glenview, IL: Scott, Foresman/Little, Brown, 1990).

2. "The New Beneficiaries of the Top 400," *Washington Post National Weekly Edition,* December 4–10, 1995, p. 7.

3. David Maraniss and Michael Weisskopf, "Cashing In," *Washington Post National Weekly Edition,* December 4–10, 1995, p. 6.

4. Thomas R. Rochon and Daniel A. Mazmanian, "Social Movements and the Policy Process," *Annals of the American Academy of Political and Social Science,* vol. 528 (July 1993): 75–87.

5. John H. Cushman Jr., "Gingrich Calls for a 'New Environmentalism,'" *New York Times,* April 25, 1996, p. A8.

6. Tom Kenworthy and Gary Lee, "A Green Roadblock," *Washington Post National Weekly Edition,* December 4–11, 1995, p. 29.

7. David Helvarg, *The War Against the Greens: The "Wise-Use" Movement, the New Right, and Anti-Environmental Violence* (San Francisco: Sierra Club Books, 1994), pp. 416–417.

8. Jacqueline Vaughn Switzer, *Environmental Politics: Domestic and Global Dimensions* (New York: St. Martin's, 1994), pp. 15–16. A 1995 *Washington Post*/ABC News survey and a similar one conducted by the Gallup Organization found that 5 percent of those questioned named problems related to the environment as either the country's first or second most pressing problem. See Richard Morin, "A Lighter Shade of Green," *Washington Post National Weekly Edition,* June 5–11, 1995, p. 37.

9. Morin, "A Lighter Shade," p. 37.

10. Willett Kempton, James S. Boster, and Jennifer A. Hartley, *Environmental Values in American Culture* (Cambridge, MA: MIT Press, 1995), pp. 4–5; and Morin, "A Lighter Shade," p. 37.

11. Kempton, Boster, and Hartley, *Environmental Values,* p. 5.

12. In Morin, "A Lighter Shade," p. 37.

13. Ibid., p. 37.

14. Paul R. Ehrlich, *The Population Bomb* (New York: Ballantine Books, 1968); and Paul R. Ehrlich and Anne H. Ehrlich, *The Population Explosion* (New York: Simon and Schuster, 1990).

15. Al Gore, *Earth in the Balance: Ecology and the Human Spirit* (Boston: Houghton Mifflin, 1992).

16. Ibid., p. 49.

17. Wallace Kaufman, *No Turning Back: Dismantling the Fantasies of Environmental Thinking* (New York: Basic Books, 1994), p. 9.

18. Gregg Easterbrook, *A Moment on the Earth: The Coming Age of Environmental Optimism* (New York: Viking, 1995), p. xvi.

19. Ibid.

20. Richard M. Stapleton, "On the Western Front," *National Parks* (January–February 1993): 33–34.

21. Janet Ellis, "Taking on Anti-Environmentalists," in John Echeverria and Raymond Booth Eby, eds., *Let the People Judge: Wise Use and the Private Property Rights Movement* (Washington, DC: Island Press, 1995), pp. 295–303.

22. Richard M. Stapleton, "A Call to Action," *National Parks* (March–April 1993): 37.

23. Stapleton, "On the Western Front," p. 35.

24. T. H. Watkins, "Fat Cats and New Voices," *Wilderness*, vol. 56, no. 198 (fall 1992): 8–9.

25. Phil Brick, "Determined Opposition: The Wise Use Movement Challenges Environmentalism," *Environment*, vol. 37, no. 8 (October 1995): 38.

26. In Timothy Egan, "Look Who's Hugging Trees Now," *New York Times Magazine*, July 7, 1996, p. 30.

27. Michael W. Robbins, "A Place for Feelings," *Audubon* (May–June 1996): 4.

28. Joan Laatz Jewett, "Scientists, Policy-makers Join in Effort to Save Salmon," *The Oregonian*, April 28, 1996, p. A26.

29. William E. Riebsame, "Ending the Range Wars?" *Environment*, vol. 38, no. 4 (May 1996): 8–9.

Acronyms

AAA   Agricultural Adjustment Act
AAM   American Agriculture Movement
ACL   Associated California Loggers
ADCA   Animal Damage Control Act
AFBF   American Farm Bureau Federation
AFC   American Freedom Coalition
ALRA   American Land Rights Association
AMC   American Mining Congress
ANEC   American Nuclear Energy Council
ANWR   Arctic National Wildlife Refuge
ARCO   Atlantic Richfield Company
AUM   animal unit month
BLM   Bureau of Land Management
BRC   Blue Ribbon Coalition
CARB   California Air Resources Board
CAWG   Clean Air Working Group
CDC   California Desert Coalition
CEI   Competitive Enterprise Institute
CEO   chief executive officer
CERES   Coalition for Environmentally Responsible Economies
CFC   chlorofluorocarbons
CFDFE   Center for the Defense of Free Enterprise
CITE   Citizens for Total Energy
CLC   Constitutional Law Center
CMA   Chemical Manufacturers Association
CSMA   Chemical Specialties Manufacturers Association
DDT   dichlorodiphenyltrichloroethane
EGA   Environmental Grantmakers Association
EPA   Environmental Protection Agency
ESA   Endangered Species Act
ESPA   Endangered Species Preservation Act
FDA   Food and Drug Administration
FIFRA   Federal Insecticide, Fungicide, and Rodenticide Act
FLOC   Fairness to Landowners Committee
FLPMA   Federal Land Policy and Management Act
FTC   Federal Trade Commission
GDP   gross domestic product

GESAC Grassroots Endangered Species Act Coalition
GMC General Motors Corporation
LASER League for the Advancement of States Equal Rights
LWCF Land and Water Conservation Fund
MCA Manufacturing Chemists Association
MSLF Mountain States Legal Foundation
NABC National Advisory Board Council
NAFTA North American Free Trade Agreement
NARPO National Association of Reversionary Property Owners
NCPC National Coal Policy Conference
NEPA National Environmental Policy Act
NFLC National Federal Lands Conference
NFWF National Fish and Wildlife Foundation
NIPCC National Industrial Pollution Control Council
NPCA National Parks and Conservation Association
NPS National Park Service
NRDC Natural Resources Defense Council
NWF National Wildlife Federation
NWI National Wilderness Institute
OCA Oregon Citizens Alliance
OHV off-highway vehicle(s)
OSM Office of Surface Management
PAC political action committee
PARC Predatory Animal and Rodent Control
PERC Political Economy Research Center
PERI Public Environment Reporting Initiative
PETA People for the Ethical Treatment of Animals
PFW! People for the West!
PLF Pacific Legal Foundation
RARE Roadless Area Review and Evaluation
RFF Resources for the Future
SHARE Shasta Alliance for Resources and Environment
SIP state implementation plan
TIA Takings Impact Analysis
USCEA United States Council for Energy Awareness
USDA United States Department of Agriculture
USFS United States Forest Service
USFWS United States Fish and Wildlife Service
USGS United States Geological Survey
VMT vehicle miles of travel
WMI Waste Management, Inc.
WRC Western Regional Council

An Environmental History and Politics Timeline

Year	Event	Government Action	Group Formation
1626		Plymouth Colony ordinance regulating timber cutting	
1710		Massachusetts protects waterfowl in coastal regions	
1803	U.S. negotiates Louisiana Purchase, doubling public domain		
1804–1806	Lewis and Clark expedition		
1832	George Catlin proposes national park		
1845	Henry David Thoreau publishes *Walden*		
1849		Dept. of Interior established	
1862		Dept. of Agriculture established	
1864	George Perkins Marsh publishes *Man and Nature*		
1866			American Society for the Prevention of Cruelty to Animals
1869	John Wesley Powell leads expedition through Grand Canyon to Colorado River		
1872		First national park (Yellowstone) established; Mining Law	

(continues)

Year	Event	Government Action	Group Formation
1875			American Forestry Association
1878	John Wesley Powell publishes report on *Lands of the Arid Region of the U.S.*		
1879		U.S. Geological Survey created	
1882			American Forestry Congress
1885			Boone and Crockett Club
1888			National Geographic Society
1891		Yosemite National Park established	National Irrigation Congress
1892			Sierra Club
1895			American Scenic and Historic Preservation Society
1898		Gifford Pinchot named head of Division of Forestry	
1899		Rivers and Harbors Act bans pollution of navigable waters	
1900		Lacey Act bans transport of illegally killed game animals across state lines	
1902		Newlands Act establishes Bureau of Reclamation	
1905		Gifford Pinchot appointed first chief of USFS	National Audubon Society
1907		Inland Waterways Commission established	
1908	Theodore Roosevelt hosts conservation conference	Grand Canyon designated national monument; National Conservation Commission directed to inventory resources	

(*continues*)

Year	Event	Government Action	Group Formation
1909	North American Conservation Conference held		
1911			American Game Protective and Propagation Association
1914	Passenger pigeon becomes extinct		
1916		National Park Service established	
1918		U.S.-Canada Migratory Bird Treaty Act	Save the Redwoods League
1919			National Parks and Conservation Association
1920		Minerals Leasing Act; Federal Water Power Act	
1922			Izaak Walton League
1924	Teapot Dome scandal; first National Conference on Outdoor Recreation	Oil Pollution Control Act; Gila National Forest designated as first wilderness area	
1928		Hoover Dam project authorized	
1930	CFCs hailed as new refrigerants		
1933		Tennessee Valley Authority formed; Soil Erosion Service created	
1934		Taylor Grazing Act enacted	
1935		Soil Conservation Service created	Wilderness Society
1936			National Wildlife Federation
1937		Federal Aid in Wildlife Restoration Act	Wildlife Society
1940		U.S. Fish and Wildlife Service designated	
1944			Soil Conservation Society of America

(continues)

Year	Event	Government Action	Group Formation
1946		U.S. Bureau of Land Management established; Atomic Energy Commission created	
1947			Defenders of Wildlife
1948	Air pollution episode in Donora, PA	Federal Water Pollution Control Act	
1949	Aldo Leopold publishes *A Sand County Almanac*		
1951			Nature Conservancy; Animal Welfare Institute
1952	Killer smog episode in London		
1953			Humane Society of the U.S.
1954			Keep America Beautiful
1956		Water Pollution Control Act	
1958		Outdoor Recreation Resources Review Commission named	
1960		Multiple Use and Sustained Yield Act	
1961			World Wildlife Fund
1962	Rachel Carson publishes *Silent Spring*; White House Conference on Conservation		
1963		Clean Air Act; Bureau of Outdoor Recreation established	
1964		Wilderness Act	
1965	National Conference on Natural Beauty	Land and Water Conservation Fund Act; Water Quality Act	
1966	Air pollution episode in New York City	Endangered Species Preservation Act	

(*continues*)

Year	Event	Government Action	Group Formation
1967			Fund for Animals; Environmental Defense Fund; American Cetacean Society
1968	Paul Ehrlich publishes *The Population Bomb*	Wild and Scenic Rivers Act	Public Lands Council; Zero Population Growth
1969	Santa Barbara oil spill	Council on Environmental Quality established	Animal Protection Institute of America; Friends of the Earth; Union of Concerned Scientists; Greenpeace
1970	Earth Day observed April 22	National Environmental Policy Act; Clean Air Act Amendments; EPA established	Environmental Action; Natural Resources Defense Council
1971		Alaska Native Claims Settlement Act	American Solar Energy Society; Clean Water Action
1972	UN Conference on the Human Environment; use of DDT phased out; Club of Rome publishes *The Limits of Growth*	Federal Water Pollution Control Act Amendments; Ocean Dumping Act; Marine Mammal Protection Act; Coastal Zone Management Act	League of Conservation Voters; Center for Marine Conservation
1973	Alaskan pipeline project begins; snail darter controversy over Tellico Dam, TN; Arab oil embargo	Endangered Species Act	Pacific Legal Foundation; American Rivers, Inc.; Cousteau Society
1974		Safe Drinking Water Act	American Wind Energy Association
1975		Nuclear Regulatory Commission established	World Watch Institute
1976		Office of Science and Technology established; Federal Land Policy and Management Act; Toxic Substances Control Act; Resource Conservation and Recovery Act	Center for the Defense of Free Enterprise; Mountain States Legal Foundation

(continues)

Year	Event	Government Action	Group Formation
1977		Dept. of Energy created; Clean Air Act Amendments; Clean Water Act Amendments; Surface Mining Control and Reclamation Act	Consumer Alert; Sea Shepherd Conservation Society
1978	Love Canal, NY, evacuated	National Energy Act	National Inholders Association; National Recycling Coalition
1979	Three Mile Island, PA, experiences near meltdown; massive oil spills in Atlantic Ocean and Gulf of Mexico		
1980	*Global 2000 Report* published; debt-for-nature swap concept proposed	Comprehensive Environmental Response, Compensation, and Liability Act; Alaska National Interest Lands Conservation Act	U.S. Council for Energy Awareness
1981			Alliance for Responsible CFC Policy; Citizens Clearinghouse for Hazardous Wastes; Earth First!
1982			Earth Island Institute; World Resources Institute
1985			Alliance for Environment; Rainforest Action Network; Resources Committee for a Constructive Tomorrow
1986	Chernobyl nuclear incident in USSR; Times Beach, MO, evacuated	Superfund Amendments and Reauthorization Act; Water Resources Development Act; Safe Drinking Water Act	California Desert Coalition; Rainforest Alliance
1987	Montreal Protocol signed; garbage barge *Mobro* searches for place to dock		Blue Ribbon Coalition

(continues)

Year	Event	Government Action	Group Formation
1988	NASA scientists warn of global warming; EPA issues warnings about indoor air pollution; beaches closed due to medical waste washing ashore; Reno, NV, conference on wise use; Ron Arnold publishes *The Wise Use Agenda*		
1989	*Exxon Valdez* oil spill in Alaska		National Wetlands Coalition; Global Climate Coalition
1990		Congress ends ban on offshore oil drilling; Clean Air Act Amendments	Environmental Conservation Organization; Sahara Club USA; Putting People First
1991	Environmental damage due to Persian Gulf War	President Bush announces "no net loss" of wetlands; Symms National Recreation Trails Act	Alliance for America; Coalition for Vehicle Choice; Defenders of Property Rights; Institute for Justice
1992	Industrial nations agree to assist environmental cleanup of Eastern Europe; court clears captain of *Exxon Valdez* of charges; nations agree to speed up ban on ozone-harming chemicals; UN Conference on Environment and Development in Rio	"God Squad" opens up Northern spotted owl habitat under Endangered Species Act	
1993	Massive oil spill off Shetland Islands; Reno Declaration of Non-Violence	President Clinton backs compromise plan to reduce Northwest timber harvest; Florida Everglades cleanup plan approved	Property Rights Foundation of America
1994		California Desert Protection Act	Stewards of the Range

(continues)

Year	Event	Government Action	Group Formation
1996	Resumption of American Forest Congress	President Clinton reverses policy on salvage timber operations; Food Quality Protection Act; Safe Drinking Water Act Amendments	

Index

AAA. *See* Agricultural Adjustment Act
AAM. *See* American Agriculture Movement
Adirondack State Park, 38–39, 255–256
AFL-CIO. *See* American Federation of Labor and Congress of Industrial Organizations
Agricultural Adjustment Act (AAA, 1933), 81
Agricultural Appropriations Act (1907), 30
Agriculture industry, 77–97; common interests within, 78, 80, 86–89; consolidation of small farms, 77, 80; cooperation with environmentalists, 84, 86, 88; and disaster aid, 82; farmworkers and pesticide poisoning, 84; Grange organizations, 80–81; irrigation issues, 33; policy impact, 86–89; beginnings of political activism, 77, 80; pollution issues, 82–83; subsidies and price supports, 78–79; transition to scientific farming, 80 81. *See also* Grazing disputes, Livestock industry
Air pollution, 6, 82, 83, 108–109, 113–117, 155. *See also* Clean Air Act *and its amendments*
Alar controversy, 85, 133
Alaska National Interest Lands Conservation Act, 262
Alaskan oil spill. *See* Exxon Valdez oil spill
Alaska pipeline project, 8
ALCOA. *See* Aluminum Company of America
Alliance for America, ix, 201, 206
Alliance for Responsible Atmospheric Policy, 116
ALRA. *See* American Land Rights Association
Aluminum Company of America (ALCOA), 33
American Agriculture Movement (AAM), 87, 89
American Cattle Growers Association, 52

American Chemical Society, 111
American Civic Association, 39
American Farm Bureau Federation, 80–81, 87–88, 192, 282
American Federation of Labor and Congress of Industrial Organizations (AFL-CIO), 273; Montana division, 202
American Forestry Association, 28
American Game Protective and Propagation Association, 2
American Land Rights Association (ALRA), 12, 248, 252, 268. *See also* Cushman, Charles
American Mining Congress, 108, 110, 157
American National Livestock Association, 42, 54
American Newspaper Publishers Association, 33
American Nuclear Energy Council, 111
American Petroleum Association, 108
American Petroleum Institute, 108
American Society for the Prevention of Cruelty to Animals (ASPCA), 2, 70
American Sportsfishing Association, 74
Andrus, Cecil, 62, 175, 252, 273
Andrus Report, 62
Animal Damage Control Act (1931), 61
Animal Liberation Front, 60
Animal rights, 49–50, 70–74; conflicts over ESA, 71–72; and environmental opposition, 50, 72; and trapping, 62. *See also* Endangered Species Act; Hunting
Animal unit month, defined, 53
Anticommunism, 42, 209, 221
Antifederalism. *See* Federalism
Antiquities Act of 1906, 181
Anti-Steel Trap League, 70
ANWR. *See* Artic National Wildlife Refuge
Arctic National Wildlife Refuge (ANWR), 105, 118, 123, 284
Arizona Cattle Growers Association, 53
Armey, Dick, 103
Armstrong, L.K., 40

Army Corps of Engineers, 35, 36, 155, 156
Arnold, Ron: and wise use movement,· 196–198, 200, 205, 206, 209, 221; and county supremacy movement, 229. *See also* Center for the Defense of Free Enterprise
Articles of Confederation, 22–23
ASPCA. *See* American Society for the Prevention of Cruelty to Animals
Associated California Loggers, 194
Atomic Energy Commission, 8, 110
Atomic Industry Forum, 110
Audubon Society. *See* National Audubon Society.
Automobiles, increased use of, 90–91
Automotive industry, 113–115, 162–163, 166; alliance with United Auto Workers, 114

Babbitt, Bruce: and 104th Congress, 121; as governor of Arizona, 181; and grazing issues, 56, 57; appointment as interior secretary, 9; and mining law, 110; and rangeland reform, 236, 295–296; and Safe Harbors program, 59
Baca, Jim, 57, 133, 239
Ballinger, Richard, 40
Ballot initiatives, 133–135
Bari, Judy, 214–215
Barrett, Frank, 41–42
Bentham, Jeremy, 1
Bhopal, India, 132, 146
Biotechnology applications, 86
Blue Ribbon Coalition (BRC), ix, corporate connections, 94–95; and ESA, 94; and outdoor recreationists, 79, 93–97; and wise use movement, 94, 201
Boone and Crockett Club, 38, 73
Boschwitz, Rudy, 107
Bottle bill legislation, 6
Boundary County (Idaho), 241
BRC. See Blue Ribbon Coalition
Brick, Phil, 13, 293–294
Brock, J. Elmer, 42
Brower, David, 6, 211, 293
Brown, Jerry: Malathion controversy, 84; and Sagebrush Rebellion, 181
Browner, Carol, 103
Budd-Falen, Karen. *See* Falen, Karen Budd- and Frank
Bureau of Fisheries, 30

Bureau of Forestry, disputes with Department of Interior, 29–30. *See also* Department of Agriculture
Bureau of Indian Affairs, 30
Bureau of Land Management: and Classification and Multiple Use Act, 92; establishment of, 53; and foreign species controversy, 71; and grazing regulations, 58; and hunters, 286; and militant opposition, 210, 216, 218, 219; responsibilities of, 53–54, 55; and Sagebrush rebels, 178–183; and wilderness expansion, 252
Bureau of Mines, 30
Bureau of Outdoor Recreation, 91
Bureau of Reclamation, 4, 34
Burford, Anne Gorsuch, 8, 180, 185, 186, 294
Burford, Robert, 180
Burke, Thomas, 21
Burns, Conrad, 286
Burson-Marstellar, 132
Bush, George, 10, 11, 105; and land purchase programs, 262; and 1990 Clean Air Act Amendments, 115, 155; and wetlands, 155–156, 258; and William Ellen, 260; and *The Wise Use Agenda*, 202
Business: advisory role in policy implementation, 156–158; alliance building, 115–117; early complacency, 7–8; 104–105; compliance costs, 104; disunity within, 105; and front groups, 111, 144–146; distinction from grassroots, 103–104, 282–285; and Earth Day, 8, 9; and fragmentation of federal agencies, 160–163; and labor unions, 109; legislative strategies, 103–125; litigation strategies, 163–165; organized opposition, 104–105; use of PACs, 104, 283; and public opinion concerns, 106, 107; as technical experts, 159–160; and trade associations, 106, 111–112; and wise use movement, 220. *See also* Congress, 104th; Greenscamming; Greenwashing; Public relations campaigns

California Air Resources Board (CARB), 142, 161–162, 166
California Cattlemen's Association, 53
California Desert Coalition (CDC), 203–205

California Desert Protection Act, 121, 203, 204

CARB. *See* California Air Resources Board

Carcinogens, 84, 112

Carey Act (1894), 33

Carhardt, Arthur, 44

Carson, Rachel, 7, 83, 198

Carter, Jimmy: energy policies, 115; and logging restrictions, 195; and property rights movement, 251; purchase of Alaskan wilderness, 262

Carthage Foundation, 212

Carver, Dick, ix, 236

Cato Institute, 141, 147, 201, 231, 257

Catron County (New Mexico), 67, 230, 231, 233–235, 236, 242–243

CAWG. *See* Clean Air Working Group

CDC. *See* California Desert Coalition

Center for the Defense of Free Enterprise (CFDFE), ix, 143, 197; and Center for Investigative Reporting, 13; and Charles Cushman, 12, 207; and county supremacy movement, 229; declaration of nonviolence, 216–217; and property rights movement, 268; and wise use movement, 201, 203–205, 207, 208. *See also* Arnold, Ron, and Gottlieb, Alan

CERES. *See* Coalition for Environmentally Responsible Economies

CFCs. *See* Chlorofluorocarbons

CFDFE. *See* Center for the Defense of Free Enterprise

Chemical industry, 107, 111–113; and pollution, 112; public relations efforts, 131; and toxics, 112–113; trade associations, 111–112

Chemical Manufacturers Association (CMA), 8, 112, 132, 146–147

Chemical Specialty Manufacturers Association Amendment (CSMA), 107

Chenoweth, Helen, 65, 118–119, 228, 238

Cherney, Daryl, 214–215

Chlorine, 113

Chlorofluorocarbons (CFCs), 113, 116, 117, 136

CITE. *See* Citizens for Total Energy

Citizens Against Government Waste, 228

Citizens for Total Energy (CITE), 203

Clark, Tom, 40

Clark, William (explorer), 2

Clark, William (senator), 37

Classification and Multiple Use Act (1964), 55, 92

CLC. *See* Constitutional Law Center

Clean Air Act (1963), 6, 104, 107

Clean Air Act Amendments (1970), xiii, 7, 107, 114, 155, 158–160

Clean Air Act Amendments (1977), 107, 109

Clean Air Act Amendments (1990), 82, 114–115, 116, 118, 152, 155, 163

Clean Air Working Group (CAWG), 116

Clean Water Act (1972), 58–59, 82, 285

Clean Water Act (1977), 107

Cleveland, Grover, 28

Clinton, Bill: appointment of Babbitt, 9; and California Desert Protection Act, 203; and Council on Economic Competitiveness, 161; farm subsidy reform, 82; Food Quality Protection Act, 84; and environmental opposition, 59–60; and grazing fees, 56–57; and land purchase programs, 262; and timber industry, 123; and War on the West, 228

Clyde, George Dewey, 55

CMA. *See* Chemical Manufacturers Association

Coal industry, 36–37, 108

Coalition for Environmentally Responsible Economies (CERES), 9, 147

Coalition of Counties, 67–68

Cohen, Richard, 152

Collins, Clark, 93, 96–97

Colonial attitudes, about environment, 1, 60, 73, 89

Colorado Rangeland Reform Working Group, 295

Committee to Abolish Sport Hunting, 74

Committee for Air and Water Conservation, 108

Commons, defined, 39–40

Commonwealth Edison, 8

Compliance costs, for business, 104; and regulatory takings, 269

Comprehensive Environmental Response, Compensation and Liability Act (Superfund, 1980): and 104th Congress, 123, 285; cost of new sites, 104; creation of, 105, 152

Congress, 104th: contrast with 103rd, 121; and grazing fees, 56; members associated with environmental opposition,

118–119, 123; openings given to policy entrepreneurs, 11; policy implications of, 7, 117–124, 205, 286, 294; and wetlands issues, 156

Congress, 105th, 124

Conservation Foundation, 8, 160

Conservationists: defined, 25; early history, 4; and preservationists 4–6, 38–41, 92. *See also* Pinchot, Gifford; Preservationists

Constitution: authority granted over nonfederal owned lands, 232; and grazing rights, 58; rules governing public lands and admission of states, 23–24, 171, 173–174, 237. *See also* Federalism; Regulatory takings

Constitutional Law Center (CLC), 165, 254

Continental Congress. *See* Articles of Confederation

Contract With America, 117, 120–122, 155, 285

Coolidge, Calvin, 37

Cooperative programs: on pesticide use, 88; Safe Harbors, 59

Coors, Joseph, 157, 164, 177

Cost benefit analysis, 121, 157

Council on Competitiveness, 119, 156, 161

Council on Economic Priorities, 147

Council on Property Rights, 254

County supremacy movement, 227–243; and county ordinances, 233; the future of, 241–243; legal theories and litigation strategies, 231–233, 237, 242; links to other movements, 229; militancy of, 237–239; philosophy and values, 227–228; policy impact, 239–241; strategies and issues, 231–232. *See also* Catron County; Nye County

Cow bloc, 42, 44

Cranston, Alan, 219, 203

Creative Act (1891). *See* General Revision Act

Crustacean Liberation Front, 71

CSMA. *See* Chemical Specialty Manufacturers Association Amendment

Cushman, Charles: and ESA, 65; as a model policy entrepreneur, 11–12; and property rights movement, 252–253, 263–264; and wise use movement, 194–195

Custom and culture theory, 233

Dawes Allotment Act (1887), 4

DBS. *See* Division of Biological Survey

DDT. *See* Diclorodiphenyltricloroethane

Defenders of Property Rights, 237, 253

Defenders of Wildlife, 64, 71, 296

Delaney clause, 84

Denver Public Lands Conference, 40

Department of Agriculture (USDA): creation of forestry division, 28–30; and disaster aid, 82; and predator and pest control, 60, 82; subsidies and price supports, 79; and water pollution, 155. *See also* Agriculture industry; Bureau of Forestry; Federal government; Grazing disputes

Department of Energy, 7, 105

Department of the Interior: forest reserves, 29–30; and grazing, 52, 54; and habitat protection, 261; and utility industry, 32–33; and water pollution, 155; during Watt and Reagan years, 8. *See also* Agriculture industry; Federal government; Grazing disputes; National Park Service

Desert Land Acts, 4

De Voto, Bernard, 43

Diclorodiphenyltricloroethane (DDT), 83, 164

Dingell, John, 114, 115, 116

Division of Biological Survey (DBS), 60–61

Division of Forestry. *See* Bureau of Forestry

Doheny, Edward, 38

Dole, Robert, 270

Dunlap, Riley, 8

Earth Day (1970), 7, 8, 288

Earth Day (1990), 8–9

Earth Day (1995), 9

Earth First!, 218, 220, 293

Easterbrook, Gregg, 13, 291

Ecofeminism, 198

Ecorealism, 291

Ecosystem. *See* Habitat protection

Edison Electric Company, 32

Edison Electric Institute, 8, 111, 140, 157

Ehrlich, Anne and Paul, 6, 13, 290

Eisenhower administration, 107

Ellen, William, 260

Emergency Planning and Community Right-to-Know Act, 109

Emerson, Ralph Waldo, 2
Endangered species: bald eagles 61, 63;
    blunt-nosed lizard, 262; California clap-
    per rail, 71; desert tortoise, 67; fairy
    shrimp, 49; golden-cheeked warbler, 66;
    Houston toad, 69; Kirtland's warbler,
    69; Mexican spotted owl, 67, 235; north-
    ern spotted owl, 195, 235; sea gulls, 61;
    sea lions, 69; snail darter, 68; wolves
    62–65
Endangered Species Act (1973), ix, 6, 7,
    59–63, 82, 104, 220, 284, 285; and animal
    rights, 62, 69; and cooperative efforts,
    296; and country supremacy move-
    ment, 230; difficulties of implementa-
    tion, 69; and economic development is-
    sues, 49, 66–70; and land purchase
    programs, 262; and livestock industry,
    63; and 104th Congress, 121; and prop-
    erty rights movements, 67–68, 254,
    261–263; public support for, 68–69; and
    timber industry, 195; and wildlife man-
    agement, 59; and wise use movement,
    220. See also Habitat protection
Endangered Species Preservation Act
    (1966), 63
End run strategy, 44–45, 151–166
Environmental Conservation Organiza-
    tion, 254
Environmental Defense Fund, 9, 136, 187
Environmental Grantmakers Association,
    139
Environmental movement: alleged ex-
    tremism of, 70, 143, 144, 209–211; and
    animal rights, 49–50, 69, 70–71; and cor-
    porate support, 138–140; and county
    supremacy movement, 240–241; dis-
    agreement within, 9; early history of, 2;
    fragmentation of, 6–7; and hunting,
    72–74; membership fluctuations,
    199–200; modern movement, 6, 7–9,
    287–290; and outdoor recreationists,
    91–93, 95–97; professionalization of,
    186; response to country supremacy
    movement, 238–241; response to overall
    environmental opposition, 13, 95, 284,
    292–294; response to property rights
    movement, 256; response to Sagebrush
    Rebellion, 186–187; response to wise
    use movement, 209, 211–218; as strate-
    gic model for opposition groups, 12,

235. See also Animal rights; Environ-
    mental opposition
Environmental opposition: alleged ex-
    tremism of, 13, 14, 70, 210–220, 256,
    273–276; and animal rights, 49–50; and
    conservatism, 13, 121, 140–144, 164,
    210–211, 228–229; 248, 294; demo-
    graphic and diversity issues, ix, 13–14;
    distinctions between business and
    grassroots, 103–104, 282–285; early his-
    tory of, x–xi, 26–37; nomenclature of,
    12–15, 208; overall policy impact,
    282–287; religious components of,
    211–212, 256. See also Agriculture indus-
    try; Business; Chemical industry; Coun-
    try supremacy movement; Livestock in-
    dustry; Mining industry; Petroleum
    industry; Property rights movement;
    Sagebrush Rebellion; Think tanks; Tim-
    ber industry; Wise use movement
Environmental policy, examples of coop-
    eration between environmentalists and
    industry, 59, 84, 87, 295–296
Environmental Protection Agency: and
    agricultural chemicals, 84; assault from
    business, 105, 285; and Clean Air Act,
    158–160, 163; and cost assessments, 104;
    discretionary powers of, 155; enforce-
    ment during Reagan years, 8; founding
    of, 7; measuring chemical and pesticide
    exposure, 112; and water pollution
    82–83, 155, 156
Environmental racism, 9
Epstein, Richard, 257. See also Regulatory
    takings
Equal footing doctrine, 173, 232
Executive Order 12630, 267
Extractive resource industries, 59,
    107–110. See also Coal industry; Mining
    industry; Petroleum Industry; Timber
    Industry
Exxon Valdez oil spill, 9, 132, 294

Fairness to Land Owners Committee
    (FLOC), 247, 248
Falen, Karen Budd- and Frank, 58, 231, 233
Farmers. See Agriculture industry
Farmers Alliance, 80
Federal Corrupt Practices Act (1925), 38
Federal Environmental Pesticide Control
    Act (1972), 7

Federal government: disputes between agencies, 29–39, 52–53, 59; fragmentation of agencies, 160–163; growth in number of agencies and laws, 7, 151; inconsistencies and shifts in policy, 3, 4–7, 61, 123; target of militancy, 210, 216–217, 218, 219, 236, 238–239. *See also* Air pollution; Endangered Species Act; Oklahoma City bombing; Public lands; Water pollution; *and specific agencies, departments, and programs*

Federal Insecticide, Fungicide, and Rodenticide Act (FIFRA, 1947), 83

Federalism, and challenges to federal authority, 42, 53, 172–174, 183, 282. *See also* Constitution, States

Federal Land Policy and Management Act (FLPMA, 1976), 55, 56, 92, 172–173

Federal Register, 153, 154, 158

Federal Trade Commission (FTC), 138

Federal Water Pollution Control Act Amendments (1972), 155

Federal Water Power Act of 1920, 33, 36

Fenton Communications, 85, 133

FIFRA. *See* Federal Insecticide, Fungicide, and Rodenticide Act

Fillmore, Millard, 36

Fishing (sport), 73–74

FLOC. *See* Fairness to Landowners Committee

Flood control 35–36

FLPMA. *See* Federal Land Policy and Management Act

Food additives, 84, 112

Food Quality Protection Act (1996), 10, 84

Ford, Gerald, 62

Foreman, Dave, 293

Forest Industries Council, 31

Forest Reserve Act (1891), 4

Forest reserves, creation of, 4, 28–29. *See also* National parks

Forest Service Organic Act (1897), 4, 29, 38

Friends of the Earth, 55, 85, 187

Front groups, 111, 144–146

FTC. *See* Federal Trade Commission

Fund for Animals, 71, 74

Garn, Jake, 68, 183

General Accounting Office, 54

General Motors Corporation (GMC), 114, 130

General Revision Act (1891), 4, 28

GESAC. *See* Grassroots ESA Coalition

Gibbs, Lois, 198

Gingrich, Newt: as a member of opposition, 119, 120, 285; proposal for cooperation with environmentalists, 286

Glacier National Park, 38

GMC. *See* General Motors Corporation

Goldwater, Barry, 176

Gore, Al, 142; reform of grazing, timber, and mining law, 228; pessimism of, 290–291

Gorsuch, Anne. *See* Burford, Anne Gorsuch

Gospel of efficiency, 3. *See also* Samuel Hayes

Gottlieb, Alan, 196–198, 200, 202, 205, 206. *See also* Center for the Defense of Free Enterprise

Gottlieb, Robert, 6

Grassroots ESA Coalition (GESAC), 65–66

Grazing disputes, 41–45, 50–59; cooperative efforts, 295; litigation about, 58–59; and NAFTA, 57; and property rights movement, 58, and Sagebrush Rebellion, 179–180. *See also* Cow bloc

Greater Yellowstone Coalition, 202, 210

Greenpeace: and Alliance for Responsive Atmospheric Policy, 116; and chemical industry, 113; criticism of PR campaigns, 132; and nuclear industry, 110; sinking of Rainbow Warrior, 214

Greenscamming, 144

Greenwashing, xiii, 9, 129, 135–140; defined, xiii, 129; liabilities of, 135

Griggs, Chauncey, 31

Group of Ten, 186

Guggenheim, Simon, 37

Gulf Coast Tenant Leadership Project, 9

Guyot, Arnold, 25

Habitat protection, 49–50, 63, 66–69, 261–263. *See also* Endangered Species Act; Wetlands; Wilderness

Hage, Wayne, 165, 251, 254

Hage v. United States, 165, 251, 253–254

Harding, Warren, 37–38

Harmer, John L., 176

Harris County (Texas), 69

Harrison, Benjamin, 28

Hatch, Carl, 42

Hatch, Orrin, 183

Hayes, Denis, 9

Hays, Samuel, 3, 104–105, 112
Hearst, George, 37
Heartland Institute, 144
Help Our Wolves Howl, 71
Helvarg, David, 13, 132, 214, 287
Henry, Joseph, 25
Heritage Foundation, 13, 141, 147, 201
Hetch Hetchy controversy, 39
Hickel, Walter, 8
Hill and Knowlton, 85, 132
Hill Country Landowners Coalition, 66
Homecroft Society, 33
Homestead Act (1862), 3, 24, 174
Homesteading, 3–4, 33, 36, 52, 77
Hoover, Herbert, 37, 41, 53
Howard, David, 255
Humane Society of the United States, 71
Hunting, and animal rights: 49, 72–73;
    and BLM land, 286; and farmers, 91; re-
    lationship with environmental move-
    ment, 72–74
Hydroelectric industry, 6, 31–32

Inholders, 11, 179. See also National In-
    holders Association
Inland Waterways Commission, 35. See
    also Waterways
Initiative campaigns. See Ballot initiatives
Internet, the, 12, 205, 206, 256
Iron triangle, 29
Iroquois peoples, 1
Issue-attention cycle, xii, 10
Izaak Walton League, 44, 91

Jackson, Leroy, 215–216
Jefferson, Thomas, 23
John Birch Society, 256, 274
Johnson, Lyndon B., 54, 92
Joint National Livestock Committee, 41
Jones, Paul, 259

Kaczynski, Theodore, 218
Kaiser, Ruth, 230
Kaufman, Wallace, 291
Kennedy, John F., 54, 172
Kerr, Andy, 215
King, Clarence, 25
Kingdon, John, 10
Kjos, Berit, 212
Kleppe v. New Mexico, 178, 242
Klyza, Christopher McGrory, 26
Knous, Lee, 44

Kuras, Bob, 263

Ladd/Bowman report, 288–289
LaGrasse, Carol, 253
Lakes-to-the-Gulf Association, 35
Lamb, Henry, 254
Lamm, Richard, xi, 180, 227–228
Land and Water Conservation Fund
    (LWCF, 1965), 91, 108, 261–262
Land Center, 231
Land ethic, 2, 3
Land Ordinance of 1785, 3, 23
LaRouche, Lyndon, 212
LASER. See League for the Advancement
    of States Equal Rights
Latin-American Club of St. Louis, 35
Laxalt, Paul, 183
League for the Advancement of States
    Equal Rights (LASER), 176, 186
League of Conservation Voters, 12
League of Private Property Voters, 12
Legal support groups, 164–165
Leopold, Aldo, 90
Lewis, Meriwether, 2
Limbaugh, Rush, 197
Lincoln, Abraham, 27, 173
Livestock industry, 49–59; beginning of
    organized opposition, 41, 51; "capture"
    of federal agencies, 54; and Clean Water
    Act, 59; economics of, 50–51; effect on
    ecology, 56; and ESA, 63–65; forage and
    grazing needs, 50–51; internal policy di-
    visions, 52; predator and pest control,
    61–65; and property rights movement,
    58. See also Cow bloc; Grazing disputes
Locke, John, 1
Logging. See Timber industry
Love Canal, 198
Lucas, David, 254, 265
Lucas v. South Carolina Coastal Council,
    265–266
LWCF. See Land and Water Conservation
    Fund

Manning, Dick, 230
Manufacturing Chemists Association, 112
Marine Mammal Protection Act (1972), 63,
    285
Marquardt, Kathleen, 72
Marsh, George Perkins, 2, 25
Marshall, Robert, 26
Marzulla, Roger, 237

Mazmanian, Daniel A., 285
McCarran, Pat, 42, 44, 183
McConnell, Grant, 6
McDonald's, 136, 146
McKey, Louis, 218
McVeigh, Timothy, 238. *See also* Oklahoma City bombing
Media: alarms about environmental opposition, 13; encouraging sectionalism, 40–41; and environmentalists, 43–44; and opposition, 40–41, 86, 137, 207–208, 210–211; talk radio, 69–70, 207, 210–211; and wise use movement, 220. *See also* Greenwashing; Public relations campaigns
Michigan Militia, 238
Mid-Atlantic Legal Foundation, 164
Militia movement, 238–239
Mill, John Stuart, 1
Mining industry, 4, 5, 27, 36–38, 110; and state laws, 110; and Teapot Dome scandal, 38; and wise use movement, 201–202
Mining Law (1872), 5, 36, 110, 202, 220, 228, 234
Misso, David Porter, 274–275
Mondale, Walter, 187
Mondell, Frank, 37
Montreal Protocol, 116
Moon, Rev. Sun Myung, 13, 211
Mormons, 2, 30–31, 58
Morrill Act (1862), 3, 80–81
Mountain States Legal Foundation (MSLF): and country supremacy movement, 231; establishment of 164–165; and Sagebrush Rebellion, 177, 185
MSLF. *See* Mountain States Legal Foundation
Muir, John, xi, 4, 25, 39, 227
Multiple purpose approach, 35
Multiple use, xi, 4, 90, 91
Multiple Use and Sustained Yield Act (1960), 54
Multiple Use Land Alliance, 12
Murray, Gil, 218
Muskie, Edmund, 114, 117, 152
MX missile controversy, 175, 179

NABC. *See* National Advisory Board Council
NAFTA. *See* North American Free Trade Agreement

Nash, Roderick, 1
National Advisory Board Council (NABC), 54
National Agricultural Wheel, 80
National Association of Manufacturers, 34, 117
National Association of Reversionary Property Owners, 256
National Audubon Society: accepting advertisements from industry, 130; and corporate funds, 138; membership during Reagan administration, 186; reaction to opposition, 13
National Board of Trade, 34
National Business Men's League, 34
NCA. *See* National Conservation Association
National Cattlemen's Beef Association, 57
National Coal Association, 109
National Coal Policy Conference, 108–109
National Conservation Association (NCA), 37, 39
National Drainage Association, 35
National Drainage Congress, 35
National Energy Act (1978), 7
National Environmental Policy Act (NEPA, 1970), 7, 157, 232, 233, 267, 285
National Farmers Union, 44
National Federal Lands Conference (NFLC), 229–230
National Grange of the Patrons of Husbandry, 79
National Industrial Pollution Control Council (NIPCC), 157–158, 159
National Inholders Association, 11, 179, 263–264. *See also* Cushman, Charles
National Legal Center for the Public Interest, 164
National Lumber Manufacturers Association, 31, 108
National Marine Fisheries Service, 63, 73
National parks, creation of, 4–6
National Parks and Conservation Association (NPCA), 6, 91, 96, 184, 212–213, 292
National Park Service (NPS): founding, 5; incorporation into Department of the Interior, 39; and inholders, 11, 179; and land swaps, 263; and 104th Congress, 123, 263; and wilderness preservation, 26, 92–93; and wildlife control and management 61–62, 65
National Parks Inholders Association, 11

National Petroleum Council, 157
National Public Domain League, 40
National Reclamation Association, 35
National Rifle Association, 192
National Rivers and Harbors Congress, 35
National Taxpayers Union (NTU), 228
National Toxics Campaign, 85–87
National Wetlands Coalition, 155
National Wilderness Institute, 145
National Wilderness Preservation System, 92, 203
National Wildlife Federation, 71–72, 139, 271
National Wildlife Refuge System, 74
National Woolgrowers Association, 42, 54, 61, 183
Native Americans, 1, 2, 182, 296
Natural Resources Council of America, 44, 57
Natural Resources Defense Council (NRDC): Alar controversy, 85, 133; and *The Amicus Journal,* 13; conflict with grassroots organizations, 9; and 1970 Clean Air Act Amendments, 160; role as scientific and legal organization, 187
Nature Conservancy: contributions from industry, 130; funding from federal agency, 143; ownership of grazing land, 58; ownership of wetlands, 258
Nelson, Gaylord, 9
NEPA. *See* National Environmental Policy Act
Nevada: controversies about statehood, 27, 173; as leader in Sagebrush Rebellion, 178, 179. *See also* Nye County
Newlands, Francis, 33–34
Newlands Act. *See* Reclamation Act
New York Audubon Society, 2
New York Board of Trade and Transportation, 38
New York Zoological Society, 13
NFLC. *See* National Federal Lands Conference
NIPCC. *See* National Industrial Pollution Control Council
Nixon, Richard: and 1972 Clean Water Act, 82–83; illegal campaign contributions from National Industrial Pollution Control Council members, 158; use of advisors from business, 157
North American Free Trade Agreement (NAFTA), 57

Northwest Ordinance (1787), 23
NRDC. *See* Natural Resources Defense Council
NPCA. *See* National Parks and Conservation Association
NPS. *See* National Park Service
NTU. *See* National Taxpayers Union
Nuclear Energy and Resources Council, 111
Nuclear Energy Institute, 111
Nuclear power industry, 110–111
Nuclear Regulatory Commission, 7, 110
Nye County (Nevada), ix, 236–237, 242, 243

Off highway vehicles (OHV): defined, 79; and lobbying activities, 93–96. *See also* Blue Ribbon Coalition; Outdoor recreationists
OHV. *See* Off highway vehicles
Oklahoma City bombing, 70, 133, 206, 216, 217, 227, 238
Omnibus National Parks Act, 11
Oregon Citizen's Alliance, 212
Oregon Lands Coalition, 56, 202
Oregon Natural Resources Council, 58, 83, 215
Organized labor, 6, 109, 114, 202, 256, 273
Outdoor recreationists, xiii, 89–97; cooperative efforts by, 296; and increased leisure time, 78, 89; lobbying by, 93; and rural landowners, 90–91. *See also* Blue Ribbon Coalition
Outdoor Recreation Resources Review Commission, 91

Pacific Legal Foundation, 164, 231, 264
Pacific Rivers Council, 58
PACs. *See* Political action comittees
PARC. *See* Predatory Animal and Rodent Control Program
Penn, William, 1
Pennsylvania Landowners' Association, 14
People for the American Way, 212–213
People for the Ethical Treatment of Animals (PETA), 70, 71–72
People for the West!, 201–202, 210
PERC. *See* Political Economy Research Center
Perot, Ross, 289

Pesticides, 83–87
PETA. *See* People for the Ethical Treatment of Animals
Petroleum industry, 36–38, 108, 109. *See also* Extractive Resource Industries
Philosophical traditions and the environment, 1–2, 26
Pinchot, Gifford, xi, 4, 25, 29, 30, 34, 37, 227; conflict with preservationists, xi, 4, 38–40; and hydroelectric industry, 32; and NCA, 37; and public lands, 29–30; and wise use, 191. *See also* Conservationists
Policy entrepreneur, xii, 10–12
Policy implementation: attempts by business to influence, 151–166; effect of vagueness on, 154–156
Policy windows, xii, 10–12; for business opposition, 107, 123; for Sagebrush Rebellion, 174; and wise use movement, 195–196
Political action committees (PACs), 104, 158, 283
Political Economy Research Center (PERC), 129, 141–142
Political Research Associates, 13
Pollard's Lessee v. Hagen, 173
Pollot, Mark, 165, 229, 254
Pollution Prevention Act (1990), 109
Pope, Carl, 103, 281
Powell, John Wesley, 2, 25, 28, 33
Pozgai, John, 260–261
Predator and pest control, 60–62. *See also* Animal rights; Endangered species; Endangered Species Act
Predatory Animal and Rodent Control program (PARC), 62
Preemption Act of 1841, 3
Preservationists, 4–7, 26, 37–39, 44–45; and grazing issues, 52; influence on wilderness preservation, 89–93; and recreationists, 89–93, 95–97. *See also* Conservationists; Pinchot
Price supports, 79–82
Prior appropriation doctrine, 250–251
Private Property Rights Act of 1994, 270
Property Rights Foundation of America, 253, 256
Property rights movement, 11–12, 14, 247–276; alleged extremism, 256, 273–276; characteristic issues in, 248;

criminal sanctions against, 259–261; environmentalists response to, 271; and ESA, 67–68, 261–263; and environmental opposition, 14, 252; federal legislative efforts, 270–272; and grazing disputes, 58; litigation efforts, 264–267; opposition to by nonenvironmental groups, 256, 273; philosophical and legal perspectives, 249–251; public relations efforts, 272–273; response of environmental movement, 256, 271, 273; state legislative efforts, 267–270. *See also* Regulatory takings
Public domain. *See* Public lands
Public Employees for Environmental Responsibility, 238
Public Environmental Reporting Initiative, 131
Public Land Law Review Commission, 54, 178–179
Public lands: and Articles of Confederation, 22–23; conversion to recreation use and wilderness, 89–93, 252; creation and definition of public domain, 21–24; disposal to private individuals, 3–4, 5, 24; disposal to states 3, 24, 53; within federal control, 173; history of federal policy, 2–7, 21–45; "Keep Public Lands in Public Lands Campaign," 286; sales to discharge national debt, 23. *See also* Grazing dispute
Public Lands Commissions, 4, 30
Public lands question, 24–26
Public opinion about the environment: and the Agricultural Adjustment Act, 81; and Clinton years, 9–10, 107, 121, 124; current and long term trends, 287–290; distraction by international events, 10; and economic difficulties, 108; and endangered species, 68; in the 1970s, 7; and predator and pest control, 60; and preservationism, 26, 38; and Reagan years, 8. *See also* Issue-Attention Cycle.
Public Rangelands Improvement Act (1978), 57
Public relations campaigns, 129–147; by chemical manufacturers, 112, 131–132; and deceptive names, 144; and Earth Day, 8–9, 132; eco-approval, 9; front groups, 111, 144–146; by petroleum

companies, 132–133; policy impact, 146–147; and product repackaging, 136–137; response from environmental organizations, 136, 139–140. *See also* Alar controversy; Ballot initiatives; Greenwashing; Greenscamming
Public trust theory, 174
Putting People First, 72

Quayle, Dan, 119, 156, 161

Ranchers. *See* livestock industry
RARE. *See* Roadless Area Review and Evaluation
Ray, Dixie Lee, 164, 210–211
Reagan, Ronald: and asset management plans, 185; business sympathies, 195; defeat of Jimmy Carter, 175; environmentalists' response to, 186–187; and land purchase programs, 262; policies of his administration, 8; and predator and pest control, 62; and regulations, 151, 161; and regulatory takings, 267; use of advisors from business, 157
Reclamation Act (1902), 34
Recreationists. *See* outdoor recreationists
Reed, Scott, 240–241, 243
Regulatory reform, 120–121, 269
Regulatory takings: and compliance costs, 269; and court rulings, 264–267; defined, 249; environmentalists response to, 271; and executive orders, 267; and property rights movement, 58, 249–250, 256–257
Reid, Henry, 57
Reid, Kenneth, 44
Reigle, Peggy, 247
Reno Declaration of Non-Violence, 216–217, 238
Rescissions Bill (1995), 123
Research institutes. *See* Think tanks
Resource Conservation and Recovery Act (1976), 7, 155, 163
Resources for the Future (RFF), 8, 142
Rest the West, 55
RFF. *See* Resources for the Future
Riparian principle, 250
Risk: acceptable levels of, 84, 112–113; assessment of, 105, 121–122
Ritter, Carl, 25
Rivers and Harbors Act (1899), 4

Roadless Area Review and Evaluation (RARE), 92, 213
Robbins, Michael W., 294
Robertson, Edward, 42
Rochon, Thomas R., 285
Roland, Ronald A., 112
Romantic vision, 2, 3
Romer, Roy, 295
Roosevelt, Franklin Delano, 81
Roosevelt, Theodore: and forest reserves, 29–31; and hunting, 73; and inland waterways, 35; and mining, 36–37; and Reclamation Act, 34; timber policy, 29–31, 40; and utility industries, 31–32
Rousseau, Jean-Jacques, 2
Ruckelshaus, William, 114, 186

Safe Harbors Program, 59
Safe Drinking Water Act (1974), 7, 104, 105
Sagebrush Rebellion, 171–189; connections to other opposition movements, 171, 252; constitutional arguments of, 172–174; early land disputes, 22, 171; legacy of, 187–189; organizations involved in, 176; reasons for decline, 184–186, 187–188; response of environmentalists, 186–187; at state level, 178–182
Sahara Club, 218–220
Santini, James, 176
Schurz, Carl, 25
Scientific resource management, 4, 26, 27–28, 52, 73
Second National Conservation Congress, 26
Sectionalism: and agricultural price supports, 81; and county supremacy movement, 227–228; and forest reserve policy, 30–31; and grazing disputes, 52; and homesteading, 52; and land purchase in the East, 40–41; and public lands, 21, 27–28, 30, 31, 40–42. *See also* County supremacy movement; Sagebrush Rebellion; War on the West
SHARE. *See* Shasta Alliance for Resources and Environment
Shasta Alliance for Resources and Environment (SHARE), 203, 204–205
Sieman, Rick, 218–219
Sierra Club: and Adirondack State Park, 39, 55, 71; and Council on Competitive-

ness, 161; divisions within, 293; fund-raising by, 12; and hunting, 73; and James Watt, 185, 186–187; and livestock industry, 56; and McDonald's, 136; and 1970 Clean Air Act Amendments, 160; protectionism, 6, 91; suit against United States Forest Service, 93; and wetlands, 258

Sierra Club Legal Defense Fund, 187

Silkwood, Karen, 214

Simplot Company, J. R., 58, 95

Sinclair, Harry, 38

Smith, Loren, 251

Smith, Zachary, 5

Snodderly, David, 194

Society of Range Management, 52

Soft money, 283

Soil Conservation and Domestic Allot-ment Act (1936), 81

Southwest Environmental Center, 240

Southwest Organizing Project, 9

Stans, Maurice, 157

States: as access point for environmental opposition, 165–166; cessation of West-ern land claims, 22–23; and Clean Water Act, 165–166; constitutional re-quirements for admission of new states, 23–24, 173–174; and ESA, 63, 67; and forest reserves, 30–31; and Native Americans, 182. *See also* Federalism; Sagebrush Rebellion

Stern, Kenneth, 275–276

Stewards of the Range, 165, 228, 253–254

Stewart (Big Bill), 27, 28

St. Louis Business Men's League, 35

Streep, Meryl, 85

Sundry Civil Appropriations Act. *See* For-est Service Organic Act

Superfund. *See* Comprehensive Environ-mental Response, Compensation and Liability Act

Surface Mining Control and Reclamation Act (1977), 7

Symms National Recreational Trails Act (1991), 93

Taft, Robert, 40

Takings. *See* Regulatory takings

Takings Impact Analysis (TIA), 267, 270–271

Taung Ming-lin, 262–263

Tauzin, Billy, 272

Taylor, Edward, 53

Taylor Grazing Act (1934), 53. *See also* Grazing disputes, 53

Teapot Dome scandal, 38

Teller, Henry, 27

Tellico Dam, 68

Tennessee Valley Authority, 68

Think tanks, 140–144, 147, 231

Thoreau, Henry David, 2, 25, 227

TIA. *See* Takings Impact Analysis

Timber and Stone Act (1878), 4

Timber Culture Act (1873), 4

Timber industry, 4, 5, 28–31, 108, 123; sup-port for wise use movement, 195. *See also* Endangered species; Endangered Species Act

Tobacco industry, 140

Toxic Substances Control Act (1976), 7, 104, 155, 285

Toxic pollution, 9

Trade associations, 105, 115–117; as "front groups," 111. *See also* Business opposi-tion

Transcendentalists, 2

Transfer Act of 1905, 30

Tucker, Cora, 198

Turner, Scott, 77

Udall, Morris, 117

United Auto Workers, 114

Union Carbide, 132, 146

United Mine Workers, 109

United States Council for Energy Aware-ness (USCEA), 111

United States Fish and Wildlife Service (USFWS), 30; annexing new wildlife re-serves, 184; and ESA, 63, 65, 68–69, 180, 261; and inholders, 179; pesticide use in wildlife refuge, 83; and water pollution, 156. *See also* Division of Biological Sur-vey

United States Forest Service (USFS), ix, 4, 26, 40; close relations with business, 29; and grazing, 43, 54; and livestock in-dustry, 43; and utilities, 32–33; and wilderness preservation, 92–93

United States Geological Survey, 25, 33, 36, 37

United States Taxpayers Association, 66

United States v. Ellen, 259

United States v. Jones, 259
United States v. Pozsgai, 260
Urbanization: creating demand for recreation spaces, 78, 90–91; influence on farming, 78; policy implications in West, 182
USCEA. *See* United States Council for Energy Awareness
USDA. *See* Department of Agriculture
USFS. *See* United States Forest Service
USFWS. *See* United States Fish and Wildlife Service
Ute Indians, 2
Utilitarian philosophy, 1
Utility opposition, 8, 31–33, 109; and Federal land policy, 31–33

Valdez Principles, 9, 147
Velie, Lester, 43–44

War on the West, 227–243. *See also* County supremacy movement
Water policy opposition, 33–36
Water pollution: and agricultural practices, 82–83; legislation regulating, 155–156; thermal, 8. *See also* Clean Water Acts *and other water quality legislation*
Water Pollution Control Act (1956), 107
Water Pollution Control Act Amendments (1956), 7
Water Pollution Control Act Amendments (1965), 104
Water Pollution Control Act Amendments (1972), 105
Water Power Act (1920), 33
Water Projects, 32–33; 68
Water Quality Act (1965), 107
Waterways, 4, 34–36
Watt, James: as "bane" of environmentalists, 8, 12, 200, 294; as a conservative 164; and property rights movement, 252; and Sagebrush Rebellion, 185, 186, 187
Waxman, Henry, 114, 117, 161
Welsh, Dick, 256
West: disputes with federal government and the East, 21, 27, 30–31, 41; early history of, 22; and federal jurisdiction, 173–174; organized opposition to federal land and timber policies, 40; settlement and expansion, 2–4, 77. *See also* County supremacy movement; Sectionalism; States; War on the West
Western Conservation League, 40
Western Land Act, 183
Western Regional Council (WRC), 115
Western States Center, 13, 212
Western States Governors, 26
Western States Public Lands Coalition, 201
Western States Water Power Conference, 33
Wetlands, 155–156; and property rights movement, 257–261
Weyerhauser, George, 31
Whitney, David, 31
Wild and Scenic Rivers Act (1968), 93
Wilderness: defined, 90; preservation of, 89–92
Wilderness Act (1964), 92, 172–173
Wilderness Society: and BLM management, 55, 185, 193, 258, 271, 292; founding, 26; fund-raising, 12; and protectionism, 6, 91, 92
Wildlife management policy, 59–70
Wildlife refuges, 61, 74, 83
Wilson, Pete, 49
Wilson, Woodrow, 41
Wise Use Address Book, ix
Wise Use Agenda, 200, 202
Wise use movement, ix, 191–222; alleged extremism, 70, 133, 206, 210, 212–220; corporate support of, 192–193; delegitimization of environment movement, 209–211, 222; early history, 194–196; ideology of, 192; leaders of, 196–198; legislative agenda, 200, 220–221; mainstream message of, 221–223; membership and alliances, 191–193, 200–205; and National Wilderness Institute, 145; networking and technology use by, 205–206; opposition to corporate sponsorship of environmentalist values, 220; and organized labor, 202; policy impact, 220–223; public relations by, 206–208; and religion, 211–212; response of environmentalists, 211–218, 221; technological expertise within, 203; umbrella organizations, 12, 200–202; women participants in, 198

Wolves. *See* Endangered species; Predator and pest control

Women: in environmental movement, 198; in opposition, 194, 198

Women in Timber, 194, 198

World Wide Web, 205, 206, 256

World Wildlife Fund, 136, 138

Worster, Donald, 250

WRC. *See* Western Regional Council

Wyoming Stock Growers Association, 53

Yellow Ribbon Coalition, 191

Yellowstone National Park: creation of, 4; ecosystem and "vision" plan, 202, 210, 292; and wolf controversy, 63–65, 295

Yosemite National Park: creation of, 4; and Hetch Hetchy controversy, 39; and inholders, 11, 194, 263; and recreational use, 221

Young, Don, 65, 118

About the Book

Although most Americans do not refer to themselves as being "anti-environmental," there has been a growing opposition to the environmental movement of the 1970s and 1980s. *Green Backlash* explores the historical, ideological, and social foundations of this countermovement, providing essential perspectives for scholars, policymakers, and citizen activists.

Switzer offers a comprehensive overview of the participants in the environmental opposition—from the corporate interests that engage in public relations campaigns, which are sometimes called "greenwashing," to the populist core, the individuals and groups in the wise use, county supremacy, and property rights movements. She examines the role of policy entrepreneurs in the opposition, and explores the effectiveness of the strategies that have been used to influence policymakers and public opinion. She considers the response of environmental groups, as well as claims that the opposition has links with the extreme right. Throughout the book, Switzer notes the divisions and shifting alliances within and between the traditional environmental groups and their opponents. Her final chapter survey the prospects for future cooperation or conflict in environmental policymaking.

JACQUELINE VAUGHN SWITZER is a writer and consultant on public policy issues. She has taught at Southern Oregon State College and University of the Redlands, and has worked as a policy and political analyst in both the public and private sectors.